# WOMEN OF KURDISTAN

## A HISTORICAL AND BIBLIOGRAPHIC STUDY

# DEDICATION


*In memory of*

Shilan Hassanpour (1951-2020)

# WOMEN OF KURDISTAN

## A HISTORICAL AND BIBLIOGRAPHIC STUDY

Shahrzad Mojab and Amir Hassanpour

TRANSNATIONAL PRESS LONDON
2021

Society and Politics: 4

Women of Kurdistan: A Historical and Bibliographic Study

By Shahrzad Mojab and Amir Hassanpour

First Published in 2021 by TRANSNATIONAL PRESS LONDON in the United Kingdom, 12 Ridgeway Gardens, London, N6 5XR, UK.

www.tplondon.com

Transnational Press London® and the logo and its affiliated brands are registered trademarks.

Requests for permission to reproduce material from this work should be sent to: sales@tplondon.com

Paperback

ISBN: 978-1-912997-96-1

Digital

ISBN: 978-1-80135-032-7

Cover Design: Nihal Yazgan

Cover Art: "Dancing in Yellow Field" by Dara Aram, Kurdish artist based in Toronto, Canada

Transnational Press London Ltd. is a company registered in England and Wales No. 8771684

# TABLE OF CONTENTS

# ABOUT AUTHORS

**Shahrzad Mojab**, a scholar, teacher, and activist, is internationally known for her work on the impact of war, displacement, and violence on women's learning and education; gender, state, migration, and diaspora; and Marxist feminism and anti-racism pedagogy. She is a professor of Adult Education and Community Development as well as Women and Gender Studies at the University of Toronto. She is the Director of Critical Studies in Equity and Solidarity; a former Director of the Women and Gender Institute, University of Toronto; and the recipient of the Royal Society of Canada Award in Gender Studies in 2010 along with the 2020 Canadian Association of Studies in Adult Education Lifetime Achievement Award. She is the editor of the Peter Lang Publishing book series on *Kurdish People, History and Politics*. Her most recent books include *Youth as/in Crisis: Young People, Public Policy, and the Politics of Learning* (co-edited with Sara Carpenter, 2017); *Revolutionary Learning: Marxism, Feminism and Knowledge* (co-authored with Sara Carpenter, 2017); *Marxism and Feminism* (editor, 2015); *Educating from Marx: Race, Gender and Learning* (co-edited with Sara Carpenter, 2012) and *Women, War, Violence, and Learning* (editor, 2010). Her current research projects are *Youth in Transition: War, Migration, and 'Regenerative Possibilities'* and *The Pedagogy and Policy of Refugee Youth Resettlement*. The Ontario Arts Council has funded her project with Roshanak Jaberi and Doris Rajan, *No Woman's Land*, which is a dance project to capture the experience of refugee women of sexual violence.

**Amir Hassanpour** (1943-2017) was a prominent Kurdish Marxist scholar, a revolutionary thinker, and Professor Emeritus of Near and Middle Eastern Civilizations at the University of Toronto. He earned his BA in English Language and Literature, University of Tehran (1964); MA in Linguistics and Ancient Languages, University of Tehran (1972); and PhD in Communications Studies, University of Illinois at Urbana-Champaign (1989) where he studied sociolinguistics and contemporary Middle Eastern history. His research and teaching interests included international communication, Canadian communication and culture, broadcasting policy, communication theory, and Middle Eastern and Kurdish politics and culture. His books, *Essays on Kurds: Historiography, Orality, and Nationalism* and *Nationalism and Language in Kurdistan, 1918-1985* are among his seminal works on Kurdish sociolinguistics, Kurdish history and nationalism, peasant and social movements, class struggle, and gender relations in the Middle East and Kurdistan. He published numerous articles in academic journals and reference works such as *Encyclopedia of Television, Encyclopaedia Iranica, Encyclopedia of Modern Asia, The New Grove*

*Dictionary of Music and Musicians, Encyclopedia of Modern Middle East, Encyclopedia of Women in Islamic Cultures, Encyclopedia of Genocide and Crimes Against Humanity* and *Encyclopedia of Diasporas.*

# ACKNOWLEDGEMENTS

This book has been many years in the making. Over two decades, it benefited from the collaboration and contribution of great scholars. I am writing this note of appreciation on behalf of myself and Amir.

We extend our deepest thanks and appreciation to all who meticulously shared resources with us. Our students, Nadeen El-Kassem, Michael Hill, and Aisha Silim remained committed and interested in this project years after their graduation. We are truly appreciative of all their contributions over the years. Martin van Bruinessen, Rohat Alakom, Heidi Wedel, Christine Robins (nee Allison), and the late Mirella Galletti, the authors who contributed to *Women of a Non-State Nation: The Kurds*, generously shared more materials to be included in this book. Our enormous thanks to all of them. Our visits to Berlin and London over many summers were invaluable in establishing everlasting friendship with Necla Açik, Siamend Hajo, Carsten Borck, Eva Savelsberg, and Şükriye Dogan, all of them helped us with collecting original materials, accompanied us in long walks throughout Berlin to discuss the building of a Kurdish studies program, and creating an International Kurdish Women's Studies Network (IKWSN). Tijen Uğuriş kindly assisted with organizing the last meeting of the IKWSN. She was a generous intellectual with deep commitment to international feminism. Her premature death devastated us all, but her memory is long-lasting.

There are other colleagues and friends whom we must name and thank because of their long and sustained exchanges with us. They are Thomas Ricks, Hassan Ghazi, Stephan Dobson, and Michael Chyet, all of whom helped us in developing sources, topics, method of referencing, and the creation of the bibliography. There are also institutions that we should thank as they responded to our inquiries and provided information, including Archiv-Bibliothek-Dokumentation (Austria), National Library of Australia, Institut kurde de Paris, University of Toronto Library, and the Library of Congress (USA).

In the last few years, I have dedicated some of my time to finish Amir's unfinished projects. One has been this book which was our political and intellectual shared project. Finally, Marlene Schäfers and Ibrahim Sirkeci provided me with the incentive to finish this book. I remain indebted to them for their encouragement and support. Sara Carpenter and Susan Benson-Lokmen read some parts of this work and offered valuable comments, for which I am most thankful. Gülay Kilicaslan helped with transliteration and translation of some keywords, I am grateful for her help in the last stage of this work. Dara Aram has generously given me permission to use his beautiful art for the cover. I remain, as ever, grateful.

With all the precious help from so many people, it was the meticulous and efficient editorial work of Danielle Stewart that finalized this work. Danielle's care went much beyond the editorial task, she understood the personal significance of this book for me and gave it that much needed attention. Surely, without her this book would not have reached its end.

At the heart of this book is the love of my life, Amir, who accompanied me through my political and intellectual journey. Surely, he expected a comprehensive and errors free text. However, any errors and lacuna in analysis are obviously mine.

# ACRONYMS

| | |
|---|---|
| **ACAT** | Action des Chrétiens pour l'Abolition de la Torture |
| **AIJ** | Alliance international pour la justice |
| **AKIN** | American Kurdish Information Network |
| **AKP** | Justice and Development Party (*Adalet ve Kalkınma Partisi*) |
| **ANAP** | Motherland Party (*Anavatan Partisi*) |
| **ARGK** | Peoples' Liberation Army of Kurdistan (*Artêşa Rizgarîya Gelê Kurdîstan*) |
| **ATO** | Adana Doctors' Association (*Adana Tabip Odası*) |
| **CAT** | UN convention Against Torture and Other Cruel Inhuman or Degrading Treatment or Punishment |
| **ÇATOM** | Multi-Purpose Social Centers (*Çok Amaçlı Toplum Merkezi*) |
| **CEDAW** | UN Convention on the Elimination of all Forms of Discrimination against Women |
| **CHP** | Republican People's Party (*Cumhuriyet Halk Partisi*) |
| **CIA** | Central Intelligence Agency, U.S.A. |
| **CILDEKT** | French initials for International Committee for the Liberation of the Imprisoned Kurdish Members of Parliament |
| **CRC** | UN Convention of the Rights of the Child |
| **CRDA** | Centre de recherches sur la diaspora arménienne |
| **DEHAP** | Democratic People's Party (*Demokratik Halk Partisi*) |
| **DEP** | Democracy Party (*Demokrasi Partisi*) |
| **DGM** | State Security Court (*Devlet Güvenlik Mahkemesi*) |
| **DHKP-C** | People's Revolutionary Liberation Front-Party (*Devrimci Halk Kurtuluş Partisi-Cephesi*) |
| **DİSK** | Confederation of Progressive Trade Unions of Turkey (*Türkiye Devrimci İşçi Sendikaları Konfederasyonu*) |
| **DSP** | Democratic Left Party (*Demokratik Sol Parti*) |
| **ECHR** | European Convention on Human Rights |
| **EKB** | Working Women's Union (*Devrimci Halk Kurtuluş Partisi-Cephesi*) |
| **ERNK** | National Liberation Front of Kurdistan (*Eniya Rizgariya Netewa Kurdistan*) |
| **FGM** | Female Genital Mutilation |
| **FIDH** | International Federation for Human Rights |
| **GAP** | Southeast Anatolia Development Project (*Güneydoğu Doğu Anadolu Projesi*) |
| **HADEP** | People's Democracy Party (*Halkın Demokrasi Partisi*) |
| **HAK-PAR** | Rights and Freedoms Party (*Partiya Maf û Azadiyan; Hak ve* |

3

|  | *Özgürlükler Partisi)* |
|---|---|
| **HEP** | People's Labour Party (*Halkın Emek Partisi*) |
| **HGP** | People's Defense Forces (*Hêzên Parastina Gel*) |
| **HKD** | Kurdish Women's Commission of Popular Culture |
| **HRA** | Human Rights Alliance |
| **HRFT** | Human Rights Foundation of Turkey (*Türkiye İnsan Hakları Vakfı*) |
| **HRK** | Kurdistan Liberation Units (*Hêzên Rizgarîya Kurdîstan*) |
| **ICAD** | International Committee Against Disappearances |
| **IFHR** | International Federation of Human Rights |
| **IFZ** | International Women Center |
| **İHD** | Human Rights Association (*İnsan Hakları Derneği*) |
| **IKP** | Institut Kurde de Paris |
| **IMF** | International Monetary Fund |
| **IMIK** | Islamic Movement of Iraqi Kurdistan |
| **IWO** | Women's Organisation of Kurdistan |
| **KADAV** | Women's Solidarity Foundation (*Kadınlarla Dayanışma Vakfı*) |
| **KADEK** | Freedom and Democracy Congress of Kurdistan (*Kongreya Azadi û Demokrasi ya Kurdistan*) |
| **KA-DER** | Association for Supporting Women Candidates (*Kadın Adayları Destekleme Derneği* |
| **KA-MER** | Women's Centre (*Kadın Merkezi*) |
| **KAV** | Kurdish Association of Victoria |
| **KCP** | Kurdistan Communist Party |
| **KDP** | Kurdistan Democratic Party (*Partiya Demokrat a Kurdistanê*) |
| **KDPI** | Kurdistan Democratic Party |
| **KESK** | Confederation of the Public Workers Unions also referred to as Public Workers Trade Union Confederation (*Kamu Emekçileri Sendikaları Konfederasyonu*) |
| **KHRP** | Kurdish Human Rights Project |
| **KHRW** | Kurdish Human Rights Watch |
| **K.Ka.DaV** | Women's Solidarity Foundation (*Kürt Kadınlarıyla Dayanışma ve Kadın Sorunları Araştırma Vakfı*) |
| **KNC** | Kurdish National Congress |
| **KOMALA** | Society of Revolutionary Toilers of Iranian Kurdistan (*Komeley Şorrişgêrrî Zehmetkêşanî Kurdistanî Êran*) |
| **KOMJIN** | Union of Women of Kurdistan (*Yekitiya Jinên Kurdistan*) |
| **KPE** | The Women's Commission Kurdistan Parliament-in-Exile |
| **KRG** | Kurdistan Regional Government (*Hikûmetî Herêmî Kurdistan*) |
| **KSP** | Kurdistan Socialist Party (*Kurdistan Sosyalist Partisi*) |
| **KURD-HA** | Kurdistan News Agency (*Kürdistan Haber Ajansı*) |

4

| | |
|---|---|
| **KWAHK** | Women's Action Against Honour Killing |
| **LAPASHRC** | Legal Aid Project Against Sexual Harassment and Rape in Custody |
| **MHP** | Nationalist Movement Party (*Milliyetçi Hareket Partisi*) |
| **MIT** | Turkish Military and Intelligence Police (*Milli İstihbarat Teşkilatı*) |
| **MKM** | Mesopotamian Cultural Centre (*Mezopotamya Kültür Merkezi*) |
| **MRAP** | Movement Against Racism and For Friendship between Peoples |
| **ÖDP** | Freedom and Solidarity Party (*Özgürlük ve Dayanışma Partisi*) |
| **OHAL** | State of Emergency (*Olağanüstü Hal*) |
| **OPFG** | Organization of People's Fedayee Guerrillas |
| **OSCE** | Organisation for Security and Cooperation in Europe |
| **OTAK** | Armed Forces Mutual Aid Corporation |
| **ÖZDEP** | Freedom and Democracy Party (*Özgürlük ve Demokrasi Partisi*) |
| **PAK** | Kurdistan Freedom Party (*Parti Azadi Kurdistan*) |
| **PASOK** | Panhellenic Socialist Movement |
| **PJA** | Free Women's Party (*Partiya Jiyana Azad*) |
| **PJKK** | Women's Labor Party of Kurdistan (*Partiya Jinên Karkerên Kurdistan*) |
| **PKK** | Kurdistan Workers' Party (*Partiya Karkerên Kurdistan*) |
| **PSK** | Socialist Party of Kurdistan |
| **PUK** | Patriotic Union of Kurdistan |
| **PWAK** | Patriotic Women's Association of Kurdistan |
| **PYD** | Democratic Union Party (*Partiya Yekîtiya Demokrat*) |
| **RAF** | Royal Air Force |
| **RCC** | Revolutionary Command Council |
| **RP** | Welfare Party (*Refah Partisi*) |
| **SAVAK** | National Organization for Security and Intelligence of Iran (*Sāzemān-e Ettelā'āt va Amniyat-e Keshvar*) |
| **SCIRI** | Supreme Council of the Islamic Revolution in Iraq |
| **SHP** | Social Democratic People's Party (*Sosyal Demkrat Halkçi Parti*) |
| **SOAS** | School of Oriental and African Studies |
| **TAJK** | Women's Movement of Kurdistan (*Tevgera Azadîya Jinên Kurdistan*) |
| **TDP** | Revolutionary Party of Turkey (*Türkiye Devrim Partisi*) |
| **TEVGER** | Patriotic Revolutionary Youth Movement (*Tevgera Ciwanen Welatparêzên Şoreşger*) |
| **THYD-DER** | Association for Solidarity with Prisoners' Families (*Tutuklu Hükümlü Yakınları Yardımlaşma ve Dayanışma Derneği*) |

| | |
|---|---|
| **TIHV** | Turkey Human Rights Foundation (*Türkiye İnsan Hakları Vakfı*) |
| **TİKKO** | Turkish Workers and Peasants Liberation Army (*Türkiye İşçi ve Köylü Kurtuluş Ordusu*) |
| **TKP-ML** | Turkish Communist Party of Turkey, Marxist-Leninist (*Türkiye Komünist Partisi-Marksist Leninist*) |
| **TKSP** | Turkish Kurdish Socialist Party (*Türkiye Kürdistan Sosyalist Partisi*) |
| **TKV** | Turkish Cultural Foundation (*Türk Kültür Vakfı*) |
| **TTB** | Turkish Doctors' Union |
| **UNHCR** | United Nations High Commissioner for Refugees |
| **WAF** | Women Against Fundamentalism |
| **WWHR** | Women for Women's Human Rights |
| **YAJK** | Free Women's Union of Kurdistan (*Yekîtiya Azadiya Jinên Kurdistan*) |
| **YJWK** | Union of Patriotic Women of Kurdistan (*Yekîtiya Jinên Welatparêzên Kurdistan*) |
| **YKD** | Patriotic Women's Union (*Yurtsever Kadınlar Derneği*) |
| **YKWK** | Union of Patriotic Workers of Kurdistan (*Yekîtiya Karkerên Welatparêzên Kurdistan*) |
| **YNK** | Patriotic Union of Kurdistan |
| **YPG** | People's Defence Unit (*Yekîneyên Parastina Gel*) |
| **YPJ** | Women's Defence Unit (*Yekîneyên Parastina Jin*) |
| **YXK** | Union of Revolutionary Youth of Kurdistan (*Yekîtiya Xortên Şoreşgerên Welatparêzên Kurdistan*) |

# PART I

# THE MAKING OF THE BIBLIOGRAPHY

## Shahrzad Mojab

Love and learning made the making of this bibliography imaginable. It began more than 20 years ago when Amir was expanding his theoretical ground for class analysis of nationalism and peasant movement in the Kurdish region of Mukriyan (Hassanpour, 2021). Simultaneously, I was engaged with debates on Marxist feminism and transnational feminism while grappling with *post-al* tendencies in feminism such as post-colonialism, post-structuralism, and post-modernism. We wanted to better understand the explanatory power and political implications of Marx's dialectical historical materialism in explicating the intersecting and refracting relations of gender, class, race, culture, nation, and nationalism. This commitment, nonetheless, did not remain in the realm of epistemology as a disembodied intellectual exercise. As a member of a dominant nation–a Shirazi born Iranian–I wanted to critically confront this national "identity" and the sense of "belonging." Amir sought to scrutinize patriarchal structures and gender relations in Kurdish history, society, culture, and nation. This intertwined mind and heart desire put us onto a path of renewed discoveries of our personal and intellectual relations. In a nutshell, this was the beginning of the making of *Women of Kurdistan: A Historical and Bibliographic Study*. Surely, it comes with sorrow to finalize this project 20 years after without Amir. But it gives me hope and strength to know that this work will enter the public realm after four decades of companionship, comradery, and collegial relations between myself and my beloved Amir; a life fully committed to revolutionary social transformation.

In the two analytical and historical sections below, "The State of Knowledge about Kurdish Women," and "Women of Kurdistan," we have addressed several themes to contextualize this historical bibliographical work. These include the biases, silences, and omissions of Kurdish women in feminist bibliographies and in women and gender studies; the stereotypical representation of Kurdish women as either/or bearer/betrayer of Kurdish culture and language or freedom fighters of/for nation; the national

7

chauvinistic and racist view of Kurdish culture where national suppression is delinked from class, patriarchy, and state violence; and dichotomized analysis of feminism/nationalism and finally, constructing Kurdish women by their single identity of being a Kurd rather than by multiple identities which frame their lives and struggles. In what follows, I plan to go further and beyond this contextualization by recounting the history of our ideas. I hope this historicization will provide a blueprint to expand this work and help us to realize that ideas are rooted in history and social reality, while being consciously formed and collectively shaped.

To advance feminist responses to colonialism, nationalism, and capitalist imperialism, Amir and I began with a series of reading groups and sustained conversations with radical activists, colleagues and graduate students in North America, Europe, and the Middle East where we (re)read Marx's original texts to enhance our knowledge and use of the method of dialectical historical materialism in centring class, race, sexuality, and culture in feminism and nationalism. The preliminary result of these efforts was presented in two books which were published simultaneously in 2001. The first one is *Of Property and Propriety: The Role of Gender and Class in Imperialism and Nationalism* which I co-edited with Himani Bannerji and Judith Whitehead. In this book, we offered a Marxist feminist critique of "subaltern," "post-colonial", and "cultural" studies and argued that,

> [T]he abundant literature on nationalism and gender prompts us to contemplate how national identities and dominant forms of moral regulation associated with national cultures have been mediated by gender identities. In our view, the relationships between gender, nationalism, and moral regulation have been inadequately analysed. Much of the existing literature on gender and nationalism has been written from a post-structural and post-colonial perspective in which all social relations are erased, and nationalism is viewed solely as a cultural contest between Self and Other, colonizing and colonized cultures…This literature has therefore failed to consider a matrix of underlying yet important social relationship that influenced the political character of anti-colonial nationalist movements. (Bannerji, Mojab, & Whitehead, 2011, p. 3)

In this collection, the question of feminism and nationalism were interrogated in the context of nationalist movements in Ireland and Finland, the anti-colonial national liberation movements in India, and the Kurdish autonomous movement of 1946. To pursue some of the theoretical themes which emerged in this work further, I decided to produce an anthology centring on the experience of Kurdish women. Thus, the second edited book, *Women of a Non-State Nation: The Kurds* (2001). This book still remains as the

8

sole English language collection on Kurdish women.[1] This anthology is thematically organized to situate the life and struggle of Kurdish women in history, politics, society, culture, language, religion, and international law. In the introductory chapter, "The solitude of the stateless: Kurdish women at the margins of feminist knowledge," I wrote:

> I did not ask the authors to address the question of statehood and nationhood in their study of the lives of Kurdish women. Uninvited, however, the state is prominently and, often violently, present in Kurdistan, a territory without "recognized borders." In this "borderless" land, however, the borders are more visibly marked than most internationally recognized borders: it is a land whose "borders bleed." (Mojab, 2001a, p. 1)

The notion of "border" here is an elucidation of social, political, geographical, historical, and cultural demarcation which enclose women's bodies. From a Marxist feminist perspective, the control over women's sexuality is connected to a range of social practices and patriarchal norms of propriety that are (re)produced through the converging interaction between colonial, capitalist, and nationalist forces as these practices and norms cross borders on land, culture, or on women's bodies.

To explore some of these ideas further, especially within the domain of knowledge production, I initiated the creation of the *International Kurdish Women's Studies Network* and wrote on the opening page of the inaugural pamphlet that the network "started as a response to a growing need for opening a space for Kurdish women in international debates on women's rights, women's studies, and promoting gender justice among the Kurdish communities in the diaspora and the Middle East" (Appendix). The network itself became a contested terrain of knowledge production. The tension between activists and academics, representational questions of whose voice, who is speaking for whom, who is speaking for Kurds, and can the Kurds speak, all were key concerns on the politics of knowledge production and the complex power/knowledge relations (Mojab, 2000a).

Before proceeding, let me pause and underline key theoretical shifts in the larger feminist intellectual milieu of the last three decades that coincided with our effort in introducing the life and struggle of Kurdish women as a distinct though complementary force.[2] In the last three decades, women's studies of the Middle East and North Africa (MENA) grew in response to the 1979 revolution in Iran and the rise of Islamism in Pakistan and Afghanistan in the

---

[1] Chapters from this book are translated into Sorani Kurdish and Persian. The entire book was translated into Turkish in 2005 (Devletsiz Ulusun Kadınları: Kürt Kadını Üzerine Araştırmalar, Istanbul: Avesta).
[2] For a Marxist feminist theorization of these debates, see Carpenter and Mojab (2017, 2011), and Mojab (2015a).

1980s. Certain topics dominated the knowledge production in this area such as Islam and secularism, modernity and traditionalism, and women's bodies/women's agency. Although Kurdish women offered much empirical evidence to alarm feminist scholars about their linear thinking to Islam-centred approach, nonetheless, they totally ignored the possibility let alone actuality of women's agency in the context of participation in armed struggle and working towards building a socialist secular nation in the region. The feminist poststructuralist, cultural relativist, identity-based approaches even dropped the possibility of studying a trans-regional/transnationalist feminist analysis of women's participation in radical national movements in the late 1970s to early 1980s from Palestine to Oman to Yemen and Kurdistan. Culturalizing women's agency in its "piety" was used as a universal truth, which was much appreciated by Islamist and nationalist forces. The alternative offered was moderate Islam and bourgeois democracy, that is, legal equality and the regime of rights. In this articulation "woman" became gender; gender, in turn, was displaced or overwritten by sexuality; feminism became the "unfit" and taboo concept; women's rights were limited to sexuality and the covering/uncovering debate. Gradually, sexuality was used as the main conceptual framework. While the concept of "woman" was overly contested in some feminist theorization, the colossal structure of capitalism and capitalist patriarchy disappeared from most analysis.

The last three decades are usually called the period of turns and twists—mostly cultural or linguistic. However, I understand their political import as conservatism and conformism. It is not surprising, therefore, that the academia and the media were astonished by the presence of secular revolutionary Kurdish women in Rojava who took up arms against the Islamic State. But those of us who have been envisioning and struggling for a secular, democratic, and free MENA region felt immediate political and historical affinity with this movement. The women of Rojava came into prominence to a large extent because they took up arms against the Islamic State and were not seen as a threat to Western imperialist interests. There is much geo-political complexity that certainly requires careful Marxist feminist analysis to realize that women's emancipation rests on the struggle against all forms of patriarchal property relations, which (re)produce capitalism and imperialism.

I contend that the hegemonic analytical tools of the last 30 years, centred on Islam, agency, authenticity, voice, and body among others, have isolated and delinked women's experience from history, social formation, and relations of powers embedded in the structure of patriarchy and capitalist imperialism. These analytical tools will not help us to analyze the complex conditions of women's lives in the Middle East and the rest of the world. Therefore, I suggest that the theorization of gender relations in general, and Kurdish women's experience in particular, should express an expansive dialectical understanding of social relations where patriarchy, nationalism, capitalism, and imperialism constitute women's lives *similarly*, though dialectically speaking, *differently*. This dialectical understanding helps us to analyze the interconnectedness of imperialist occupation, the rise of violence against women, and the proliferation of women's "empowerment" projects, NGOization of women's movements, and re-emergence of Kurdish women as a revolutionary force.

I have suggested so far that theories are not equal in their explanatory power. We will not break new ground by a simple exchange or interchange of some feminist theoretical approaches to culture, Islam, agency, or gender governance for class, patriarchy, and capitalism. Liberal feminist theories usually stay with the state or outside it, and in both cases leave intact and strengthen the patriarchal capitalist state. We can surely move away from the problematization of women's emancipation as a question of rights, and the regime of rights and equality, and instead treat women's lives as a major divide in world history, one that needs historical and materialist understanding. This requires a radical rupture with current theorization which confuses essences with essentialism, structures with structuralism, and universalism with totalitarianism. Bannerji suggests, "[I]t is only adopting a feminist historical materialist perspective that we can see the inextricable and constitutive relationship between social organization, relations and values of property and propriety, between capital, class and patriarchy in *any* society" (2011, p. 124). She also indicates that if women

> . . . do not work on an even-handed critique of all forms of domination, they become the instruments of imperialism or ethnic/cultural nationalism of the West or the East. The mainstream Western feminists in the context of Afghanistan or Palestine, provide perhaps in all good faith, the shock troops of imperialism, while women in the service of traditional/cultural nationalism not only betray themselves and all other women, but all possibilities of social justice and political agencies. (Bannerji, 2011, pp. 125-26)

The making of *Women of Kurdistan: A Historical and Bibliographic Study* is framed within these analyses. It is a first step in documenting knowledge on, for, and with Kurdish women. It certainly closes one century (though it is more precise to say it began in the latter part of the nineteenth century and ends in the beginning of the twenty-first century) and carves the path for new directions and a renewed mode of documenting and archiving knowledge production. In the 20 years since Amir and I started this project, the intellectual and political grounds of patriarchal, capitalist, imperialist world order have intensely shifted and has transformed not to ameliorate social relations of class, gender, race, sexuality, and nationalism, but rather to reconstitute these social cleavages differently and disproportionally, particularly for Kurdish women. The start of this project coincided with major global changes: the dismantlement of socialist projects, the expansion of military aggression in the Middle East (in particular, the occupation of Afghanistan since 2000 and Iraq since 2003), the rise of neoliberalism and authoritarianism, and the revitalization of nationalism and xenophobia. This book comes to an end under the condition of a global pandemic that Arundhati Roy calls a "portal," as in a

> "gateway between one world and the next. We can choose to walk through it, dragging the carcasses of our prejudice and hatred, our avarice, our data banks and dead ideas, our dead rivers and smoky skies behind us. Or we can walk through lightly, with little luggage, ready to imagine another world. And ready to fight for it" (Roy, 2020, para. 47).

Under this unprecedented global condition, the carceral states of Iran and Turkey continue to arrest, torture, and execute Kurds. Turkey's military aggression against Rojava has not been halted even with COVID-19 ravaging the region. Pondering our current state, I am reminded of Brecht's line "truly I [we] live in dark times." Brecht noted these dark times in 1940, when fascism in Europe was on the rise. The poem is titled "To those born later" and depicts the condition of poverty, violence, and ruthless humanity, but most significantly it calls upon humanity to resist and survive with dignity.

**One last note for readers**: Amir and I planned to prepare a comprehensive, thorough, well organized historical and bibliographical study of the lives and resistance of Kurdish women in English, French, and German. Certainly, there are shortcomings, as we have indicated in the sections below. Our goal was to produce a multilingual and annotated subject bibliography which covers a span of more than a century of writings on Kurdish women. Thus, this subject bibliography should be considered as the annotation of the life and struggle of Kurdish women in the twentieth century. There has been a *knowledge explosion* on Kurdish women in the last decade that is inspiring, imaginative, and original. This includes historical analysis of Kurdish women's movements, memoirs, novels, and further artistic expressions in music, film, poetry, and songs (see for example Cansiz, 2018; Çaglayan, 2019; Dirik, 2021; Ghobadi, 2020; Homa, 2020; Nammi & Attwood, 2020; Ghaderi & Scalbert Yücel, 2021; Mahmoud, 2021). Coincidently, this book reaches its end at the time of the reprint of Margaret Kahn's influential book, *Children of the Jinn*, which was originally published in 1980. The book is Margaret's memoir of her travels in the mid-1970s to the Kurdish region of Iran and Iraq. It is her account of women's lives in Mahabad, the first Kurdish town that I ever visited in 1978, that always captivated me. *Children of the Jinn* makes me look with longing toward *Deçmewe Sablax* [Going Back to Sablagh/Mahabad], as Shilan Hassanpour titled her extraordinary memoir.[3]

As I mentioned above, I am not a Kurd. I claim neither internal/external researcher relations to Kurdish women, nor the "informant" of the culture and lived experiences of Kurdish women. I have, however, developed a long and lasting solidarity with the struggle of Kurdish women. I have been in this movement for four decades, and over the years have conducted extensive research with, and among, Kurdish women on the mountains of Kurdistan with women peshmergas, in the women's community centres in Kurdish cities of Bakur and Bashur, and in the Kurdish diaspora in Europe and North America. I recall vividly when I presented my first paper on Kurdish women at the 1994 MESA annual conference ("Gender, Ethnicity, and Nationalism," in the Middle East Studies Association Annual Conference, MESA, Phoenix, Arizona, U.S.A. November 19-22). Professor Nikki Keddie, a prominent historian of the Middle East with expertise on women and Iranian history, dismissed my paper and commented that "Kurdish women's experience can't teach us anything new." I decided to dedicate my intellectual and political life to a struggle that's longevity, perseverance, and vitality that continues.

The end of a project is the beginning of much more work to complete, as Amir always said, to denote the dialectic nature of knowledge production that is constantly evolving, fluid, and contestable. In the last few years, I have received more invitations than a decade ago to write endorsements or introductions for books on Kurdish women, to review manuscripts for journals on Kurdish women, or to serve on doctoral thesis committees on Kurdish women. The academic year of 2020-2021 also began with the reinstitution of the *Kurdish Women's Studies Network* where a yearlong lecture series is organized, including nine panels with 32 paper presentations covering a wide range of topics such as politics, state violence, literature, ethnography, language, religion, diaspora, art, stories, love, sexuality, resistance, trauma, war, and prison. This burst of knowledge production is remarkable. It is a new beginning to push the boundaries of Kurdish feminist knowledge and practices and with it, the entire cannon of Kurdish studies. We know that no genuine social transformation is possible without a critical knowledge of the historical and social relations that need to be transformed.

---

[3] Shilan Hassanpour (1951-2020) wrote *Deçmewe Sablax* [Going Back to Sablagh/Mahabad] in an eloquent Sorani Kurdish in 2012. For an English review of it see Mojab, 2015b.

# THE STATE OF KNOWLEDGE ABOUT KURDISH WOMEN

There are serious, systemic obstacles to the creation and dissemination of knowledge about Kurdish women. This is in spite of the fact that Kurds are one of the world's large transnational nations, living in a strategically important part of the world. Their status as a suppressed non-state nation plays a major role in creation and dissemination of knowledge about Kurdish women.

Feminists and Marxists, among others, reject the political, juridical, and economic neutrality of the state. Many feminist theorists treat the state, both modern and pre-modern, as a patriarchal institution (Murray, 1995). However, as is the case in the juridical domain, where the state "grants" rights and has the power to mediate in the course of their violation or implementation, in the realm of the construction of knowledge, the absence of Kurdish statehood has constrained the creation of knowledge about Kurdish women. No doubt, the non-state status of the Kurds could be less debilitating if the nation-states ruling over the Kurds were more tolerant of the Kurds. The reality of statelessness has meant, for instance, that limited, if any, census data about Kurds or Kurdish women are provided by any government in the Middle East. It also means the exclusion of books and journals from library holdings, blocking access to archives, and the use of the postal and customs services to prevent the import and export of books, journals, film, and other material. In Turkey, where the names "Kurd" and "Kurdistan" are banned in official circles, there can be no talk of Kurdish women in government contexts. Even if they have to be addressed as a collective, they can only be mentioned as women of the "southeast." In Iran, where a Kordestan (or Kurdestan, the spelling of Persian pronunciation) province exists, census data are available for this administrative entity, which includes only parts of the Kurdish region of the country. Statelessness also means that Kurdish women cannot have access to state-centred international arenas, such as the United Nations (UN) and its agencies such as UNICEF or UNIFEM.

The ability of non-democratic states to obstruct the creation of knowledge is much more extensive, however. In the absence of academic freedom and university autonomy, institutions of higher education, which are major locations of teaching and research in the region, do not allow or encourage research or teaching on Kurdish women. This has been especially true in Turkey, Iran (under the Pahlavi monarchy, 1925-79), and Syria (since the 1960s). Women's studies, like many domains of contemporary academic research and teaching, emerged first in the West. The earliest academic

14

programs of women's studies began in the United States in the 1970s, and the spread to other parts of the world has been slow. However, by 2005 several institutions were offering women's studies programs in Iran and Turkey. So far much of the research about women, with or without such programs, has not been responsive to the ethnic diversity of these countries. These nation-states are in a position to control the production of knowledge not only by their citizens but also by international researchers, which we will elaborate on further. In spite of these restrictions, there is much interest in Kurdish women's studies in academic institutions. As this bibliography demonstrates, research on Kurdish women has already begun in universities in Turkey, Iran, and Iraq.

In Iraq, Kurds had demanded the establishment of a university since the 1920s. However, they had to wait until 1968 to get the first institution of higher education. Under the Regional Government of Iraqi Kurdistan, formed in 1992, this institution developed into three poorly equipped universities; their libraries are still impoverished in every area of knowledge, especially women's studies. Graduate students, however, show much interest in writing their theses on women. If the institution of the state is the main locus of censorship of knowledge about Kurdish women, the market works as the principal censor in the West. No doubt, in both contexts, the market and the state, far from being independent entities, act together in complex ways.

Middle Eastern studies, as a Western area of knowledge, has a rather long history. Although this "Orientalist" tradition had to deal with the women of the region, it did not treat them as a worthy entity of study. In the wake of the fall of the Pahlavi dynasty and its replacement by an Islamic theocracy in 1979, Western governments, media, academia, and the publishing industry discovered a new player, the "Muslim woman." Within a decade, courses on "Muslim women" or "women and Islam" began to be offered in a few institutions. The publishing industry, too, has heavily invested in this new area of interest. To give an example, in the course of two centuries, between 1800 and 1999, a total of 110 book titles about Iranian women appeared in English (Mojab, 2000b). The data is based on a WorldCat search for "women AND Iran OR Persia"). Of these 110 titles, 78, essentially, about 71%, appeared during the 20 years after the coming to power of the Islamic theocracy in 1979.

In the West, the institution of the state, much more than academic curiosity, has shaped the formation of Middle Eastern studies programs. These programs have largely focussed on Arabic, Hebrew, Persian, and Turkish (state) languages, the history of the Ottoman and Iranian empires, and the post-WWII nation-states. They have studied the Middle East not from the points of view of social movements, but rather within the perspectives of their own states, the interstate system, or Middle Eastern regimes. This "Muslim" woman is usually ethnically Arab, Turkish, or Iranian, and more often urban, and rarely, if ever, working class. In this ideologically shaped preference, there was little room for Kurdish women's studies. That academia continues to reduce the diverse women of the Middle East to "Muslim women" exposes the tendency to ignore a century of women's struggles rooted in secular, socialist, and nationalist politics. For decades, academic studies had celebrated the "liberation" of women by pro-Western secular and nationalist leaders such as Atatürk in Turkey and Reza Shah in Iran but had not been as approving of similar projects of "state feminism" initiated by adversaries like Jamal Abel Nasser of Egypt. It is not surprising, therefore, that there is little notice of the women of non-state nations such as the Assyrians, Baluchis, or Kurds.

The marginalization of the Kurds and Kurdish women in academic knowledge creates a vicious circle of omission. The lack of courses on Kurdish women reduces to the point of elimination publishers' interest in producing textbooks, reference works, and journals on Kurdish women; in the absence of teaching, university libraries, and adequate funds, individuals will be less likely to acquire material on Kurdish women; the absence of resources, in turn, reduces interest in conducting research, even writing term papers; faculty with no expertise on Kurdish women are less likely to supervise or encourage graduate thesis work; under these conditions, research funding is generally not readily forthcoming; faculty hiring, too, may be shaped by all of these mechanisms of exclusion; there will be more interest in hiring one with expertise on Arab, Turkish, Iranian, or Muslim women. Thus, cause and effect transform into each other, and perpetuate processes of exclusion for Kurdish women's studies.

The vicious circle of exclusion is further exacerbated by the ability of Middle Eastern states to censor academic research in the West. For instance, Turkey, Iran, Syria, and Iraq intervene in the creation of knowledge in other countries. This is done by various means such as issuing or denying research permits to foreign researchers. With the exception of Iraq under the monarchy (1932-58), Turkey, Iran, and Syria have rarely issued permits for research on the Kurds (for more on Turkey, see Hassanpour, 2000). Also, these states offer money to establish "chairs" of study in Western institutions, grant scholarships, donate books and journals to libraries, and invite academics and students for visits, conferences, and other events. If these states are interested in shaping knowledge about women, they will promote them as Iraqi, Turkish, Syrian, or Muslim (Iranian) women.

State interest can also be seen in the ways in which empire building and war is impacting the creation of knowledge about women. The U.S. war in Afghanistan (2001-) and Iraq (1991 and 2003) brought not only the army to these two countries but also a host of media reporters, aid workers, human rights groups, peace activists, NGOs, and even academics to the war zone. All of this generated academic interest ranging from student term papers to graduate theses, course offerings, conferencing, and publishing activity. This bibliography records the impact of these wars on Kurdish women's studies.

While the interests of the state and the market have generally been critical in obstructing the creation of knowledge about Kurdish women, the resistance of women to patriarchal state and domestic violence is working against the complex regime of censorship sketched above. In Turkey, resistance to patriarchal state violence, especially by victims and their lawyers, alerted international and diaspora human rights organizations, and finally Turkish academia and media to the atrocities being inflicted. Turkish lawyers produced one of the first studies of sexual violence while in custody (some are reported in this bibliography). At the same time, resistance against domestic violence, especially honour killing, generated much activism and research. The spread of feminist knowledge in the region and diaspora-homeland feminist interaction is also a factor in the growth of research interest.

Although much of the current production of knowledge is reacting to the horrors of state and family violence against women, it generates both feminist consciousness and research interest. The literature documented in this bibliography, although not written in the languages spoken in Kurdistan, demonstrates extensive activism and writing by the Kurds themselves. One can find, in this literature, a history of Kurdish struggle against oppressive gender relations. Patriarchy is an ancient social formation and, as the experience of two centuries of feminist struggle in the West attests, it cannot be easily displaced, let alone dismantled, without organized feminist intervention.

The new Kurdish diasporas also contribute to women's studies by, among other means, publishing, art, academic research, media activities, and human rights activities. The first and second generation of diasporans write graduate theses on women. The Kurdish Human Rights Project in London has produced excellent reports on sexual violence in custody and the repression of lawyers in Turkey. We hope that this bibliography will encourage libraries to contribute to the advancement of Kurdish women's studies by developing specialized collections.

## Bibliographies: The Unequal Distribution of Knowledge

Although knowledge, especially in writing, has been male centred throughout the world, its creation and dissemination, too, has been unequal and hierarchical. For instance, much of the available literature is about Western

17

women, and women in the rest of the world appear less often either as creators, knowledge producers, or as subject of the study. The disparity can be gauged to some extent by looking at the sources of knowledge available in libraries, archives, or databases. For instance, a keyword search on February 24, 2005 on WorldCat for "women" modified by "American," "Chinese," "Arab," "Iranian," "Turkish," and "Kurdish" revealed the following results displayed in Table 1.

**Table 1.** WorldCat Keyword Search of Women

| Country/People | Total in All Languages | Of Which in English |
|---|---|---|
| American Women | 83,251 | Not provided |
| Chinese Women | 5,382 | 2,880 |
| Arab Women | 2,425 | 1,184 |
| Iranian Women | 441 | 308 |
| Turkish Women | 655 | 298 |
| Kurdish Women | 74 | 31 |

These figures include books, articles, visual materials, serial publications, sound recordings, computer files, Internet resources, archival materials, musical scores, and maps. However, in each case the majority of records are books. In the area of bibliographic studies, too, the disparity is remarkable. A keyword search for "bibliography" and "women" modified by "American," "Chinese," "Arab," "Iranian," "Turkish," and "Kurdish" provided the following results in Table 2.

**Table 2.** WorldCat Keyword Search of Bibliographies on Women

| Country/People | Total in All Languages | Of Which in English |
|---|---|---|
| American/Women/Bibliography | 3,607 | 3,498 |
| Chinese/Women/Bibliography | 160 | 120 |
| Arab/Women/Bibliography | 146 | 69 |
| Iranian/Women/Bibliography | 24 | 17 |
| Turkish/Women/Bibliography | 37 | 1 |
| Kurdish/Women/Bibliography | 4 | 4 |

It must be emphasized that these are not all monographs, and many of them, including the four Kurdish women's bibliographies, are nothing more than a few pages of bibliographic references within the covers of books. Another trend is the dominance of English even in bibliographies about women of non-Western, non-Anglophone, societies.

Libraries, too, are biased in acquiring their resources. Many books and journals never make it to any library, while some are acquired by thousands. The processes of inclusion and exclusion are complex but not difficult to comprehend. Much depends on where, in what language, by whom, and for whom a book or a periodical is published. WorldCat provides information on which "worldwide libraries" hold a particular item. Many publications about Kurdish women listed in the bibliography cannot be found in any libraries, even in the countries where they are published.

## The Idea of a Bibliography of Kurdish Women's Studies

Almost anyone who studies the Kurds, their history, and society, will find references to the status of Kurdish women as being different, in essence, enjoying more freedom, than their neighbouring Arab, Persian, or Turkish sisters. However, even specialists find it difficult to acquire information about these women.

While living in Kurdish environments both in Kurdistan and in Kurdish diasporas, engaging in activism and conducting research, we conceived, in 1998, the idea of compiling a comprehensive bibliography. Knowing, like everyone else, that there is a dearth of research, we envisaged compiling a multilingual, multi-author, bibliography in 12 languages, including Arabic, Danish, Dutch, English, Italian, French, German, Kurdish, Persian, Russian, Swedish, and Turkish. We wrote a proposal, sent it to researchers who work in these languages, and invited them to participate in the project. All the respondents emphasized that there was not enough material for compiling a book-length bibliography. To give a couple of examples, a well-known specialist on the Kurds, who has published research about Kurdish women, sent us (November 30, 1998) all the items on "gender" and "women" in his multilingual "personal bibliography." This list included a total of 38 items, of which nine were in English, eight in German, and none in French. Another researcher, a Kurdish student working in France on a doctoral dissertation about the Kurds sent us 12 French language references on Kurdish women, and noted: "Believe me, as much as I have searched French sources, I have not found more than this on Kurdish women; writing on Kurdish women is very rare (I mean in French)" (personal communication, February 18, 2002).

We finally decided to reduce the number of languages to English, French, and German. This decision had nothing to do with the dearth of resources on Kurdish women. It was, rather, due to limitations of time in an environment of heavy teaching loads, lack of financial resources, and limited access in Canada to material in Middle Eastern languages or even Western languages such as Danish, Italian, or Russian. We were originally optimistic about the existence of more literature on Kurdish women, our initial estimates ranged between 200 and 500 items.

Progress in bibliographic studies of the Kurds began in the 1960s with the appearance of the first multilingual monographic bibliography of Zh. S. Musaelian, *Bibliografiia po Kurdovedeniiu* (Moscow, Akademiia Nauk SSSR, 1963), which recorded 2,690 books and articles with an addendum of 79 entries, mostly in Western languages. This was the basis for Silvio van Rooy and Kees Tamboer's *ISK's Kurdish Bibliography* (Amsterdam, International Society of Kurdistan, 1968) with 9,350 entries including leaflets and news reports. Although literature on Kurdish women was included in these works, they were not organized under the heading of "women" or any related term that would allow the user to locate them conveniently. The second rather detailed general bibliography, in essence, the two-volume work by van Rooy and Tamboer, does not use the category of "women" in its subject index.

Even the most detailed, multilingual general subject bibliography, Zh. S. Musaelian's *Bibliography po Kurdovedeniyo (Nachinaia s XVI Veka)/ Bibliography on Kurdology (Since 16th Century;* St. Petersburg Institute for Oriental Studies, Russian Academy of Sciences, two volumes, 1996; 8,764 entries), an updated version of the 1963 work, does not use "women" as a subject heading or subheading. In this important effort, works on Kurdish women are hidden under the broad category of "History. Ethnography," which is itself divided according to language (Russian and non-Russian), and time periods of centuries and decades. In the absence of a subject index, the user must peruse through 125 pages and no less than 1,800 citations in order to find the literature on Kurdish women.

There is more adequate inclusion of women in the latest bibliographies. For instance, Karin Kren's *Kurdologie, Kurdistan und Kurden in der Deutschsprachigen Literatur: Kommentierte Bibliographie* (2000) is an annotated author bibliography of German language literature on "Kurdish studies, Kurdistan and the Kurds." It lists 814 entries, and has *Frauen,* "women," in its subject index, which refers to 25 items with a cross-reference to three more sources.

Another major bibliography is Lokman I. Meho and Kelly L. Maglaughlin's *Kurdish Culture and Society: An Annotated Bibliography* (Westport, Connecticut: Greenwood Press, 2001). It includes a total of 931 entries in Arabic (15%), English (60%), French (5%) and German (5%), organized under 22 subheadings, one of which is "women" (pp. 285-91). Its subject index offers the following headings: Women (29 entries, with cross-references to marriage, social life and customs, urbanization, and weddings), women and war (7), women and politics (6), women and Islam (2), women rulers (1), and women's studies (1). Of the last five headings, which total 17 entries, only one is not listed under the heading "women." Thus, adding up the number of entries under these headings and leaving out repeated citations, we get a total of 30 items. It must be noted that, as an annotated work, this bibliography does not aim at a comprehensive coverage of the literature.

Moving from bibliographies about the Kurds to specialized bibliographies on women, we find a similar trend. For instance, Michelle R. Kimball and Barbara R. Von Schlegell's *Muslim Women Throughout the World: A Bibliography*

(Boulder, Colorado: Lynne Rienner Publishers, 1997) has 2,905 entries with only seven on Kurdish women. To give another example, Eleanore O. Hofstetter's *Women in Global Migration, 1945-2000: A Comprehensive Multidisciplinary Bibliography* (Westport, Connecticut: Greenwood Press, 2001) provides three references out of no less than 5,100 entries. In the *Encyclopedia of Women & Islamic Cultures* (EWIC, 2005) there are nine entries under Kurdish women, nine under Kurdistan, 20 for Kurds, and 50 for Kurdish.[4]

## This Bibliography

Given the peripheral presence of women in general bibliographies, there is an urgent need for compiling bibliographic studies of the women of Kurdistan in different languages. We believe that all reference works are, far from being neutral or objective, political and ideological undertakings. In order to make up for bibliographic silences, this work aims to be as comprehensive as possible in covering literature on Kurdish women in English, French, and German. The silence is, however, systemic or structured, with many factors contributing to its production and reproduction. We will elaborate on some of the challenges of collecting, indexing, and retrieving information on the women of Kurdistan.

The users of this bibliography will soon find out that there are few books dealing with Kurdish women. Apparently, the first monographic work on Kurdish women is a Soviet book produced by N. A. Smirnov, *Kurdskaia Zhenshchina* (Kurdish woman), published in Moscow in 1927. The second book is Henny Harald Hansen *Daughters of Allah* (London: Purnell and Sons Ltd., 1960), which was a translation of the original Danish book *Allah's Døtre* published in 1958. Hansen's next work, *The Kurdish Woman's Life: Field Research in a Muslim Society, Iraq* (Copenhagen: Nationalmuseet, 1961), provided the first major anthropological study of Kurdish women.

While there is a dearth of monographic works on Kurdish women, most books on the Kurds provide some information about women. It is simply difficult to select from this literature in so far as any information may have research value. We have included book chapters about Kurdish women as well as shorter references in travel accounts, missionary literature, and other

---

[4] Shahrzad serves on the Advisory Board of the *Encyclopedia of Women & Islamic Cultures* (EWIC) and in an October 2020 meeting, Suad Joseph, the General Editor, reported (see also https://sjoseph.ucdavis.edu/ewic) the EWIC Print I, consisting of 6 volumes (1,246 articles, 2 million words, on 410 topics), was written by 907 scholars from around the world and published between 2003-2007. EWIC Online produced 20 supplements between 2010-2020. Two supplements were uploaded every year aiming at 100,000 words per supplement. EWIC Online added 42 new topics, in addition to the 410 of EWIC Print I. EWIC Online produced nearly 2 million words, written by 292 authors, covering 126 topics. EWIC Online also included all the articles from EWIC Print I. EWIC Online was launched in 2009 and published consistently through 2020. EWIC Online took a sabbatical in 2020 and will resume in 2021.

sources. One example is Rev. Samuel Graham Wilson's *Persian Life and Customs* (Second Edition, Edinburgh and London: Oliphant Anderson and Ferrier, 1896), which has, like other literature of this genre, some references to Kurdish women, and, more significantly, is one of the few sources reporting an event that is still alive in the memory of the people in Mukri Kurdistan. This story, known locally as "the year of the Armenian girl" (*salî kiçe Hermenî*), is about the eloping of an Armenian girl and a Kurdish man, which led to a diplomatic war involving Iran, Britain, and Ottoman Turkey, as well as the deployment of the Iranian army in 1891.

This bibliography aims at covering diverse sources of knowledge including books, articles, news reports, films, video documentaries, graduate dissertations and theses, book and film reviews, and "ephemeral publications" of political parties and individuals. Quite often, a news report, an obscure pamphlet, or a film review constitutes an important source, especially for feminist understanding of gender relations. Although academic works have prominent presence in libraries and bibliographies, and it has been easy to collate them, we have also tried to cover non-academic sources as much as possible. Much of the ephemeral literature is usually available in private possession, if at all. We hope that this bibliography will encourage the launching of an online library of this type of literature.

Not included in this bibliography are Internet materials, which are readily available, but more short-lived than ephemeral sources in print. Women in Kurdistan have had more limited access to the Internet compared with men. Many feminists believed that cyberspace was radically different from realspace, only to find out that patriarchy dominates both spaces. In spite of limited presence and access, knowledge about Kurdish women is available through this medium (Mojab, 2001d). Tracking ephemeral literature is extremely difficult. To give one example, in Europe we had acquired a few issues of *Jiyan-Kovara Yekîtiya Jinén Kurdistan - Kurdische Frauenzeitschrift*, the "magazine of the Union of Women of Kurdistan," published in Köln, Germany, in German, Kurdish, and Turkish in the 1990s by KOMJIN, the women's branch of KOMKAR, a Kurdish political organization in Europe. However, communicating with KOMKAR to access all the issues proved unsuccessful. A doctoral student at a North American university, who was doing research on the Kurds in Germany and had friends in the group, asked them for help to no avail. In April 2002, we finally received some of the issues we were missing thanks to a response received from a staff member of the Kurdistan Solidarity Committee, London, publisher of *Kurdistan Report*. However, even this publisher could not provide us with issues No. 1, 2, 3, 20, 21, 22, 26, and 27, and it was impossible to access the French and German versions of this publication.

# The Politics and Ideology of Bibliographic Studies

If omission and commission are political undertakings, indexing any selected item rests on equally political and ideological considerations. While we have not eliminated any source of knowledge for its political or ideological positions, we have consciously taken sides in indexing the selected material. Our goal is to provide a feminist bibliography of information on the women of Kurdistan.

The bibliography is organized under 19 broad subject headings, with 101 sub-headings arranged in alphabetical order. We have used the *European Women's Thesaurus*, which describes itself in the title page as "a structured list of descriptors for indexing and retrieving information in the field of the position of women and women's studies" (International Information Centre and Archives for the Women's Movement, 1998). It provides 20 general categories such as "The Arts," "Anthropology," and "Building/Housing." The *Thesaurus* takes a feminist approach in its listing of terms, organizing, and structuring them. For instance, it lists the word "companies" as an indexing term that has "a women's aspect," (p. iii) and gives its *related term* or *similar meaning* as "women's companies." The *Thesaurus* notes that it has made an "important ideological choice" (p. iii) by regarding women's companies as a "related term" of "companies" instead of its "*narrower term*," and thus placing women's companies "on the same level as 'ordinary' (general/men's) companies and hence not... as something different or inferior" [a "narrower term" is "a more specific term, often of a lower hierarchical level e.g., 'film' is a NT of 'audiovisual material'"] (p. iii).

The cited example reveals the gendered nature of indexing. However, we find the *Thesaurus* lacking in several areas, especially in dealing with male violence against women and the gendered nature of war. The *Thesaurus* places "violence" under three of its 20 categories, namely "health/the body," "psychology," and "social relations" for the purpose of covering all aspects of the term. It then notes that "violence" is a "collective term" in scope, which is used for "aggression"; the broader term of "violence" is identified as "social problems," while its more specific terms are "mental cruelty, physical violence, sexual violence," and its related terms (similar meanings) are given as "criminal law, offenders, power, self-defence, victims." Among these referred terms, mental cruelty, physical violence, sexual violence, criminal law, offenders, power, self-defence, and victims are listed as "preferred terms," in essence, "terms in the thesaurus which are used to index a document" (p. ii). Listed under "sexual violence" are narrower terms of "incest, indecent assault, rape, sexual harassment," and related terms "criminal law, pornography, prostitution, sex industry, traffic in women."

The terms listed above do not cover all the types and sites of violence against women as identified, for instance, in the 1993 U.N. "Declaration on the Elimination of Violence against Women." This document refers to "physical, sexual, and psychological violence occurring in the family . . . within the general community . . . [and] perpetrated or condoned by the state, wherever it occurs" (article 2). However, the *Thesaurus* does not relate male violence to the sphere of the state or even the community. Also, unlike the U.N. document, it does not treat female genital mutilation as a form of violence, and places it under categories of "anthropology" and "health/the body."

Another limitation of the *Thesaurus* is its inadequate treatment of the gendered nature of war and peace; it has very few terms dealing with war, and its related references do not cover the extensive ways in which war affects women; in fact, it does not use terms such as genocide, war crimes, and crimes against humanity. Moreover, it does not include "torture," "femicide," "honour killing," "stoning," or "gendercide," although the latter was not well known when the *Thesaurus* was published in 1998.

Our bibliography records extensive literature on violence perpetrated by the family, community, and the state. We have let the entries suggest subject headings and subheadings, have created new ones, and refined the ones which have already been used. This is necessary because the literature on the women of each country has its particularities, which should be considered to enrich indexing and retrieving. The Republic of Turkey, for instance, has committed sexual violence against women in custody, in hospitals and clinics (conducting "virginity tests"), and through the legal and judiciary processes, which have been lenient on honour killers.

We have tried to avoid the fashionable state-centred scholarship, which sanitizes processes of nation-building and state-building and disguises their violence. Moreover, we distinguish between violence against women in times of peace and war. As will be discussed further below, the region where Armenians, Assyrians, and Kurds have lived is identified by one historian as a "zone of genocide" (Levene, 1998). Here, the state has violated what is known variously as the laws of war, international humanitarian law, or international law of armed conflict by committing genocide, war crimes and crimes against humanity (for the case of Turkey, see Human Rights Watch, *Weapons Transfers and Violations of the Laws of War in Turkey*). However, violations are considered war crimes and crimes against humanity if the conflict is international. Under these conditions, the rape of women in custody, for instance, is considered both a war crime and a crime against humanity. Placing these cases in a bibliography under the heading of "violence against women" amounts to decriminalization of these war crimes. Following the cited Human Rights Watch document, we consider the 1984-2000 war between Turkey and the armed forces of Workers' Party of Kurdistan (Partiya Karkerén Kurdistané, PKK) as no less than an "internal armed conflict," which "passed well beyond the level of violence required to be considered an internal armed conflict" (HRW, 1995, p. 160). The intermittent wars between the various Iraqi regimes and the Kurds in 1961-91 should also be considered in the same light. Even when they have not officially declared war on each other, these governments have accused each other of interfering in their internal affairs, and the Iraq armies have crossed international borders in their war on Kurdish armed groups. In placing an entry under the headings of "war crime" or "crime against humanity," we have also used the frameworks of the International Criminal Court, as codified in their 2013 document, *Elements of Crimes*.

Reference books are compiled and used under conditions of the division of human beings into nation-states with their international borders, which criss-cross the ethnic mosaic of the world, ignore ethnic diversity, and often try to eliminate it. These works, therefore, contribute to the (re)production of the nation and its state, as well as its inter-state or "international" order. Bibliographies may be state centred in many ways, including their organizing of entries according to the number of states, and ignoring non-state entities. This is the case even of the *European Women's Thesaurus*, cited above, which offers a list of "geographic descriptors" to be "used to index documents by area, country or other geographical aspect" (1998, p. vi). For non-state peoples, it recommends that "[p]opulation groups without a country may be used as free descriptors... 'Kurds' and 'Palestinians' are examples" (p. x). Our bibliography ignores international borders, which divide the geoethnic entity known as Kurdistan, and treats the Kurds as a transnational, non-state, or nation. At the same time, it uses the nation-state divisions in so far as many entries are about women in particular states.

In the context of ongoing transnationalization and globalization, it is nationalism, nativism, ethnicization, or indigenization of feminism and women's movements that are being promoted. Rooted in the nationalist urge to control women and women's movements, this politics of fragmentation of women along ethnic lines converges with currently fashionable trends in Western social theory, which privilege "difference" and particularism, and treat feminist internationalism and even "feminism," "patriarchy," and "woman" as oppressive "grand narratives." In this work, we do not privilege ethnicity as a marker of human beings, states, or politics, and treat Kurdistan as a land of the Kurds as well as several non-Kurdish ethnic peoples. Thus, the bibliography covers non-Kurdish women, although it does not do so in any comprehensive way. The literature on non-Kurdish women such as Armenians, Assyrians, and the Jews, who have shared the land with the Kurds for millennia demands specialized bibliographies. We have tried to include literature that deals with inter-ethnic gender relations.

The user of this bibliography should also be alerted to silences and emphases that are apparent but may be misleading. For instance, there are many entries on honour killing, which may give the wrong impression that Kurdish society, Kurdish culture, or the Kurdish people are more violent than their counterparts in Turkey, Iran, or in the West. Racists and national chauvinists have already promoted this kind of politics, which keeps silent about the persistence of patriarchal violence among the members of their own "race" or nation, and thus endorses their own regime of male supremacy. In treating the Kurds as exceptionally or inherently violent, racial supremacists engage in misogynism in so far as they ignore the extensive resistance of Kurdish women against patriarchal violence. In their approach to gender relations in Kurdish society, they divide the women of the world into two races, one of which is free and the other subjected to violence, permissive of it, incapable of understanding its subordination, and thus unable to resist it. The bibliography rejects these racist mythologies by documenting the non-exceptional status of Kurdish women, and their active resistance against male violence.

If racism and national chauvinism of the dominant nations constitute misogynist politics, many Kurdish nationalists play into this by underestimating the seriousness of indigenous male violence, by psychologizing it and, even worse, relating it to fictional, foreign, origins such as an Arab and Islamic past. This position, in essence, blaming indigenous violence on other nations and races, is itself no less than racist patriarchal politics. It is not difficult to note that thousands of women lose their lives, often in obscurity every day and everywhere in the world, due to male violence. The cases of honour killing committed by the Kurds in Europe have attracted media attention to the extent that in some countries the name Kurd is associated with femicide. Many Kurds, reacting to the overt racism of neo-fascists and ultra-conservative supremacists or the covert racism of the mainstream media, resent any publicity about Kurdish honour killings. The coverage of these crimes in a bibliography turns, thus, into a clearly political issue. We discuss one case next.

In Britain, the father who killed his daughter, Heshu Yones, in October 2002 was sentenced to life imprisonment. Although the crime itself did not attract much local or national attention, the sentencing became an international news item only because it was covered by BBC World Service television on September 30, 2003. Within a month, a Google web search for "Heshu" produced 1,340 results (October 28, 2003), and 1,910 results by February 27, 2005. Although the event led to controversy, much of the international reporting was the republication, often with only a change of the headlines, of British media reports. No doubt, including all the recycled reports in the bibliography will be useful for various research purposes, such as media construction of honour crimes, the role of a major media outlet such as BBC in creating and distributing knowledge about gender crimes, media and racism, or media and Islamophobia. One can envisage research on headlines alone, which will reveal racial, gender, national, and religious biases. At the same time, the inclusion of all these reports, even if only the ones written in English, would inflate the section on violence against women with entries on one case only. We have tried to cover different reports of the event by print media in English and have included some of their reprints outside Europe in order to show the geographic spread of the news. We believe that media attention to crimes against women is much desired, although how they are covered should be subjected to critical scrutiny.

The user of the bibliography will also notice the visibility of Leyla Zana, the first and only Kurdish woman member of parliament in Turkey, who was tried and jailed for advocating the rights of the Kurds. Media coverage of her life and struggle is extensive, and she has emerged, among the Kurds and in Europe, as a symbol of resistance. Still, the bibliography has not covered all the literature in its three languages.

The image depicted of the women of Kurdistan in this bibliography is shaped also by the languages we have chosen. It is a record of material in languages that are not spoken by the majority of the Kurds. It will, therefore, be different from a bibliography of works in the Kurdish language, which have a majority of Kurdish authors, with more entries on topics such as poetry, fiction, education, or sport. Still, a considerable number of the entries in this bibliography are written by the Kurds themselves. Many have appeared in publications issued by Kurdish groups and targeted at an international readership.

The bibliography is more or less silent on the women of Syria and Iran. This is largely due to the dearth of research on the Kurds of these two countries in general and Kurdish women in particular. As for the Kurds of the Soviet Union, currently Commonwealth of Independent States, there is a considerable body of research in Russian but very little in the languages of this bibliography.

This bibliography is a compromise between annotation and simple listing of entries. Instead of evaluating each entry, we have tried to provide information on its content, more than what one can glean from the title. This is done through the use of "keywords," which at times amount to long phrases and sentences. The key wordings are uneven in quality and quantity. Sometimes, it is not easy to keyword an entry, especially when it is fiction or poetry. Entries without keywords are the ones we have not read or seen. When entries do not carry the name of their author, compiler, or producer we have assigned them a name, often the name of the publication or publisher, in order to allow for more efficient treatment in the indexes. All bibliographic entries, here as elsewhere, are complex and polysemic, and do not, as a result, lend themselves to placement under one category. Like other bibliographies, we address this problem by cross-referencing for many entries.

# WOMEN OF KURDISTAN

## The People and the Land

Kurdish women, in this study, are members of a non-state nation, the Kurds, who live in their homeland, Kurdistan, a contiguous territory divided since 1918, among the neighboring countries of Turkey (southeast), Iran (northwest), Iraq (north), and Syria (northeast).[5] They also live in small and large communities dispersed outside Kurdistan in each of the four countries (especially northeast Iran, central and western Turkey, in major cities like Istanbul, Baghdad, Damascus, and Tehran), Caucasus (Armenia, Azerbaijan, Georgia) and Central Asia, and as refugee and immigrant communities in Lebanon, Europe, North America, Australia, New Zealand, Japan, and other countries (see Table 4).

In the absence of census figures, estimates of the size of the Kurdish population vary between 25 to 35 million, making them the fourth largest ethnic people of the Middle East, outnumbered by Arabs, Turks, and Persians (see Table 3). While the population in much of Kurdistan is densely Kurdish, other peoples such as Armenians, Assyrians, and Jews have shared the region with the Kurds. The women of Kurdistan, in this bibliography, include not only Kurdish women but also women of such non-Kurdish ethnic peoples.

**Table 3**. Population of the Kurds (Estimation)

| Country | Number of Kurds | Percent of the Population |
|---|---|---|
| Turkey | 13,700,000 | 24.1 |
| Iran | 6,600,000 | 12.4 |
| Iraq | 4,400,000 | 23.5 |
| Syria | 1,300,000 | 9.2 |
| Europe* | 700,000 | |
| Ex-USSR* | 400,000 | |
| Total | 27,100,000 | |

*McDowall (2000, p. 3-4).

---

[5] In recent years, it is more common to refer to different Kurdish regions by their geographical location. Therefore, the Kurdish region of Turkey is called Bakur (Northern Kurdistan), Iraq is Başur (Southern Kurdistan), Syria is Rojava (Western Kurdistan), and Iran is Rojhelat (Eastern Kurdistan).

The Kurds are often depicted in both the Middle East and the West as a nomadic and tribal Muslim people. However, Kurdish society, throughout its recorded history, has been complex including tribal-nomadic, rural-feudal, and urban non-agrarian social and economic formations, and it is now highly differentiated in terms of social class, profession, politics, religion, and culture.

Language is a major indication of the national identity of the Kurds. The Kurdish language is a member of the Iranian branch of Indo-European languages with four dialect groups, namely Kurmanji (or Northern), Sorani (or Central), Zaza/Dimili and Hawrami/Gorani, and Southern dialects. The language has been written for about five centuries, predominantly in Arabic script, but as of the 1930s also in Cyrillic and Roman alphabets. The nation-states of Turkey, Iran, Iraq, and Syria formed in the wake of WWI, and pursued a policy of assimilating the diverse ethnic peoples into the dominant nation, in part, by suppressing their language. The Kurdish language was subjected to harsh policies and practices of linguicide, the deliberate killing of language. This bibliography reflects the gender dimension of this policy.

Religious life in Kurdistan is diverse, although the Kurds are predominantly Sunni Muslims, with several religious minority groups such as Alevis, Ahli-Haq (Ahl-e Haqq), Baha'is, Christians, Judaists, Shi'is (Shiites), and Yezidis. In spite of the genocide of the Christian population (Armenians and Assyrians) by the Ottoman state during WWI, many Kurdish cities continue to have churches, though some exists only in ruins. The Jewish population in Kurdistan was scattered, although there were sizeable rural populations especially in Iraq, speaking their language and practicing religion in their synagogues; most of the Jewish population in both rural and urban areas immigrated to Israel. The Ahl-e Haqq and Yezidis, too, have survived systemic persecution.

Although citizens of several nation-states, many Kurds identify their homeland as Kurdistan: land of the Kurds. This land includes the northern parts of what was called Mesopotamia and the eastern parts of Anatolia. The first mention of the land of the Kurds (*ard al-akrād* in Arabic) was apparently in a map drawn in 1076 (Chaliand & Rageau, 1983). A century later, the Saljuq monarch, Sultan Sanjar (1086?-1157), conquered the Kurdish territory and turned it into an administrative unit called Kurdistan. Written sources, produced by the Kurds themselves, date back to the sixteenth century. While the name Kurdistan appears in the Kurdish oral literature recorded since the mid-nineteenth century, the earliest delineation of its borders in a written source is in the "history of the Kurds" known as *Sharaf-Nāme* and written by prince Bidlisi in 1596-97, ruler of Bidlis principality (Bidlisi, 1964, pp. 24-25).

**Table 4.** The Size of Kurdish Diasporas

| Region | Country | Numbers |
| --- | --- | --- |
| Europe | Germany | 500,000 |
| | France | 100,000-120,000 |
| | Netherlands | 70,000-80,000 |
| | Switzerland | 7,531 |
| | Belgium | 50,000-60,000 |
| | Austria | 50,000-60,000 |
| | Sweden | 25,000-30,000 |
| | United Kingdom | 20,000-25,000 |
| | Greece | 20,000-25,000 |
| | Denmark | 8,000-10,000 |
| | Norway | 4,000-5,000 |
| | Italy | 3,000-4,000 |
| | Finland | 3,916 |
| | Russia | |
| | Siberia | 35,000 (30,000 in Vladivostok) |
| | Krasnodar | 30,000 |
| Central Asia | Kazakhstan | 30,000 |
| | Turkmenistan | 50,000 |
| | Kirghizia | 20,000 |
| | Uzbekistan | 10,000 |
| | Tajikistan | 3,000 |
| Caucasia | Armenia | 75,000 |
| | Azerbaijan | 12,000-30,000 |
| | Georgia | 40,000 |
| Middle East | Lebanon | 75,000-100,000 |
| North America | Canada | 7,140 |
| | United States | 15,000-20,000 |
| Oceania | Australia | 2,845 |
| | New Zealand | 603 |

*Note.* From Mojab, S., and Hassanpour, A. (2004). Kurdish diaspora. In I. Skoggard (Ed.) *Encyclopedia of diasporas* (pp. 214-24). Diasporas. Human Relations Area Files, Inc.

In the absence of Kurdish state power, Kurdistan does not have internationally recognized borders. Within each country, too, the state's ruling over the Kurds pursue a policy of assimilating them, and thus have refused Kurdish demands for identifying the borders of the Kurdish region, administratively or cartographically. In Iran, a part of the larger Kurdish territory carries the name "Kordestan," while in Iraq, it is only after the 2003 invasion of Iraq by Western allied forces led by the US that "Northern Iraq" is now being referred to as Iraqi Kurdistan. In Turkey, using the names Kurd and Kurdistan has been, since the mid-1920s, considered a crime against the "indivisibility of the Turkish nation" and the "territorial integrity of the state" (terms from the Constitution of Turkey). Not surprisingly, in the context of coercive erasing of the contours of the Kurdish homeland, Kurdistan's "borders bleed" (Kashi, 1994). In order to isolate Iraqi Kurdistan from the Kurdish parts of Iran and Turkey, the Iraqi Ba'ath regime destroyed hundreds of border villages in the late 1970s. Similarly, Iraq and later Iran, in the late 1980s, planted tens of millions of land mines in border passes to prevent the movement of Kurdish nationalist forces, known as *peshmarga* (defined as one who faces death, or freedom fighter) across the borders.

While forced displacement was practiced throughout the history of the region, two developments in the latter part of the twentieth century led to major uprooting of Kurdish populations, within the region and internationally. One was ongoing coercive assimilation, which led to increasing Kurdish resistance, including armed conflicts between the Kurds and the governments in Iraq (intermittently from 1961-2003), Iran (1967-68, 1979-present), and Turkey (1984-present). Western powers and regional states were involved in these and other inter-state conflicts (Iraq-Kuwait, Iran-Iraq) which turned the area into an active and enduring war zone.

The second development was the economic boom of Western Europe in the 1960s, which relied on a large number of "guest workers" especially in Germany but also, on a more limited scale, in Belgium, the Netherlands, Denmark, France, and Sweden. Many guest workers were from Turkey. By the late 1990s, Germany hosted Europe's largest Kurdish population, estimated at about half a million.

## Kurdistan: A Historical Sketch

Although the Kurds are apparently an Indigenous people of Western Asia, their territory was home to numerous civilizations and peoples, most of which (except for Assyrians, Armenians, and Jews) are extinct or assimilated. The area is the site of the first agrarian and urban revolutions. The landscape is decorated with relics of monumental construction projects ranging from ancient irrigation networks to bridges to citadels side by side with records of continuing destruction of life and property through conquest, wars, massacres, and forced population movements.

After the conquest of the region by Islamic armies in the seventh century, we hear more about the Kurds. Kurdistan, which is very close to Baghdad, the capital of the Islamic caliphate, was the site of incessant wars among the caliphs, their armies and governors, Kurdish rulers, and conquerors coming from as far as the Roman empire in the west and Mongolia in the east. While the conflicts were primarily over land, taxes, and recruiting military service

31

from the population, ethnic and religious differences provided justifications for conquest and subjugation. Unrestrained violence including atrocities against both civilians and combatants was widespread and aimed, in part, at intimidating the adversary and the population into submission (Minorsky, 1986).

The arrival of Oghuz Turks into the region from the Asian steppes in the eleventh century, the formation of the Saljuq dynasty (eleventh through thirteenth centuries), and Turkoman dynasties (Aq Qoyunlu and Qara Qoyunlu), followed by the fall of the caliphate in 1258 in the wake of the Mongol invasion, reshaped the ethnic composition of Western Asia. While "the Kurdish element was exhausting itself" (Minorsky, 1986, p. 453) in these unceasing wars, according to one historian, it is during this period that the Kurds emerge as a distinct people, their territory becomes identified by outsiders as Kurdistan, and Kurdish statehood emerges in the form of mini-states and principalities.

Some of the Indigenous populations of Kurdistan including the Armenians, Assyrians (Christians), Kurds (mostly Muslims), followers of minority religions (such as Yezidis), as well as scattered minorities such as the Jews survived the intensive colonization of the region by Turkic (Oghuz, Turkoman, Ottoman), Mongol nomadic, and tribal peoples from central Asia. While centuries of conversion, forcible population movements, and massacres acted as ethnically homogenizing forces, the feudal states failed to centralize power and assimilate conquered subjects into the language, culture, and religion of the conquerors. Equally important in preventing total annihilation of populations was the labour-intensive nature of feudal agrarian production. Without a sizeable productive labour force, the fertile lands of Armenia, Azerbaijan, Kurdistan, and Mesopotamia could not sustain elaborate state structures. Thus, while some Kurdish territories were Turkicized due to conquest, violent elimination of Kurdish ruling families (especially by the Aq Qoyunlu dynasty, 1378-1508), through massacres and deportations, Kurdish mini states were, at the same time, gaining ground (Minorsky, 1986). By the end of the sixteenth century, about 40 small and large emirates ruled all over Kurdistan (Vasil'eva, 1967, 1976). The administrative structure of the mini states was similar to the system of the larger states in the region, especially the Ottoman empire (van Bruinessen, 1992).

Western Asia was, by the early sixteenth century, under the rule of two rival and ever-expanding Turkish dynasties, the Ottomans and Safavids. In 1639, in the wake of major wars, they drew their borders along the Zagros mountain range, thus dividing Armenia and Kurdistan into two pieces. The two empires pursued a policy of administrative centralization by removing hereditary Kurdish principalities and appointing governors from the centre.

However, these mini-states benefitted from their rivalry, and some continued to rule until the mid-nineteenth century. Shah Abbas I (1588-1626), suspicious of the loyalty of the rulers of Biradost and Mukri principalities, supervised and personally participated in the massacres of the rulers and their subjects (1610-11), resettled Turkish tribes in their territory, and deported some 15,000 Kurds from another region of Kurdistan to Northeastern Iran. An eyewitness to the mass killings, the Shah's official chronicler Eskandar Monshi (1979, pp. 791-800, 806-12) detailed with pride the "general massacre" of Mukri Kurds and noted that the Shah's "fury and wrath" could not be allayed "but by shedding the blood of those unfortunate ones..." (p. 813), and that the "slicing of men" and the "enslavement of women and girls... had been inscribed on the annals of time by destination" (p. 814). He labeled the Kurds as "base-born" (p. 701), "human beings of savage disposition" (p. 792), and "impious" (p. 813). In Biradost principality, women in the besieged Dimdim fortress committed suicide in order not to fall into the hands of the Shah's forces.

The 1639 Ottoman-Iranian border survived frequent wars between the two states, and, with minor modification, still constitutes the borders between Iran and Turkey as well as Iran and Iraq. In the mid-nineteenth century, European style administrative and military centralization of state power began in Ottoman Turkey and Iran. The two states used military force in order to overthrow the six remaining Kurdish principalities and extended their direct rule over all parts of Kurdistan.

With the emergence of modern style nation-states in Iran (after the Constitutional Revolution of 1906-11) and Ottoman Turkey (especially after the 1908 Young Turk revolution), the Kurds were incorporated into the state as citizens rather than a distinct people enjoying the right to self-rule. While feudal and tribal relations continued to prevail in the predominantly rural society of Kurdistan, Kurdish nationalist ideas began to appear in the poetry and journalism in the last decade of the nineteenth century.

WWI turned Kurdistan into a battlefield between the Ottomans, Russians, Iranians, and the British. Armenia and Kurdistan changed hands between the Ottoman and Iranian armies. The Ottoman government undertook a genocide of Armenians and Assyrians in 1915, as well as the forcible transfer of some 700,000 Kurds to Western Turkey in 1917 (Andrews, 1989). At the same time, the Czarist Russian army conducted massacres of the Kurds in Sauj Bulagh (present-day Mahabad, Iran) in 1915, Rawandiz (presently in Iraq), Khanaqin (Iran), and throughout the eastern parts of Kurdistan. As in previous wars, both armies committed crimes against humanity including enslavement, murder, extermination, rape, sexual slavery, sexual violence, persecution, as well as war crimes such as willful killing, inhuman treatment, unlawful deportation and transfer, attacking civilians, pillaging, and cruel treatment (for a brief account see Jwaideh, 2006). The Russian army also committed gendercide in the massacre of Sauj Bulagh by killing adolescent and adult males and carried away some 400 women and girls for abuse. While Armenian and Assyrian militia participated in the Russian massacres (Fossum, 1918; Jwaideh, 2006), some Kurdish tribal, feudal, and religious leaders acted as accomplices in the genocide of Armenians and Assyrians. At the same time, many Kurds sheltered Armenian victims (Ussher, 1917), and Assyrians helped starving Kurds.

The dismantling of the Ottoman empire in WWI led to the division of its Kurdish region and its incorporation into the newly created states of Iraq (under British occupation and mandate, 1918-32), Syria (under French occupation and mandate, 1918-46), and Turkey (Republic of Turkey since 1923). The formation of these modern type nation-states entailed the forced assimilation of the Kurds into the official or dominant national language and culture, in essence, Turkish (Turkey), Persian (Iran), and Arabic (Syria, and, in a more limited scope, Iraq), and, especially in Turkey and Iran, the uprooting of the political power of religious, tribal, and feudal leaders. State violence was the principal means of integration and assimilation. According to one historian, Ottoman Turkey and the Republic of Turkey turned Eastern Anatolia, which includes Armenia and Kurdistan, into a zone of genocide from 1878-1923 (Levene, 1998) to present day (Fernandes, 1999).

## Kurdish Women: A Historical Sketch

## Women in Tribal and Feudal Formations

The dearth of evidence and the near absence of research on the history of gender relations do not allow us to sketch the life of Kurdish women until the nineteenth century. *Sharaf-Name*, the first history of the Kurds, written four centuries ago by the Kurdish prince Sharaf al-Din Bidlisi, is a chronicle of Kurdish dynasties, mini-states, and principalities. More or less silent on women and non-princely classes, it makes references to the women of the ruling land-owning class, and their exclusion from public life and the exercise of state power. According to this source, the Kurds, following Islamic traditions, took four wives and, if they afforded it, four maids or slave girls (*jāriya*; 1964, p. 33). This regime of polygyny was, however, practiced by a minority, which included primarily some of the members of the ruling land-owning class, the nobility, and the religious establishment. Daughters and sisters were given or exchanged in marriage as means of settling wars and blood feuds. When one side was defeated, the victor could take over the women of the enemy as booty and as proof of the humiliating defeat of the adversary (p. 184).

The exercise of state power and institutions of the feudal states were patriarchal. Although ruling was hereditary in the male lineage, Bidlisi mentions three women who, after losing their husbands, took the rein of power in order to transfer it to their sons upon their adulthood (pp. 176, 226, and 497). While referring to women in degrading words such as "weakling" (p. 508), Bidlisi extolled the ability of these women to rule in the manner of males, and called one of them a "lioness" (p. 228). Even as interim rulers, women had to act as men and in the interest of the male gender.

In the mid-seventeenth century, the Turkish traveler Evliya Çelebi confirmed the picture depicted by *Sharaf-Nāme*. He was associated with the Ottoman court and stayed in a number of Kurdish cities as the guest of Kurdish rulers. In the court of the powerful Bidlis principality in the capital city of Bidlis, which he visited three times in 1655 and 1656, the esteemed guest found the female members of prince's family, together with maids or slave girls, confined to the *harem*. Apparently exaggerating, he noted that women were not allowed into the marketplace, and would be killed if they did. Although Çelebi was seeking information about women, their dress, and names, he could inquire only from "close friends" (Çelebi, 1990, p. 77). He noted, "I do not know about women, since I have not seen them in the marketplace; but they themselves [the men] praise them as chaste, veiled beauties. They are certainly covered" (Çelebi, 1990, p. 75). However, in his travels to other parts of Kurdistan, Çelebi noted that in Kurdish principalities women did occasionally assume power, to the extent that the Ottoman state accepted the succession of a male ruler by a female in Kurdistan (manuscript of Çelebi's travelogue cited in van Bruinessen, 2001, pp. 98-99).

Travelers not associated with a court depict a different picture of gender relations. Pietro della Valle (1586-1652), the Italian visitor who passed through Kurdistan in 1617, reported that "women go about freely and unveiled and talk spontaneously with men both natives and foreigners" (Della Valle, 1667, cited in Galletti, 2001, p. 210). The traveler and his wife were received warmly by a woman, who was ruling a region in the absence of her husband. Other travelers to Kurdistan had similar experiences of gender relations. A century after della Valle, another Italian visitor, Domenico Sestini (1750-1832), wrote in 1786 that Kurdish women "are pretty, tall, strong and able to make efforts. They go unveiled as heroines... In spite of their sex, women are not less ferocious than men" (Sestini, 1786, as cited in Galletti, 2001, p. 211).

By the mid-nineteenth century, European travel literature had established the myth of the relative freedom of Kurdish women. The claim that Kurdish women enjoy more freedom than their Arab, Persian, and Turkish sisters is based on observations such as absence of veiling in villages, women's freedom to socialize with men, their tradition of receiving male guests, mixed

35

dancing, and a history of women rulers. This myth was picked up by Kurdish nationalists when they emerged in the beginning of the twentieth century, discussing the "woman question" in the context of the suffragist movements in Nordic countries, and the beginning of the politics of women's rights and the rise of women's journalism in the Ottoman empire (Klein, 2001). No doubt European travel literature and scholarship also record the subordinate position of Kurdish women. The myth of relative freedom is, however, dominant. If this Orientalist regime of knowledge and the future Kurdish nationalist literature failed to depict extensive patriarchal constraints on the freedom of Kurdish women, a learned Kurdish mullah in the mid-nineteenth century noted the unity and conflict of opposites in the Kurdish patriarchy of his time.

Writing the first indigenous reflections on the status of Kurdish women in his *Customs and Manners of the Kurds* (1963; originally written in 1858-1859), Mullah Mahmûdê Bayazîdî, did not totalize the position of Kurdish women as either sovereign or subordinate. He vividly depicted both freedom and unfreedom of women in the context of rural Kurdish society. Instead of searching for an essential, a-historical "Kurdish woman," he made sharp distinctions between women living in tribal-nomadic formations and in settled agrarian communities. The gender division of labour was different in the two social formations. Nomadic women did all the work related to animal husbandry, which constituted of the mode of production of the tribe. All domestic work was also done by women. When the tribe was attacked, women took part in war side by side with men. Comparing women of nomadic and settled Kurds, he wrote that "the women of nomadic Kurds are indeed unparalleled (*nadiret-ol-zeman*) because they are at the same time wives, slaves (*xulam*), and guards (*pawan*), and during wars if necessary they are [men's] friend (*yar*) and companion (*yoldaş*) outside the home" (1963, pp. 99-98). By contrast, settled rural women were much less involved in the dominant mode of production, in essence, agriculture, and were not as courageous as nomadic women. Here, men were in charge of all domestic work except baking bread, cooking, and washing. These differences were so consequential that there was no intermarriage between settled and nomadic communities, because the latter believed that women and children of the settled would be weaklings unfit for the harsh life of nomadism.

Bayazîdî noted that, in both communities, the majority of marriages were monogamous; girls and women were not free to choose their spouses; fathers and brothers arranged marriages and women could not disobey (p. 180); women did not veil (pp. 75, 115), and together with men participated in singing, dancing, and other entertainment. At the end of the day, young men would gather in front of houses or tents and play javelin, while young women, spined their distaff, and the elderly watched them. After dinner, they would gather and begin dancing and singing until the morning (p. 83). In winters, too, "the youth, boys, girls and brides, get together at a home every night for a night party. If they have an instrument, they would play it. If they do not have instruments, singer boys and brides and girls mix together and sing and dance until early morning. Then everyone disperses and goes to her/his home. There is a night party every two or three nights in Kurdish villages" (1963, pp. 105-106; see also, p. 160).

Bayazîdî emphasized the freedom of Kurdish women by comparing them with the women of Europe, and claiming that they were equally free in socializing with men (1858-59, p. 190). However, the boundaries of this freedom were clearly delimited: women were denied control, possession, or ownership of their own bodies and sexual desire. This was the domain of the exercise of power by males. The visible freedom of socializing with men was strictly constrained by the codes of propriety and the status of women as the property of the husband, father, and brother. The family would kill women, with impunity, if they violated the codes of propriety, which was first and foremost engaging in extra- or pre-marital sexual relations. Bayazîdî emphasized the seriousness of this rule by noting, among other things, that the Kurds were strongly against taking anyone's life, to the extent that they did not kill men who were taken prisoner during violent conflicts such as war and robbery:

> But of course they do kill men who commit bad deeds (*şûla xirab*). They even kill their own wives, daughters, mothers, and sisters. And for [punishing] such bad deeds, women also kill; for instance, mothers strangle their daughters in the night or poison and kill them, and mothers-in-law do it to their daughters-in-law, and sisters to sisters. No chief (*agha*) and no elder (*rîspî*) asks why you have killed this [woman]. (1963, pp. 191-90)[6]

Throughout the text, Bayazîdî uses the words "bad deeds" to refer to pre-marital or extramarital sexual intercourse of both women and men. He noted then that Kurdish

> ...women and girls do not hide away from anyone and are free, too, like the people of Europe. However, [they are free] because it is believed that they do not engage in bad deeds, otherwise if one of them commits a bad act there is no alternative but killing her. (1963, p. 190)[7]

In spite of such violent disciplining, this patriarchal regime was challenged by

---

[6] The pages are in descending order because of the way Arabic script text has been paginated as a supplement to Cyrillic texts.

[7] Bayazîdî repeatedly referred to the freedom of Kurdish women to socialize with men including strangers and the absence of veiling (pp. 115-16, 147-48).

women and men. Faced with unwanted arranged marriages, women and men resisted by eloping. Elopement (*kiç rifandin, redûkewtin*), according to Bayazîdî, was not considered a disgrace (*'eyb*) if the woman consented to it. The man and the woman would, however, be killed by the woman's family if they could be located and captured. Although the risk of being killed in elopement was high, once the eloping couple found a mediator, usually a chief or a religious figure, the woman's family would accept a compromise (pp. 181-80). Bayazîdî graphically depicts the strict codes of women's modesty and the violent punishment of deviating from its dictates:

> Jealousy (*komreşî*) and mistrust (*bedgumanî*) are not a habit among the Kurds. For instance, their young women talk, laugh, and socialize (*rûnîn û rabûn*) with stranger men without [evoking] any suspicion. However, when they [men] see wrongdoing (*xirabî*) [by women] and are assured of it, without delay they kill the woman and the man, too. Their blood is then wasted. No one will claim them. (1963, p. 179)[8]

He notes that there is much respect for Kurdish women. However,

> when they [women] commit a bad deed, no one will intercede and they are killed since if this is not done this way, Kurdish women will not abstain from people [men] and will then be involved in much bad deed, but they are scared of (*ditirsin*) being killed. (pp. 175-74; see also, p. 113)

Bayazîdî emphasizes that killing instills fear in women and it is because of this fear that they self-discipline their modesty (p. 174; see also, p. 113). Punishment for adultery is also killing, in which case no one will intercede (*rica û şifa'et*). The author notes that in non-sexual "hideous acts" (*qebahet*), families claim blood money and also mediate for saving a killer or a thief, but in cases of adultery the family of the adulterous woman will kill both of the adulterers immediately.[9] Even if the family of the woman did not witness the act of adultery but found out about it,

> they will immediately kill the woman by stabbing and burying her. None of the neighbors and relatives and no other person will ask the killer why you did this (the killing), and there will be no condolence and no mourning. And then the woman's family will always be on guard to find the opportunity to kill the man who was involved in the

---

[8] He notes, again, that women were killed only when they engaged in wrongdoing (*şula xirab*), and it was the fear of being killed that disciplined their behaviour (pp. 175-74). The author re-emphasized the freedom of Kurdish women to socialize with male strangers without raising their husbands' suspicion, but any violation of modesty codes invited killing (pp. 114-13).

[9] The word "family" was used here for Bayazîdî's "waris." The latter means "inheritor" or "successor," which implies that anyone in the woman's family or even a relative was in a position to kill her.

bad deed. (1963, pp. 113-12)

Killing happened also when the groom and the family of the bride claimed that she was not virgin. The guests at a wedding stay in the groom's house until they are sure that the bride proves to be virgin in the first intercourse. According to Bayazîdî,

> It is very shameful if the groom cannot have intercourse in the [wedding] night, because people may suspect that the bride is not a virgin girl... God prohibit, if the bride was found not to be virgin; it will be a big disgrace. They will send the bride back to her father's home and they will take back the bride-price (*qelen*), and the owners [i.e., family of the woman] kill the bride... But if it happens that the bride is not a girl and she realizes her situation, while the preparations for the wedding are made, she will take poison and will die before the wedding, and will not live until that day. (1963, pp. 80-79)

Bayazîdî was describing the conditions under which women were disciplined by killing. He mentioned three situations which would lead to unquestionable killing – premarital sex (loss of virginity), extramarital sex (adultery), and eloping. The common thread that connects these forms of violence was the feudal patriarchal system's almost total control of the sexuality and body of the woman. A woman, married or unmarried, must be chaste, loyal, pure, obedient, and subordinate. In the feudally and tribally organized rural environment described by Bayazîdî, women were not veiled, secluded, or segregated. However, a woman was the carrier or embodiment of the honour of her husband, and, through him, that of the family and the whole community. In the absence of the husband, other male members of the family, in essence, the father, brothers, and uncles acted as the guardians of honour. Bayazîdî emphasized the participation of mothers in killing their daughters. The codes of honour were clearly inscribed in culture, tradition, custom, religion, and the economic system.

In spite of the subordinate position of women, Bayazîdî believed that they were morally and mentally better than men:

> Kurdish women are much wiser (*be'eql*), accomplished ([*be*] *kemal*), perceptive ([*be*] *idrak*) and humane ([*be*] *mirovayî*) than men. They are very affectionate (*dilovan*) and are very compassionate with those from other lands (*xerîb*) and strangers (*bîyaniyan*). They are very content (*ehlê qena'et*) and obedient. At home, they have much authority (*sahib ixtîyar*) and engage in taking and giving in the absence of men. (1963, pp. 139-38)

The Kurdish woman was, therefore, the embodiment of a web of contradictions, which were not rooted in their nature or, contrary to racist construction, to their ethnicity but, rather, in the history of the social formations in which they lived. They were, in Bayazîdî's account, both resilient and obedient, strong and weak, free and subdued, resistant and subordinate, and compassionate and unforgiving. In the labour-intensive agrarian and transhumant economies of rural Kurdistan, women constituted a major economic resource. Not only were they needed to reproduce the male lineage, but their labour was also vital in domestic work as well as agrarian production. This explains why Bayazîdî found nomadic women the best of all since they were good, obedient wives and at the same time were slave-type labourers, guardians of the household, and fighters in wars. However, the patriarchal order made a clear distinction between women and all other forms of property. A woman was the *namûs* or "honour" of the whole family but especially its male members. The loss of property due to theft, natural disaster, and other factors was tolerated but there was no tolerance for the loss of honour. *Droit du seigneur*, (right of the lord) the right to sleep the first night with the bride of a peasant, which was a right prevalent in medieval Europe that was also exercised by Kurdish feudals.

Until the late twentieth century the majority of women lived in rural areas. Unlike rural women, urban women, especially in well-to-do families, were largely confined to the domestic realm. Until the late twentieth century, the majority of women were illiterate. Literacy was limited to the male clergy, scribes, and certain members of the feudal and mercantile classes; however, some women in these social milieus acquired literacy through private tutoring. Thus, a few female names appear in the list of poets who lived before WWI. The only well-known female intellectual, Mah Sharaf Khanim, known as Mastura Kurdistani (1805-47), was a member of the court of Ardalan principality, part of Iran. She was a poet, writer of a brief work on Islamic doctrine, and is known as the first female historian of the Middle East. A considerable part of her poetry is lamenting the untimely death of her husband, the young ruler of the principality (Māh Sharaf Khānum, 1998). In her work, there is no evidence of consciousness about gender inequality or women's rights (Mojab, 2001c).

Kurdish oral tradition, collected since the latter part of the nineteenth century, depicts a complex regime of gender relations. In oral literature, one finds both the patriarchal regime presented in the written sources cited above, and a tribal quasi-matriarchal order in, for instance, *Beytî Las û Xezal* (Ballad of Las and Khazal recorded in 1901-03, as cited in Mann, 1906). In this ballad, two women, each ruler of a tribe, openly compete over a lover, Las, a man who chooses one and freely socializes with the other. Xezal exercises full authority over her lover, allows him to visit her rival, Xanzad, who is the chief of his tribe, but forbids him from making love with her. Las is obedient and acts according to Xezal's wishes. The Kurdish poet Hemin noted that the ballad was probably composed under conditions of matriarchy. In fact, in the region where the story originated and the ballad was collected, traces of matriarchy can be seen in a male's surname, which continues to be the name of his mother.

While the Ballad of Las and Khazal is apparently the only one depicting matriarchal relations, other ballads find peasant women subjected to the violence of male feudal lords, for example, in *Beytî Kake Mîr û Kake Şêx* (Ballad of Kaka Mir and Kaka Sheikh, both texts in Mann 1906). In other stories, women resist to be sold as property or exchanged in marriage in the interests of the male members of the family; this resistance takes the form of eloping with their lovers, an act which leads to the loss of life, for example *Beytî Xec û Syamend* (Ballad of Khaj and Syamand), or leaving their family and tribe in search of their lovers, for example, *Beytî Şoř Mehmûd û Merzîngan* (Ballad of Shor Mahmud and Marzingan; text in Fattāhī Qāzī 1970). It is significant that all these stories, their plots, characters, and contexts are Kurdish, and although they may readily fit the international motifs depicted by folklorists, they depict the complex values of Kurdish society in the realm of gender relations.

Kurdish proverbs, too, treat women in conflicting, though patriarchal, ways, ranging from "source of life" to "pain" (Rohat, 1994).[10] Quite often proverbs such as "A lion is a lion, whether male or female" are cited as evidence of a tradition of equal treatment of women. There are, however, numerous proverbs conferring on women subordinate status. The study of Kurdish language from a feminist perspective has just begun. Like other languages studied so far, Kurdish is lexically and semantically androcentric, sexist, and misogynist, although it has emerged, at the same time, as one of the sites of struggle for gender equality (Hassanpour, 2001).

## The Era of Capitalism, Nationalism, and Socialism

The regime of principalities came to an end due to the military action of the Ottoman empire and Iran in the mid-nineteenth century. This was a project of centralization of state power through legal, administrative, financial, and military reforms first launched in Ottoman Turkey. The reforms occurred, in part, due to the pressure from emerging liberal-minded elites and nascent democratic movements, and, to some extent, under the pressure of Western powers interested in a safe environment for their economic pursuits. The fall of Kurdish principalities eliminated the last trace of Kurdish self-rule, and extended Ottoman and Iranian power over all parts of Kurdistan; however,

---

[10] It must be noted, however, that Rohat depicts in Kurdish proverb the sovereignty of Kurdish women.

rural areas and their population remained largely under the control of tribal and feudal chiefs.

The constitutionalization of monarchical regimes in Ottoman Turkey (1876 and 1908-09) and Iran (1906) did not immediately turn subjects (*ra'āyā*) into citizens. Inspired by European constitutions, the Iranian and Ottoman documents denied women full citizenship. The emerging nation-state was, like its Western counterparts, a male entity, which denied women the right to participate in the exercise of state power. Women were expected to contribute to nation-building primarily by producing and nurturing good sons and daughters. While state power remained male gendered, it was also ethnicized on the basis of Turkish ethnic identity. In the same vein, the Iranian state emerged as a patriarchal unitary regime centred on Persian ethnicity.

In the wake of the defeat of the Ottoman state in 1918, Ottoman Kurdistan was re-divided, and incorporated into the newly formed states of Iraq (under British rule,1918-32), Syria (under French rule, 1920-46), and Turkey. The small Kurdish population of Russia came under Soviet rule by 1921. The five states–Turkey, Iran, Iraq, Syria, and the Soviet Union–pursued different policies in integrating women into their nation-building projects, and thus shaped the lives of Kurdish women in diverse ways.

Modern state- and nation-building has often entailed the use of violence. This region, as mentioned previously, was identified as a "zone of genocide" (Levene, 1998), the Ottoman regime and the Republic of Turkey eliminated the Armenian and Assyrian peoples in the course of genocidal campaigns from the late nineteenth century to 1923. Beginning in 1917, the government forcibly moved hundreds of thousands of Kurds to the Western parts of the country; many perished during these operations. State violence in the form of genocide, ethnocide, linguicide, or ethnic cleansing continued throughout the twentieth century in Republican Turkey, Iraq under the Ba'ath regime, and to varying degrees, in other countries (Fernandes, 1999). The gender dimension of this violence has not received adequate research attention.

## Women in the Kurdish Nationalist Project

Nationalist and feminist consciousness emerged, more or less simultaneously, in the Ottoman empire in the latter part of the nineteenth century. Kurdish nationalism, too, emerged in the late nineteenth century primarily among exilic groups in Istanbul and, on a more limited scale, in Kurdish urban environments. Unlike its Arab, Persian (Iranian), and Turkish counterparts, however, it failed to achieve statehood. The Kurdish aristocrats and intellectuals exiled in Istanbul formed literary, political, and journalistic circles, which promoted the idea of a distinct Kurdish nation with claims to self-rule within the Ottoman state. The circle, led by the uprooted Badir Khan rulers of Botan principality, launched *Kurdistan*, the first Kurdish newspaper in Cairo in 1898. One of the members of this group, Haji Qadir Koyi (1817-1897), a mullah and poet, emerged later as the ideologue of Kurdish nationalism. He encouraged the Kurds to embrace modern science and education, and learn from the national liberation movements of the time. Part of his nascent modernist politics was advocacy of women's education. Referring to Prophet Mohammad's saying that Muslims should search for knowledge by going to as far as China, Koyi addressed the Kurds: "There is no difference between males and females in this saying, if the mullah forbids it [women's education], he is a nonbeliever" (Koyi, 1986, pp. 186-87). The emerging modernist Kurdish intelligentsia, mostly males, developed this nascent idea of gender equality into a full-fledged nationalist discourse on the "woman question" between the 1908 constitutional revolution and the formation of the Turkish Republic in 1923.

For the intelligentsia, the Kurds constituted a nation because they possessed a homeland, a distinct language, a literary tradition, and their own culture and history. They conferred on women a special role in these early efforts to map the conditions of a modern Kurdish nation. Women constituted half the nation, and had to be equal to men in certain areas such as education. Moreover, women, especially those in rural areas, were the bearers of authentic Kurdish language and culture, which distinguished the Kurds from the Turks, and conferred on them national rights including self-determination. Rural women were the proof of a distinct nation in so far as they enjoyed more freedom than Muslim Turkish women, and at the same time, were bearers of a pure language and culture not tainted by the Turkification rampant in the cities. However, women whose illiteracy and domestic life had protected them from assimilation into the dominant nation had to be educated so that they could contribute to Kurdish nation-building (Klein, 2001). Religion was not a constituent of nationhood and womanhood since the Kurds were, like their adversary the Ottoman state, predominantly Muslims. Nationalists founded the first Kurdish women's organization (*Kürd Kadınları Teali Cemiyeti*, "Society for the Advancement of Kurdish Women") in 1919 in Istanbul where the size of the Kurdish population had been growing due to forced migrations and war (Alakom, 2001).

In spite of initial successes towards self-rule in the wake of WWI, Kurdish nationalists failed to achieve statehood. In the Treaty of Sèvres of 1920, European victors of the war designed a project for the creation of Armenian and Kurdish states in the territory that is now Eastern Turkey. However, this project was abandoned in 1923 in the Treaty of Lausanne. In Iraq under British Mandate, too, an autonomous government led by the religious figure Sheikh Mahmud (fall 1918-June 1919, October 1922-July 1924) was allowed to exist only in order to serve the military interests of Britain. In the early years of Soviet rule, the Kurdish communities of Caucasia and Turkmenistan were granted cultural and linguistic rights. In 1923-29, there was a Kurdistan administrative unit (*Kurdistanskii uzed*) in Caucasia.

In the wake of WWI, Kurdish women were fragmented into five states with different socio-economic systems and new politics of gender relations: European colonialism (France in Syria, Britain in Iraq), monarchy (Iran) and republican regime (Turkey), and Soviet socialism (Armenia, Azerbaijan, etc.). Women loomed large in the politics of nation-building of these states. While the project of the creation of "Soviet woman" aimed at liberating Kurdish women from the bonds of tribalism, feudalism, and religion, and transforming them into conscious agents of socialist construction, Turkey and Iran's projects of "new Turkish woman" and "Iranian woman" pursued their integration into the bourgeois nation in the process of being made. State feminism played a less prominent role in the early stages of state building in Iraq and Syria, although in these cases, too, urban, middle class, Arab "Iraqi woman" and "Syrian woman" were the model for all female citizens. With the formation of the Islamic theocracy in Iran, the state used coercion in order to de-secularize, and Islamize "Iranian woman"; the ideal "Muslim woman" was assigned the role of reversing a century of secularization of culture and society. Kurdish womanhood emerged in the course of these conflicts, which were part of the broader process of suppressing Kurdish nationhood in Turkey, Iran, Iraq, and Syria.[11]

***Turkey.*** In 1919-22, Turkish nationalists led by army officer Mustafa Kemal Pasha, later celebrated as Atatürk, "Father of the Turks", defeated the invading foreign armies which had dismantled the Ottoman empire, and were occupying the territory now known as Turkey. They declared the formation of the Republic of Turkey in 1923. Formally abolishing the Ottoman sultanate, Atatürk replaced it by a secular, Western-type, and nationalist order based on Turkish ethnic identity. Women were assigned a special role in this nation-building project, which included reforms such as the separation of state and religion, and Westernization of dress and calendar. Unveiled women, studying in coeducational institutions, participating in public life, and enjoying suffrage rights (as of 1934), were a hallmark of the modernizing state.

The Kemalist project of building a unitary, secular, and ethnically Turkish

---

[11] The brief historical sketch provided below for each country does not cover major events or the geopolitical shift in the region, which had significant impact on the Kurds. These changes most notably are the 2011 Arab Uprising, the emergence of the Islamic State of Iraq and Syria (ISIS) in 2013, and the protracted military aggression of Turkey against the Kurds in Bakur and Rojava since 2014. However, due to the rise of a significant resistance movement in Syria, that section briefly touches on post-2014 development.

nation-state met considerable resistance by Kurdish religious and nationalist leaders. A series of revolts from 1925-38 were brutally suppressed. The suppression of the Dersim revolt of 1937-38 has been identified as genocide. The army targeted males and females, and many women committed suicide in order to escape rape and abuse (McDowall, 2000; van Bruinessen, 2000). Ethnic cleansing projects were extensive and intensive, including forced resettlements of the Kurds in central and western provinces, banning of all expressions of Kurdish identity including the names Kurd and Kurdistan, and the criminalization of Kurdish culture and the use of the Kurdish language in speaking and writing. All Kurdish organizations, including the women's society of 1919, and Kurdish publishing disappeared after the 1925 revolt.

In the early decades of the republic, the state, its educational system, mass media, and popular culture constructed the Turkish nation as a military-nation (ordu-millet or asker-ulus; Altinay, 2004). Official propaganda and the media identified Kurdish resistance to Turkification as tribalism, feudalism, religious fanaticism, reactionary politics, backwardness, and banditry all directed against a civilizing state. The "emancipated women" of the republic were recruited to highlight the civilizing role of the Turkish nation. Sabiha Gökçen, an adopted daughter of Atatürk, was promoted as the world's first woman combat pilot, who dropped the bomb that killed the leader of the Dersim revolt and brought it to a successful end (Altinay, 2004; Mojab, 2001a). The modern Turkish woman, herself "emancipated" by the national army, was now in a position to save the nation, its indivisibility and territorial integrity, through military action. The only alternative open to the Kurds, women or men, was to discard their "traditional" ways of life, culture, and language, and become Turks.

While the Turkish nation-state was able to ethnically cleanse the Armenian and Assyrian peoples, it failed to eliminate the Kurds or assimilate them. By the mid-twentieth century, tribalism and religion had suffered setbacks, in part due to state intervention. After a long silence in the wake of the genocide of Dersim, a new wave of Kurdish opposition movements emerged in the 1960s and 1970s. These movements were different from the revolts of the 1920s and 1930s in so far as they were urban, secular, cultural, political, and led by communists, leftists, and nationalists. One of these groups, the PKK, survived the 1980 military coup d'état and began armed struggle against the state in 1984 in order to create a Kurdish state. Turkey responded with full power. Military operations against the PKK included the destruction or evacuation of more than 3,500 villages, the uprooting of the population, forced urbanization, and many disappearances and extrajudicial killings. During the "counterinsurgency operations" against the PKK, Turkey declared a state of emergency in parts of the southeast (i.e., Kurdistan), and committed, according to Human Rights Watch (HRW), "gross violation of its international commitments to respect the laws of war" (HRW, 1995, p. 7). This included forced displacements, indiscriminate fire, summary executions, disguising the identity of perpetrators, as well as violations of international law, including torture, forcible displacement of civilians, pillage, destruction of villages, failure to care for civilians displaced by government forces, injury of civilians, destruction of civilian property, inhumane and degrading treatment, kidnaping of civilians to act as porters and as human shields against attack, disappearances, life-threatening conditions of detention and inadequate medical attention leading to death. The United States, Turkey's close ally and its major weapons supplier, was "deeply implicated," and, much like NATO, chose to "downplay Turkish violations for strategic reasons" (p. 13).

These violations of the laws of war, now as in the past, have been gendered. Women in custody of armed and security forces were systematically subjected to various forms of "sexual torture," including rape. Amnesty International reported in 2003 that

> Although all women are at risk of violence, due to specific patterns of discrimination in Turkey Amnesty International is concerned that Kurdish women, particularly those living in the south-east, and women who hold political beliefs that are unacceptable to the government or the military, have been at increased risk of violence at the hands of agents of the state. Such violence is in violation of their internationally guaranteed right to be free from torture and inhuman and degrading treatment. Women who have the courage to speak out about their experiences have extreme difficulty in obtaining justice and both state and society combine to silence them. (Amnesty International, 2003, pp. 3-4)

The Amnesty International report also noted that

> In a study published in 2000, two per cent of women situated in Turkey's mainly Kurdish south-east reported being the victims of sexual violence at the hands of security forces... This figure is likely to be even higher given the reluctance of women to report such abuses because of fear of retaliation, ostracism or forced marriage... women detained are frequently stripped naked by male police officers during periods of questioning in police custody or in prison... the majority of women who report sexual violence by state security forces are Kurdish, or express political opinions that are unacceptable to the military or the government. Sometimes a woman is subjected to sexual violence in the presence of her husband or family member, apparently as a means of forcing her husband or family member to "confess," or,

in a cynical utilization of the concept of "honour," as a way of demeaning her family and her community. (p. 15)

According to this document, Turkey violates several treaties which it has ratified: the European Convention for the Protection of Human Rights and Fundamental Freedoms, the Convention against Torture and Other Cruel, Inhuman or Degrading Treatment or Punishment, the Convention on the Elimination of All Forms of Discrimination against Women, and the Convention on the Rights of the Child. Even lawyers who defend sexually tortured women are subjected to suppression:

Lawyers representing women in Turkey who have been sexually assaulted in custody have been subjected to official, media, and peer persecution. This makes it even more difficult for survivors of sexual violence to obtain justice, and contributes to the silence surrounding sexual crimes. For speaking about rape and torture by security officials, Eren Keskin is facing trial. She commented publicly, "The peace mothers - were blindfolded, stripped naked and sexually ill-treated by soldiers young enough to be their grandchildren. They were harassed and insulted using names such as 'whore' and 'bitch.'" For this statement, she was charged with "insulting the state security forces ..." Eren Keskin has been the subject of 86 lawsuits in relation to her human rights activities... Seven of these relate to statements she has made in her role as head of a legal aid project which supports women who have been sexually assaulted in custody. She has also been the subject of death threats and insults. (Amnesty International, 2003, p. 35)

The destruction or evacuation of more than 3,500 villages, and the uprooting of a population of around two million, forced urbanization, and many disappearances and extrajudicial killings between 1984 and 1999 has destroyed the fabric of Kurdish rural life. This large-scale violence has unleashed the patriarchal violence of not only the state, as indicated above, but also non-state actors in rural and urban areas.

The destruction of rural society led to the sudden explosion of urban population, which in turn led to the disruption of urban life, and the aggravation of all social, especially gender, conflicts. Women bore the brunt of displacement, exacerbated by poverty, unemployment, a failing economy, and a state that treated all Kurds as enemy. Desperate to defeat both the PKK and the new wave of Kurdish nationalism, the government appealed to Kurdish tribalism and religion, and capitalized on religious cleavages. It used and, according to some observers, created a fundamentalist Hizbullah party to conduct counter guerrilla operations (Gürbey, 1996) against the PKK.

Under these conditions, the traditional gender regime and its complex apparatus of male control of women also experienced major disorders. The outcome was the unleashing of male violence in the private domains of family and household. If under "normal conditions," male power was exercised by "normal" means of disciplining and surveillance, it now resorted to the most violent means such as killing and even, in one case, stoning to death. While the state's "village guards," organized and financed by the state and the armed forces themselves, were free to engage in extrajudicial killing, males also found it expedient to engage in the extrajudicial killing of women in the name of honour.

Turkey's feminist and women's groups could hardly remain neutral in the face of widespread patriarchal violence of the state and civil society. Turkish feminism had until the early 1990s been, by and large, the watchdog of Kemalism, in essence, the official form of Turkish nationalism. Feminists endorsed the official policy of nation-building through Turkification of non-Turkish peoples even through the use of violence. However, if the state had failed to Turkify the Kurds, Turkish feminism, state and non-state, also failed to transform Kurdish women into the ideal Kemalist "Turkish woman." Sixty years after the foundation of the republic, the Kemalist nation-state had created its antithesis. The new Kurdish nationalist movement under PKK, unlike the armed resistances of the 1920s and 1930s which were led by patriarchs and in sharp contrast with the all-male Turkish army, created its own guerrilla army with thousands of women in its ranks. These women successfully engaged large detachments of the high-tech, sacrosanct Turkish army. The Turkish state responded to the presence of women guerrillas with violence, both physical and symbolic. The state and the pro-state media revealed their patriarchal nationalism by vilifying women fighters as "bitches and prostitutes" (KIC/KSC Publications, 1992, p. 32), while various government organizations unleashed sexual violence against Kurdish women.

The critique of Kemalist state feminism had emerged by the late 1990s. Turkish feminists of a critical persuasion argued that male dominance and patriarchal structures remain intact in spite of the progress made in legal equality and remarkable advances in women's access to public domains of life (Arat, 1994; Müftüler-Bac, 1999). It was also obvious that if state feminism had failed to displace patriarchy in Turkey, it also was unable to assimilate Kurdish women into its ethnicist project. In fact, in part due to gender differences, Kurdish women were less Turkicized than men in so far as they had more limited access to non-domestic and public domains such as formal education, business, art, and government.

In spite of limited female integration into the non-household/formal, urban economy, the number of educated women in Kurdish provinces was increasing by the mid-twentieth century, and, in the 1980s, a stratum of professionals and intellectuals had already changed the face of Kurdish society. No doubt, the Kurdish socialist and nationalist movements since the 1960s, involving mostly students and the youth, continued to be male dominated. Still, by the time the leaders of the 1980 military coup d'état had suppressed leftist movements and crushed any trace of civil society, the Kurdish Marxist director Yilmaz Güney raised the question of women's oppression in his film *Yol* [Road] (1982), and strongly condemned the patriarchal violence prevalent in rural Kurdish society (Benge, 1985). After the 1980 coup, women in Turkey undertook independent feminist initiatives, and feminism gained more currency. This trend was still Kemalist, and denied the existence of Kurdish women. Under conditions of harsh state violence against the Kurds, gender consciousness was overshadowed by nationalist consciousness.

Another development was the resurgence of Islamist political movements in Turkey and throughout the Middle East in the wake of the establishment of the Islamic Republic of Iran in 1979. Turkish Islamist movements, in spite of their own cleavages, do not deviate from the Kemalist line of denying the Kurds national rights. While they share with Kurdish Islamists a politics of Islamization of gender relations, their devotion to Turkish ethnicity distances them from the Kurds. At the same time, the secular Turkish state, faced with the challenge of Kurdish nationalism, has used Islam and religious divisions among the Kurds including the Alevi/Sunni divide against this nationalism. For its part, the secular PKK responded by endorsing religion as a legitimate component of Kurdish life, and thus recruiting Islamists and Alevists. Under these conditions, ethnic, national, and religious cleavages created a regime of ever shifting alliances (Houston, 2001), which undermined the potential for non-sectarian feminist organizing. By 2002, Turkey took new steps in extending legal gender equality. However, in Kurdish provinces, violations of women's rights were prevalent in, for instance, domestic violence including honour killing, polygyny, wife exchange, and early, forced, arranged, and child marriages. Women were not aware of their rights under the existing legal system (Ilkkaracan, 1999). However, non-official and non-party feminist initiatives emerged in Istanbul and major cities, which ranged from "Islamic feminisms" to radical secular projects. While the words "Kurdish woman" were officially considered "separatist propaganda" and a crime against the "indivisibility of the Turkish nation," Kurdish women had launched feminist journals (e.g., *Roza* and *Jujîn* both launched in 1996), and formed their own feminist initiatives such as rights advocacy groups (e.g., K. Ka. DaV, The Foundation for Solidarity with Kurdish Women and Research on Women's Question, Istanbul), shelters and literacy and skills training programs (e.g., Ka-Mer: Women's Center in Diyarbakir), and mothers of the disappeared.

The failure of the unitary nation-state and its state feminism has led to a diverse and fragmented environment where Kurdish women and feminists are increasingly present. It is in this diversity that feminists can overcome fragmentation and achieve unity against patriarchy. Turkish feminists have already begun evading the traps of nationalism, which divides women and allows patriarchy unobstructed reign (see Altinay, 2004). Such unity between Turkish and Kurdish women has already emerged in the course of resistance to state violence against women in custody. Kurdish nationalist belonging, too, is in conflict with feminism. If Turkish feminists have already launched a serious, though still limited, challenge to "their" nation, Kurdish feminists have yet to confront "their" nationalism. While nationalism still pervades the lives of both Kurdish and Turkish women, feminists from both sides have already engaged in dialogue.

***Iran.*** Demands for the reform of gender relations in Iran date back to the late nineteenth century, when nationalist and liberal intellectuals questioned the oppression of women, especially veiling, segregation, polygyny, seclusion, and illiteracy. During the Constitutional Revolution of 1906-11, social democrats and radical members of the new parliament demanded women's suffrage rights, and there was considerable women's grassroots organizing in the Caspian region. The violent suppression of the revolution in 1911 silenced radical voices, although outside the sphere of the state, women continued their organizing activities, journalism, advocacy of equal rights, and opening of girls' schools (Afary, 1996). Most of these activities were confined to Tehran and major cities, leaving Kurdish provinces and much of the country marginally affected. Opposition to women's demands came especially from conservatives among the clergy and in the government.

Kurdish women, as mentioned previously, were a target of the armies of Russia and Ottoman Turkey when they invaded the northern parts of Kurdistan during WWI. In 1915, the Russian army massacred the male population of Sauj Bulaq (Mahabad) and took away some 400 women for abuse (Fossum, 1918). State intervention in gender relations in Kurdistan was more visible after the 1921 coup d'état, when the central government further expanded its military and civil administration to all the cities and towns. Reza Shah, army officer and founder of Pahlavi dynasty (1925-79), established a highly centralized dictatorial regime largely through the use of military power. By the early 1930s, he suppressed all independent women's activism and crushed the religious centres of power. Much like Republican Turkey, and inspired by it, the Pahlavi monarchy was a nationalist, secular, modernizing, and Westernizing unitary state, which assigned women a major role in its patriarchal nation-building project. In this multiethnic and multicultural country, women had to be modern, Westernized, and Persian(ized).

The most visible intervention in gender relations, Reza Shah's 1936 decree on the unveiling of women, was enforced largely through coercion. According to confidential government correspondence of the period, there was no need for unveiling in the rural and tribal areas of the country, especially in Kurdistan, where women were always unveiled. However, the colourful and distinctly Kurdish clothing of women was treated as "ugly and dirty," and had to be replaced by the "attire of civilized women," (Iran National Archives, 1992, pp. 171, 250, 249, and 273), in essence, Western-type dress. In Kurdistan, the state-imposed "unified dress" was known as Pahlavi or Persian ('ecemî) rather than European clothing. Another official initiative was the opening of the first and few public schools for girls in Kurdish cities in the 1930s.

The USSR and Britain occupied Iran during WWII, and replaced Reza Shah with his son Mohammad Reza in 1941. Soon after the war ended, Kurdish and Azerbaijani nationalists established their short-lived autonomous governments in Northwestern Iran in 1946. The National Government of Azerbaijan granted women suffrage rights, while the Kurdish Republic encouraged women's participation in public life outside the sphere of the family. The Kurdistan Democratic Party, founder of this mini-state, launched a Women's Party (Hizbî Jinan), which promoted women's education, and rallied them in support of the republic. Women teachers and students from girls' schools appeared unveiled in official ceremonies and other public spaces wearing their uniforms and appearing in the Kurdish national dress.

The short-lived experience of the two governments, overthrown within a year through Tehran's military offensive, demonstrated the failure of the Pahlavi monarchy to integrate non-Persian women into its unitary ethnicist state. In fact, Kurdish nationalists created their own alternative, in essence, a Kurdish state based on Kurdish ethnicity—its language, culture, history, homeland (niştman), i.e., Kurdistan, with its own ideal "Kurdish woman." This Kurdish woman shared more with the women envisioned by the Kurdish nationalists of the late Ottoman period than the modern "Iranian women" fostered by the Pahlavi state (Mojab, 2001b).

Participants in the 1978-79 revolution against the monarchy were extremely diverse both socially and politically, and pursued different goals. In Kurdistan, the struggle was predominantly nationalist and secular, and the demand was autonomy within a democratic and federal state structure. The Islamic theocracy is, like the monarchical regime, a unitary state rooted in Persian ethnicity (its language, religion, and culture), and rejects the idea of self-rule or autonomy for non-Persian nationalities. "Muslim women" were given a special role in the theocratization of the ancient monarchical state; they were expected to play a leading role in reversing the social and cultural changes that had occurred in Iran since the constitutional revolution. In Kurdistan, resistance against the Islamization of gender relations assumed a nationalist dimension, although religious cleavages were marginally present (most Kurds are Sunnis while Iranian theocracy is Shiite). Women's resistance included, among others, using Kurdish, non-Islamic, female names and violating Islamic dress codes by wearing Kurdish clothing.

Kurdish opposition parties engaged in armed resistance when the army launched a major offensive, in August 1979, to wipe out the autonomy movement. One of the political organizations, Komele, the Kurdistan Organization of the Communist Party of Iran, and other leftist groups recruited hundreds of women into their military and political ranks. Komele's military camps formed a sharp contrast to the gender apartheid regime imposed throughout Iran. By 2000, the Islamization of gender relations had failed in Kurdistan, where the active presence of "Kurdish woman" was in sharp contrast with the state-sponsored "Muslim woman" promoted at the centre. Kurdistan was not, however, the only source of resistance to the Islamizaiton of gender relations. In fact, the Islamic regime's first major intervention in the lives of Iranians was its offensive against the women in the form of dismissing female judges and imposing the head cover, the *hijab*. Islamization developed into a regime of gender apartheid in, for instance, sports, buses, pools, government offices, schools and universities, and beaches. This theocracy subjected women to pre-modern forms of subordination such as requiring permission of the husband or male guardians to travel, discrimination in inheritance, lowering the marriage age to nine years, capital punishment for lesbian relations, and stoning married adulterers to death (on the penal codes affecting women, see Afkhami & Friedl, 1994). It is not surprising, therefore, that women have offered the most persistent and extensive resistance to the Islamic state. They have resisted theocratic patriarchy by challenging various impositions ranging from Islamic dress codes to bans on riding bikes or studying engineering. In Kurdistan, resistance was equally diverse, including the use of Kurdish dress, singing and mixed dancing in weddings, and celebrations of New Year (*newroz*).

While a considerable number of Kurdish women had entered the non-domestic labour force, both skilled and unskilled, a female intelligentsia has been in the making consisting of an increasing number of poets (e.g., Miryam Hula and Zhila Huseni), writers (e.g., Nasrin Ja'fari and N. J. Ashna), musicians (e.g., Qashang Kamkar), academics, teachers, and artists. In the early 2000s, women had formed non-government organizations in a number of Kurdish cities mostly aimed at providing relief, aid, and welfare for the poor, although demands for rights were being expressed increasingly. At the same time, the unprecedented increase in women's suicide, especially through self-immolation, exposed the pressures of both theocratic patriarchy and domestic violence (Yūsifī & Yūsifī, 1997), exacerbated by poverty and a ruined economy. Not surprisingly, feminist consciousness and activism have different trajectories in each part of Kurdistan. For instance, unlike Turkey, where several Kurdish feminist journals have appeared, there is still no feminist or women's press in Iranian Kurdistan. This is in spite of the fact that women are actively involved in publishing and journalism in Tehran and the major urban centres.

*Iraq.* Formed under British Occupation (1917-20) and Mandate (1920-32), and supervised by the League of Nations, the newly formed Iraqi state accepted the existence of the Kurds as a people with limited rights to use their language in primary schools, publishing, and broadcasting. However, Britain created Iraq as a unitary state, and rejected Kurdish demands for autonomous status, fearing that it would spread Kurdish nationalism to the neighbouring countries, and inhibit the integration of the Kurds in the emerging state. Unlike the nationalist regimes of Turkey and Iran, Britain did not adopt an official project of "women's emancipation" or "state feminism" in the course of building Iraq as a monarchical Arab state. In fact, British authorities complained to the League of Nations about excessive Kurdish educational demands (see Great Britain, 1930, pp. 139-40), including more girls' schools. After Iraq's independence in 1932, the monarchical regime (1932-58) continued the policy of ignoring gender equality. The Communist Party of Iraq, like its counterparts in Iran, Syria, and Turkey, while often underground and brutally suppressed, was the most vocal in advocating women's rights.

Iraq was the only country, in addition to the Soviet Union, where the existence of the Kurds was not denied. However, a policy of containing Kurdish nationalism through Arabization was in place. Resisting assimilation into the Arab state, Kurdish nationalists emphasized their ethnic, linguistic, cultural, territorial, racial, and historical distinctness, which included the claim to the relative freedom of Kurdish women. However, the autonomous government of Sheikh Mahmud formed in the early 1920s was a patriarchal, feudal regime with no interest in women's rights. Still, intellectuals, ranging from religious to nationalist to communist, denounced the oppression of women. Abdullah Goran (1904-62), the most prominent modern poet and a communist, condemned through his poetry gender and class violence, especially honour killing (see the English translation of the poem in Mojab, 2004a). The Kurdistan Democratic Party (KDP) of Iraq published, clandestinely, the first issue of *Dengî Afret* "Woman's Voice" in 1953. In the more or less open environment following the overthrow of monarchy in 1958, the communist party's powerful women's organization cooperated with the Union of Kurdish Women, and lobbied for legal reform, which brought marriage under civil control, and abolished the tribal custom of honour killing.

A new round of armed conflicts began in 1961 between the Kurds and the republican regime led by Abdul-Karim Qassem. The first Ba'ath regime, which came to power for less than a year in 1963, launched a major offensive against the Kurds, and massacred the communists. The Mongolian People's Republic asked the U.N. General Assembly to discuss "the policy of genocide carried out by the government of the Republic of Iraq against the Kurdish people," (U.N. General Assembly, 1963, pp. 109-14) and the Soviet Union referred the case to the Economic and Social Council (also see Vanly, 1970, pp. 210-16, 381-84).

The second Ba'ath regime (1968-2003) constructed a *cordon sanitaire* along its northern borders with Iran and Turkey by destroying hundreds of Kurdish villages soon after the defeat of the Kurdish armed resistance in 1975. In 1983, it killed all the adolescent and adult males of Barzani Kurds numbering about 8,000, and used chemical weapons against the Kurds in a number of settlements including the town of Halabja (March 16, 1988) and against Iranians during its war with Iran (1980-88). This was in violation of the 1925 Geneva Protocol. Moreover, the oil-rich Kirkuk region was Arabized by forcibly uprooting Kurds from the city and villages. The campaign of mass murder of 1988 code-named Operation *Anfal* ("spoils of war," title of a chapter in the Koran), widely considered a genocide, entailed the killing of more than 100,000, disappearance of tens of thousands of non-combatants, destruction of villages (4,006, according to Kurdistan Regional Government), the forced displacement of hundreds of thousands of villagers, arbitrary arrest and jailing under conditions of extreme deprivation of thousands of women, children, and elderly, and the destruction of rural life (HRW, 1993). The coercive institutions of the state institutionalized rape as a method of torture and punishment. At the same time, a project of gendercide eliminated the entire adult male population of the Barzani tribe and kept women in concentration camps subjected to rape and terror (Makiya, 1993, pp. 135-50).

After the defeat of Iraq in the Gulf War of 1991, much of Kurdistan came under the rule of two Kurdish organizations, the KDP and Patriotic Union of Kurdistan (PUK), which created the Kurdistan Regional Government (KRG). Six of the 105 members of the parliament, about 6%, were women. However, in the course of parliamentary elections, male and female voters were segregated at the voting centres. Although virtually independent from Baghdad, the KRG, especially its KDP faction, refused to repeal the Ba'ath regime's personal status codes and other laws that were lenient on honour killing. In 1994, women marched from Sulaimaniya to Irbil in protest to the civil war between KDP and PUK, which lasted, intermittently, until 1996, and led to the formation of two Kurdish governments. Much like Turkey, the 1988 genocide, the long war against Kurdish autonomists, the Iraq-Iran war of 1980-88, and the 1991 U.S.-led Gulf War destroyed the fabric of Kurdish society, and unleashed extensive male violence including honour killing.

Suicide through self-immolation, a rare phenomenon in the past, was ubiquitous. In the wake of continuing organized protest, however, the PUK-led government issued resolutions aimed at criminalizing honour killing, although they remained only on paper. The KDP justified patriarchal violence as part of Islamic and Kurdish traditions (Çingiyanî, 1993), although it also had to criminalize the practice later.

The Ba'ath regime's policy of transforming Kurdish women into the "new Iraqi woman," in essence, a secular, Ba'athist, educated, and obedient citizen of an Arab state, failed largely due to national oppression and Kurdish resistance against it. As in Turkey and Iran, Kurdish nationalism confronted the ethnicist state project by advancing the idea of "Kurdish woman," which is equally secular, nationalist, and rooted in Kurdish ethnicity and nationalist aspirations. The experience of self-rule between 1991 and 2003 revealed that Kurdish nationalism in power, like other cases, pursues women's loyalty to the state.

The second U.S. war against Iraq, aimed at changing the Ba'athist regime of Saddam Hussein, met resistance from the anti-war and feminist movements of the world. However, the leaders of the two major Kurdish parties, as well as the majority of Iraqi Kurds, supported the war hoping that it would remove the Ba'athist regime, and replace it with a better alternative. After the fall of Saddam, women in the Arab regions of Iraq were subjected to extreme violence, including abduction and rape, and were unable to leave home without protection. Iraqi Kurdistan, already independent of Baghdad, was not a theater of war, and remained relatively quiet. Women for Women International, an American aid group working in Iraq, concluded in a report in January 2005 that "Iraqi women have been marginalized and excluded by both the U.S.-led Transitional Governing Authority and its successor, the Iraqi Governing Council" (Women for Women International, 2005, p. 7). Very few women were invited to participate in the April 2003 meetings, which planned the creation of an interim government, and only three women were nominated to the Interim Governing Council. No women were included in the nine-member rotating presidential council or the 24-member committee, which drafted the interim constitution. If women were excluded from the nation-building process, tribal and feudal lords, religious patriarchs, returning exiled nationalists, former Ba'athist dissidents, aristocrats, pro-American technocrats and bureaucrats, and American advisors worked as architects of the new state (Mojab, 2009).

Even after the elections of January 2005, in which the Shiites and the Kurds were top winners, the future of the Iraqi state remained unclear, although it was rather obvious that the Shiite leadership pursued a theocratic regime, which the Kurds, along with many Iraqis, opposed. At the same time, extremist Islamist forces were ruling the streets all over Arab Iraq and had already imposed on women a theocratic regime of gender relations.

Under the rule of Kurdistan Regional Government (1991-2003), several women's organizations were formed, each with its own publication, although they were all tied to political parties. The Kurdish government boasted itself as multiparty and democratic, but was not tolerant of a small communist group, which was the first to expose the rise of honour killing, was vocal in criticizing nationalist patriarchy, and established the first shelters in the region.

Unlike Iran, and much like Turkey, Kurdish women's journalism appeared in the 1990s, and by the early 2000s feminist writing appeared in the form of journal articles and research. Under conditions of national conflict, Kurdish feminists find it expedient to claim that feminism is a Western phenomenon, which needs to be appropriated in nationalist terms. In spite of the prevalence of this feminist nationalism, the critique of indigenous national patriarchy has already begun.

*Syria.* Built under French rule (1920-46), the Syrian state was, like Iraq under British rule, without a "state feminist" project. The majority of the Kurds lived in rural areas of the northeast, although there were sizeable Kurdish settlements in Damascus, Aleppo, and other cities. A nationalist movement emerged in the 1920s among the urban notables and intelligentsia, but there was no Kurdish women's movement. However, individual women of the aristocratic families were active in education and culture in the 1930s and 1940s.

The ruling Ba'ath party has eliminated all opposition movements since it came to power in the mid-1960s. Although the Kurds of Syria have not engaged in armed conflict with the state, they were targeted for ethnic cleansing beginning in the early 1960s. Some 120,000 Kurds were stripped of Syrian citizenship, with plans for the depopulation of Kurdish regions by creating an "Arab belt" along the Turkish border, evicting peasants from 332 villages, and replacing them with Arab settlers (MEW, 1991). There has been a resurgence of nationalist activism since the early 1990s. As this bibliography demonstrates, there is a dearth of research on the Kurds of Syria in general, and women in particular.[12]

The Kurds of Syria (Rojava) had a number of political parties in 2011 when resistance against Bashar al-Assad's regime began as part of the continuation of the 2011 Arab Uprising. By early 2014, when the Syrian regime withdrew its forces from Rojava, one of the Kurdish parties known as the Democratic Union Party (Partiya Yekîtiya Demokrat, PYD) declared an autonomous regime in three parts or cantons of Rojava, which are not contiguous. The

---

[12] For excellent contemporary history of Syria see Reilly, 2019 and Schmidinger, 2018.

Democratic Union Party is a leftist nationalist organization ideologically and politically affiliated with the Kurdistan Workers' Party, or PKK, in Turkey.

The formation of these autonomous cantons was opposed by the Syrian opposition groups including the Free Syrian Army, Turkey, the U.S., and even the Kurdistan Regional Government in Iraq. Islamic fundamentalist forces were staunch enemies of the Kurds, and ISIS launched a major offensive in order to topple the autonomous cantons. This war centred on the city of Kobanê in September 2015; it attracted the attention of the media, and people throughout the world were inspired by the women partisans who defended the city and defeated ISIS in the course of a few months that left the city in ruins. Many observers compared Kobanê to Stalingrad and Madrid during the anti-fascist struggles of the previous century. Images from the battlefield dramatized a sharp contrast between young women in fatigues with machine guns fighting a brutal theocratic and misogynistic army. The women of Kobanê showed a side of the Middle East which had been obscured by the media and academia: Women are ready to fight patriarchal, misogynist forces by all means. The women of Rojava have their own military organization called Women's Defence Unit (YPJ), which together with the male People's Defence Units (YPG) form the military wing of the Democratic Union Party. This party leads the struggle in Rojava.

Rojava women have put up a valiant resistance against the violent forces of theocratic misogyny. In the realm of theory, they have implemented and have extensively developed the thought of the PKK leader, Abdullah Öcalan, on women's liberation, known as *Jineolojî*. Often referred to as an alternative women's science or a paradigm, Jineolojî is presented as theoretical and methodological substitute for positivist, euro-centrist, nationalist feminisms. It is beyond the scope of this section to engage comprehensively with this highly contested conception of women's liberation theory and praxis (for further discussion on Jineolojî, see Çaglayan, 2019; Dirik, 2021; Neven and Schäfers, 2017). There is much to celebrate in every advance that women make in overcoming patriarchy in Rojava. Women are a new and major force for revolutionary change. The women of Rojava have powerfully demonstrated this revolutionary potential. While women's resistances are widespread, there is much need for more knowledge and more theorization about how to build a new world without all of the current forms of oppression and class exploitation. Revolution is a conscious intervention in the course of historical change. This intervention will not lead to revolutionary change without revolutionary theory.

***The USSR (1921-91).*** Women were granted suffrage rights once Soviet power was established in 1921 over Caucasian regions of Armenia and Azerbaijan, where most Kurds lived in rural areas. Tribal-feudal socio-economic relations, considered the engine of patriarchy, were promptly dismantled; women were expected to be active in the building of socialist society and economy (Abdal, 1960). In sharp contrast to other parts of Kurdistan, where female illiteracy rates are highest in villages, illiteracy was eliminated in the Soviet Union by the early 1930s. The reform of gender relations entailed extensive educational and ideological work in the newly established Kurdish print media, film, and schools. By the mid-1950s, a generation of professional women were active in areas such as teaching, journalism, broadcasting, medicine, agriculture, and music. Also, sharply different from Turkey and Iran, Kurds enjoyed the freedom to use their language and maintain their culture. However, thousands of Caucasian Kurds were subjected to two waves of forced deportation to the Central Asian republics of Kazakhstan, Kirgizia, and Uzbekistan in 1937 and 1944 (Kren, 2000). During the disintegration of the Soviet Union, the Muslim Kurdish population of Armenia and Nagorny-Karabakh was largely displaced in the course of the war between Armenia and Azerbaijan in 1990-94, when both countries "systematically violated the most basic rule of international humanitarian law" (HRW, 1992; see also, McDowall, 2000, pp. 490-94; Russo, 2000).

## The Diasporas and Transnationalization

The Kurdish diasporas that have emerged since the 1960s in the West and elsewhere consist of around one million "guest workers" (mostly in Germany), refugees, and immigrants in other European countries, Lebanon, North America, Australia, and New Zealand. The 1918 division of Kurdistan among four countries has endured not only in the Middle East but divides diasporic communities, too. The persistence of national oppression, and violent repression of Kurdish nationalism in the "homelands" of the Middle East, shapes diasporic politics, and reinforces feelings of belonging to the homeland nation. Thus, this *transnationalization* of the Kurds has only further fragmented the nation. In other words, Kurdish transnationalism is a set of fragmented nationalisms that thrive on the ongoing national oppression perpetrated by the four nation-states, and often extends to diasporas. Equally constitutive of diaspora nationalism are hostland racism, xenophobia, unemployment, and exploitation, which make it difficult for diasporans to experience hostland citizenship beyond the domain of legal equality (Mojab, 2006).

Kurdish transnationalization is also generated by the imperatives of global capitalism, for example, labour migrations (guest workers), population displacements in Turkey (one of the world's major hydroelectric and irrigation networks, the Southeast Anatolian Project launched in 1983), uneven economic development, war, and militarization. This trans*nationalism* is in conflict with *inter*nationalism, whether democratic, socialist, or feminist.

The Kurdish guest workers in Germany, for instance, came mostly from the milieu of Kurds resettled in Western Turkey where they had generally been assimilated into the Turkish population. However, many acquired Kurdish nationalist consciousness in Germany, and their participation in German or European labour movements, solidarity with homeland labour or socialist movements, or feminist solidarity are either lacking or overshadowed by their involvement in Kurdish nationalist politics (on German-Kurdish politics, see Østergaard-Nielsen, 2003; on British-Kurds, see Griffiths, 2002; for a comparative study of Finnish- and British-Kurds, see Wahlbeck, 1999). Diasporic communities have, thus, immersed in nationalism and are less influenced by radical feminism.

No doubt, in spite of its status as a regime of parcelized nationalisms, transnationalism creates conditions for internationalism, which may emerge in the course of conscious intervention, including displacing nationalism. The hybridization of the Kurds has already occurred in so far as some members of the first and second generation identify themselves in hyphenated terms such as Kurdish-Americans, Euro-Kurds, or Swedish-Kurds. However, these hybridizations emerge within the framework of host country nationalisms.

Cleavages such as gender, class, race, religion, alphabet, and dialect are reproduced in the diaspora. In the realm of gender relations, for instance, a small minority of diasporans expect women, much more than men, to be loyal to the traditional patriarchal regime of the homeland, to the extent that they deny their daughters the right to participate in coeducational activities such as swimming or field trips. The European extremist rightists and neo-fascists treat honour killing and other practices as evidence of a "barbaric culture" that must be discarded together with "the immigrants." At the same time, some European states have taken, with good intention, a cultural relativist policy, which advocates diversity and respect for "difference" by denying diasporan women full citizenship rights guaranteed in the civic nation. This policy is, thus, ethnocentric in so far as it does not accept secularism and a century of feminist struggles as genuine components of Kurdish and Middle Eastern immigrant cultures. Some Euro-Kurds, fearing violent racist backlash, take shelter in nationalism by denying that honour killing is part of their patriarchal culture, and treat it as borrowed (from Arab and Islamic culture), imposed (Islamization), marginal (rural), and incidental (individual madness). In some European countries such as Sweden, White supremacists and, to some extent, the mainstream media, equate the name "Kurd" with violence against women. Western White racism and its various forms of national chauvinism display their misogynism in treating Euro-Kurdish males as inherently or racially violent; their politics is in conflict with feminism, which treats male violence as universal, both Eastern and Western. In spite of the ubiquity of nationalism, diasporic resistance to patriarchal violence has been mounting, leading to increasing feminist consciousness and organizing (Mojab & Hassanpour, 2002). At the same time, integration into the new host societies is accelerating in the second generation. Kurdish women, for instance, have already formed as a growing milieu of intelligentsia and professionals including poets, writers, researchers, journalists, members of parliament (Sweden, European Parliament), diplomats (U.S.), physicians, broadcasters, and academics.

## Conclusions

The life of Kurdish women at the beginning of the twenty-first century is characterized by webs of contradictions, which have yet to be recorded and understood in all their complexity. While disruptions of their lives within the twentieth century are spectacular, continuities are equally startling. They went through the disintegration of the Ottoman empire, several genocides, ethnic cleansing, unbridled sexual violence by the state, the rise and fall of socialism in Caucasia and Central Asia, the destruction of rural life, large scale displacements, the coming to power of theocracy, direct Western colonial rule, and new rounds of dispersion throughout the world. One trend in the lives of Kurdish women is the failure of the modernizing projects of the nation-states to transform them into the "Iranian woman," "new Turkish woman," "new Iraqi woman," or "Muslim woman." Eight decades of forcible assimilation have, in fact, contributed to the formation of the polity of "Kurdish woman."

Kurdish womanhood has emerged, to a large extent, in conflict with its Arab, Persian, and Turkish counterparts, and is fragmented along the lines of the nation-states, which have divided the Kurds since 1918. With the formation of new diasporas, "Kurdish womanhood" is further fragmented into a transnational entity that continues to be largely nationalist. While there is no single definition of Kurdish womanhood, the ideal "Kurdish woman" is predominantly nationalist, secular, and modern.

The persistence of tribal-feudal forms of Kurdish patriarchy and the failure of Kurdish nationalism to democratize gender relations have invited women's opposition and organizing. This resistance is more spontaneous or reactive than conscious or planned. In Iraq, Turkey, and the European diasporas, for instance, the rise in male violence, especially honour killing and media coverage of it, has led to action. This activism, limited in scope and depth, occurs in the context of the absence of strong feminist or women's movements in the West. This is especially the case in North America, where new waves of anti-feminism pervade popular culture (Hammer, 2002).

The picture we have depicted above and the knowledge documented in this bibliography challenge the Western Orientalist view of women in the Middle

East and North Africa. Much of the knowledge, both liberal and conservative, about the region reduces women to carriers of identities, and, in turn, essentializes their identities as one of eternal loyalty to Islam. Thus Arab, Baluch, Kurdish, Persian, or Turkish women are treated as "Muslim women" in spite of their enormous diversity in terms of class, social background, politics, language, culture, education, geography, and culture. This construction of women as Muslims is sexist and racist in so far as it denies a substantial number of women of the region identities rooted in secularism, atheism, feminism, socialism, and internationalism.

The growing literature on the women of the Middle East is framed in identity politics, post-structuralist, post-colonialist, and post-modernist theories, and like the Orientalist trend also promotes the idea of women as Muslims. What connects this body of knowledge with Orientalism is its theoretical privileging of the concept of "difference" and its disdain for "sameness." Any idea of sameness, even in the struggle against male violence, is rejected as a grand narrative or essentialism. Working within an either/or framework, these theoretical perspectives fail to treat universality and particularity as the unity and struggle of opposites. They find it difficult to make sense of the simple observation that male violence, for example, is universal (practiced in all contemporary societies) although it takes historically and culturally specific forms (Mojab, 2004b). The treatment of feminism as a derivative discourse, coming from such discourses of "difference," appeals to nationalists, nativists, and Islamists who brand feminism as a Western phenomenon, and thus, question its validity for non-Westerners.

Under these conditions, the emerging Kurdish feminism is in a position to draw on the Western theoretical package of identity and difference, and to entertain nationalism in theory and practice. As we have seen, the conflict between nationalism and feminism has already emerged outside the sphere of theory, and in the inability of nationalist regimes to confront patriarchy. It seems that current feminist theories prefixed with *post-* contribute to the resolution of this conflict by inviting women to enter into "negotiation" with national, religious, ethnic, and tribal patriarchy.

## References

Abdal, A. (1960). La structure sociale des Kurdes de la Transcaucasie. In M. B. Nikitine (Ed., Trans.) *L'Afrique et l'Asie*, pp. 61-66.

Afary, J. (1996). The Iranian constitutional revolution, 1906-1911: Grassroots democracy, social democracy, and the origins of feminism. Columbia University.

Afkhami, M., & Friedl, E. (1994). Appendix II: The Islamic penal code of the Islamic Republic of Iran: Excerpts relating to women. In M. Afkhami & E. Friedl (Eds.), *In the eye of the storm: Women in post-revolutionary Iran* (pp. 180-87). Syracuse University Press.

Alakom, R. (2001). Kurdish women in Constantinople at the beginning of the twentieth century. In S. Mojab (Ed.), *Women of a non-state nation: The Kurds* (pp. 53-70). Mazda

Publishers.

Altinay, A. G. (2004). The myth of the military-nation: Militarism, gender, and education in Turkey. Palgrave Macmillan.

Amnesty International. (2003). Turkey: End sexual violence against women in custody!

Andrews, P. A. (Ed.). (1989). *Ethnic groups in the Republic of Turkey*. Wiesbaden.

Arat, Z. (1994). Kemalism and Turkish women. *Women and Politics*, 14(4), pp. 57-80. DOI: 10.1300/J014v14n04_05

Bannerji, H., Mojab, S., & Whitehead, J. (2001). Of property and propriety: The role of gender and class in imperialism and nationalism. University of Toronto Press.

Bannerji, H. (2011). Demography and democracy: Essays on nationalism, gender and ideology. Canadian Scholars' Press.

Bayazîdî, Mullah Mahmûdê. (1963). 'Adat we Risûmatnameyî Ekradîye [*Customs and manners of the Kurds*]. Nravy i Obychai Kurdove (M. B. Rudenko, Ed. & Trans.). Akademiia Nauk SSSR. Izdatel'stvo Vostochnoi Literatury Kurdov.

Benge, A. (1985). Güney, Turkey and the West: An interview. *Race and Class*, 26, 31-46.

Bidlisi, Amir Sharaf Khan. (1964). *Sharaf Nāmi: Tārikh-e Mufassal-e Kordestān* [Book of {Amir} Sharaf {Khan Bidlisi}: History of Kurdistan]. Mohammed 'Abbasi (Ed.). 'Elmi.

Çaglayan, H. (2019). Women in the Kurdish movement: Mothers, comrades, goddesses. Palgrave Macmillan.

Cansiz, S. (2018). *Sara: My whole life was a struggle* (J. Biehl, Trans.). Pluto.

Cansiz, S. 2019. *Sara: Prison memoir of a Kurdish revolutionary* (J. Biehl, Trans.). Pluto.

Carpenter, S., & Mojab, S. (Eds.). (2011). *Educating from Marx: Race, gender, and learning*. Palgrave MacMillan.

Carpenter, S., & Mojab, S. (2017). *Revolutionary learning: Marxism, feminism and knowledge*. Pluto.

Çelebi, E. (1990). Evliya Çelebi in Bıtlıs: The relevant section of the Seyahatname. Vol. 1 (L. Dankoff, Ed. & Trans.). Vol. 2 of Evliya Çelebi's Book of Travels: Land and People of the Ottoman Empire in the Seventeenth Century: A Corpus of Partial Editions (Klaus Kreiser, Ed.). E.J. Brill.

Chaliand, G., & Rageau, J.- P. (1981). *A strategic atlas: Comparative geopolitics of the world's powers* (T. Berrett, Trans.). Harper Collins.

Çingiyanî, C. (1993). An interview with four women belonging to the Union of the Women of Kurdistan. *Xermane*, Nos. 9-10, 119-26.

Dirik, D. (2021). The Kurdish women's movement: History, theory, practice. Pluto.

Encyclopedia of Women & Islamic Cultures. (2005). *Encyclopedia of Women & Islamic Cultures* (S. Joseph, Ed.).

Fattāhī Qāzi, Q. (Ed. & Trans.). (1970). *Mandūmi-yi kurdî-yi shur mahmūd va marzīngān* [The Kurdish epic poem of Shur Mahmud and Marzingan]. Tabriz University of Literature and Humanities.

Fernandes, D. (1999). The Kurdish genocide in Turkey, 1924-1998. *Armenian Forum*, 1, 57-107.

Fossum, L. O. (1918). The war-stricken Kurds. *The Kurdistan Missionary*, 10(1), 5-6.

Galletti, M. (2001). Western images of the woman's role in Kurdish society. In S. Mojab (Ed.), *Women of a non-state nation: The Kurds* (pp. 209-225). Mazda Publishers.

Ghaderi, F., & Scalbert Yücel, C. (2021). *Women's voices from Kurdistan. A selection of Kurdish Poetry*. Transnational Press London.

Ghobadi, G. (2020). Poppies Garden: The untold stories of women fighters of Iranian Kurdistan. Noghteh Publisher.

Great Britain. Colonial Office. (1930). Report by His Majesty's Government in the United Kingdom of Great Britain and Northern Ireland to the Council of the League of Nations on the Administration of Iraq for the year 1929. H.M.S.O.

Griffiths, D. (2002). *Somali and Kurdish refugees in London: New identities in the diaspora.*

Ashgate.

Gürbey, G. (1996). The Kurdish nationalist movement in Turkey since the 1980s. In R. Olson (Ed.), *The Kurdish Nationalist Movement in the 1990s* (pp. 9-37). The University Press of Kentucky.

Hammer, R. (2002). Antifeminism and family terrorism: A critical feminist perspective. Rowman and Littlefield Publishers.

Hansen, H. H. (1960). *Daughters of Allah*. Purnell and Sons.

Hansen, H. H. (1961). The Kurdish woman's life: Field research in a Muslim society. Nationalmuseet.

Hassanpour, A. (2000). The politics of a-political linguistics: Linguists and linguicide. In R. Phillipson (Ed.), *Rights to language: Equity, power, and education* (pp. 33-37). Lawrence Erlbaum Associates.

Hassanpour, A. (2001). The (re)production of patriarchy in the Kurdish language. In S. Mojab (Ed.), *Women of a non-state nation: The Kurds* (pp. 227-63). Mazda Publishers.

Hassanpour, A. (2020). Essay on Kurds: Historiography, orality, and nationalism. Peter Lang.

Hassanpour, A. (2021). The peasant uprising of Mukriyan, 1952-1953. Iran Namag.

Hassanpour, S. (2012). *Deçmewe Sablax* [Going Back to Sablagh/Mahabad]. Apec Förlag AB.

Hofstetter, E. O. (2001). *Women in global migration, 1945-2000: A comprehensive multidisciplinary bibliography*. Greenwood Press.

Homa, A. (2020). *Daughters of smoke and fire*. Harper Perennial.

Houston, C. (2003). Profane knowledge: Kurdish diaspora in the Turkish city. In C. Houston (Ed.), *Islam, Kurds and the Turkish nation state: New technologies, new cultures* (pp. 113-32). Routledge.

Human Rights Watch. (1992). Bloodshed in the Caucasus: Escalation of the armed conflict in Nagorno-Karabakh.

Human Rights Watch. (1993). *Genocide in Iraq: The Anfal campaign against the Kurds*. A Middle East Watch Report.

Human Rights Watch. (1995). Weapons transfers and violations of the laws of war in Turkey.

Ilkkaracan, P. (1999). Exploring the context of women's sexuality in Eastern Turkey. *Reproductive Health Matters, (6)*12, pp. 66-75.

Institut kurde de Paris. (2003). *The Kurdish diaspora*.

International Criminal Court. (2013). *Elements of crimes*.

International Information Centre and Archives for the Women's Movement. (1998). *European women's thesaurus: A structured list of descriptors for indexing and retrieving information in the field of the position of women and women's studies*. Author.

Iran National Archives. (1992). *Khoshonat va farhang: Asnad-e mahramaneh kashf-e hejab, 1313-1322* [Violence and culture: Confidential records about the abolition of hijab, 1313-1322]. Iran National Archives.

Jwaideh, W. (2006). *The Kurdish national movement: Its origins and development*. Syracuse University Press.

Kahn, M. (2020). *Children of the Jinn: The story of my search for the Kurds and their country*. Pearlnote Press. (Original work published 1980)

Kashi, E. (1994). *When the borders bleed: The struggle of the Kurds*. Chatto and Windus.

Kimball, M., & Von Schlegell, B. R. (1997). *Muslim women throughout the world: A bibliography*. Lynne Rienner Publishers.

Klein, J. (2001). En-gendering nationalism: The 'woman question' in Kurdish nationalist discourse of the late Ottoman period. In S. Mojab (Ed.), *Women of a non-state nation: The Kurds* (pp. 25-51). Mazda Publishers.

Hacî Qadirî Koyî. (1986). Dîwan, collected poetry of Haji Qadir Koyi. S. Hamid Miran & K. Mistafa Sharaza (Eds.). *Emîndarêtî Giştî Roşinbîrî w Lawanî Nawçey Kurdistan*,

Baghdad.

Kren, K. (2000). *Kurdologie, Kurdistan und Kurden in der Deutschsprachigen Literatur: Kommentierte Bibliographie* [Kurdology, Kurdistan and Kurds in German-language literature: Annotated bibliography]. Münster.

KIC/KSC Publications. (1992). We fight for a free Kurdistan and the liberation of Kurdish women [Interview with Medya, a member of the YJWK in *Kurdish women: The struggle for national liberation and women's rights*, London, Kurdistan Information Centre/Kurdistan Solidarity Committee, pp. 31-35.

Kurdish Human Rights Project. (1996). *Kurds in the Former Soviet Union*. KHRP.

Levene, M. (1998). Creating a modern "zone of genocide": The impact of nation- and state-formation on Eastern Anatolia, 1878-1923. *Holocaust and Genocide Studies, (12)*3, 393-433.

Māh Sharaf Khānum (Mastūri Kurdistānī). (1998). *Divan of Mastūr-i-yi Kurdistānī*. Sadīq Safīzādī (Ed.). Amirbahadoor.

Mahmoud, H. (Ed.). (2021). *Kurdish Women's* Stories. Pluto Press.

Makiya, K. (1993). Cruelty and silence: War, tyranny, uprising and the Arab world. W. W. Norton & Company.

Mann, O. (1906). *Die Mundart der Mukri-Kurden* [The dialect of the Mukri Kurds]. G. Reimer.

McDowall, D. (2000). *A modern history of the Kurds*. I. B. Tauris.

Meho, L. I., & Maglaughlin, K. L. (2001). *Kurdish culture and society: An annotated bibliography*. Greenwood Press.

Middle East Watch. (1991). Syria unmasked: The suppression of human rights by the Asad Regime. Yale University Press.

Minorsky, V. (1986). Kurds, Kurdistan. iii. History. In P. Bearman, T. Bianquis, C. E. Bosworth, E. van Donzel, & W. P. Heinrichs (Eds.), *The Encyclopedia of Islam: Vol. 2* (pp. 447-64). E.J. Brill.

Mojab, S. (2000a). Educational voyaging in a globalizing planet: The conference of the rich, the poor, and the oppressed. *Atlantis, 24*(2), 124-34.

Mojab, S. (2000b). Introduction: Iranian women's studies: Steps in the internationalization of feminist inquiry. In S. Mojab & A. Hojabri (Eds.), *Women of Iran: A subject bibliography* (pp. i-xii). Iranian Women's Studies Foundation.

Mojab, S. (2001a). Introduction: The solitude of the stateless: Kurdish women at the margins of feminist knowledge. In S. Mojab (Ed.), *Women of a non-state nation: The Kurds* (pp. 1-21). Mazda Publishers.

Mojab, S. (2001b). Women and nationalism in the Kurdish Republic of 1946. In S. Mojab (Ed.), *Women of a non-state nation: The Kurds* (pp. 71-91). Mazda Publishers.

Mojab, S. (2001c). Theorizing the politics of 'Islamic feminism.' *Feminist Review, 69*, pp. 124-146.

Mojab, S. (2001d). The politics of 'cyberfeminism' in the Middle East: The case of Kurdish women. *Race, Gender and Class, 8*(4), 42-61.

Mojab, S. (2004a). No 'safe haven': Violence against women in Iraqi Kurdistan. In W. Giles & J. Hyndman (Eds.), *Sites of violence: Gender and conflict zones* (pp. 108-33). University of California Press.

Mojab, S. (2004b). The particularity of 'honour' and the universality of 'killing': From early warning signs to feminist pedagogy. In S. Mojab & N. Abdo (Eds.), *Violence in the name of honour: Theoretical and political challenges* (pp. 15-37). Bilgi University Press.

Mojab, S. (2006). Gender, nation and diaspora: Kurdish women in feminist transnational struggles. In H. Moghissi (Ed.), *Muslim diaspora: Gender, culture and identity* (pp. 116-32). Routledge.

Mojab, S. (2009). Imperialism, 'Post-war Reconstruction' and Kurdish Women's NGOs. In N. Al-Ali & N. Pratt (Eds.), *Women and war in the Middle East: Transnational perspectives* (pp. 99-128). Zed Books.

Mojab, S. (Ed.). (2015a). *Marxism and feminism.* Zed Books.

Mojab, S. (2015b). *Deçmewe Sablax* [Going Back to Sablagh; Review of the book by Shilan Hassanpour]. *The Middle East Journal, 69*(3), Summer, pp. 488-89.

Mojab, S., & Hassanpour, A. (2002). The politics and culture of 'honour killing': The murder of Fadime Şahindal. *Pakistan Journal of Women's Studies: Alam-e-Neswan, 9*(1), 57-77.

Mojab, S., & Hassanpour, A. (2004). Kurdish diaspora. In I. Skoggard (Ed.), *Encyclopedia of diasporas* (pp. 214-24). Diasporas. Human Relations Area Files.

Müftüler-Bac, M. (1999). Turkish women's predicament. *Women's Studies International Forum, 22*(3), 303-15.

Murray, M. (1995). The law of the father? Patriarchy in the transition from feudalism to capitalism. Routledge.

Musaelian, Z. S. (1963). *Bibliografiia po Kurdovedeniiu* [Bibliography on Kurdish studies]. Akademiia Nauk SSSR.

Monshi, E. B. (1979). *History of Shāh 'Abbās the Great, Vol. I* (Tārīk-e 'Ālamārā-ye 'Abbāsī; R. M. Savory, Trans.). Persian Heritage Series, 28. Westview Press.

Musaelian, Z. S. (1996). *Bibliography po Kurdovedeniyo (Nachinaia s XVI Veka)* [Bibliography on Kurdology (Since 16th Century)]. St. Petersburg Institute for Oriental Studies, Russian Academy of Sciences.

Nammi, D., & Attwood, K. (2020). *Girl with a gun: Love, loss and the fight for freedom in Iran.* Unbound.

Neven, B., & Schäfers, M. (2017, November 25). Jineology: From women's struggles to social liberation. *ROAR Magazine.*

Østergaard-Nielsen, E. (2003). *Transnational politics: Kurds and Turks in Germany.* Routledge.

Reilly, J. (2019). Fragile nation, shattered land: The modern history of Syria. I.B. Tauris.

Rohat, A. (1994). *Di folklora Kurdî de Serdestiyeke Jinan* [The sovereignty of women in Kurdish folklore]. Weşanên Nûdem.

Roy, A. (2020, April 3). The pandemic is a portal. *Financial Times.*

Russo, D. (2000). Azerbaijan and Armenia: An update on ethnic minorities and human rights. Kurdish Human Rights Project.

Schmidinger, T. (2018). Rojava: Revolution, war and the future of Syrian's Kurds. Pluto Press.

Smirnov, N. A. (1927). *Kurdskaia Zhenshchina* [Kurdish woman]. Okhrana materinstva i mladenchestva.

United Nations General Assembly. (1963). *U.N. Economic and Social Council. 36th Session.* 109-14. UN Doc. A/5429.

United Nations Human Rights Office of the High Commissioner. (1993). *Declaration on the elimination of violence against women.*

Ussher, C. D. (1917). An American physician in Turkey: A narrative of adventures in peace and in war. Houghton Mifflin Company.

van Bruinessen, M. (1992). Agha, Shaikh and state: The social and political structures of Kurdistan. Zed Books.

van Bruinessen, M. (2001). *Kurdish ethno-nationalism versus nation-building states.* Collected Articles. The ISIS Press.

Van Rooy, S., & Tamboer, K. (1968). *ISK's Kurdish Bibliography.* International Society of Kurdistan.

Vanly, I. C. (1970). *Le Kurdistan irakien: Entité nationale. Etude de la révolution de 1961* [Iraqi Kurdistan: National entity. Study of the 1961 revolution]. Éditions de la Baconnière.

Vasil'eva, E. I. (1967). Predislovie. In Sharaf-Khān ibn Shamsaddīn Bidlīsī (Ed.), *Sharaf-Nāme: Vol. I* (pp. 613-19). Nauka.

Vasil'eva, E. I. (1976). Predislovie. In Sharaf-Khān ibn Shamsaddīn Bidlīsī (Ed.), *Sharaf-Nāme: Vol. II* (pp. 347-50). Nauka.

Wahlbeck, Ö. (1999). *Kurdish diasporas: A comparative study of Kurdish refugee communities.*

Macmillan Press.

Wilson, S. G. (1896). *Persian Life and Customs* (2nd ed). Oliphant Anderson and Ferrier.

Women for Women International. (2005). Windows of opportunity: The pursuit of gender equality in post-war Iraq.

Yūsifī, M. H., & Yūsifī, F. (1997). A survey of the causes of self-immolation in the city of Sanandaj in 1995-96. *Abidar*, 8(5).

# PART II

# WOMEN OF KURDISTAN: A BIBLIOGRAPHIC STUDY

**NOTE:** This bibliography does not include the extensive literature that are published from 2006 onward. This work is a bibliographical archive of Kurdish women's life, thought, and struggle. It certainly can be improved, corrected, and expanded. The main headings, sub-heading, and all entries are alphabetically organized. There will be differences in spelling and perhaps terminology within keywords, as these reflect the preference of the author. Cross-references are provided where appropriate. Some entries have missing or incomplete publication information. Many materials are no longer available, however, we felt it was important to include what we could to show the amount and type of coverage given to Kurdish women.

# GENERAL WORKS

**Aziz, Namo**. (1992). Frauen [Women]. In Namo Aziz (text), *Kurdistan. Menschen, Geschichte, Kultur* (pp. 71-78). Nürnberg: DA Verlag Das Andere. ISBN 3-922619-20-7. Two colour photos (pp. 73, 74).

> **Keywords:** Europeans impressions of Kurdish women; class; strength of Kurdish women; Kurdish women's position compared to other Muslim women; patriarchy; marriage; divorce; women reduced to their reproductive role; brothers' inheritance of their deceased brothers' wives; women's work; legends about Kurdish women.

**Bedir Xan, Dr. Kamiran Ali**. (1933). La femme kurde [The Kurdish woman]. *Hawar: Qovara Qurdî, Revue kurde*, Année 1, Numéro 19, 17 Avril, pp. 6-8. Reprinted without author's name in *Le Jour Nouveau: Quotidien kurde*, Troisième Année, Numéro 49, 16 juillet 1945, pp. 1-2.

> **Keywords:** absence of gynecaeum, separate area for women in Greece, among the Kurds; Kurdish approach to women similar to that of the ancient Romans; authors agree that Kurdish women are freer than all the women of the Orient; life of a girl; as fiancé; in marriage; rarity of divorce; women in popular literature; as poets and composers; Pura Halim chief of Kafourouchi tribe and Quah Nerkiz, chief of Chouvan tribe in Pichder region before WWI, fought the Ottomans after they killed their husbands; political life of women; Adile Hatoun [Khatoun] died in 1924, ruled in Haleptche [Halabjah], and was in charge of social and political life of the Djaff tribe for 15 years; Hafsekhan, sister of Cheikh Mahmoud, defended the rights of women.

**Bois, Thomas**. (1965). *Connaissance des Kurdes* [Knowledge of the Kurds]. Beirut: Khayats. Text (pp. 1-158), bibliography (pp. 159-161), author bibliography (pp. 163-164), map of Kurdistan (unnumbered back page).

> **Keywords:** history; nomadism; art; tribal system; family life; childhood; education; songs; music; festivals; religion; superstition; literature; nationalism; the absence of lesbianism; the absence of prostitution; marriage; Kurdish proverbs about women.

**Boulanger, Philippe**. (1998). *Le destin des Kurdes* [The fate of the Kurds]. Paris: L'Harmattan.

> **Keywords:** women in the PKK: guerilla fighting; as commanders; PKK as a vehicle for emancipation; joining the PKK to escape violence and bad conditions in family life and community; illusion of

the emancipated woman in Kurdish society as opposed to other Middle-Eastern societies; women as the keepers of tradition.

**Garrer, Hanneke and Adrienne Schürenberg**. (1978). Frauen in Kurdistan Ein Bericht aus dem Leben der kurdischen Frauen [Women in Kurdistan. A report from the life of Kurdish women]. In Jürgen Roth (Ed.), *Geographie der Unterdrückten,* (pp. 145-170). Reinbeck bei Hamburg: Rowohlt Taschenbuch Verlag. ISBN: 3 499 17125 2. Six black and white photographs (pp. 146, 151, 153, 155, 157, 165).

**Keywords:** family relations; domestic life of Kurdish women; domestic violence; health problems; farming; livestock; inter-ethnic relations in Turkish Kurdistan; childbirth; childhood; marriage; bride price (dowry); henna night.

**Hansen, Henny Harald**. (1961). *The Kurdish woman's life: Field research in a Muslim society, Iraq.* Copenhagen: Nationalmuseet. Preface (pp. vii-viii), note on transcription (pp. xi-xii), introduction (pp. 1-4), text (pp. 5-186), notes (pp. 187-197), list of Kurdish terms employed (Normalized by Professor K. Barr; pp. 205-208), list of ethnographical specimens (pp. 209-210), list of illustrations (pp. 211-213). 101 black and white illustrations. Maps (pp. 2, 3). Reviewed: Thomas Bois. (1962, 15 mai). Une Danoise parle de la femme kurde. *Le Soir* [Beyrouth], No. 4737, 15 mai 1962, No. 4738, 16 mai 1962.

**Keywords:** history; statements concerning the Kurdish woman; village life; material culture; women's work; women's dress; life cycle; marriage; death; women and Islam; importance of virginity; honour killing; divorce; superstition; magic; veiling; women's possibility of moving and of seclusion; women and authority; structures of power; women's potentials for emancipation; Lady Adela.

**Hitchens, Christopher**. (1992). Struggle of the Kurds. *National Geographic, 182*(2), 32-61. Map (p. 37), 23 colour photographs by Ed Kashi (pp. 32-33, 34-35, 36, 38, 39, 40, 41, 42, 43, 44-45, 47, 49, 50-51, 52, 53-54, 54, 56-57, 58-59, 59, 61).

**Keywords:** effects of war; women's work; Kurdistan in Turkey, Syria, Iran, and Iraq; religion; language; history of the Kurds and Kurdistan; Sabry Ahmed, a Kurdish woman who lives in Qalat Dizah; Kurds of Lebanon; the Kurdish Uprising following Operation Desert Storm; the "carefree mixing of the sexes" in Kurdistan; Kurdish women's lack of seclusion or veiling; Fadime Kirmizi, a female law student in Diyarbakir; Masoud Barzani; Jalal Talabani; destruction of villages in Iraqi Kurdistan; mass graves in Iraqi Kurdistan; Halabjah; Amina Mohammed Amin, a witness to the chemical bombing of Halabjah, and a victim of the poison agents dropped; Kurdish organizations and communities in Germany; Kurdish youth gangs in Germany; Jewish Kurdish community of Jerusalem; PKK; Yildiz Alpdogan, a woman sentenced to 12.5 years in prison in Turkey for membership in the PKK; cultural assimilation in Turkey; Mahsum Korkmaz Academy in Lebanon; Milan, a Kurdish teenager from Australia who joined the PKK; an interview with Abdullah Ocalan regarding views on feudalism and the Kurdish role in the Armenian Genocide; Beritan Tribe of Turkish Kurdistan; nomadism; Aso Ağace, a Kurdish woman who works at the Hînbûn women's center in Berlin; difficulties facing Kurdish women in Germany; Institut Kurde de Paris; the Kurdish Library and Museum of New York; Kurdish community of San Diego; the absence of women at a Kurdish gathering in Chula Vista, a suburb of San Diego.

**Kahn, Margaret**. (1980). *Children of the Jinn: The story of my search for the Kurds and their country*. New York: Seaview Books. Introduction (pp. xi-xiv), map (p. xv), text (pp. 3-302), 15 black and white photographs (unnumbered centre pages), ISBN 0-87223-564-5.

**Keywords:** inter-communal relations; women's position in society; Rezaiyeh; Mahabad; Republic of Mahabad; Assyrians; tribal system; Herkis; nomadic life; Azeri discrimination against Kurds; Kurdish honorific titles for women; female khans; hierarchy of Kurdish villages; Kurdish women's dress; feudalism; polygamy; SAVAK; education; Shikak tribe; illiteracy among Kurdish women; Mullah Mustafa Barzani; KDP; Shah Reza Pahlavi; Ba'ath Party; CIA; the White Revolution; Talabani; Sheikh Avdila; female refugees; Haji Ismail; village relations; blood feuds; refugee camps; refugee schools; student strikes; segregation of the sexes; Kurdish folk tales; veiling; Dustan; Mawana; divorce; Naqadeh; Herki migration.

**Keist, Dorothea and Cristina Karrer** (Directors). (1994). *Jîyana Me - Unser Leben: Vier Frauen aus Kurdistan* [Jîyana Me – our life: Four women from Kurdistan]. German Version, KeKa Production, Zürich, video Beta-SP, 73 minutes, Music by Othman Serkar. Distributer: KeKa Production, c/o Dorothea Keist, Sihlfeldstr. 26, CH-8003 Zürich, Switzerland.

**Keywords:** women's lives; a peasant woman from Iraqi Kurdistan; a physician from Iraqi Kurdistan; a Komele member from Iranian Kurdistan; the nationalist movement; political parties; Barzan; PKK; emigration; Suleymanya; Saqqiz.

**KIC/KSC Publications**. (1992). Women in Kurdistan: a history of their

71

struggle since the '70s. In *Kurdish women: The struggle for national liberation and women's rights* (pp. 1-4). London: KIC/KSC Publications. One photograph.

**Keywords:** women and nationalism; women and colonialism: men taking out their aggression on women because of humiliation suffered at the hands of domination; women as commodities: sale of women; women solely as child bearers; the oppression of women in traditional Kurdish family structures; role of the PKK in bringing about equality between men and women and changes in the traditional family structure; 1970s: women becoming politically and nationally conscious; mid-1970s: theoretical stages of independence struggle; participation of female students in debates and possibilities for struggle, eventually becoming active in the struggle; women and family honour; pressure to marry and have children; controlling the movements of female family members; ostracization from the community for making non-traditional choices; participation in youth propaganda activities, marches and protests; armed struggle: participation arose from the need to combat the agents of the 12 September coup; Besey Anus, Turkan Derin, and Azime Demirtas: amongst the first Kurdish women to die in armed combat; female prisoners: torture; stripped naked; rape; sexual abuse as a weapon against Kurdish men; hunger strikes; effects of imprisonment of males on female relatives: role of support; suffered harassment, assault, abuse; unable to communicate with imprisoned relatives; organization and action of relatives of prisoners; women as maintainers of national culture and education; negative reaction of male Kurds to women's actions; training of female guerillas; women in positions of power in the guerilla forces; Hanim Yaverkaya, Nafiye Oz, Cicek Selcan, Reyhan Kal, Rahime Kahraman; Sultan Yavuz: women who died in armed struggle; arrests of female relatives of men wanted by the police; Kurdish women in the cities and in the Diaspora: spreading of national consciousness amongst women; founding of the YJWK.

**Meho, Lokman I. and Kelly Maglaughlin.** (2001). Women. In Lokman I. Meho and Kelly Maglaughlin (compilers) *Kurdish culture and society: An annotated bibliography* (pp. 285-91). Westport, CT: Greenwood Press. ISBN 0-313-31543-4 (hb).

**Keywords:** rise of Islamism; female politicians in Kurdistan; matriarchy; women's liberation; KDP; PUK; mothers; life companions; political leaders; militants; Kurdish nationalist movement and women; rape and the Iraqi army; Saddam Hussein's war on the Kurds; fertility; women in politics and war; nationalism; patriarchy; eurocentrism; migration; gender roles; female strategies; male hegemony; tribalism; prison; Leyla Zana.

**Mojab, Shahrzad** (Ed.). (2001). *Women of a non-state nation: The Kurds.* Costa Mesa: Mazda Publishers. 263 pages.

> **Keywords:** statelessness and Kurdish women; the state as a patriarchal and class formation; Armenia and Kurdistan as a "zone of genocide"; Turkish feminists as nationalists, denying Kurdish national rights; Turkish Kemalist state uses state feminism against Kurdish women; misogynist propaganda against PKK women guerrillas; Turkish feminism as watchdog of nationalism; women in the modernization policies of the Iraqi and Iranian states; Persianization in Iran; the demand for Kurdish women's education in Iraq; Britain's resentment at the demand for more education; patriarchal nature of state nationalism and Kurdish nationalism; the incompatibility of nationalism and feminism; the absence of Kurdish women's studies as a product of statelessness; the politics of Kurdish women's studies in the Middle East and its political economy in the West; cyberfeminism and Kurdish feminist studies; the emerging conflict between Kurdish nationalism and feminism: Kurdish feminist and women's journalism.

**Mojab, Shahrzad**. (2015). Kurdish women. In Suad Joseph (General Editor), *Encyclopedia of women and Islamic cultures: Vol. II. Family, Law and Politics* (pp. 358-66). Leiden: Brill.

> **Keywords:** historical sketch of "Kurdish woman" in early histories and travelogues; Kurdish women in nomadic, tribal, feudal, and urban environments in the nineteenth century; freedom of nomadic and tribal women and the strictness of codes of honor and propriety; instilling fear in women by killing them for extra- or non-marital sexual relations; women rulers and poets; the diversity of gender relations in oral traditions; the claim to the "relative freedom" of Kurdish women (compared with Arab, Persian, and Turkish women); the division of Kurdistan among the new nation-states of Iraq, Iran, Turkey, Syria, and the Soviet Union after WWI; fragmentation and transnationalization of women; rise of Kurdish nationalism and its identification of women as bearers of pure Kurdish culture and language; patriarchy and nationalism; Kurdish nationalist resistance to assimilation; the patriarchal nature of the nation-states; their projects of nation-building through the construction of "new Iraqi woman," "Turkish woman," "Iranian woman," and "Muslim woman"; the formation of the polity of "Kurdish woman"; the failure of these projects and the formation of Kurdish womanhood, as a nationalist, secular, and modern identity.

**Sammali, Jacqueline**. (1995). *Être Kurde, Un Délit?: Portrait d'un peuple nié,* Paris: L'Harmattan. ISBN 2-7384-3772-9. Preface (pp. 9-13), introduction (pp. 15-30), text (pp. 33-279), appendixes (pp. 282-288), maps (pp. 282, 284), bibliography (pp. 289-294), chronology (pp. 295-298).

> **Keywords:** cultural denial; historical background; origins of Kurds; the structure of Kurdish society; tribalism; nomadism; hospitality; status of women; religion; Mazdaism; Yezidism; Islam; Alevism; language; oral literature; written literature; revolts; division of Kurdistan; origins of cultural denial in Turkey; Kemalism; Sheikh Said; Mount Ararat Revolt; Dersim Revolt; political opposition; survival of Kurdish identity; new Kurdish organizations; Maraş massacre; struggle for independence; effects of cultural denial; climate of fear; tourists and denial; peasants; way of life; Kurdish humor; role of women; language rights; childhood; literacy; education; denial in regions with mixed populations; assimilation; collective action; PKK; resistance; geography of Kurdistan; honor killing.

**Schumann, Gerd, Alexander Goeb, and Guenay Ulutunçok**. (1992). *Ez Kurdim - Ich bin Kurdin. Kurdische Frauen im Aufbruch,* München: Marino Verlag. ISBN 3-927527-54-8.

> **Keywords:** migration; change; feudalism; equality; guerillas; Kurdish women in the "secret" capital of Kurdistan (Diyarbakir/Amed); Kurdish women in Istanbul; Kurdish women in Köln; Kurdish women in Leverkusen; Leyla Zana; herstory (women's history of Kurdistan); Musa Anter on the role of women in Kurdish culture; women in theatre, film, literature, and everyday culture; Abdullah Öcalan; PKK; Feridun Yazar; HEP; history, geography.

**Thornhill, Teresa**. (1995). Women and Kurdistan. In *Resistance: Women in Kurdistan* (pp. 32-34). London: KIC/KSC Publications. One photograph.

> **Keywords:** research on Kurds in Iraq: done from the point of view of men; very little written about or by Kurdish women, about their experiences and contribution to the Kurdish struggle; Teresa Thornhill: visited Iraqi Kurdistan in 1993; conducted interviews with 40 Kurdish women; most of them had been, or were, politically active and/or affiliated; contacts and introductions came mostly through women who were affiliated with the PUK or KDP; honour and shame: Kurdish saying: "Everything a woman does is shameful"; long term effects of the culture of shame; family honour dependent on sexual purity of the female members of the family; imposition of strict social controls on females to protect family honour; female peshmerga: in general did not fight; service role of cooking, building camps, nursing

the wounded, carrying ammunition and messages; most in the mountains with their husbands; only some were single; no privacy; separation from children; suffering of women whose husbands became peshmerga; exploitation of culture of shame and honour during interrogation by police forces; rape, sexual harassment systematic practices within Iraqi detention centres; rejection by families upon release from prison; psychological and physical trauma; widows; assumption of traditionally male jobs in order to support families; humiliation and anger at having to work in "male" jobs to survive; since the 1991 Kurdish uprising life has become more difficult for Kurdish women; women and political participation: seven female MPs in the Kurdish parliament one of whom is Minister of Tourism and Municipalities, Kafia Sulayman; 1992 campaign to reform the family law code; women from the main political parties came together to form an all-women's committee to draft law reform proposals; aided by Khajor, a Turkish Kurdish activist, and some female lawyers; the proposals were not adopted.

## I. CONFERENCES

**Gallier, C**. (2002). Un acte de solidarité, *Presse de la Manche,* 21 February 2002, reprinted in *Institut Kurde de Paris: Information and Liaison Bulletin, 203*, p. 90.

> **Keywords:** international conference on Kurdish women, "Femmes, violence et moyens de mobiliser la résistance: le cas des femmes kurdes," Paris, February 22, 2002.

**Gallier, C**. (2002). Un acte de solidarié [An act of solidarity]. *La Pressse de la Manche*, reprinted in *Institut Kurde de Paris, Information and Liaison Bulletin, 203*, p. 90.

> **Keywords:** news about the forthcoming conference on Kurdish women to be convened in Paris on February 21.

**Gallier, C**. (2002). La violence faite aux femmes kurdes est un problème universel, *La Presse de la Manche*, reprinted in *Institut Kurde de Paris: Information and Liaison Bulletin, 203*, February 25, pp. 88-89.

> **Keywords:** international conference on Kurdish women, "Femmes, violence et moyens de mobiliser la résistance: le cas des femmes kurdes," Paris, February 22, 2002; violence against women is universal; organizers: Kurdish Institute of Paris; Kurdish Women Action Against Honour Crimes; International Network of Kurdish Women's Studies; France-Libertés.

International Conference: Women, Violence and the Politics of Mobilizing Resistance: The Case of Kurdish Women, Conference Programme. (2002). *Institut Kurde de Paris, Information and Liaison Bulletin, 203*, February 22, pp. 16-18.

**Keywords:** Kurdish Institute of Paris; Kurdish Women Action Against Honour Killing; International Kurdish Women Studies Network; France Libertés; Nazand Begikhani (KWAHK), Kurdish Institute of Paris; Danielle Mitterrand (President of France-Libertés); *Session 1: Explaining the Dynamics of Violence*: Margaret Grieco, Professor, Napier University; Juliette Minces, author and specialist on Islam and women, Paris; *Session 2: Women in Armed Conflict*: Nebahat Akkoç (KA-MER Women's Centre, Diyarbakir), "The effects of displacement on Kurdish women and children in Diyarbakir and women's response"; Fatma Karakaş (lawyer, Legal Aid Project for Women Raped or Sexually Abused in Custody, Istanbul), "Sexual violence against women..."; Meral Daniş Beştaş (lawyer, Diyarbakir Bar Association, Women's Commission), "The situation of Kurdish female prisoners..."; Necla Açik (researcher, Manchester), "Women images and self-sacrifice in the Kurdish national struggle"; Messages from Leyla Zana; Shirin Fattah Amedi (President of the Kurdistan Women's Union, Erbil), and Kafia Suleiman (General Secretary of the Kurdistan Women's Union of Suleimanieh); *Session 3: "Politics of Extermination: The Anfal Campaign in Iraqi Kurdistan"*: Pakhshan Zangana (Journalist, Cologne), "The Anfal campaigns..."; Wazira J. Saaid (editor-in-chief of *Bergri* magazine, Suleimaniya), "Anfal and the women's movement in Iraqi Kurdistan"; Karin Mlodoch (psychologist, Berlin), "The psychological situation of women Anfal survivors in the Garmian area"; Inga Rogg (journalist and cultural anthropologist, Munich): "Violent voices, silenced voices: Anfal and memory"; *Session 4: Nationalist Violence The Practice of Violence Against the Bodies of Women and Strategies of Resistance*: Roonak Faraj (researcher, Women Information Centre, Suleimaniya), "Notions of shame and honour: The practice of honour killings in Iraqi Kurdistan"; Narmeen Karadakhy (lawyer, Erbil), "The functioning of the law and the situation of women in the KDP controlled area"; Nazaneen Rasheed (project co-ordinator, Kurdish Women Action against Honour Killing , London), " The Aram shelter for women in Suleimaniya..."; Nazand Bagikhani, "Kurdish women and political Islam"; *Session 4: Kurdish Women in the Diaspora: The Dialectics of Violence and Resistance*: Rachel Gorman (researcher, University of Toronto), "Learning for life: Kurdish women's tales of war and diaspora"; Mounireh Moftizadeh (chairperson, Kurdish Women Organisation and KWAHK, London), "Kurdish women's life in exile"; Carina Grosser-Kaya (researcher,

Leipzig), "Between resistance and adaptation: The everyday life of Kurdish women in Leipzig, Germany"; Isabelle Rigoni (researcher, Warwick University), "Concluding remarks."

**Jacob, Antoine**. (2004). En Suède, un conférence internationale dénonce les crimes 'd'honneur' [In Sweden, an international conference denounces "honor crimes"]. *Le Monde*. December 10.

**Keywords:** international conference on "Combating Patriarchal Violence Against Women: Focusing on Violence in the Name of Honour," held in Stockholm on December 7-8, 2004 sponsored by the Swedish government; 200 participants; gender inequality among new Swedish citizens (immigrants); one-sixth of Swedish population of foreign origins with limited integration, leading to recourse to origins, culture, and identity; participants resolve that "it is unacceptable to invoke customs, traditions or religious considerations to avoid obligations to eradicate violence against women and girls, including violence in the name of honour"; the root causes of all patriarchal violence is "perceptions of male superiority and female subordination."

*See also* Honour Killing

**Kurdish Human Rights Project**. (2003). KHRP at Iranian Women's Conference. In *KHRP Newsline*, 23, Autumn, pp. 18.

**Keywords:** June 2003: KHRP invited to make a presentation at the 14th annual conference of the Iranian Women's Studies Foundation (IWSF) that focused on globalization and its impact on women.

**Kurdish Human Rights Project**. (2003). Participation at events. In *Kurdish Human Rights Project, Annual Report 2003*, pp. 49-50.

**Keywords:** June 2003: KHRP invited to make a presentation at the 14th Annual conference of the Iranian women's Studies Foundation (IWSF) that focused on globalization and its impact on women.

**Kurdish National Congress of North America**. (1990) *Proceedings of the Third Annual Kurdish National Congress Conference*. Fullerton, California. August 4-5, 10 pages.

**Keywords:** session on the "Role of Kurdish Woman"; speakers: Dela Jaff; Soraya Mufti, and Dr. Kejal Rahmani; Kurdish women freer than Turkish, Persian, and Arab women; progress in women's participation in politics; need for more women's activism.

**Kurdistan Report**. (1992). "We take our strength from our people, which is becoming ever freer, from the fact that we are in the right and from our organized resistance." *Kurdistan Report, 6*, February, pp. 21-23. Also appeared in *Kurdish Women: The struggle for national liberation and women's rights.* (1992). London: KIC/KSC Publications, pp. 19-23.

> **Keywords:** Sara Akan, representative of the YKD interviewed by the monthly, Özgür Halk; exploitation of women's labour; difficulties facing urban and rural Kurdish women; women and capitalism; the buying and selling of women; women's sexual identities; women and education; women's (lack of) access to health care; women and reproduction; importance of giving birth to male offspring; assimilation of Kurdish women in Turkish cities; male-female relations within the home; sexist proverbs regarding women; mothers of martyrs; women fighters/guerrillas; female revolutionaries; women and solidarity movements.

**Kurdistan Report**. (1994). Resolution passed at the international conference of Kurdish women. *Kurdistan Report, 18*, p. 36.

> **Keywords:** International Women's Day, 8 March 1994, Cologne, Germany; solidarity; Leyla Zana; International Conference of Women from Kurdistan; TAJK; International Women's Conference of the U.N. in Beijing, 1995; International Committees in Solidarity with the Free Women's Movement of Kurdistan; Kurdish Women's Week.

**Levallois, Jean**. (2002). L'identité facteur de dignité [Identity as a factor of dignity]. *Presse de la manche,* reprinted in *Institut Kurde de Paris: Information and Liaison Bulletin, 203*, February 22, pp. 90-91.

> **Keywords:** national identity; the division of Kurdistan by four states; activism; violence against Kurdish women and honour killings; international conference organized by Mme. Danielle Mitterrand, the Fondation France libertés and the Institut Kurde de Paris at the Senate of France.

**Levallois, Jean**. (2002). Point de vue: L'identité facteur de dignité [Point of view: Identity as a factor of dignity]. *La Pressse de la Manche,* reprinted in *Institut Kurde de Paris, Information and Liaison Bulletin, 203*, February 22, p. 90.

> **Keywords:** comments on the conference on "Women, Violence and the Politics of Mobilizing Resistance: The Case of Kurdish Women" (February 22, Paris).

**Ouest-France**. (2002). Femmes du Cotentin et femmes kurdes réunies au

Sénat; J.-P. Godefroy: un engagement amical. *Ouest-France*, reprinted in *Institut Kurde de Paris, Information and Liaison Bulletin, 203*, February 26, p. 91.

**Keywords:** international conference on Kurdish women, "Femmes, violence et moyens de mobiliser la résistance: le cas des femmes kurdes," Paris, February 22, 2002; mobilization of Kurdish women; Kurdish female victims of violence; rape; sexual abuse; forced migration; deportations; domestic violence; honour crimes.

**Petrini, Barbara and Dominik Schaller.** (2000). Research in progress workshop on Kurdish gender studies. Katzow, Germany. Berlin Society for the Promotion of Kurdology and the project "Kurdish Studies" at the Research Center for Intercultural Studies (FiSt) of the University of Cologne, Kurdish Studies. Katzow, Germany, Heft 1, September 23-25, 172-177.

**Keywords:** topics covered in papers presented: Dilşah Deniz, "Positive effects of migration on Kurdish women in Istanbul"; Marrianne Rugkåsa, "Political mobilization and gender ideology among Kurdish migrants in Oslo"; Isabelle Rigoni, "Kurdish visible actions in Western Europe and the role of women"; Geoffrey Haig, "The gender system in the Kurdish language: Structural and sociolinguistic aspects"; Paul White, "The formation of Kurdish national identity among diaspora women from Turkey in north-western Melbourne, Australia"; Minoo Nemati, " The boundaries of diaspora; The influence of gender on the construction of national identity within the Kurdish diaspora"; Christiane Lembert-Dolber, "Assyrians in Augsburg between tradition and modernisation: The change of social structure and gender relations"; Eva Savelsberg, "Teenagers of Kurdish origin and their conceptions of marriage and partnership."

**La Presse de la Manche.** (2002). Les femmes au Kurdistan: état des lieu [Women in Kurdistan: State of play]. *La Pressse de la Manche*, reprinted in *Institut Kurde de Paris, Information and Liaison Bulletin, 203*, February 25, p. 89.

**Keywords:** 18th and 19th century Western travellers' views on the relative freedom of Kurdish women; the impact of war (in Turkey and Iraq); Kurdish proverb about gender and power; the privileged status of Kurdish women in the Muslim world; the division of Kurdistan; the disintegration of Kurdish cultural and social structures; war; repression; displacement of populations; the destruction of Kurdish elites; Islamism; suicide of young Kurdish women in Turkish Kurdistan; honour; deportation under Saddam Hussein; the destruction of Kurdish villages and towns in Iraq; disappearances under Saddam Hussein; chemical weapons; Halabja; the role of women in Iraqi Kurdistan; the abolition of Iraqi legislation regarding honour killings in Iraqi Kurdistan; the double oppression of Iranian Kurdish women; Syrian Kurdish women.

**Sullivan, Laura**. (1994). International conference of Kurdish women: An Irish visitor's perspective. *Kurdistan Report, 18*, May/June 1994, pp. 35-36. Also appears in *Resistance: Women in Kurdistan.* (1995). London: KIC/KSC Publications, pp. 29-48, one photograph.

> **Keywords:** International Women's Day; comparisons between the movement for Irish freedom and that for Kurdish freedom; reflections on the state of equality for women in England and Kurdistan; peace as a woman's demand; the PKK's views on the equality of women; Kurdish women's double oppression; women guerrillas; PKK; solidarity movements.

## II. STATISTICS

**Agace, Asiye, Marina Sabinasz, and Sonja Reuter**. (1981). In Astrid Albrecht-Heide (Ed.) *Bildungs- und Sozialstatistik türkischer und kurdischer Frauen in der Türkei, der Bundesrepublik Deutschland und in Berlin (West), einschließlich einer nach Problemen gegliederten Bibliographie,* Berlin: Technische Universität Berlin. 189 pages.

> **Keywords:** statistics; Turkish and Kurdish women; migration; Turkey; Federal Republic of Germany; West Berlin.

**Akhan, Okan**. (1997). The most recent development in connection with the trial against the Rehabilitation Center in Adana, Turkey. *Quarterly Journal on Rehabilitation of Torture Victims and Prevention of Torture (7)*4, (Copenhagen, Denmark) reprinted in *Institut Kurde de Paris, Information and Liaison Bulletin, 152-153*, November/December 1997, pp. 90-93.

> **Keywords:** HRFT; the Documentation Center Project; the Treatment and Rehabilitation Centers Project; human rights violations in Turkey; torture survivors; legal difficulties of HRFT and Rehabilitation Centers; torture statistics; murders by unidentified assailants; disappearances; extrajudicial executions; torture; health reports; torture of women; rape/harassment; torture of children; Human Rights Association (IHD); limits on freedom of expression; oppression of NGOs.

**Institut Kurde de Paris**. (1997). Turkey's population now numbers 62 million according to the Nov. 1997 census. In *Institut Kurde de Paris, Information and Liaison Bulletin, 152-153*, November/December 1997, pp. 12-13.

**Keywords:** Kurdish population; children in Turkey; poverty; homelessness; children in prison; illiteracy; girls' lack of access to education; emigration; war in Kurdistan; gender discrimination in census; male-centric collection of occupation data.

**UNICEF Tehran**. (1998). *The status of girls and women in Kurdestan province in the Islamic Republic of Iran.* Tehran, Iran: UNICEF, 1377. ISBN: 964-6513-16-6. Photo credits: UNICEF/photo: H. Zolfaghari and Sedigheh Akbarzadeh. Introduction (pp. 1-2), text (pp. 3-94). photographs (32 photographs, unnumbered page and pp. 1, 2, 5, 6, 7, 11, 14, 19, 22, 26, 28, 31, 34, 39, 41, 46, 48, 51, 52, 55, 58, 62, 63, 64, 71, 74, 79, 81, 85, 88, 91) 13 graphs (pp. 13, 14, 15, 16, 41, 42, 43, 44, 45, 46, 47, 49).

**Keywords:** Kurdestan, "one of the most deprived frontier provinces in Iran"; main purpose of research: "to obtain a true portrait of girls and women in Kurdestan, the role they play in family life, in the town, the village, or in society, and the status they enjoy within the family, village, town, and society as a whole"; statistics; population; education; literacy; health and medical care; marriage; polygamy; divorce; poverty; prostitution; the production, consumption, and sale of alcohol; bribes; domestic abuse; child labor; immigration; employment; girls and women's awareness of their civil and social rights.

# ARTS AND CULTURE

## I. FILM

**Institut Kurde de Paris**. (2004). Kurdish Film Director, Bahman Ghobadi, Receives the 'Golden Seashell' at the 52nd San Sebastian Film Festival for his film, 'Turtles Can Fly. In *Institut Kurde de Paris, Information and Liaison Bulletin, 234*, September, pp. 4, (summary).

**Keywords:** *Turtles Can Fly:* Iran-Iraq war; refugee camp; main female character: young girl raped by Saddam Hussein's army.

**Lavalley, Jean**. (2004). Quand les dunes de Biville prennet un air de Turquie [When the dunes of Biville take on an air of Turkey]. *La Press de la Manche,* reprinted in *Institut Kurde de Paris, Information and Liaison Bulletin, 236,* November 2004, pp. 18, three photographs.

**Keywords:** Xecê: character in film, *Seredan,* by Kurdish director, Suayip Adlig, was raped and tortured by the Turkish army; in order to save her family from dishonour, she leaves Turkey for Great Britain, where her brother is living; Adlig says the film is based on reality; estimates of Kurdish women who have been raped are 20,000 even if only 400 have reported it.

**The Herald Magazine**. (2005). You're a failed assassin. You've seen members of your family murdered in Iraq. And you'll always be an exile. What do you do? Look on the bright side. *The Herald Magazine*, January 29, reprinted in *Institut Kurde de Paris, Information and Liaison Bulletin, 240*, March, pp. 89-90.

> **Keywords:** *Vive la mariée...et la liberation du Kurdistan*: film by Hiner Saleem; Kurdish audience had divided reaction; women liked it; men were not pleased with his portrayal of their treatment of women.

**Institut Kurde de Paris**. (2000). A Spanish documentary on Leyla Zana blasted by the Turkish Press. *Institut Kurde de Paris, Information and Liaison Bulletin, 187*, p.10.

> **Keywords:** La Espalda del Mundo; Leyla Zana; Mehdi Zana; Turkish press.

**Institut Kurde de Paris**. (2002). At the demand of the police, the Turkish Ministry of Culture bans the film that had received the most awards in Turkey. *Institut Kurde de Paris, Information and Liaison Bulletin, 203*, pp. 9-10, and *204*, March 2002, p. 6.

> **Keywords:** The Turkish High Control Committee of Films, Video and Music bans the film *Büyük Adam, Küçük Aşk* (Great Man, Small Love); the Golden Orange Festival; the story of a little Kurdish girl, Hejar, who speaks Kurdish only, and shows extrajudicial killing by the police; Police Directorate bans the film because of its "attacks on the territorial and national integrity" of Turkey.

*See also* Language

**McKiernan, Kevin** (Director). (2000). *Good Kurds, Bad Kurds*. Edited by Thomas G. Miller. Associate Producer: Catherine Boyer. Cinematography by Haskell Wexler and Kevin McKiernan. Original Music by Bronwen Jones. U.S.A.: IMDbPro

> **Keywords:** U.S. foreign policy; U.S. arms trade; U.S. immigration policy; attacks on Kurdish villagers in Turkey and Iraq with American weaponry; Gulf War; American support for, and withdrawal of support for Kurdish uprisings in Iraq under Barzani and during the Gulf War; war; insurrection; Kurds in the diaspora; Kani Xulam; AKIN; history of Kurdistan; Abdullah Öcalan.

**Rois, Emmanuèle**. (2005). Bahman Ghobadi et l'innocence perdue [Bahman Ghobadi and the lost innocence]. *Le Figaro*, reprinted in *Institut Kurde de Paris, Information and Liaison Bulletin, 239*, February 2005, pp. 79, one photograph.

> **Keywords:** *Turtles Can Fly:* Iran-Iraq war; refugee camp; main female character: young girl raped by Saddam Hussein's army.

**Saleem, Hiner** (Director). (1998). *Vive la mariée et la liberation du Kurdistan* [Long live the bride and the liberation of Kurdistan]. Actors: Georges Corraface, Marina Kobakhidzé, Fatah Soltani, Schahla Aalam, Tuncel Kurtiz. Length: 100 minutes. France, Reviewed in *The Globe and Mail*, March 23, 2000, p. R5.

> **Keywords:** Kurdish refugees in France; arranged marriages; patriarchal family relations; difficulties facing Kurdish women in France.

## II. MASS MEDIA

**AFP**. (1993). Offensive turque: 25.000 personnes réfugiées dans les montagnes, selon le Comité du Kurdistan [Turkish offensive: 25,000 refugees in the mountains, according to the Kurdistan Committee]. *AFP*, reprinted in *Institut Kurde de Paris, Information and Liaison Bulletin, 101-102*, August/September, p. 67.

> **Keywords:** Kurdistan Committee; PKK; *Özgür Gündem*; Aysel Malkoç.

**Amnesty International**. (1993). Action Urgente [Urgent Action]. *Amnesty International, Section Française*, reprinted in *Institut Kurde de Paris, Information and Liaison Bulletin, 105*, December, pp. 72-73.

> **Keywords:** Gürbetelli Ersöz; *Özgür Gündem*; torture.

**Ersöz, Gurbetelli**. (2004). To the Court (Friends of *Özgur Gündem*, Ed., Trans.). In *Gurbetelli Ersöz's Defence: An Impassioned Plea for Free Speech in Turkey* (pp. 4-19). London: Friends of *Özgur Gündem* and Action for Kurdish Women.

> **Keywords:** media; arrests and torture of journalists; murder of journalists; decree 156; press freedom; *Özgur Gündem*; Turkish penal code; Anti-Terror Law.

**Gamk**. (1995). Ayşe Nur Zarakolu" l'éditrice du livre d'Yves Ternon sur le Génocide, est condamnée à 2 ans et demi de prison [The editor of Yves Ternon's book on the genocide sentenced to 2.5 years in prison]. *Gamk*,

83

reprinted in *Institut Kurde de Paris, Information and Liaison Bulletin, 118-119*, January/February 1995, p. 174.

**Keywords:** Armenians and Kurds in Turkey; breaking of taboos regarding the Armenian Genocide; imprisonment of publishers.

**Gamk.** (1997). La Revue de Femmes Kurdes Roza poursuivre par la Justice Turque. *Gamk,* reprinted in *Institut Kurde de Paris, Information and Liaison Bulletin, 144-145,* March/April 1997, p. 52.

**Keywords:** Fatma Kayhan; Ayşe Nur Zarakolu; State Security Court; monetary fine imposed on *Roza*; charge of separatism.

**L'Humanité.** (1993). Députés et journalistes kurdes sous la menace [Kurdish deputies and journalists under threat]. *L'Humanité,* reprinted in *Institut Kurde de Paris, Information and Liaison Bulletin, 105,* December 1993, p. 131.

**Keywords:** DEP; Leyla Zana; PKK; *Özgür Gündem.*

**L'Independent.** (1992). Au moins 56 journalistes tués en 1992 [at least 56 journalists killed in 1992]. *L'Independant,* reprinted in *Institut Kurde de Paris, Information and Liaison Bulletin, 93,* December 1992, p. 15.

**Keywords:** murder of journalists; *Özgür Gündem.*

**Mardikian, Varoujan.** (1998). Ayché Zarakolu reçoit le *Prix de la Liberté de Publier* à la Foire du Livre de Francfort [Ayché Zarakolu receives the Freedom to Publish Award at the Frankfurt Fair]. *La Lettre de L'UGAB,* reprinted in *Institut Kurde de Paris Information and Liaison Bulletin, 162-163,* September/October 1998, pp. 126-127.

**Keywords:** Ayşe Nur Zarakolu; CRDA; Belge Yayınları; Ermeni Tabusu; difficulties facing the translators and publishers of the translation of a book by Yves Ternon regarding the Armenian Genocide.

**Paringaux, Roland-Pierre.** (1998). Les Zarakolu, vigies de la conscience turque [The Zarakolu, lookouts of the Turkish conscience]. *Le Monde,* reprinted in *Institut Kurde de Paris, Information and Liaison Bulletin, 164-165,* November/December 1998, pp. 203-204.

**Keywords:** Ayşe Nur Zarakolu; Ragip Zarakolu; Armenian Genocide; Belge Publishing House.

**PEN.** (1993-1994). Focus On: Torture. *Centre to Centre: Newsletter of the Writers* *in Prison Committee of International PEN*, December 1993-January 1994, reprinted in *Institut Kurde de Paris, Information and Liaison Bulletin, 106-107*, January/February 1994, pp. 9-10.

**Keywords:** *Özgür Gündem*; Necmiye Arsanoğlu; Nalan Alıcı; torture.

PEN. (1995). Ayşenur Zarakolu, Turkey. In *Newsletter of the Writers in Prison Committee of International PEN*, cited in *Institut Kurde de Paris, Information and Liaison Bulletin, 120*, March 1995, p. 2.

**Keywords:** first and only woman director of a Turkish book distribution house; imprisonment of publishers in Turkey.

PEN. (1999). Half-Yearly Caselist to 30th June 1999. *International Pen Writers in Prison Committee*, reprinted in *Institut Kurde de Paris, Information and Liaison Bulletin, 174*, September 1999, pp. 73-79.

**Keywords:** Konca Kuriş; Serpil Güneş; Selma Kubat; Aynur Koruç; Hatice Ödemiş; Fatma Harman; Ayten Öztürk; Yazgül Güder Öztürk; Asiye Güzel Zeybek; Fatma Sesli; Sakine Topoğlu; Nuray Yazar; Hatun Yıldırım; Gülsüm Cengiz; Ayşe Nur Zarakolu.

PEN. (2000). Half-Yearly Caselist to 30 June 2000. *International PEN Writers in Prison Committee*, reprinted in *Institut Kurde de Paris Information and Liaison Bulletin, 184-185*, July/August 2000, pp. 1-6.

**Keywords:** Leyla Arçil; *Vatan*; torture; prison sentences of journalists; Lütfiye Aygün; Sevilay Çalışkan; Derya Duman; Özgül Emre; Selma Kubat; Özlem Kütük; Arzu Demir; *Özgür Bakış*; Sakine Yalçın; Manolya Gültekin; Ayça Taşkaya; Seval Uzun; *Alınterimiz; Özgür Barikat;* Serpil Güneş; Fatma Harman; *Atılım*; Nuray Yazar; *Proleter Halkın Birliği;* Yazgül Güder Öztürk; Kurtuluş; Nazan Yılmaz; Asiye Güzel Zeybek; Sultan Seçik; Mukkades Çelik; Nadire Mater; Ayşe Nur Zarakolu; International Freedom to Publish Award; Ayşe Tosun; Fatma Sesli; Serpil Kaplan; Ayşe Oyman; Fatma Sesli; Sakine Topoğlu.

PEN. (2001). Turkey: Asiye Güzel Zeybek - Four years in prison without trial. *Centre to Centre: Newsletter of the Writers in Prison Committee of International PEN*, reprinted in *Institut Kurde de Paris, Information and Liaison Bulletin, 194*, May 2001, p. 30.

**Keywords:** Asiye Güzel Zeybek; Marxist-Leninist Communist Party; rape; torture.

**PEN American Center.** (1993). Letter to Tansu Ciller and Mehmet Gazioğlu. *PEN American Center*, reprinted in *Institut Kurde de Paris, Information* *and Liaison Bulletin, 101-102*, August/September 1993, pp. 21-23.

**Keywords:** DEP; PKK; *Özgür Gündem*; Aysel Malkaç; missing journalists; attacks on the press; killing of journalists.

**PEN American Center.** (1993). Letter to the Turkish authorities, reprinted in *Institut Kurde de Paris, Information and Liaison Bulletin, 105*, December 1993, pp. 81-83.

**Keywords:** Gurbetelli Ersöz, chief editor of *Özgür Gündem*; torture; Leyla Akgül.

**Platt, Steve.** (1994). Özgur Gündem in the front-line of Turkish state oppression. In *The New Statesman* and *Gurbetelli Ersöz's Defence: An Impassioned Plea for Free Speech in Turkey*. London: Friends of *Özgur Gündem* and Action for Kurdish Women, November 1994, pp. 23-24.

**Keywords:** article 168, paragraph 2; persecution of journalists; Özgur Gündem; *Özgur Ülke*; PKK; war; refugees; burning of villages; Leyla Zana; the Council for Security and Cooperation in Europe's Copenhagen Declaration on the rights of minorities; Turkish Human Rights Foundation, murder of journalists and newspaper distributors; banning of books and publications; disappeared people; police raids; unsolved murders; war casualties in Kurdistan; burning and evacuation of villages.

**Reporters Sans Frontieres.** (1999). RSF saisit le président Clinton de la situation de la presse en Turquie [RSF tells President Clinton about the press situation in Turkey], *Reporters Sans Frontieres*, press release, reprinted in *Institut Kurde de Paris, Information and Liaison Bulletin*, pp. 19-20.

**Keywords:** Asiye Zeybek Güzel; *Özgür Gündem*.

**Rugman, Jonathan.** (1993). Atrocity Times. *The Guardian,* 23 August 1993, Reprinted in *Institut Kurde de Paris, Information and Liaison Bulletin, 101-102,* August/September, p. 74. Also appeared in *Kurdistan Report, 16,* October/November, p. 7.

**Keywords:** Aysel Malkaç; *Özgür Gündem*; PKK; Amnesty International; Gurbetelli Ersöz; intimidation campaigns against the press.

**Stapleton, Barbara.** (1994). Gürbetelli faces terror of death threats. *Gurbetelli Ersöz's Defence: An Impassioned Plea for Free Speech in Turkey,* London: Friends of Özgur Gündem and Action for Kurdish Women, pp. 20-22. Also appeared in *Kurdistan Report, 19,* September/October 1994, p. 12. Also appeared in

*Resistance: Women in Kurdistan.* London: KIC/KSC Publications, 1995, pp. 5-6, three photographs.

**Keywords:** article 19 of the Anti-Terror Law; Gurbetelli Ersöz; torture; use of the threat of rape to obtain a confession; *Özgür Gündem*; trial of Gürbetelli Ersöz. Editor of *Özgur Gündem*; torture in prison; death threats; discrimination against Kurds; ethnic cleansing; extra-judicial executions.

**Turkish Daily News**. (1994). *Özgür Gündem* bombed. *Turkish Daily News,* reprinted in *Institut Kurde de Paris, Information and Liaison Bulletin, 106-107,* January/February, p. 121.

**Keywords:** Özgür Gündem; PKK.

**Turkish Daily News**. (1994). Blasts rock offices of pro-PKK daily in Istanbul and Ankara. *Turkish Daily News,* reprinted in *Institut Kurde de Paris, Information and Liaison Bulletin, 116-117,* November/December, p. 110.

**Keywords:** *Özgür Ülke*; PKK; attacks on the press.

**Turkish Daily News**. (1993). Courts take action against writers on Kurdish issue. *Turkish Daily News,* reprinted in *Institut Kurde de Paris, Information and Liaison Bulletin, 103,* October, p. 43.

**Keywords:** Gunay Aslan; Yunus Nadi literature award; The Truncheon Republic.

**Turkish Probe**. (1996). Journalist found murdered. *Turkish Probe,* reprinted in *Institut Kurde de Paris, Information and Liaison Bulletin, 130-131,* January/February, p. 43.

**Keywords:** Aysel Malkaç; missing journalists; murdered journalists; *Evrensel*; PKK.

## III. MUSIC

**Anquetil, Gilles**. (2000). La voix des Alevis [The voice of the Alevis]. *Le Nouvel Observateur,* reprinted in *Institut Kurde de Paris, Information and Liaison Bulletin, 189,* December, p. 21.

**Keywords:** Sabahat Akkiraz; Imam Ali; Pir Sultan Abdal; Ataturk; *cem*; *dede*; Karacaahmat Sultan Dergahi; *zikir; semah; saz*; "female ambassador of the Alevi religion"; Alevi devotional music.

**Bois, Thomas**. (1946). La femme kurde aussi est racee [Kurdish women are also a race]. In *L'Ame des Kurdes: À la lumière de leur folklore. Les cahiers de l'est*, *No. 5-6*: Beirut, pp. 31-46.

**Keywords:** perception of Kurdish women by the French author in 1946; women in Kurdish folk songs; women as caregivers; women and the home; according to the author there are no unmarried people amongst the Kurds; prostitution does not exist; they do not have a word to describe it; marriage: they marry very young; boys at 15 or 16 and girls at 12; Muslim but not polygamous amongst common people; heads of communities do sometimes have more than one wife in order to form political alliances; Said Beg: head of the Yazidis; author met him when he had six wives but considers that for a Kurdish woman it is a blessing to be noticed by him because he is almost divine in origin; divorce is infrequent; honour killing: in order to repudiate a woman she might be killed according to a folk song that says that pretty women cannot be abandoned by cruel men but should be killed; if the wife is guilty than the husband who kills her is protected by the community; the woman is considered to be equal to the man in Kurdish culture; Kurdish women do not wear headscarves; she handles household affairs and money matters; she takes part in discussions where males are present; Kurdish folk songs reflect equality between Kurdish men and women; women as songwriters: Kurdish women have written most of the popular Kurdish songs including war songs and love songs; working songs: "Berdolavî; Pehîzok; Zozan;" Kurdish women all share the same characteristics no matter what their location: tenderness, devotion, coquettish; exoticism; marriage choices (when choosing a wife): look at her family; marriage between cousins; importance of dowries: the future husband has to present the father of the bride with a sufficient dowry; virginity testing on wedding night; patriarchal family structure; importance of childbearing and childrearing; Kurdish women are superstitious; women and love of the nation; Perîxan: to avenge the death of her father who was killed during a Kurdish revolt in Turkish Kurdistan, hid a bomb in a bouquet of flowers that she was to present to the Turkish governor; it exploded and a revolt was commenced; quite frequently women will become the heads of tribes after the death of their husbands; women as mothers of the nation.

**Institut Kurde de Paris**. (1996). Death of Kurdish singer Aysha Shan. *Institut Kurde de Paris, Information and Liaison Bulletin, 141*, December, p, 8.

**Keywords:** Ayshe Shan; *dengbêj* [bard]; first Kurdish record in the Turkish Republic; first Kurdish woman to sing in public in Turkey; asylum in Germany; Muhamed Arif Cirawi; Isa Berwari.

**Institut Kurde de Paris.** (2002). The Diyarbekir Cultural Festival: A group of women singers arrested and charged with singing in Kurdish and wearing Kurdish dress. *Institut Kurde de Paris, Information and Liaison Bulletin, 207,* June, p. 8.

> **Keywords:** Diyarbekir Cultural Festival; Koma Asmin, an amateur group of 11 young girls from Istanbul's Mesopotamia Cultural Centre charged with singing in Kurdish and also provoking the authorities; Feridun Çelik.

**Kurdistan Report.** (1993). "For me, music means above all the chance to free myself from isolation and colonialism." *Kurdistan Report, 16,* October/November, pp. 35-36.

> **Keywords:** Beser, lead singer of Koma Ciya; MKM; Kurdish women and the arts; women resisting feudalism; Kurdish women's role in the transmission of Kurdish culture; Kurdish women's role in the preservation of the Kurdish language and cultural traditions; Meryem Xan; Mizgin; Kurds in the diaspora; HUNERKOM, an association of Kurdish artists based in Germany.

**Mirzeler, Mustafa Kemal.** (2000). The formation of male identity and the roots of violence against women: The case of Kurdish songs, stories and storytellers. *Journal of Muslim Minority Affairs, 20(2),* pp. 261-269.

> **Keywords:** Kiremithane; Kurdish masculine identity; songs; stories; forced migration; maternal attachment; storytellers; Kurdish clothing; the songs of Kurdish women; women's ways of expressing themselves; work songs; weddings; funerals; heroes; heroines; henna night; male virtues; mourning rituals; female virtue; shame; honour; honour killing; suicide.

**Ouest France.** (1993). Mahmut et Françoise interprètent des chants kurdes [Mahmut and Françoise perform Kurdish songs]. *Ouest France,* reprinted in *Institut Kurde de Paris, Information and Liaison Bulletin, 95-96,* February/March, p. 7.

> **Keywords:** Kurdish Alevi music; Aysen Güven; diaspora life.

**Özgür Politika** (2002). Musicians detained at Diyarbakir Festival for singing Kurdish song. Reprinted in *Institut Kurde de Paris, Information and Liaison Bulletin, 207,* June, p. 28.

> **Keywords:** Diyarbakir Cultural Festival; Koma Asmin, an amateur group of 11 young girls from Istanbul's Mesopotamia Cultural Centre

charged with not only having sung in Kurdish but also with having provoked the authorities; DGM; Feridun Çelik; detained girls: Besime Yagi; Kadriye Senses; Gülbahar Kavcu; Serap Sönmez; Nurcan Değirmenci; Yeşim Coşkun; Arife Düztaş; Zelal Gökçe; Selda Sezgin; Kader Baştaş; Ruken Gökçe.

## IV. PAINTING

**Bulteau, Marie**. (2003). Un artiste aux sources de ses origines 'Peindre est une thérapie' [An artist at the source of his origins: "Painting is therapy"]. *Le Républicain,* reprinted in *Institut Kurde de Paris, Information and Liaison Bulletin, 218-219,* May/June, p. 51, one photograph.

> **Keywords:** Nüvidé Mahieu, a Kurdish artist from Diyarbekir, emigrated to France; Mahieu's father did not allow her to learn Kurdish for fear of state repression; painting as therapy; exhibition at the Kurdish Institute in Paris.

**Journet, Christophe**. (1995). Inayat, le peintre des femmes kurdes, de la Syrie à l'Anjou [Inayat, the painter of Kurdish women, from Syria to Anjou]. *Le Maine Libre/Le Courrier de l'Oeust,* reprinted in *Institut Kurde de Paris, Information and Liaison Bulletin, 128-129,* November-December, p. 155.

> **Keywords:** Afrin, Syrian Kurdistan; Mouhamad Inayat; paintings of Kurdish women; paintings of Kurdish women in traditional dress.

**Kurdistan Report**. (1994). Zohra: 'In my work I try to catch the Kurdish colours and the spirit of the Kurdish people's struggle'. *Kurdistan Report, 17,* February/March, pp. 44-45.

> **Keywords:** Zohra, a Kurdish refugee artist from Eastern Kurdistan in Iran; Sanandaj; Zohra's politics and style of painting; views on the history of the Mahabad Republic; the impact of the Islamic Republic on Kurds, women, and on artists; the difficulties facing female artists in Iran; her exhibitions.

## V. PHOTOGRAPHY

**Bruni, Mary Ann Smothers**. (1995). *Journey through Kurdistan.* Texas Memorial Museum, The University of Texas at Austin. ISBN 0-944671-01-1. Acknowledgements (pp. 4-7), map (pp. 8-9), foreword by William G. Reeder (p. 11), introduction (12-15), text (pp. 15-121), glossary (p. 122), select bibliography (pp. 123-124), photographs (list, pp. 125-127, 83 colour photographs).

**Keywords:** Exodus 1991; Anfal; Iraqi Kurdistan; Kurdish Parliament Elections 1992, Regional Government of Iraqi Kurdistan; Kurdistan in Turkey; political parties (KDP, PKK, PUK); villages; cities; map of Kurdistan; women travellers (1991-93).

**Bruni, Mary Ann Smothers**. (1996). The Zhinan. In *The National Peace Corps Association Worldview, (9)*4, Fall. pp. 11-16. One map (p. 12), eight colour photographs (pp. 11, 13, 14, 15, 16).

**Keywords:** history; woman and war; murder; pillage; rape; chemical attacks; peshmerga; KDP; PUK; inter-Kurdish fighting in Northern Iraq; Kurdish women's resistance to inter-Kurdish fighting; female PKK guerillas; Kurmanji; Sorani; elections in Kurdistan; women's participation in elections; Massoud Barzani; Jalal Talabani; Hero Talabani; women's education; Anfal; women's resilience; Barzan widows; Zhinan women's organization.

**Guerrin, Michel and Claire Guillot**. (2003). La revanche des peshmergas [Revenge of the peshmerga]. *Le Monde*, reprinted in *Institut Kurde de Paris, Information and Liaison Bulletin, 217*, April, p.1.

**Keywords:** Newsha Tavakolian, an Iranian photographer who lived with, and photographed, the peshmergas in Iraqi Kurdistan; Qara Anjir village; Ansar al-Islam; American bombardment of Biara village; Komala Islam; Al-Qaida; the participation of women in the peshmerga; Tavakolian comments that the Kurds do not differentiate between men and women; she comments on her work for the first Iranian women's journal; Photojournalism Festival of Perpignan; she finds it easier to work in Iraqi Kurdistan than in Iran.

**Kurdistan-AG AstA FU [Freien Universität Berlin]** (Eds.). (1996). *Glücklich, wer sich Türke nennen darf": Bilder aus Kurdistan* [Happy if you can call yourself Turkish: Pictures from Kurdistan]. Berlin: AstA FU. ISBN: 3-926522-09-7. 22 black and white photographs. 22 pages.

**Keywords:** internally displaced women; female seasonal workers on plantations in Mersin; displaced women in Van; displaced women in Adana; *Özgür Gündem;* IHD; death squad killings; Kurdish refugees from Turkey in Iraqi Kurdistan; attacks by the Turkish authorities on Kurds in Iraq; destruction of Kurdish villages by the Turkish army; special teams; torture; the use of German weapons by the Turkish military; Gurbetelli Ersöz; attacks on the press and murders of journalists; the bombing of *Özgür Gündem* buildings in 1994; *Özgür Ülke;* PKK.

**Maro, R.** (1995). *Kurdistan.* Text by R. Ofteringer, photographs by R. Maro. Berlin: ID-Archiv. ISBN: 3-89408-046-9. Text (pp. 7-123), chronology (pp. 124-125). 118 black and white photographs.

**Keywords:** internally-displaced Kurdish women in Turkey; the pogroms against Alevis, Communists, and Kurds in 1970s Turkey; the cutting open of pregnant Alevi women's stomachs by supporters of the MHP in 1978; the cutting off of Alevi women's hands by supporters of the MHP in order to steal their gold bracelets; the returning of refugees to their villages in Iraqi Kurdistan; women labourers; female victims of the chemical attacks on Halabja; al-Anfal; IHD; PKK; special teams; Iraqi Kurdish women demonstrating in the Kurdish refugee camps in Turkish Kurdistan; female doctors among the Kurdish guerrillas in Iraqi Kurdistan; female PKK guerrillas in Bekaa, Lebanon; female PKK guerrillas in Zale Camp, Iraqi Kurdistan; female KOMALA guerrillas; women voting in Iraqi Kurdistan; mines; mine victims; Iranian bombardment of Kurdish villages; reconstruction of Kurdish villages in Iraqi Kurdistan.

**Renard, Jean-Claude.** (2000). Des femmes-courage [Women of courage]. *Politis,* reprinted in *Institut Kurde de Paris, Information and Liaison Bulletin, 189,* December 2000, p. 63.

**Keywords:** Anne Delassus; photographs of Kurdish women; Iran-Iraq war; PKK; Turkish army; Badinan; French photographer traveling to Iraqi Kurdistan in spring 1992, summer 1994, winter 1997; Kurdish women and memory; Kurdish women and territory; Kurdish women and war: widows, rebuilding post-Iran Iraq war; Kurdish women and national identity; Kurdish women and family.

**Tanör, Bülent and Bahadır Taşkin.** (1995). *Fotoğraflarla Türkiye'de İnsan Hakları [1839-1990] Human Rights in Turkey: A Photographic Account.* Istanbul: Türkiye Ekonomik ve Toplumsal Tarih Vakfı. Turkish text (pp. 5-30), English Text (pp. 33-62). 43 black and white photographs.

**Keywords:** women's rights; history of human rights in Turkey; military; death penalty; massacres; freedom of thought; European Court of Human Rights; transvestites; health conditions; emigration; unions; right to strike; Kemalism; Article 438 (which reduces the penalty when a prostitute is raped); Varlık Vergisi; Kahramanmaraş; Alevis; Armenians; Kurds.

**Taroni, Magda.** (1986). *Die Frauen von Isabey* [Isabey's wives]. Köln: Pahl-Rugenstein. ISBN 3-7609-1030-0. 96 pages.

**Keywords:** Turkey; photography; Kurdish women.

## VI. THEATER

**Smith, Helena**. (2004). Play shakes audiences where women fall victim to gruesome honour killings. *The Guardian*, January 28, reprinted in *Institut Kurde de Paris, Information and Liaison Bulletin, 226*, January, pp. 84-85.

**Keywords:** Diyarbakir; Semse Allak; rape; honour killing; Kurdish-language play depicting the murder of Semse Allak; Human Rights Week; Mehmet Farac, author of the book *Women in the Grip of Tribal Customs;* Recve Aslan, a woman killed by her brother for having been raped at the age of 11; lack of identity cards for some women; modesty; chastity; honour; Nilufer Narli, a sociologist who studies honour killings; bride money (dowry); high suicide rates among women in Batman and Diyarbakir; Yalim Village; domestic violence; marital rape; laws in Turkey; Pınar İlkkaracan who leads the Women for Women's Rights group in Istanbul.

*See also* Honour Killing

# CUSTOMS AND BELIEFS

**Al Karadaghi, Mustafa**. (1992). The median people: Ethnic type, moral characteristics, habits and customs, customs in war, and median dress. *Kurdistan Times*, *1*(2), Summer, pp. 35-38. ISSN 1057-8668.

**Keywords:** "remarkable stature and beauty" of Median women.

**Kren, Karin**. (1994). La Culture Matérielle des Kurdes Syriens et Turcs [The material culture of Syrian and Turkish Kurds]. *Peuples Méditerranéens, 68-69*, July/December, pp. 95-106. ISSN 0399 1253.

**Keywords:** material culture of the Syrian and Turkish Kurds; women's clothing; jewelry; pottery; carpet making; tanning.

**Mater, Nadire**. (1992). Newroz celebrations in Kurdistan in Turkey. *Kurdistan Times, (1)2*, Summer, pp. 285-287. ISSN 1057-8668.

**Keywords:** Cizre; IHD; PKK; Leyla Zana; Kurdish women talk about Newroz and what it means to them.

## I. CLOTHING

**Andrews, Peter Alford**. (1992). Kurdish clothing in Persia. *Encyclopedia Iranica, Vol. V*, pp. 824-825.

**Keywords:** continuation of the article by Shirin Mohseni; vocabulary of Kurdish dress; female and male dress; differences in head coverings for married/unmarried women of Kermanshah province.

**Andrews, Peter Alford and M. Andrews**. (1992). Turkic and Kurdish clothing of Azerbaijan. *Encyclopedia Iranica, Vol. V*, pp. 836-840. Four photographs.

**Keywords:** Turkic dress of Azeris, Shasevan, Qaradaghi, costume of Milan, Zarza, Harki, and Mahabad Kurds; vivid colors, contrasts and "generic resemblance" to Azeri costume.

**Beyhaqī, Hosayn-'Alī**. (1992). Clothing of Khorasan. *Encyclopedia Iranica, Vol. V*, pp. 833-836. Two sketches.

**Keywords:** male and female dress of the Kurds of Northern Khorasan, Iran; four types of women's dress, in the northern border area, Qaramani Kurds, "the Kurds of the plain" around Quchan, Faruj and south of Shirvan, and Layeni women.

**Dziêge, Leszek**. (1984-85). Iraqi Kurdish Traditional Costume in its Process of Europeanization. *Acta Ethnographica Academiae Scientiarum Hungaricae, 33*(1-4), pp. 93-112. Map of Northern Iraq (p. 93), three black and white photographs (pp. 96, 99, 109).

**Keywords:** women's dress; veiling; Kurdish women's head gear; Halabja skull-caps; regional variations in dress; European and Arab influences; differences in dress for married/unmarried women; urban/rural variations in dress; class differences and clothing; jewelry; children's clothes; "Europeanization of Kurdish national costume" slow in rural areas and rapid in towns.

**Mohseni, Shirin**. (1992). Kurdish Clothing in Persia. *Encyclopedia Iranica, Vol. V*, pp. 822-840. Six black and white photographs.

**Keywords:** "distinctive features" of Kurdish dress and regional differences; Kurdish female dress in Western Azerbaijan and Sanandaj, Kermanshah and Quchan; male dress.

**Mohseni, Shirin**. (1991). *Le Vêtement kurde et son évolution de XIXème siécle à nos jours: Le cas des Mokris à Mahâbâd* [Kurdish clothing and its evolution from the

19th century to the present day: The case of the Mokris in Mahâbâd]. UFR d'Anthropologie et Sciences des Religions. Mémoire de DESS d'ethnométhodologie et d'Anthropologie. Soul la direction de M. Meyer. Université de Paris VII, 163 pp.

Keywords: female and male clothing of the Kurds of Mahabad; adults and children; differences according to socio-cultural contexts (age, ceremonies, regional identity, and social origin), seasons; clothing in literature, poetry, proverbs, and travel literature.

Schwartz-Beeri, Ora. (1992). Clothing of the Kurdish Jews. *Encyclopedia Iranica, Vol. V*, pp. 825-826. Two sketches.

Keywords: clothing of the Kurdish Jews from Iran and Iraq, based on field work in Israel, and Northern Iran; transition from hand-made to synthetic fabrics.

Turkish Daily News. (1994). Cindoruk: Parliament is not a disco - no miniskirts. *Turkish Daily News*, reprinted in *Institut Kurde de Paris, Information and Liaison Bulletin, 116-117,* November/December 1994, p. 3.

Keywords: Turkish Women's Association; dress regulations for civil servants.

## II. FOOD/COOKING

Dziegiel, Leszek. (1981). Traditional food and daily meals in Iraqi Kurdistan today. *Ethnologia Polona, 7*, pp. 99-113.

Keywords: women's tasks in food preparation and daily meals in Iraqi Kurdistan; drawing water; making fuel for heating and cooking purposes; today, kerosene and gas primus stoves more common; cooking; bread making; women smoking; food storage; segregation of women from men at mealtimes; tea preparation.

Kattan, Naïm. (2003). Kurdish cuisine. *Queen's Quarterly, 110*(3), Fall, pp. 427-429. One photograph.

Keywords: Fahima: Kurdish woman living in Paris, archaeologist preparing her doctoral thesis on Christin churches in Northern Iraq; stereotypes about Kurdish women, cooking; working without papers in order to survive in Paris; working in stereotypically female jobs such as housecleaning, babysitting, etc.

Meridional. (1989). Découvrez la cuisine kurde[ [Discover Kurdish cuisine]. *Meridional,* reprinted in *Institut Kurde de Paris, Information and Liaison Bulletin, 49-*

*50-51*, April-June 1989, p. 31.

Keywords: Cenet Yanar; lahmacun.

Le Montagne-Centre France. (1990). Zayka Saïd: bonne comme son pain [Zayka Saïd: Good as her bread]. *Le Montagne - Centre France*, reprinted in *Institut Kurde de Paris Information and Liaison Bulletin, 69*, December 1990, p. 14.

Keywords: women's preparation of bread; importance of bread in Kurdish culture.


# DISPLACEMENT, REFUGEES, AND MIGRATION

Albrecht-Heide, Astrid, Helene Kaselitz, and Elisabeth de Sotelo (Eds.). (1984). *Analyse der Lebenswelt türkischer und kurdischer Frauen in zwei Berliner Bezirken und die Möglichkeit von Bildungs- und Weiterbildungsmaßnahmen mit ihnen: Abschlußbericht zum Modellprojekt in Berlin, West* [Analysis of the world of Turkish and Kurdish women in two Berlin districts and the possibility of educational and further training measures with them: Final report on the model project in Berlin, West]. Berlin. 623 pages.

Keywords: Kurdish and Turkish women; migration; living conditions; education; Berlin.

Alyamaç, Serdar. (2002). The report: Obligatory migration one of the worst dramas in Turkey history. *Turkish Daily News*, April 25, reprinted in *Institut Kurde de Paris, Information and Liaison Bulletin, 205*, April, pp. 71-72.

Keywords: GÖÇ-DER; Sefika Gurbuz, chairwoman of GÖÇ DER; forced migration; OHAL; food embargo; NGOs; Kurdish women's inability to speak Turkish; health; education; unemployment; poverty.

Black, Richard. (1994). Political refugees or economic migrants? Kurdish and Assyrian refugees in Greece. *Migration, 25,* pp. 79-109.

Keywords: gender-specific statistics regarding employment of refugees in Greece; comparison of Kurdish and Assyrian refugees from Iraq and Turkey.

Cheney, Peter. (1991). I'll never use the word courage carelessly again. *Toronto Star*, April 18, pp. A1. Two photographs.

Keywords: conditions in the Uludere refugee camp in Southeast Turkey.

**Colville, Rupert**. (1996). Le drame continue au Kurdistan iraquien [The drama continues in Iraqi Kurdistan]. *Réfugiée*, (HCR-Haut Commissariat des Nations Unies pour les réfugiés), IV, reprinted in *Institut Kurde de Paris, Information and Liaison Bulletin, 144-145*, March/April 1997, pp. 113-115.

Keywords: KDP; PUK; refugees; Operation Provide Comfort; PKK; U.N.; plight of women and children in refugee camps.

**Crisp, Jeff**. (1989). Fending for themselves. *Refugees*, November, pp. 17-18.

Keywords: difficulties facing Kurdish asylum seekers in Britain; deportations; homeless Kurdish women and children in London.

**Crisp, Jeff**. (1991). A terrible tragedy. *Refugees*, May, pp. 5-7.

Keywords: an interview with a Kurdish woman refugee from Iraq in Iran; hunger; health conditions.

**Frelick, William**. (1992). Kurdish refugees and the New World Order. *Kurdish Studies, 5*(1&2), Spring-Fall, pp. 45-53.

Keywords: Turkish refugee policies regarding Kurds and non-Europeans; conditions within the camps where Kurdish refugees from Iraq live in Turkey; the poisoning of refugees; Resolution 688 and the "Safe Haven."

**Gomez, Ferreira and Ana Cristina**. (1991). Notizen zum Frauenalltag in einem Flüchtlingslager: Kurdische Frauen an der türkisch-irakischen Grenze [Notes on everyday life in a refugee camp: Kurdish women on the Turkish-Iraqi border]. *Frauen in der Einen Welt*, 3-4, Frankfurt, Verlag für Interkulturelle Kommunikation, pp. 186-190.

Keywords: Kurdistan; refugee camps.

**Hardi, Choman**. (2005). Kurdish women refugees: Obstacles and opportunities. In David Ingleby (Ed.), *Forced migration and mental health: Rethinking the care of refugees and displaced persons* (pp. 149-68). New York: Springer.

Keywords: Kurdish refugee women in Britain; paper dedicated to Heshu Yunis (Yones), victim of an honour killing in London; problems facing refugee women upon arrival: uncertainty about the future; loss of relationships, social and material status, employment, qualifications; becoming familiar with a new environment; learning a new language; possible reversal in power relationships in family; change in family and community structure; women as the keepers of tradition; narrative therapy (writing workshops) as a means of empowerment for refugee women; activism and women's groups as a form of empowerment; KWAHK; Nazand Bagikhani (Begikhani) founder of KWAHK; employment and education as a means of empowerment; women as being more "free" in the UK; the "West" and gender equality.

**Hoffmann-Walbeck, Katrin and Susanne Prior** (Eds.). (1988). *Mein Leben ist wie ein fremder Fluß: der Weg ins Asyl - Frauen erzählen*, [My life is like a strange river: The way to asylum - women tell]. Reinbeck bei Hamburg: Rowohlt. ISBN 3-499-12380-0. 201 pages.

**Keywords:** refugee women; reasons women flee their homelands; struggle for freedom; Kurdistan; Middle East; Sri Lanka; Ghana.

**The Initiative for Human Rights in Kurdistan**. (1990). *Silence is killing them: A report on the situation of the Kurdish refugees in Turkey*. The Initiative for Human Rights in Kurdistan, Bremen. Introduction, July, (pp. 1-4), text (pp. 4-41), appendix (pp. 42-44).

**Keywords:** chemical weapons attacks on Kurds in Iraqi Kurdistan; Kurdish refugees from Iraq in Turkey; women's work in the camps; health conditions; sanitary conditions; poisoning of the refugees in the camps; repression against the refugees in the camps; denial of schooling to the refugee children; limitations placed on the refugees' freedom of movement; attitudes of the Indigenous Kurdish population towards the refugees from Iraq; UNHRC projects.

**Institut Kurde de Paris**. (1991). The Exodus. *Institut Kurde de Paris, Information and Liaison Bulletin, 73*, April, pp. 1-374.

**Keywords:** Kurdish revolt; refugees; genocide; "safe" haven.

**Institut Kurde de Paris**. (2001). In a single week over a thousand Kurds illegally transported to the Greek coasts. *Institut Kurde de Paris, Information and Liaison Bulletin, 200-201*, November/December, pp. 11-12.

**Keywords:** Kurdish refugees; the smuggling of people.

**International Human Rights Law Group and Kurdistan Human Rights Project.** (1994, August). *Report of the Law Group and KHRP Delegation to Iraqi Kurdistan*. International Human Rights Law Group and KHRP. Text (pp. 1-8), annexes (pp. 9-14), maps (pp. 15-16).

**Keywords:** widows; Kurdish refugees from Turkey in Iraqi Kurdistan; tensions between local Kurds and the Kurds from Turkey; PKK;

Human Rights Association of Turkey; the destruction of Kurdish villages in Turkey; the bombing of Kurdish villages in Turkey; village guard system; hunger strike by Kurdish refugees.

**KeKa-Produktion**. *Destên me wê bibin bask em ê bifirin herin/ Wenn unsere Hände zu Flügeln werden - fliegen wir*...[When our hands become wings – we fly]. (1996). Produced by the MKM/Mesopotamischen Kulturzentrums Vertrieb in Europa: KeKa-Produktion, Istanbul. Original version in Kurdish and Turkish. With German or English subtitles. VHS, 27 minutes.

**Keywords:** Kurdish refugees; migration; mass flight of Kurdish villagers to Istanbul; destruction of villages by the Turkish military; exile; war; IHD.

**Kilbracken, Lord**. (1974). Mass return of educated exiles. *The Irish Press*. Photograph reprinted in *Kurdistan, Annual Journal of the Kurdish Students Society in Europe, Vol. XVII*, 1974, May 1, p. 43.

**Keywords:** 1974 Iraqi war in Kurdistan; women nurses in liberated areas.

**Kurdistan Times**. (1990). "Among the people I met in Kiziltepe Refugee Camp in Turkey I remember a Kurdish mother, Gulla." *Kurdistan Times, 1*, Winter, pp. 150-152.

**Keywords:** refugee woman in Turkey; conditions in the refugee camp; health; poisoning of the Kurdish refugees; Kurdish mothers.

**Kutschera, Chris**. (2002). Exodus. *The Middle East. Institut Kurde de Paris, Information and Liaison Bulletin, 210*, September 2002, pp. 130-133.

**Keywords:** Kurdish women in Europe; women and emigration; KDP; PUK; al-Anfal; Halabja; a Christian Kurd from Zakho; Kurdish Women's Defence Committee linked to the Workers Iraqi Communist Party; dress restrictions imposed on women; divorced women; domestic abuse of Kurdish women; UNHCR; women and asylum; widows; Zohra, from Penjwin, a divorced Kurdish woman refugee in Ankara; Munira from Sulaimaniya, a woman who divorced her Islamist husband and fled to Turkey; poverty of Kurdish refugees in Turkey; Nilova from Kirkuk who fled to Turkey to escape her ex-husband; Sahira from Kirkuk, a hairdresser who was pressured to marry her dead husband's brother (in accordance with Kurdish tradition); hairdressers killed by Islamists in Iraqi Kurdistan.

**Mahsman, David L**. (1991). When "eyes see eyes." *Lutheran Witness, 110*(6),

June, pp. 1-3.

**Keywords:** Doa, a Kurdish girl from Iraq who died in a refugee camp in Turkey; health conditions in the camps in Turkey.

**Marshall, Ruth.** (1995). Refugees, feminine plural. *Refugees Magazine, UNHCR, 100,* Refugee women, June, pp. 3-9.

**Keywords:** food distribution: all the distributors appointed by UNCHR were men; no food was going to families headed by women; results: malnutrition, exploitation, suffering; since 1991 situation has improved; emergency teams and long-term field staff receive extensive training to help them identify and respond to the needs of refugee women and children; sexual violence and exploitation are prevalent; burdens of sanitary protection, child-rearing, domestic tasks; health care and contraception issues.

**Mohseni-Sadjadi, Chirine.** (1991). La communauté des réfugiés kurdes irakiens en France: Modes de vie et integration [The community of Iraqi Kurdish refugees in France: Modes of life and integration; Doctoral dissertation, Orient et Monde arabe, Institut d'Études Iraniennes. Université Paris II-Srobonne Nouvelle].

**Keywords:** women; family; Iraqi Kurdish refugees; culture; life in exile; identity and resistance; exodus; family cohesion; women's clothing; families and children.

**Rogge, John R.** (1991). Report on the medium and longer term resettlement and reintegration of displaced persons and returning refugees in the proposed Kurdish autonomous region of Iraq. Disaster Research Unit, Prepared for the United Nations Development Programme, University of Manitoba: Manitoba. Executive summary (pp.1-2), introduction (pp. 3-5), map of Iraqi Kurdistan (p. 4), text (pp. 5-49), itinerary (p. 50).

**Keywords:** the depopulation of Kurdistan; returnees and displaced persons; mine awareness and clearance program; employment opportunities for women; aid to female-headed households; programs for vulnerable groups (women, the handicapped and amputees); women's work; tradition of women tending beehives.

**Roulet, Annick.** (1991). Healing the scars. *Refugees, 86,* June, pp. 23-25.

**Keywords:** the return of refugees to Iraqi Kurdistan from Turkey and Iran; health conditions; poverty; sanitary conditions.

**Silence.** (1996). Femmes Kurdes et Asile Politique [Kurdish women and political asylum]. *Silence,* 209, reprinted in *Institut Kurde de Paris, Information and Liaison Bulletin, 139-140,* October/November 1996, p. 96.

**Keywords:** women refugees; Turkish army; repression in Turkish Kurdistan; violation of women by the Turkish army; honour.

**Sirkeci, Ibrahim.** (2000). Exploring the Kurdish population in the Turkish context. *Genus,* pp. 149-175.

**Keywords:** literacy amon Kurdish women; fertility among Kurdish women; Kurdish population of Turkey; demographics of Kurdish women; internal migration; international migration; displacement; geography of Kurds in Turkey.

**Spoo, Eckart.** (1983). Kurdisch Familie ohne Warnung abgeschoben [Kurdish family deported without warning]. *Frankfurter Allgemeine,* reprinted in *Institut Kurde de Paris, Information and Liaison Bulletin, 3,* November 1983, unnumbered page.

**Keywords:** deportation of women and children Kurdish refugees; deportation of Yezidi refugees; German court rejects Yezidis' fear of persecution.

**The Sunday Telegraph.** (1987). Kurds to be deported. *The Sunday Telegraph,* reprinted in *Institut Kurde de Paris, Information and Liaison Bulletin, 26,* May 10, p. 12.

**Keywords:** Iraqi Kurdish woman and her son attempt suicide rather than be deported; immigration; refugees.

**Thallmayer, Claudia.** (1994). Unerwünscht. Exil in Österreich [Undesirable. Exile in Austria]. *Frauensolidarität, 48,* Vienna, pp. 30-32. Z A 30.

**Keywords:** Iran; Austria; right of asylum; refugees; interview; Kurdistan; female migrants; refugee camps.

**Al-Tschauschli, Samia.** (1996). Kurdistan und die Lage der Kurdinnen [Kurdistan and the situation of the Kurdish women]. In Ilse Nagelsmidt (Ed.) *Frauenforscherinnen stellen sich vor I* (pp. 197-206). Leipziger Uni-Vlg.

**Keywords:** migration; refugees; Iraqi Kurdistan; geography; history; religion; art; culture; politics; situation of refugee women in Europe; situation of refugee women in Germany; women and immigration status; refugee women in the former East Germany; media.

**Turkish Daily News**. (1994). Villagers who lost homes seek refuge in Ankara. *Turkish Daily News,* reprinted in *Institut Kurde de Paris, Information and Liaison Bulletin, 115,* October, p. 117.

**Keywords:** Yellikıran; Kağızman; Fatma Çelik; bombing of Kurdish villages by the Turkish military; village guard system; Kars province; language difficulties of Kurdish women in Ankara; Bahçecik; PKK.

*See also* Language

**UNHCR.** (2000). *Background paper on refugees and asylum seekers for Iraq.* Geneva: UNHCR Centre for Documentation and Research. June, Introduction (p. 1), text (pp. 1-19), tables (pp. 20-26), bibliography (pp. 27-28).

**Keywords:** torture; the threat of the raping of detainees' female relatives as a means of psychological torture; the use of Faili Kurds as experimental subjects in Iraq's outlawed chemical and biological weapons programs; Arabization campaigns; a 1990 law which provides immunity for the perpetrators of honour killings; the psychological trauma suffered by women who are raped in custody; statistics regarding asylum seekers.

**Unterstützerkreis Kirchenasyl Weißenburg**. (1998). *Leben in Angst: Eine kurdische Familie im Kirchenasyl* [Living in fear: A Kurdish family in sanctuary]. Treuchtlingen: Verlag Walter E. Keller. ISBN: 3-924828-89-X. Foreword by Hermann von Loewenich (pp. 8-9), foreword by Thomas Miederer (pp. 12-13), text (pp. 14-206), appendix (pp. 208-218).

**Keywords:** solidarity with a Kurdish Alevi family seeking asylum; church asylum; human rights abuses in Kurdistan; difficulties obtaining political asylum in Germany; Elbistan; DİSK; DSP; Turkish policies regarding minorities; oppression of Alevis in Turkey.

**U.S. Committee for Refugees.** (1991). *Mass exodus: Iraqi refugees in Iran.* American Council for Nationalities Services. July, 14 pages.

**Keywords:** interview with Tali Amin Hassan, a Kurdish refugee from Khidrikhan village, living in Bahramabad, Iran; women who have lost their sons; widows; restrictions placed upon Kurdish refugees from Iraq in Iranian Kurdistan; refugee needs in Iran; health conditions.

**U.S. Committee for Refugees.** (1999). *The wall of denial: Internal displacement in Turkey.* Immigration and Refugee Services of America. ISBN: 0-936548-03-7. Text (pp. 1-39), endnotes (pp. 40-44) map of Turkey (p. 3), seven black and white photographs (pp. 7, 12, 17, 19, 25, 29, 39).

**Keywords:** emergency rule; destruction of villages; internal displacement and its causes; PKK; village guard system; flight from the countryside to urban slums; gecekondus; torture; NGOs; U.N.

# EDUCATION

**Hedges, Chris.** (1992). Wintry classrooms warmed by Kurdish dreams. *New York Times International*, reprinted in *Institut Kurde de Paris, Information and Liaison Bulletin, 93*, December 1992, p. 52.

**Keywords:** education; female teachers; economic effects of the embargo.

**Institut Kurde de Paris.** (2000). Flagrant educational inequalities between the Kurdish provinces and the rest of Turkey. *Institut Kurde de Paris, Information and Liaison Bulletin, 183*, June, p. 10.

**Keywords:** statistics regarding education; illiteracy among women; Kurdish women's unequal access to education.

# ETHNIC FORMATIONS

## I. ARMENIANS

**Wilson, Rev. Samuel Graham (1858-1916).** (1896). *Persian life and customs* (2nd ed.). Edinburgh and London: Oliphant Anderson and Ferrier. ISBN 0-404-06996-7. Third Edition reprinted from the 1900 Edition, New York, by AMS Press Inc, New York, 1973. Contents (pp. [5]-6), list of illustrations (p. 7), map of Northwestern Persia (pp. [322]-323), appendix (pp. 323-328), index (329-333).

**Keywords:** Urmia; Armenians and Kurds at Shatanabad (Shaitanawa) village; unsafe travel conditions; Kurd robbers; Sulduz and Ushmuk (Shino in Kurdish); Laj and Daraluk (Daralak) villages; Soujbulak; Leilajan (Lajan in Kurdish) region; women non-veiled; elopement of Armenian/Christian girl, daughter of a British citizen, in 1891; conversion into Islam; Britain's intervention and demand for the return of the girl; internationalization of conflict over eloping; Iran's military action under pressure from Britain; the girl stated her free will in eloping and converting.

## II. ASSYRIANS/CHALDEANS

**Ingrams, Doreen**. (1983). Minorities. In *The awakened: Women in Iraq* (pp. 31-39). London: Third World Centre for Publishing and Research Ltd., ISBN: 0-86199-061-1.

> **Keywords:** General Federation of Iraqi Women; Kurdish women's dress; lack of veiling among Kurdish women; marriage; Turkoman minority; Nestorians; Gregorians; Jacobites; Armenians; Chaldeans; Assyrians.

**Mauriès, René**. (1967). Les Fils de Ninive [The sons of Nineveh]. In *Le Kurdistan ou la Mort* (pp. 143-169). Paris: Robert Laffont.

> **Keywords:** Nestorians; Chaldeans; Assyrians; Marguerite Georges, "Joan of Arc of Kurdistan"; Ninive; Mullah Mustafa Barzani; emigration of Assyrians; Kurdish-Assyrian relations.

**Yousif, Ephrem-Isa**. (1993). *Parfums d'enfance à Sanate: Un village chrétien au Kurdistan irakien* [Childhood perfumes in Sanate: A Christian village in Iraqi Kurdistan]. Paris: L'Harmattan. ISBN 2-7384-1517-2. Text (pp. 7-138).

> **Keywords:** Sanate; social conditions in Kurdistan; Assyro-Chaldeans; Assyrian migration from Turkish to Iraqi Kurdistan; Aramaic; honour killing in Sanate; rape by Iraqi soldiers; suicide; Zakho; Mossul; marriage; village life; government repression.

## III. JEWS

**Brauer, Erich**. (1993). *The Jews of Kurdistan*. Detroit, Michigan, USA: Wayne State University Press. ISBN 0-8143-2392-8. Completed and compiled by Raphael Patai. Illustrations (pp. 13-14), preface (pp. 15-22), preface to the Hebrew edition (pp. 23-30), publications by Erich Brauer (pp. 31-32), abbreviations (p. 33-36), text (pp. 37-366), notes (pp. 367-400), bibliography (pp. 401-406), glossary (pp. 407-429).

> **Keywords:** peasants; nomadic shepherds; inter-communal relations; migration; agas; Nestorians; wine production and sale; domestic culture; clothing; food; marriage; birth; childhood; Kurdish Jewesses; death and burial; agriculture; trade; handicrafts; social organization; education; synagogue; the Sabbath; holidays.

**Frankel, Daniel G., Dorit Roer-Bornstein, and Robert A. Levine**. (1982). Traditional and modern contributions to changing infant-rearing ideologies of two ethnic communities. *Monographs of the Society for Research in Child Development*, pp. 1-53. 14 Tables, three figures, one appendix, 28 references.

**Keywords:** modernization of child-bearing ideologies; Kurdish Jewish women; comparison between Kurdish Jewish and Yemenite Jewish communities.

**Ronnen, Meir.** (1984). Unique portrayal of daily life in Kurdistan. *The Jerusalem Post,* December 29, reprinted in *Institut Kurde de Paris, Information and Liaison Bulletin, 14,* September 1985, p. 20.

**Keywords:** Jews of Kurdistan; Kurdish immigrants in Israel; religious life; domestic life; dress of Kurdish women; women's crafts; women rug makers; women's amulets; origins of Kurdish Jews.

**Sabar, Yona.** (1995). The famous Barazani family of Rabbis of Kurdistan. *Kurdistan Times, 4,* November, pp. 186-188. ISSN 1057-8668.

**Keywords:** Barazan; Amadiya; Asnat, the daughter of Rabbi Shamuel who became head of an academy in Mosul and a female Rabbi; Kurdish attitudes towards women; lack of veiling among Kurdish women; bestowal of the title of Tanna'it, or female Talmudic scholar, upon Asnat; the prenuptial contract between Asnat and her husband that she not be made to do housework which would interrupt her scholarship; the admiration expressed by male colleagues towards Asnat.

**Sered, Susan-Starr.** (1987). The liberation of widowhood. *Journal of Cross Cultural Gerontology, 2,* April, pp. 139-150.

**Keywords:** Kurdish Jewish women in Jerusalem; religiosity and age; widowhood and religiosity; synagogues; senior citizen's day centres; cemeteries; holy tombs.

**Sered, Susan-Starr.** (1992). The Synagogue as a sacred space for the elderly Oriental women of Jerusalem. In Susan Grossman and Rivka Haut (Eds.), *Daughters of the king: Women and the Synagogue: A survey of history, Halakhah, and contemporary realities* (pp. 205-216). Philadelphia: Jewish Publication Society.

**Keywords:** elderly Kurdish Jewish women living in Jerusalem; religion; religiosity.

**Sered, Susan-Starr.** (1992). *Women as ritual experts: The religious lives of elderly Jewish women in Jerusalem* (pp. 161-69). New York: Oxford University Press. 174 pages with bibliographical references.

**Keywords:** women's religion; women's loss of power; village-based support networks; modernization and women's lives; women and religious change; female-oriented religious traditions; day center

105

women; Kurdish Jewish women.

**Sered, Susan-Starr**. (1996). The religious world of Jewish women in Kurdistan. In Shlomo Deshen and Walter P. Zenner (Eds.), *Jews among Muslims: Communities in the precolonial Middle East* (pp. 197-214). New York: New York University Press.

Keywords: Kurdish Jewry; feminist anthropology; religiosity; women and religion; Kurdish Jewish women.

# FEMINIST AND WOMEN'S MOVEMENTS

## I. FEMINISM AND WOMEN'S STUDIES

**Borck, Carsten, Şükriye Dogan, Siamend Hajo, and Eva Savelsberg**. (2004). Zur Einführung: Kurdische Studien und Genderstudien - eine Positionsbestimmung [Introduction: Kurdish and gender studies - . . . ]. In Siamend Hajo, Carsten Borck, Eva Savelsberg, & Şükriye Dogan (Eds.), *Gender in Kurdistan und der Diaspora* (pp. 7-14), Kurdologie Series Vol. 6, Münster: UNRAST-Verlag, ISBN 3-89771-014-5 (pb).

Keywords: Kurdish studies; gender studies.

*See also* Diaspora

**King, Diane E**. (2003). The doubly bound world of Kurdish women. *Al-Raida, 20*(101-102), Spring/Summer, pp. 63-68. Reprinted in *Voices: A Publication of the Association for Feminist Anthropology, 6*(1), November, pp. 1 and 8-10.

Keywords: critical remarks on photograph depicting women as Kurdish refugees in Amnesty International's 2000 wall calendar; meeting Kurds in California in search of a research topic in anthropology; researcher situated as a female Western anthropologist studying the Kurds and living in the Arab world; situating Kurdish girls and women within the larger body politic of Kurdish communities: the double bind of living in a situation of political instability and state violence as well as living in "a heavily male dominated society"; doing field work in Iraqi Kurdistan in 1995, 1997; repression of the Kurds in Turkey, and impossibility of doing research on the Kurds; the researcher's dependence on Kurdish girls and women; opposition to the 2003 U.S. war against Iraq in the Western and Lebanese/Arab academic environment and support for the war by the Kurds; an "Edward Saidian dilemma": tell your story of the support of the Kurds for the war; fall of one oppressor, Saddam and the persistence of oppression; Kurdish painter Azhar Shemdin.

**Manushi**. (1997). Lifting the veil: Reform vs tradition in Turkey, an interview with Nilofer Gole. *Manushi*, *100*, May-June, pp. 7-12.

**Keywords:** Nilofer Gole; sociology professor at the Bogazici University in Istanbul; feminist acknowledgement of Kurdish rights.

**Mojab, Shahrzad**. (2001). Theorizing the politics of "Islamic feminism." *Feminist Review, 69*, Winter, pp. 124-146.

**Keywords:** Mah Sharaf Khanum Kurdistani; gender relations; Qurrat al-'Ayn; Bibi Khanum Astarabadi; Shari'a; veiling; Nazira Zain al-Din; Islamization of gender relations; Khomeini; Reza Shah; International Women's Day; custody laws in Iran; Council of Guardians; Islamic feminism; absence of feminist consciousness.

**Wedel, Heidi**. (1998). Internationales Netzwerk für kurdische Frauenstudien [International network for Kurdish women's studies]. *femina politica, 2*, pp. 117-119

**Keywords:** International Kurdish Women's Studies Network; Shahrzad Mojab; women of a non-state nation: the Kurds; Know How Conference on the World of Women's Information; orientalism; international women's solidarity.

## II. FEMINIST AND WOMEN'S JOURNALISM

**Açık, Necla**. (2004). Nationaler Kampf, Frauenmythos und Frauenmobilisierung: Eine Analyse zeitgenössischer kurdischer Frauenzeitschriften aus der Türkei [National struggle, women's myth, and women's mobilization: An analysis of contemporary Kurdish women's magazines from Turkey]. In Siamend Hajo, Carsten Borck, Eva Savelsberg, & Şükriye Dogan (Eds.), *Gender in Kurdistan und der Diaspora* (pp.149-182). Kurdologie Series Vol. 6, Münster: UNRAST-Verlag. ISBN 3-89771-014-5 (pb).

**Keywords:** Kurdish National Movement in Turkey; Kurdish feminist groups in Turkey; K.Ka.DaV; ARJİN; JİYAN Kadın Kültürevi; *Jujîn* magazine; *Roza*, the first Kurdish-feminist magazine in Turkey; sexism; *Yaşamda Özgür Kadın* magazine; *Jin û Jiyan* magazine; PKK; sexuality; domestic violence; virginity; AIDS; Partiya Sosyalîst a Kurdistan; gender-specific mobilization of the Kurdish national movement; patriarchy; the awakening of Mesopotamian women; patriotic mothers; unpatriotic mothers; women's role as cultural markers/bearers; migration; sexual abuse of women; *Emekçi Kadınlar Birliği Bülteni;* Pelin Demirhan, the director of ÇATOM; *Pazartesi* magazine; Fatma Kayhan; identity politics.

## III. FEMINIST INTERNATIONALISM

**Biemann, Ursula**. (1996). *Frauensichten. Reisebericht der Schweizer Frauendelegation in die Türkei und nach Türkisch-Kurdistan vom 16. Bis 21* [Women's views. Travel report of the Swiss women's delegation to Turkey and Turkish Kurdistan]. Zürich, February, 58 pages.

**Keywords:** Turkey; solidarity movements; human rights abuses; travelogue; women's movement; human rights work; Kurdish women; Kurdistan; activists.

**Dossier du Kurdistan**. (1988). Sur les traces de Rosa Luxemburg et de Klara Zetkin [In the footsteps of Rosa Luxemburg and Klara Zetkin]. *Dossier de Kurdistan, 18,* January-February, p. 19.

**Keywords:** March 8th International Day of Working Women; YJWK; ERNK.

**Institut Kurde de Paris**. (1996). Women's campaign for the release of Leyla Zana. *Institut Kurde de Paris, Information and Liaison Bulletin, 141*, December, p, 6.

**Keywords:** Leyla Zana; women's delegation travels to Turkey to demand Leyla Zana's release.

**Kurdistan Report**. (1992) Kurdish women celebrate 8 March. *Kurdistan Report, 9*, May, p. 26.

**Keywords:** March 8th celebrations organized by IHD; YKD; Halk-Evi (Peoples House); Eğit-Sen (Trade Union education); PKK; Women's Day celebrations in Diyarbakir and Erzincan; Istanbul Women's Day demonstration; police brutality; YJWK; Women guerillas of ARGK; Leyla Zana; Kurdish women's celebrations in the diaspora.

**Kurdistan Report**. (1994). Scandalous cost of border. *Kurdistan Report, 18*, May/June, p. 38 (extract from an article in *An Phoblacht Republican News*).

**Keywords:** international solidarity between Kurdish and Irish women; International Women's Day; Kurdish woman expresses her support for Irish independence; women's struggles against racism and war.

**Kurdistan Report**. (1997). Freedom for Leyla Zana. *Kurdistan Report, 25,* July/August, p. 56.

**Keywords:** Leyla Zana; Wir Frauen women's initiative's visit to Ankara to deliver an appeal "One Day for Leyla Zana" to President Süleyman Demirel; women protest in front of Ankara Central Prison; International Women's Day; signatories of the "One Day for Leyla Zana" appeal.

**Kurdistan Report**. (1997). A challenge for Turkey. *Kurdistan Report, 25,* July/August, p. 57.

**Keywords:** Leyla Zana; 1995 Sakharov Peace Prize; DEP; European Court of Human Rights; Freedom for Leyla Zana international women's initiative; Action for Kurdish Women/Peace in Kurdistan Campaign; Union des Femmes Francaises-Femmes Solidaires; Nederlandse Frouwenbeweging; PKK.

**Loepfe, Koni**. (1996). Aus dem Schweigen treten. *DAZ,* reprinted in *Institut Kurde de Paris, Information and Liaison Bulletin, 130-131,* January/February, pp. 176-177.

**Keywords:** Swiss women's delegation to "Turkish" Kurdistan; Angeline Fankhauser; imprisonment of Swiss members of the delegation in Turkey; Diyarbakir; war; Kurdish women and war; Marianne Roth; repression; Marina Widmer; virginity tests; Kurdish women visiting the graves of killed sons and husbands; guerillas; villages where almost everyone is a woman; cultural repression; MKM; Mothers of the Disappeared; Nuray Sen; Habitat II; Swiss women attempt to have the Swiss authorities accept oppression of women as a grounds for the granting of refugee status.

**Stickler, Ines**. (1997). Ein Tag für Leyla Zana [A day for Leyla Zana]. *Frankfurter Rundschau,* reprinted in *Institut Kurde de Paris, Information and Liaison Bulletin, 144-145,* March/April 1997, p. 52.

**Keywords:** women from all over the world offer to spend a day in prison for Leyla Zana's release.

**Die Tageszeitung (Berlin)**. (1997). Ein Tag im Gefängnis für Leyla Zana [A day in prison for Leyla Zana]. *die tageszeitung,* reprinted in *Institut Kurde de Paris Information and Liaison Bulletin, 144-145,* March/April 1997, p. 46.

**Keywords:** initiative by women to have Leyla Zana freed from prison.

**Tandberg, Olof G**. (1999). Nordic solidarity work 1966-1970 and the cultural experience of Kurdish women. In Petra Sundqvist (Ed.), *The Kurds: Perspectives on a unique culture* (pp. 55-60). Helsinki: Suomen Rauhanliito YK-yhdistys.

> **Keywords:** Swedish Kurd Committee formed in March 1966 to investigate whether genocide was being committed against the Kurds in Iraq; Kurdish women exercised political leadership tribes; women rulers; Kurdish society still live in a traditional patriarchal society; division of labor in rural and urban areas; women survivors of chemical bombing of Halabja; women in the diaspora; Sweden has emerged as "the leading publishing centre for Kurdish educational materials."

## IV. WOMEN'S MOVEMENTS AND ORGANIZATIONS

**Akan, Sara**. (1992). Appeal by the Patriotic Women's Association (YKD) in Istanbul. In *Kurdish Women: The struggle for national liberation and women's rights* (p. 24). London: KIC/KSC Publications. One photograph.

> **Keywords:** arbitrary closing of the Patriotic Women's Association in Istanbul; seizure of documents; women and nationalism.

**Altun, Solmaz**. (1995). Tevgera Azadiya Jinen Kurdistan (TAJK) - Freie Frauenbewegung Kurdistans [Kurdistan Women's Freedom Movement]. In *Terre des Femmes Rundbrief* (pp. 21-23), *2*, ISSN 09460373.

> **Keywords:** DEP; Dersim; destruction of Kurdish villages; role of Turkish women; masculine nation; state feminism; Sabiha Gökçen; the role of Kurdish women in the struggle for freedom; the independent women's movement; YJWK; TAJK; women's army; female guerrillas; Leyla Zana.

**Amnesty International**. (1998). Turkey: Listen to the Saturday Mothers. *Amnesty International*, November, pp. 1-10. Six photographs.

> **Keywords:** relatives of the disappeared in Turkey; weekly vigil since May 1995 in central Istanbul; group known as the Saturday Mothers; gather every Saturday at midday in front of the Galatasaray Hight School in Istiklal Street; police harassment, detentions, and ill treatment of group.

**Arbeiskreis Kurdistan "Botan"**. (1993). *Jinê rabe! Frau, steh auf!* [Woman get up!] Berlin: GNN Verlag. Photos by Gesine Jäger. Table of contents (p. 3), editorial (pp. 4-5), text (pp. 6-71), notes (p. 72), bibliography (p. 73), map (p. 74).

**Keywords:** Binefş Agal (Berivan); national oppression; economic oppression; situation of Kurdish women; family and children; women and reproducers of the nation; arranged marriages; lack of education for Kurdish women; Iranian Kurdistan: more interaction between women and men than in Iraqi or Turkish Kurdistan; women, Islam, and oppression; the role of Kurdish women in the battle for Sanandaj; female guerrillas; YKD; Women's Union of Diyarbakir; YJWK; PKK; ARGK.

**Begikhani, Nazand**. (1999). Etre femme, kurde et irakienne [Being a woman, Kurdish and Iraqi]. *Monde arabe Maghreb Machrek*, *163*, January-March, pp. 194-195.

**Keywords:** women living separate from men in Koy Sanjâq (Iraq); gender roles: women as mothers and submissive, men as dominators of women; loopholes in Iraqi law; women and nationalism; nationalism as a patriarchal ideology; nationalism and feminism.

**Frauenverband Courage**. (1994). *Frauen im Aufbruch: Dokumentation zum internationalen Frauenkongreß "Frauen verbinden Welten - Frauen kämpfen international* [Women on the move: Documentation on the international women's congress "women connect worlds - women fight internationally"]. Ebersbach: eFeF Verlag. ISBN: 3-905493-71-3, October. Frauenverband Courage (Ed.), foreword by Monika Gärtner (pp. 7-80), text (pp. 9-165), 29 black and white photographs (p. 8 and unnumbered centre pages).

**Keywords:** women's solidarity; class-consciousness; Shirin Fatah; Women's Union of Kurdistan; imprisoned Kurdish women; the disappeared; poverty; patriarchy; religion; Rezan Ali; honour killings in Iraqi Kurdistan; Farideh Ali; Nassrin Saber Mohiedin; interview with Leyla Zana; politicization of Kurdish women in Turkey; hunger strikes by Kurdish women in Turkey; PKK; female members of parliament in Turkey; criminalization of the PKK in Germany; female freedom fighters; the arranged marriage of Leyla Zana; poverty in Kurdistan; TAJK; Dersim Uprising of 1938; women and resistance; female guerillas; DEP; Abdullah Öcalan's views regarding women; YJWK; genocide; women's army; Zeynep Baran; IHD; village burnings; depopulation of villages in Turkish Kurdistan; Kurdish women in Germany organizing opposition to German support for Turkey; International Women's Conference in Cologne; Leyla Zana; Kurdish women march in Mannheim.

**Free Women's Association of Kurdistan**. (1995). Appendix 5: Resolution of international conference. In *Resistance: Women in Kurdistan*. London:

KIC/KSC Publications, pp. 60.

**Keywords:** solidarity with female guerillas; women and nationalism; solidarity with women suffering in prisons; condemnation of the arrest of Leyla Zana; demand for international recognition of YAJK as a non-governmental organization; official admission of participation in the International Women's Day 8 March Conference in Beijing, China (1995); solidarity with other women's organizations; organization of delegations to visit other countries to establish links with other organizations; organize a Kurdish women's week (meetings, seminars, and cultural events); publish a half-yearly magazine; celebration of March 8th International Women's Day.

**Greaves, Alan**. (1992). The events during Newroz have strengthened national unity, and the PKK is seen more as the legitimate representative of the people. *Kurdistan Report, 9*, May, p. 22.

**Keywords:** an interview with the management committee of the Diyarbakir Patriotic Women's Association; women organizing relief efforts for wounded Kurds; obstacles to women's participation in politics; honour; women and religion; urban/rural dichotomy; passivity of city women; Hezbollah attacks; Newroz 1992; women and nationalism.

**Hamburger Frauen Zeitung**. (1998). Ihr habt unsere Kinder lebendig genommen, also gebt sie auch lebendig zurück [You took our children alive, so give them back alive, too]. *Hamburger Frauen Zeitung, 54*, December-March, pp. 42-45.

**Keywords:** Mothers of the Disappeared; Emine Ocak; Mother's Day; IHD; Aysel Ocak; hunger strikes; solidarity with the hunger strikers; police brutality against the Mothers of the Disappeared; Eren Keskin; Amnesty International; Zübeyde Tepe; *Özgür Gündem*; Asena Türkoğlu; Hatice Toroman; Hamburg Committee for the Support of the Saturday Mothers (Mothers of the Disappeared) in Turkey and Kurdistan.

**Harsan, Novin**. (1995). Speech by Novin Harsan, Chairman of the Kurdish Women's National Committee, during UN Fourth World Conference on Women, "Action for Equality, Development and Peace," Beijing, China, September 1995.

**Keywords:** discrimination; exploitation; genocide; torture; female illiteracy; destruction of Kurdish villages in Turkish Kurdistan; Menice Kiray; rape of Kurdish women by the Turkish military; Halima Murian;

Cemilie Sanik; decapitation of prisoners; Islamic law and Kurdish women; destruction of Kurdish villages in Iranian Kurdistan; Iran-Iraq war and Kurdish women; Halabja; Al-Anfal; destruction of Kurdish villages in Iraqi Kurdistan; women deprived of citizenship in Syrian Kurdistan; economic problems of "Syrian" Kurdish women who are deprived of citizenship; assimilation policies.

**Harvie, Susan**. (2003). This is what democracy looks like? *Alternatives Newspaper*, *7*(8), April 25. One photograph.

**Keywords:** women's movement in Iraqi Kurdistan; until 2002 consisted of a series of isolated groups controlled by political parties, ethnic groups or religious organizations; in 2002 groups came together to lobby for funds to build two shelters in the two major Kurdish cities for widows, abandoned women, and women fleeing domestic violence; out of this action 20 women's groups established a network to represent the women's movement and to increase its impact; key role in changing public policy and opinion; Kurdish administration abolished the "honour" defense for murder as a result of the impact of the network; in the process of abolishing polygamy; network opposing a ruling that women teachers must wear Islamic dress.

**Hervé, Florence**. (1996). Der Aufruf. *Wir Frauen* [The call U.S. women]. Düsseldorf, *4*, p. 20, Z G 20.

**Keywords:** Turkey; campaign; Kurdish women; activist women; Leyla Zana.

**Hervé, Florence**. (1996). Nachtrichten aus einem Land, das es offiziell nicht gibt [News from a country that does not officially exist]. *Wir Frauen*, Düsseldorf, *4*, pp. 18-19, Z G 20.

**Keywords:** Turkey; human rights violations; Kurdish women; Kurdistan; female activists; Leyla Zana; Saturday Mothers; Mehdi Zana.

**Honner, Monika**. (1997). Soli Netzwerk für Kurdinnen gegründet [Soli network for Kurdish women founded]. *die tageszeitung*, reprinted in *Institut Kurde de Paris, Information and Liaison Bulletin, 148-149*, July/August 1997, p. 44.

**Keywords:** cooperation between Kurdish women activists and women researchers; illegality of Kurdish language in Turkey; women in Turkish prisons; international women's network; repression of women in Kurdistan; feminism in war situations; Fatma Kayhan;

Hatice Yaõar; Heidi Wedel; Martin van Bruinessen; Irma Leisle; *Hînbûn*.

**L'Humanité.** (1997). Les mères d'Istanbul [Istanbul mothers]. *L'Humanité*, reprinted in *Institut Kurde de Paris, Information and Liaison Bulletin, 146-147*, May/June 1997, p. 34.

**Keywords:** Mothers of the disappeared; women fighting for justice.

**Husni, Mariwan, Narmen Koye, Zack Z. Cernovsky, and John Haggarty.** (2002). Kurdish refugees' view of politically motivated self-immolation. *Transcultural Psychiatry, 39*, pp. 367-375, McGill University.

**Keywords:** according to this study, gender is not related to the support, or rejection of self-immolation as a means of struggle for an Independent Kurdistan.

**İlkkaracan, Pınar.** (1997). *Women's movements in Turkey: A brief overview.* Istanbul: Women for Women's Human Rights and Women Living Under Muslim Laws. ISBN 975-7014-02-8. Preface by WWHR (p. 5), text (pp. 7-28), references (pp. 30-32) 17 black and white photographs (pp. 1, 7, 8, 9, 11, 12, 13, 14, 15, 17, 20, 21, 23, 24, 25, 26), three colour photographs (front cover).

**Keywords:** the women's movement during the Ottoman era; the Kemalist revolution; women's movement as a new social movement; women in the Islamic movement; religion and women; migration; women and the rise of the Welfare Party; nationalism; militarism; racism; failure of Turkish women's movements to forge solidarity with Kurdish women; female sexuality; NGOs.

**Institut Kurde de Paris.** (1997). A foundation for the defence of Kurdish women's rights founded in Istanbul. *Institut Kurde de Paris, Information and Liaison Bulletin, 144-145*, March/April, p. 18.

**Keywords:** The Foundation for Solidarity with Kurdish Women; Kurdish emigres in Istanbul; destruction of Kurdish villages by the Turkish army; war; violence against women; repression; deprivation of education; research about the state of Kurdish women in Turkey; the creation of a documentation center; the establishment of a legal aid center; rape.

**Institut Kurde de Paris.** (2001). Read in the Turkish press: The evidence of Zekiye Doğan, a Kurdish mother, wife and sister of men who have "disappeared." *Institut Kurde de Paris, Information and Liaison Bulletin, 194*, May, pp. 10-11.

**Keywords:** Zekiye Doğan; disappearances; assassinations; "Week for the Disappeared"; Ancak (Drêjan); village guards; burning of villages; Dilan; Akyol; beating and detention of the Saturday Mothers (Mothers of the Disappeared); court cases against the Mothers of the Disappeared.

**International Committee Against Disappearances (British Section).** (1999). Women's Delegation to the Saturday Mothers. *International Committee Against Disappearances (British Section) Bulletin, 12*, pp. 7-15. Four photographs.

**Keywords:** delegation of women from Britain went to Istanbul from January 8-10, 1999 to protest with the Saturday Mothers; organized by The International Committee Against Disappearances, Peace in Kurdistan Campaign, London Saturday Mothers Support Committee, Lawyers International Forum for Women's Human Rights; response to increasing brutality of police against the Saturday Mothers; Eren Keskin: lawyer, president of the Istanbul branch of the IHD; spoke about sexual violence against women while in custody; EKB: founded in 1992 to struggle against sexual, national, and class oppression; EKB run weekly women's university to discuss women's issues.

**International Herald Tribune.** (1996). Kurdish women. *International Herald Tribune*, reprinted in *Institut Kurde de Paris, Information and Liaison Bulletin, 141*, December 1996, p. 42.

**Keywords:** history; strength of Kurdish women; women's march aimed at ending fighting between Kurdish parties.

**Karaca, Sevinç.** (1997). Kurdish women's foundation opened in Istanbul. *Turkish Daily News,* reprinted in *Institut Kurde de Paris, Information and Liaison Bulletin, 144-145*, March/April 1997, p. 74.

**Keywords:** The Foundation for Solidarity with Kurdish Women and Research for Women's Questions; working class district of Istanbul; Zeynep Baran; migrant Kurdish women; oppression and violence against Kurdish women; language difficulties in Turkish cities; unemployment; oppression of Kurdish women by families and husbands; PKK; human rights violations; poverty; honour system; patriarchy; bride price; pressure to bear male children; feudalism; Kurdish women as the sexual property of men; rape and sexual harassment of Kurdish women by village guards and the security forces; exploitation of Kurdish labour force in Turkish cities; poor living conditions in Turkish cities.

**KIC/KSC Publications**. (1995). Appendix 4: Turkey: Mothers of "disappeared" take action. In *Resistance: Women in Kurdistan* (p. 55). London: KIC/KSC Publications.

> **Keywords:** Emine Ocak: mother of the "disappeared," served 12 days imprisonment in Ankara Central Closed Prison; May 14, 1995, Mother's Day: established Mother's Appeal; announced thousands of women had signed an appeal for an end to "disappearance" and extrajudicial executions in Turkey.

**KIC/KSC Publications**. (1995). Appendix 6: PKK 5th congress resolution: The women's army and the free women's movement. In *Resistance: Women in Kurdistan* (p. 61). London: KIC/KSC Publications.

> **Keywords:** women and nationalism; role of women in the Kurdish nationalist movement; to address the potential of women: PKK created a women's army in order to destroy the class status quo; will achieve independence of women from men; military camps for women; eventual independent operation of women's armies; under centralized leadership a women's conference will be held every year.

**Kurdish Human Rights Project**. (1998). Trial of Foundation President. *KHRP Newsline, 4*, July-September, p. 3.

> **Keywords:** Zeynep Baran: President of KADAV; trial against her at the Istanbul State Security Court; accused under Article 312 of the Turkish Penal Code of "inciting people to enmity" for founding the organization; sentenced to a fine and two-years imprisonment.

**Kurdish Human Rights Project**. (2000). Peace Mothers arrested and tortured. *KHRP Newline, 11/12*, Summer/Autumn, p. 4.

> **Keywords:** a delegation of five Kurdish women from Turkey were detained and tortured as they crossed the Iraq/Turkey border; members of the *Peace Mothers Initiative*, an organization that campaigns for peace in the border regions; experience as mothers who have lost loved ones in the Kurdish struggle have moved them to struggle for peace; accused of helping the PKK; held for four days without access to lawyers or family; some had been stripped naked and taunted with sexual threats; released after 35 days of detention.

**Kurdish Human Rights Project**. (2003). Focus on Kurdish women's rights. *KHRP Newsline, 21*, Spring, p. 16.

> **Keywords:** Kurdish Women's Charter: KHRP's Legal Officer held meetings with the Action Group on the Kurdish Women's Charter;

joint missions and research to establish the basis for a Kurdish Women's Charter to raise awareness of the problems faced by Kurdish women; KHRP plans to carry out a number of projects focusing on the rights of Kurdish women throughout 2003.

**Kurdish Human Rights Project**. (2003). Raising awareness of the rights of Kurdish women. *KHRP Newsline*, *22*, Summer, p. 6.

**Keywords:** Kurdish Women's Charter: KHRP's Legal Officer held meetings with the Action Group on the Kurdish Women's Charter; joint missions and research to establish the basis for a Kurdish Women's Charter to raise awareness of the problems faced by Kurdish women; KHRP plans to carry out a number of projects focusing on the rights of Kurdish women throughout 2003.

**Kurdish Human Rights Project**. (2003). Women's rights lawyer Eren Keskin visits London. *KHRP Newsline*, *22*, Summer, p. 8. One photograph.

**Keywords:** Eren Keskin visited London; met with parliamentarians and Lords to inform them of the use of rape as a form of torture in Turkey.

**Kurdish Human Rights Project**. (2003). Kurdish women's rights and charter. *KHRP Newsline*, *23*, Autumn, p. 19.

**Keywords:** Kurdish Women's Charter: KHRP's Legal Officer held meetings with the Action Group on the Kurdish Women's Charter; joint missions and research to establish the basis for a Kurdish Women's Charter to raise awareness of the problems faced by Kurdish women; KHRP plans to carry out a number of projects focusing on the rights of Kurdish women throughout 2003.

**Kurdish Human Rights Project**. (2004). KHRP and KWP launch Kurdish women's charter. *KHRP Newsline*, *26*, Summer, p. 8.

**Keywords:** publication of the "Charter for the Rights and Freedoms of Women in the Kurdish Regions and Diaspora"; in English, Kurmanji, Sorani, and Arabic languages.

**Kurdish Human Rights Project**. (2004). Charter for the rights and freedoms of women in the Kurdish regions and diaspora. *KHRP Newsline*, *26*, Summer, p. 11. One photograph.

**Keywords:** developed to ensure that the needs and wishes of women in the Kurdish regions and the diaspora are addressed and identified; encourages international and domestic bodies to incorporate the rights identified in the charter, domestically.

**Kurdish Observer**. (2001). Let's reveal the strength of motherhood. *Kurdish Observer,* May 15.

**Keywords:** Mother's Day; effects of war on Kurdish and Turkish mothers; effects of economic crisis on Kurdish and Turkish mothers; women opposing patriarchy.

**Kurdish Observer**. (2000). We must stand up for our efforts. *Kurdish Observer,* September 11.

**Keywords:** HADEP Central Women's Wings; preparations for Women's Congress; Fatma Kurtalan.

**Kurdish Observer**. (2000). Women lend support to the municipality. *Kurdish Observer,* September 12.

**Keywords:** HADEP; women help municipality provide clean drinking water; women help lay pipes and replace sidewalk tiles.

**Kurdish Students Society in Europe**. (1974). Kurdish popular organisations–Kurdistan Women's Federation. *Kurdistan,* Annual Journal of the Kurdish Students Society in Europe, Vol. XVII, p. 20.

**Keywords**: KDP-Iraq, Yekêtî Afretanî Kurdistan; history and emblem of organization; role in the autonomist movement.

**Kurdistan Info**. (1988). Zum Internationalen Frauentag 1987. *Kurdistan Info,* 6, July/August, p. 26.

**Keywords:** Kurdistan-Komitee West-Berlin; Iranian refugees in Germany; 8 March 1979 demonstration against hijab in Iran; Kurdish women's dance groups; autonomous Iranian women's pantomime group; solidarity movements; the participation of a guerrilla woman in West-Berlin's Women's Day celebrations.

*See also* Germany

**Kurdistan Report**. (1993). Women occupy city council in Diyarbakir. *Kurdistan Report, 16,* October/November, p. 21.

**Keywords:** women protest against the lack of running water since the beginning of summer.

**Kurdistan Report**. (1993). IHP and DEP women demand resignation.

*Kurdistan Report, 16,* October/November, p. 21.

**Keywords:** demonstration to protest the rape of Sukran Aydin during her arrest and detention in the gendarmerie station in Derik; demanded the resignation of the Minister of Interior, Gazioğlu, stating that "women in Kurdistan are continuously exposed to sexual harassment by state forces and that women who are detained are often threatened with rape."

**Kurdistan Report**. (1993). Kurdish women occupy Reuter News Agency in London. *Kurdistan Report, 16,* October/November, p. 21.

**Keywords:** Kurdish women and children occupied the News Agency in protest against the murder of Ferhat Tepe, an *Özgür Gündem* correspondent and the abduction of Aysel Malkac.

**Kurdistan Report**. (1993). 100 Kurdish women on hunger strike. *Kurdistan Report, 16,* October/November, p. 23.

**Keywords:** protest the actions of the Turkish state against the Kurds; positive response to action from political organizations, especially women's groups; hoping to increase the interest and support of women of the plight of Kurdish women.

**Kurdistan Report**. (1996). Mothers of the "disappeared" take action [Special issue]. *Kurdistan Report, 23,* March-May, p. 66. One photograph.

**Keywords:** women as mothers/bearers of the nation; women's role in Kurdish national struggle; protest in Istanbul in March; Emine Ocak: mother of the "disappeared," served 12 days imprisonment in Ankara Central Closed Prison.

**Kurdistan Solidarity Committee and Kurdistan Information Centre**. (1992). *Kurdish women: The Struggle for national liberation and women's rights.* London: KSC-KIC Publications. KSC-KIC, "Women in Kurdistan: a history of their struggle since the 70s" (pp. 1-4); Claire Pointon, "This is Kurdistan and we'll fight for it" from *the Independent,* 4 April 1991 (pp. 5-6); Evin Aydar, "I'm part of my people. I'm firmly grounded in reality and I have nothing to lose," interview by Radio Duisburg (pp. 9-14); "The first Kurdish woman elected to Parliament," interview with Leyla Zana from *Yeni Ülke,* 27 October 1961 (pp. 15-16); Alistair Lyon, "Kurdish deputies cause uproar in Turkish parliament" (pp. 16-17); Sara Akan, "We take our strength from our people, which is becoming ever freer, from the fact that we are in the right and from our organized resistance," interview conducted by *Özgur Halk,* 15 July 1991 (pp. 19-24); Thea A. Struchtemeier, "Kurdish women in the political and military struggle" (pp. 25-28); Medya, "We fight for a free Kurdistan and the liberation of Kurdish women," interview with Medya, a member of the YJWK (pp. 31-35); Beritan, "Our struggle is for all of humanity, not just for the Kurdish people," interview by Alan Greaves (pp. 36-37); "Virginity test leads to two suicides"(p. 37); Gülsin, "I want to go back to my country soon..." interview by Teresa Allen (pp. 39-40); solidarity message by the Patriotic Women's Association of Kurdistan to the International Women's Day Rally in London, 8 March 1991 (p. 40). 18 black and white photographs by Richard Wayman (cover, pp. 7,8, 10, 18, 29, 30), Ed Kashi (p. 4), Tony Banda (pp. 14, 24, 35, 38), and David Sillitoe (p. 38), back cover and p.17.

**Keywords:** oppression of Kurdish women by Kurdish men; colonization; Kurdish society; Kurdish family; Kurdish women's role in the armed struggle; women in prison; coup of 12 September 1980; fascist-military junta; torture; women in military training camps; women in the Kurdish National Uprising; Kurdish women in the cities and in Europe; YJWK; Kurdish uprising in Iraq; Halabja; Marxism; PKK; Dersim Uprising of 1938; Siirt Human Rights Organization; Hatip Dicle; NATO; Assyrian Christians; Arabs; Kurdish language law; Leyla Zana; Mehdi Zana; YKD; women's liberation; HEP; SHP; Kurdish women in the Turkish cities; virginity tests; suicide; refugees; solidarity; International Women's Day.

**Lacrampe, Corine**. (1997). Les Samedis de Galatasaray [Saturdays in Galatasara]. *Humanité Dimanche, 373*, 8 May 1997-14 May 1997, reprinted in *Institut Kurde de Paris, Information and Liaison Bulletin, 146-147*, May/June 1997, p. 31.

**Keywords:** Mothers of the Disappeared; women fighting for justice; Alevis; leftists; pacifists; humanists; Amnesty International.

**Mater, Nadire**. (2002). Appendix: Women movement against sexual assault in custody. In Abida Samiuddin, and R. Khanam (Eds.), *Muslim feminism and feminist movement Middle-East Asia: Vol. 2* (pp. 353-56). New Delhi: Global Vision Publishing House.

**Keywords:** Eren Keskin: lawyer; founder of Turkey's first group to offer legal aid to victims of sexual assault in custody; women's testimony against attackers: not very common; fear of reaction of husbands, fathers, families, communities; in four months, 31 women took the rise; Keskin jailed in 1993 on charges of "separatism"; rape and sexual assault in custody: far more widespread than her group's caseload indicates; Turkish law includes provisions against rape and sexual harassment in custody but they are hard to apply against police and prison officials; Sukran Aydin: raped in front of her mother by paramilitary gendarmes after she was detained as a suspected supporter of Kurdish guerillas; local prosecutor refused to bring charges against the accused; group also directs victims to psychological help.

**Najmadin, Badria**. (1995). Kurds must unite for their future. *Kurdistan Times, 4*, November, pp. 93-97. ISSN 1057-8668.

**Keywords:** internal conflict between the PUK and the KDP; Kurdish women's Peace March from Suleymaniyeh to Hawler (Arbil); Kurdish women's demands made to the Kurdish parliament; Badria Najmadin's views on the reasons for the internal conflict; poverty in Kurdistan; Badria Najmadin's suggestions for a solution to the conflict; attacks on journalists in southern Kurdistan; murder of Lissy Schmidt.

**Patriotic Women's Association of Kurdistan**. (1992, October). Solidarity message by the Patriotic Women's Association of Kurdistan to the International Women's Day rally in London, 8 March 1991. *Kurdish Women: The struggle for national liberation and women's rights* (p. 40). London: KIC/KSC Publications.

**Keywords:** solidarity message to *Women Against the Gulf War* from the Association of Patriotic Kurdish women (associated with ERNK); triple burden: sexual and social oppression, racism, cultural deprivation; American lead actions in Iraq will not improve the situation of Kurdish women.

**Schmidt, Lissy (Milena Ergen)**. (1994). *Wie teuer ist die Freiheit? Reportagen aus der selbstverwalteten kurdischen Region 1991-1993* [How expensive is freedom? Reports from the self-governing Kurdish region 1991-1993]. Köln: ISP Verlag. ISBN: 3-929008-56-4 (pb). Two maps (pp. 7, 37), introduction by Lissy Schmidt (pp. 9-13), text (pp. 14-203), glossary (pp. 204-207), chronology (pp. 208-227), six black and white photographs (pp. 63, 85, 90, 97, 138, 153).

**Keywords:** interviews with female sympathisers of the KDP; female factory workers; women's participation in the uprising of 1991; women of the Kurdistan Front; interviews with female academics in Sulaymania; interview with a female teacher in Sulaymania; interview with a women factory worker; women and reconstruction; segregated voting; women's work; housewives; poverty; mines; PUK; KDP; PKK; Turkish use of napalm bombs in the "safe haven"; women's views of freedom.

**Solmaz, Altun**. (1995). Freie Frauenbewegung Kurdistans [Free Women's Movement in Kurdistan]. *Terre des Femmes-Rundbrief,* Tübingen, *2*, pp. 21-23.

**Keywords:** women's movements; liberation movements; Kurdistan; guerrillas.

**Tabari, Azar and Nahid Yeganeh** (compilers). (1982). Women's organizations in Iran–Society of Militant Women of Saqqez (Jame'a-e Zanan-e Mobarez-e Saqqez). In *In the Shadow of Islam: The Women's Movement in Iran* (pp. 222-23). London: Zed Press. ISBN 0-86232-022-4 and 0-86232-039-9 (pb).

**Keywords**: Society of Militant Women of Saqqez (Jame'a-e Zanan-e Mobarez-e Saqqez, formed in Saqqez, Iranian Kurdistan, 1979); aims; program; membership.

**Weşanên KOMJIN**. (1990). *Jinên Kurdistan. Frau in Kurdistan. Kürdistan'da Kadın* [Women of Kurdistan]. Cologne, Germany: Weşanên Komjin/Komjin Publikationen. Introduction in Turkish (p. 7), introduction in Kurdish (Kurmanji; p. 41), text in Turkish (pp. 9-39), text in Kurdish (Kurmanji; pp. 42-66), text in German (pp. 67-88), black and white photographs (pp. 12, 17, 22, 32, 40, 45, 49, 58, 71, 74, 82, 84), statistical tables (pp. 14, 16, 19, 46, 48, 50, 52, 70, 73, 75).

**Keywords:** Kurdish women's organization in Germany; history of Kurdistan; Kurdish women's education; health; socio-economic situation of Kurdish women; Kurdish women in Germany; working women; unemployed women; language; health; refugee status in Germany; cultural differences; legal situation in Germany; economic situation in Germany.

**Wesselingh, Isabelle**. (1998). Fatma, femme, kurde et militante [Fatma, woman, Kurdish and militant]. *La Croix*, reprinted in *Institut Kurde de Paris, Information and Liaison Bulletin, 160-161*, July/August 1998, p. 108.

**Keywords:** Fatma Kayhan; Kurdish Women's Association in Istanbul; *Roza*; Turkish feminist organizations failure to appeal to Kurdish women; racism; repression by the Turkish state.

# GENDER RELATIONS

## I. FAMILY AND HOME

**Aykan, Hakan and Douglas A. Wolf**. (2000). Traditionality, modernity, and household composition: Parent-child co-residence in contemporary Turkey. *Research on Aging*, *22*(4), July pp. 395-421.

**Keywords:** analysis of married adult children living with their parents in Turkey; Kurdish ethnicity distinguished in study from Turkish because Kurdish couples live primarily in the East, often seen as the least developed region of Turkey; Kurdish is associated with traditionality; this argument, that being of Kurdish ethnic origin is associated with traditionality and thus increases the chances of co-residence, is not supported by findings; interethnic marriages rare in Turkey: 92%, indicating Kurdish women do not marry outside their ethnicity.

**Dziegiel, Leszek**. (1982). The life cycle within the Iraqi Kurd family. *Ethnologia Polona, 8,* pp. 247-60.

**Keywords:** Kurdish family: institution run by women in practice although decisions are made by the father; arranged marriages; marriage amongst relatives; traditionally no dating; girl can refuse marriage to a particular candidate but it would cause a scandal; divorce is not very common, especially in rural communities; emphasis on women's rights in Kurdistan as opposed to other Middle Eastern groups by European travelers; Kurdish women do not wear veils.

**Mcfayden, Melanie**. (1995). Hell on the doorstep. In *Resistance: Women in Kurdistan*. London: KIC/KSC Publications, p. 13. One photograph. Originally appeared in *The Guardian*, March 9, 1995.

**Keywords:** feudal culture: women are not expected to work outside of the home; dependence on male relatives; rape while under police custody.

**Nikitine, Basile**. (1956). La Famille Kurde: Habitation, Costume, Nourriture, Role de la Femme, Rites Familiaux [The Kurdish family: Housing, costume, food, role of women, family rites]. In *Les Kurdes: Étude Sociologique et Historique* (pp. 87-118). Paris: Imprimerie Nationale.

**Keywords:** settlement patterns; clothing; diet; food; Kurdish proverbs regarding women and food; famine; war; status of women; lack of veiling among Kurdish women; absence of prostitution among Kurds;

marriage; prevalence of romanticism among Kurds; platonic love; love poetry about women; Kurdish respect for women; lack of harems for women; divorce; Kurdish dance; individuality among Kurdish women; Adela Khanum; children; hygiene; nomads; female tribal leaders; authority of women in domestic life; familial hierarchies; songs sung by women; music.

**Nikitine, Basile**. (1992). La vie domestique kurde [Kurdish domestic life]. *Revue d'Ethnographie et des Traditions Populaires, 3*(12), pp. 334-44.

**Keywords:** reference made to Eghazarian's study of domestic Kurdish life in Armenia, published in Russian in *Bulletins de la Société Géographique* in Tiflis, Georgia; houses among the Kurds of Hakkari; food; clothing; Mokri Kurds (Iran); birth rituals and women; marriage; funeral rites; superstitions.

**Pointon, Claire**. (1992). The is Kurdistan and we'll fight for it. In *Kurdish Women: The struggle for national liberation and women's rights,* October, (pp. 5-8). London: KIC/KSC Publications. Two photographs.

**Keywords:** changes in traditional family structures: Kadriye: not allowed to go to school because her older brothers convinced her parents that it would dishonour the family; taught herself to read as an adult and became nationally conscious; Kadriye's daughter: university student; politically active; mother wishes she would get married and have children; blaming Islam for patriarchy in Kurdish culture; women in non-traditional roles; leading demonstrations; standing trial; guerilla fighters; Sakine: served 12-year prison sentence; upon release gave up idea of having a family to become a "professional revolutionary"; raising of consciousness while in prison; repercussions of young women and men joining the guerillas in the mountains: changes in family structures; increase in birthrates as families try to keep up numbers to compensate for loss of people to armed struggle; women as bearers of the nation.

**Yalçin-Heckmann, Lale**. (1989). On kinship, tribalism and ethnicity in Eastern Turkey. In Peter A. Andrews (Ed.), *Ethnic groups in the Republic of Turkey* (pp. 622-31), Wiesbaden: Dr. Ludwig Reichert Verlag.

**Keywords:** household organization in Eastern Turkey: "ideal" type of household: conjugal couple, sons, unmarried daughters, the sons' wives and children; deviations common: dominant trend toward nuclear family especially in urban settings; "ideal" prevails mostly in villages; residential proximity: common to live close to kin; marriages: relations and customs vary from rural to urban settings; arranged marriages made with considerations of social, economic, and political interests; romantic love is a valid way of defying these decisions and abductions and elopement are common but cause continuous conflicts; inheritance: women do not inherit property through tribal laws; in the civil law it is to be distributed equally to all siblings of both sexes; Islamic law dictates that property should be distributed according to the ration of 1:2 shares for heiress: heir; in villages tribal laws are most common.

## II. MARRIAGE

**Agence France Presse**. (2000). L'armée tente de lancer le mariage civil dans le sud-est [Army tries to launch civil marriage in Southeast]. *Agence France Presse*, reprinted in *Institut Kurde de Paris, Information and Liaison Bulletin, 187*, October, pp. 29.

> **Keywords:** civil marriage campaign launched by the army in Southeastern Turkey in order to eliminate religious marriages that are banned under Turkish laws.

**Anter, Musa**. (1996). Musa Anter: My memoirs [Special issue] (I. Ozden, Trans.). *Kurdistan Report, 23*, March-May. One photograph.

> **Keywords:** marriage to a Kurdish woman to maintain links to Kurdish nation; marriage to a "respectable" family rather than an individual.

**Arif, Parween N.** (1997). Marriage customs in Kurdistan: Sulemani Case Study. *Kurdistan Times, 2*(1), November, pp. 79-89. ISSN 1057-8668.

> **Keywords:** marriage customs of southern Kurdistan; arranged marriage; custom of marrying cousins; Zen be Zen marriage - two men marry each other's' sisters; dowry; Kurdish folklore; honour killing; honour; jewelry purchasing; clothes purchasing; henna night; women's hammam party.

**Barth, Fredrik**. (1970). Father's brother's daughter marriage in Kurdistan. In Louise E. Sweet (Ed.), *Peoples and cultures of the Middle East: An anthropological reader: Vol. 1. Cultural depth and diversity* (pp. 127-36). New York: The Natural History Press.

> **Keywords:** marriage; Kurdish lineage system; bride price; arranged marriages; exogamy; land ownership and marriage.

**Gündüz-Hosgör, Ayse and Jeroen Smits**. (2002). Intermarriage between Turks and Kurds in contemporary Turkey: Inter-ethnic relations in an urbanizing environment. *European Sociological Review*, *18*(4), pp. 417-432.

**Keywords:** Turkish-Kurdish intermarriage: takes place between Kurdish males and Turkish females; takes place more in larger cities or in regions where their own group is small; education: highest intermarriage tendencies found among Turks with a low educational level and among Kurds with a high educational level; low tendency toward intermarriage; Kurdish females tended to be married much less with Turks than Kurdish males, however, over time, increase in the tendency towards intermarriage was stronger among Kurdish females than among the Kurdish males.

**Hutchinson, Rev. Henry Neville**. (1974). *Marriage customs in many lands.* Detroit: Gale Research Company (Original work published in 1897). ISBN - 0-8103-3971-4. Preface (pp. v-vii), text (pp. 2-341), index (pp. 342-48), 24 black and white illustrations (pp. 6, 10, 14, 22, 42, 50, 56, 78, 94, 114, 140, 168, 202, 210, 212, 226, 230, 242, 266, 272, 278, 302, 310).

**Keywords:** Kurdish wedding ceremony; ease with which a Kurd may obtain a divorce.

**Kahn, Margaret**. (1981). Behind the invisible veil. *Connexions, 2,* Fall, pp. 4-5.

**Keywords:** Urumiyeh; polygamy; education; clothing; arranged marriage; division of labour.

**Mokri, Mohammad**. (1970). Le mariage chez les Kurdes [Marriage among the Kurds]. In *Contribution Scientifique Aux Études Iraniennes* (pp. 35-61). Paris: Librarie Klincksieck.

**Keywords:** religious aspects of marriage; constitution of the family; social and economic aspects of marriage; desired attributes of a young girl; birth; marriage contract; *mâra brîn*; elderly women and marriage; henna night; *rûmat garden*.

**Nazdar**. (1966). A Kurdish wedding. *The Kurdish Journal, (III)*3, September, pp. 5-6.

**Keywords:** marriage in city and village; engagement; the contract; dowry; wedding ceremonies; wedding ceremonies.

**Lescot, Roger**. (1943). Tawûsparêz, Le mariage chez les Kurdes [Marriage among the Kurds]. *Hawar: Qovara Qurdî, Revue kurde, 10*(52), January 20, pp. 12-16.

**Keywords:** like the rest of the Orient, celibacy is abnormal among the Kurds; boys marry at 15 or 16 and girls from 12; Charaf Khan, Kurdish historian, notes polygyny among the Kurds; marriage in different social classes; the ruined ruling aristocracy, popular classes, and nomads; no marriage between Yezidi castes of *chaykh, pir,* and *murid*; inter-tribal marriage, and conflict and reconciliation; prevalence of marriage between cousins; forced marriage and resistance to it; prevalence of arranged marriages even though boys and girls not separated in rural contexts; stages of marriage: *rûdînî,* visiting and assessing the would-be bride by one or two women; *here kirin; xwezgîn,* betrothal or *şêranî;* bride-price; *destgîran* engagement; *dawet,* wedding, *xeyl-evanî* or *xêlvanî,* bridal procession [*xêlî,* wedding procession] or *berbûrî,* practice of matron accompanying bride; description of the days of wedding; marriage and wedding in princely families: in the story of *Mem û Zîn* and the Ardelan; description of Yezidi marriage in the book *Peacock Angel* by Lady Drower (London, 1941).

**Vega, Anne.** (1990). Mariage et accouchement chez les kurdes de Turquie: Reprsentations de l'alliance et de l'enfantement des femmes kurdes immigrées de la région Parisienne [Marriage and childbirth among Kurds in Turkey: Representations of the alliance and childbirth of Kurdish immigrant women from the Paris region; Master's thesis]. Université Paris X, Nanterre.

**Keywords:** Kurds from Hakkari region in Paris suburbs; family and lineage (*mal*); terminology of family relations; Kurdish family relation system in the Arabic, Persian, and Turkish linguistic context; choice of partner; matrimonial transactions; bride price *"naxt"*; wedding; giving birth in Kurdistan; sterility; feeding; sexuality; images of Kurdish women in tribes, villages, Kurdish towns and large cities of Turkey and in Paris; modernity and feudalism.

## III. PATRIARCHY

**Bedr-Khan, le Prince Sureya.** (1936). Le femme Kurde et son rôle social [The Kurdish woman and her social role]. *XVI International Congress of Anthropology and Prehistoric Archeology; 6th General Assembly of the International Institute of Anthropology,* Brussels, pp. 719-725.

**Keywords:** equality between Kurdish men and women as compared with other Muslim populations; Kurdish women as completely autonomous and free individuals enjoying all of the same rights as Kurdish men; management of the household done by women; coquettish nature of Kurdish women; child-rearing and cleaning as the tasks of women; arranged marriages not common.

**Boland, Vincent**. (2004). Turkish education plan brings charges of "hidden Islamic agenda." *Financial Times,* reprinted in *Institut Kurde de Paris, Information and Liaison Bulletin, 230,* May 2004, pp. 14. One photograph (women in headscarves studying).

**Keywords:** fears that the AKP will force women to wear headscarves.

**Dzięgiel, Leszek**. (1992). The Kurdish knot: Culture, history and struggle for survival (K. Kwaś niewicz, Trans.). In Leszek Węzeł Dzięgiel (Ed.), *kurdyjski. Kultura.Dzieje. Walka o przetrwanie* (pp. 430-46). Kraków: Universitas. ISBN: 83-7052-088-X.

**Keywords:** family life; patrilocal marriage; bride price; importance of a bride's virginity; difficulties for women seeking a divorce; polygamy; women's dependence upon the will of their fathers, husbands, and brothers; emigration; women's work; women's preparation of food; women's dress; jewelry; women's hairstyles; health care; women's quarters in a home; religion.

**International Herald Tribune**. (2004). Ankara, chastened, steps away from adultery law. *International Herald Tribune,* reprinted in *Institut Kurde de Paris, Information and Liaison Bulletin, 234,* September, p. 52.

**Keywords:** Van; Kurdish region of Turkey; popularity of the AKP; traditional Kurdish political parties in power in region; appeal partly its conservatism; Van and surrounding rural areas "strongly tribal"; common for men to have four wives; 80% of women illiterate; women's groups and human rights groups have reported honour killings; criminalizing adultery will bring more harm to women in the region according to the Women's Association.

**Koç, Serpil**. (1993). Turkish colonialism and the oppression of women in Kurdistan: The Ottoman concept of masculinity. *Kurdistan Report, 16,* October/November, pp. 22, 24. Also appeared as "Turkish colonialism and the oppression of women in Kurdistan," in *Resistance: Women in Kurdistan.* London: KIC/KSC Publications, 1995, pp. 38-41. Two photographs.

**Keywords:** YXK, YJWK; male domination; matriarchal society; patriarchy; the family and women's oppression; feudalism; tradition; custom; imperialism; colonialism; the Ottoman legacy in modern-day Turkey; power structures in Kurdistan; traditional masculinity; honour; sexist proverbs; segregation of the sexes.

**Leach, Edmund R**. (1940). *Social and economic organisation of the Rowanduz Kurds.* London: Percy Lund, Humphries and Co. Introduction (pp. 1-3), preliminary note on Kurdish names (pp. 3-4), the field of investigation (pp. 4-9), method of analysis (p. 9), text (pp. 9-62), diagram of kinship terms (p. 63), appendices (pp. 64-70), three maps (pp. 71-73); list of photographs (p. 74), 12 black and white photographs (pp. 75-80).

**Keywords:** social organization; marriage; bride price; divorce; pregnancy; sale of unwanted girl children (the girls being known as Kurdiya); slave servant girls; economic organization; warfare; religion; nomads; Soran tribes; Balik tribes; land tenure; blood feuds; women as part of blood money payments; honour; legality of honour killing; kinship.

**Masters, William M**. (1953). *Rowanduz: A Kurdish administrative and mercantile center* (Doctoral dissertation, University of Michigan). Ann Arbor and London: University Microfilms International. Abstract (unnumbered front pages), preface (pp. ii-iv.), table of contents (p. v), list of illustrations (p. vi), text (pp. 1-346), bibliography (pp. 347-48), appendix (pp. 349-58), three maps (pp. 16-18); diagrams of Kurdish kinship system (pp. 235-36).

**Keywords:** women's mourning rituals; elopement; honour; virginity; dowry; honour killings; class system; ethnic groups of Rowanduz; religious groups of Rowanduz; ethnic divisions; religious divisions; women and class differences; women's solidarity; societal hierarchies; widows; polygamy; milk mothers; kinship; mothers as confidants; women's power as intermediaries between father and offspring; women's domestic work; respect for the elderly; grandmother's position of influence; paternal and maternal aunts; hierarchy among brothers and sisters; veiling; gender segregation; importance of giving birth to a son; women's position as affected by her socio-economic status; pregnancy; birthing rites; nursing; superstition; wedding ceremonies; divorce; fertility; infertility as cause for divorce; leisure time; folktales told by women; prostitution; Kurdish nationalism; gossip; women's mosque; burial rites; women's work; Bayin Amina; women and the consumption of alcohol; women's dress; Lali Khan; women's jewelry.

**Reuters**. (2004). Turkey's head scarf ban is upheld by rights court. *International Herald Tribune*, reprinted in *Institut Kurde de Paris, Information and Liaison Bulletin, 231*, June 2004, pp. 83.

**Keywords:** the European Court of Human Rights rules that banning head scarves in state schools does not violate the freedom of religion and is a valid way to counter Islam.

**Rotivel, Agnès**. (2004). Konya la conservatrice observe l'Europe avec prudence [Konya the conservative watches Europe cautiously]. *La Croix*, reprinted in *Institut Kurde de Paris, Information and Liaison Bulletin, 231*, June 2004, pp. 46-47.

Keywords: banning of veiling in university in Turkey; female unemployment.

## IV. SEXUALITY

Dunda, Can. (2001). Sans certificat de virginité, pas d'études [Without virginity certificate, no studies]. *Courrier International, 561*, reprinted in *Institut Kurde de Paris, Information and Liaison Bulletin, 196-197*, July-August 2001, p. 103.

Keywords: Osman Durmuş; MHP; sex crimes; compulsory virginity testing; women's access to education; virginity certification; sexual repression.

Halisdemir, Orya Sultan. (1995). Another form of state oppression: "Virginity tests." *Turkish Probe*, reprinted in *Institut Kurde de Paris, Information and Liaison Bulletin, 118-119*, January/February 1995, p. 204.

Keywords: expelling of non-virgin females from secondary schools; forced virginity tests for female students; influence of religion in state schools; honour; Islamization; Islamic revival; suicide; virginity tests performed on dead girls.

Halisdemir, Orya Sultan. (1995). Education minister and undersecretary contradict each other on virginity test. *Turkish Daily News*, reprinted in *Institut Kurde de Paris, Information and Liaison Bulletin, 118-119*, January-February 1995, p. 193.

Keywords: virginity tests; virginity control.

İlkkaracan, Pınar. (1998). Exploring the context of women's sexuality in Eastern Turkey. *Reproductive Health Matters, 6*(12), pp. 66-75, one photograph. Also appeared in Women Living Under Muslim Laws, *Dossier 22*, November 1999, pp. 100-113. Also appeared in Pınar İlkkaracan ed. *Women and Sexuality in Muslim Societies*. Women for Women's Human Rights: Istanbul. 2000, pp. 229-244.

Keywords: control of female sexuality through customary and religious law; impact of customary and religious laws on rural and urban women in Eastern Turkey; study done of 599 women in the region; most were, or had been, married; results of study: early marriage and polygamy prevalent; religious marriage takes place earlier than civil marriage and religious marriage is not legally binding; forced marriages occur and arranged marriages are still most common; more and more younger women expect to be able to choose their partners; most women feel unable to seek divorce if their husbands had committed adultery; most women fear the custom of honour killing if they are suspected of having an extra-marital affair; almost none of the women sought legal recourse against domestic violence or marital rape even though both are common occurrences; to address the results: a human rights training program for women; public awareness campaign against honour killings of women accused of adultery; campaign to alter the Turkish Criminal Code; causes of dire situation of women in Eastern Turkey: high rate of female illiteracy; desolate economic situation in Eastern Turkey as opposed to Western Turkey: disproportionately effects women over men; customary and religious practices in breach of official laws; situation worsened by ongoing conflict between Turkish security forces and the PKK.

**Köhler, Gesa and Dorothea Nogga Weinell.** (1984). *Azade: vom Überleben kurdischer Frauen* [The survival of Kurdish women]. Photos by Abidin Sönmez. Bremen, Germany: Edition CON. ISBN 3-88526-140-5. Forward by Johannes Beck (p.7), introduction (pp. 8-9), text (pp. 10-146), map (p. 11), bibliography (p. 147-52), nine black and white photographs (pp. 40, 57, 94, 117, 132, 136, 139, 143, 152).

**Keywords:** physical Kurdistan; history of Kurdistan; political situation of Kurds in Turkey since WWII; terror and repression under military rule; Kurdish refugee women in Germany; childhood; youth and families in Kurdistan; marriage; meaning of virginity for Kurdish women; pregnancy and birth; gynaecology; abortion; birth control; polygamy; divorce; emigration to Germany; poetry; Qur'anic schools; sexuality; rights; working conditions in Germany; religion.

## V. STRUGGLE AGAINST VIOLENCE

**Alouf, Marie-Édith.** (2001). La justice violée [Justice violated]. *Politis*, reprinted in *Institut Kurde de Paris, Information and Liaison Bulletin, 192*, March 2001, p. 44.

**Keywords:** Eren Keskin; Kurdish women taking legal action against their aggressors; destruction of Kurdish villages; murder of Kurdish civilians; refugees; exiles; violation of women; destruction of Kurdish women's social and collective identities; *Des épines au coeur. Eren Keskin, une avocate kurde accuse.*

**Hamid, Surma**. (2001). The moon rises after sunset: A life story based on a struggle for women's rights (Toma Hamid & Muhammad Kamal, Trans.). In Gina Lennox (Ed.), *Fire, snow and honey. Essays: Voices from Kurdistan. Life stories, poems, short fiction and fables contributed by people from Kurdistan* (pp. 372-81). Foreword by Danielle Mitterrand. Sydney, Australia: Halstead Press.

**Keywords:** war on women in Iraqi Kurdistan beginning in 1991; killing women for sexual "misconduct" or "disobedience"; honor killing maintained by tradition, Iraqi law, and Islamic or Shari'a laws; women "scapegoats for a traumatised society" in the aftermath of the 1991 war and the civil war of 1994-98; the campaign of the Workers' Communist Party of Iraq against honor killing; KDP support of honor killing, and attacks on activists; the Islamist fundamentalist violence against women and activists; female circumcision; formation of the Independent Women's Organization in Sulaimani in 1993; the KDP and PUK attacks on IWO and its women's shelters; the Islamist fundamentalist violence against IWO, and Surma; escaping to Australia; continuing pressure of the family of the husband to reunite with him.

*See also* Australia; Communism and Socialism

**Institut Kurde de Paris**. (2001). Kurdish women are being put on trial by the Turkish Courts for having denounced rape and harassment in Kurdistan. *Institut Kurde de Paris, Information and Liaison Bulletin, 195*, June, p. 8.

**Keywords:** rape; sexual harrassment; Gülizar Tuncer; Fatma Kara; Nahide Kilici; Zeynep Ovayola; Fatma Karakaş; Kamile Çığcı; State Security Court.

**Mohammed, Sara**. (2002). Never forget Pela! (interview by Sohaila Sharifi; Special English edition). *Medusa: Journal of the Centre for Women and Socialism*, December, pp. 71-72.

**Keywords:** Sara, born in Iraqi Kurdistan and activist and organizer of "Never Forget Pela," an organization against male violence in Sweden; Pela, Swedish-Kurdish girl murdered by her father and uncle; critique of Swedish government policy of not granting new citizens gender-based equal rights; citizens born in other (non-Western) cultures should not be allowed to discriminate and commit violence against women; the need for legal reform in Sweden.

**Moore, Molly**. (2001). Turkish women who complain of police brutality pay heavy price. *International Herald Tribune*, reprinted in *Institut Kurde de Paris, Information and Liaison Bulletin, 194*, May, p. 51.

**Keywords:** Nazli Top; torture; rape; Turkey's first public conference on the abuse of women in police custody; sexual violence against women; Fatma Karataş; Nahide Kiliç; Initiative Against Sexual Abuse and Rape in Custody; Amnesty International.

**Schaller, Angélique.** (2001). Eren contre Goliath [Eren against Goliath]. *L'Humanité Hebdo,* reprinted in *Institut Kurde de Paris, Information and Liaison Bulletin, 196-197,* July/August 2001, pp. 13-14.

**Keywords:** Eren Keskin; sexual violence against prisoners; stigma regarding sex; difficulties facing women who complain of sexual violence; Suna Parlak; Dicle Kadın Kültür ve Sanat Merkezi; PKK.

## VI. VIOLENCE AGAINST WOMEN

### A. Female Genital Mutilation

**Rahim, Runak F.** (2004). *Kurdish community and female genital mutilation : a social field and theory research in southern part of Kurdistan* (Nasrren I. Rahim, Trans,). Suleimaniyah, Iraqi Kurdistan, 172 pages, pp. 51 and 77 photographs. Kurdish section: *Xetenekirdinî Kiçan.*

**Keywords:** questionnaire-based interviews with women in the cities of Erbil, Duhok, and Suleimaniyah; the goal was to identify the practice, its geographical spread, and working towards abolishing Female Genital Mutilation; FGM is practiced in the region but it is ascribed to Islam rather than "part of principal Kurdish traditions"; of a total of 40,480 females studied, 30,324 were circumcised and 10,352 were 1 to 16 years old.

### B. Non-State Violence

#### 1. Honor Killing

##### a. Films, documentaries, and reviews

**A World to Win.** (1985). Homage to Yilmaz Güney. *A World to Win, 1,* pp. 68-82. Photographs (pp. 68, 69, 70, 72, 74, 76, 78, 80, 81).

**Keywords:** *Yol;* an interview with Costa Gavras, co-winner of the 1982 Palm d'Or; excerpts of interviews with Yilmaz Güney; TKP-ML member writes of Güney's life, work, struggles and death; an interview with Nihat Behram.

**Benge, Alfreda.** (1985). Güney, Turkey and the West: An interview. *Race and Class, XXVI(3),* pp. 31-46.

133

**Keywords:** Golden Palm at Cannes awarded to Güney for *Yol*; critique of Roger Scruton's right-wing review of *Yol*; the West and Turkey; interview with Yilmaz Güney; Güney's life story; the making of the film; the ideology of Turkish cinema; heroes; the audience in Turkey; feudalism and capitalism in Güney's films; Güney's Kurdish identity; life in exile; the West and the Kurds of Turkey.

**Gabbay, Alex (Director)**. (2000). *In the name of honour*. Television Trust for the Environment: Bullfrog Films. ISBN: 1-56029-861-8. Colour, 24 minutes, series editor: Robert Lamb, executive producer: Jenny Richards, series producer: Luke Gawin.

**Keywords:** Northern Iraq; honour killings; domestic abuse; women's shelter; women fighting oppression; female lawyers; female activists; female guerillas; women and laws in Iraqi Kurdistan; women's movement in Iraqi Kurdistan; women and literacy; women and education.

**Güney, Yilmaz**. (1982). *Yol* [Road]. Feature film in Turkish with subtitles in English, French, and German. Colour. Shot in Turkey and Kurdish provinces. Screenplay by Güney. Directed by Şerif Gören

**Keywords:** five prison inmates on a 10-day furlough; honour killing; *Reviews*: Scruton, Roger; Benge, A.; and *A World to Win*.

**Kinzer, Stephen**. (1999). *Yol* [Road]. *New York Times*, p. 29.

**Keywords:** 1982 Cannes Palme d'Or awarded to *Yol*; blood feuds; honour; the banning of *Yol* by the Turkish government; lifting the ban in 1992; the first screening of *Yol* in Turkey in 1999.

**Scruton, Roger**. (1983). The rule of honour and the rule of law. *Times Literary Supplement*, January 21, p. 59.

**Keywords:** honour; the Kurdish tradition of a man marrying his brother's widow; arranged marriage; critique of *Yol*'s depiction of the oppression of women and the Turkish state; criticism of Güney's concentration on "the cruelty of the code of honour, which denies freedom to women and justice to men"; attack on the Turkish left; honour versus justice in rural life; Yaşar Kemal's views on women contrasted with Güney's.

## b. News reports

**Juurus, Kati**. (2002). Leila and Abdoulmajid and their dangerous love. *Helsingin Sanomat, International Edition*, February 5. Home Section. One photograph.

> **Keywords:** Leila Abdulkadir and Abdoulmajid Hakki: a Kurdish couple, married by a mullah against the wishes of their families; Leila: Kurd from Syria who lives in Sweden; Abdoulmajid: Finnish citizen from Iranian Kurdistan; met on Kurdish internet chat room; Leila's brother had beat her and threatened to kill her and her fiancé; brother came after them after they were married but hasn't found them; Fadime Sahindal: reaction of the couple to her murder; not surprised; not the only murder "of its kind"; change in Leila's brother when they moved to Sweden: became more controlling; Hakki's cousin moved his family back to Kurdistan from Norway after he had given birth to a daughter because he did not want her to grow up in Norway; Hakki links religion to the failure of immigrants to integrate; cultural relativism: Finnish police ignore domestic violence in immigrant homes because it is seen as part of the culture; Hakki's activism on behalf of Kurdish women: has been told he will be killed for talking about the position of women in Kurdish culture.

**Libération**. (2001). Le meurtre d'une jeune Kurde divise la Suède [Murder of young Kurd divides Sweden]. *Libération*, January 11. One photograph.

> **Keywords:** Barin: 20-year-old sister of the victim of an honour killing, Pele; accused her two uncles of the murder of her sister; her father Agid, escaped; debate about the failure of "integration" in Sweden.

**Moore, Molly**. (2001). Honor killings follow women to the city. *International Herald Tribune*, reprinted in *Institut Kurde de Paris, Information and Liaison Bulletin, 196-197*, July/August 2001, p. 112.

> **Keywords:** honour killing; Dilber Kına; Pınar İlkkaracan; decreased sentences for perpetrators of honour killings; decreased penalties for rape of non-virgins; urbanization; Mehmet Farac; feudalism; patriarchy; Canan Arin; Women's Rights Centre of the Istanbul Bar Association.

**Ortaq, Nükte V**. (2004). Kurdistan: l'honneur tue [Kurdistan: Honour kills]. *L'Express*, reprinted in *Institut Kurde de Paris: Information and Liaison Bulletin, 228*, March 2004, p. 29.

> **Keywords:** honour killings; mobilization in Turkey against honour killings; Kader, a 16-year-old-girl killed by her brother, Ahmet; Semsa

Allak; KA-MER; Nebahat Akkoç, president of KA-MER: some women condemned to death by family council for simple disobedience; Zulal Erdoğan, a lawyer in Diyarbakir.

**Pope, Nicole**. (2003). Turquie: Meurtres en Famille [Turkey: Family murders]. *Le Monde,* reprinted in *Institut Kurde de Paris, Information and Liaison Bulletin, 222,* September 2003, pp. 28-29.

**Keywords:** honour killings; Semsiye Allak, a Kurdish woman killed by her family; Sevdiye Uyanik, a Kurdish woman killed by her family; Leyla Pervizat, coordinator of a project for the prevention of "honour crimes"; women living in fear of honour killings; forced marriages; polygamy, *berdel,* the exchange of women of "equal value"; bride price, the money paid for a bride; consanguine marriages; girls as the property of their fathers; Pınar İlkkaracan of the Association of Women for Women's Rights, who organized seminars to familiarize the women of the region with their rights; the prevalence of arranged marriages in Turkish Kurdistan; the failure to consult girls regarding arranged marriage; co-spouses; religious marriage (*imam nikah*); the marriage of girls prior to the legal age of consent; Yalimköy Village; Elif Atilgan, a 15-year-old victim of honour killing; PKK; Nebahat Akkoç, founder of KA-MER; domestic violence.

**Reuters**. (2002). Sweden arrests Kurd in immigrant "honor killing." *Reuters,* July 24.

**Keywords:** Asrin Masifi: 21-year-old television presenter: father arrested in Sweden on the suspicion of killing his daughter who was planning to marry her Kurdish boyfriend against his wishes; case likely to fuel debate about Sweden's ability to integrate a large immigrant population where honour killings take place; initially it was thought that Masifi had hung herself but an inquest found that she had been strangled; her sister was arrested as an accomplice; neither father nor sister had been charged; three weeks before this murder Fadime Sahindal was murdered by her father because she had a Swedish boyfriend; her father was sentenced to life imprisonment.

**Zaman, Amberin**. (2000). In modern Turkey, women continue to pay the price for honor. *Los Angeles Times,* reprinted in *Institut Kurde de Paris, Information and Liaison Bulletin, 186,* September 2000, pp. 55-58.

**Keywords:** rape victims; women perpetuating honor killings; shame; honor; honor killings; legislation and honor killings; patriarchy; virginity tests; adultery, elopement, rumours of unchaste behaviour and their implications for women; state-run women's shelter;

participation of entire family in honor killings; Ferda Güllüoğlu; women's rights activism; government development schemes; tribal structure; material benefits of honor killings for family of murdered victim; bride price; girls as commercial assets; trading and selling of girls; forced marriages; suicide.

## c. Research

**Akkoç, Nebahat**. (2004). The cultural basis of violence in the name of honour. In Shahrzad Mojab & Nahla Abdo (Eds.), *Violence in the name of honour: Theoretical and political challenges* (pp. 113-25). Istanbul: İstanbul Bilgi University Press. ISBN 975-6857-98-6.

**Keywords:** Anna Lindh, Swedish Minister of Foreign Affairs, supporter of Kurdish women; the work of KA-MER against honor killing in Diyarbakır, and other Kurdish regions of Turkey; the stoning of Şemse Allak; the case of Kadriye Demirel; brief survey of 21 cases; the goal of male violence is to "maintain the secondary status of women" and "to preserve slavery status" for women; the successes and limitations of KA-MER's activism.

**Arat, Zehra F.** (2003). A struggle on two fronts. Carnegie Council on Ethics and International Affairs, *Human Rights Dialogue*, Violence Against Women, 2(10), Fall, p. 32.

**Keywords:** response to Leylâ Pervizat's article, "In the Name of Honor;" misconception that honor killing is somehow an Islamic practice; ancient Mediterranean practice; pervasive patriarchal norms and values lie at the core of the issue; constitutional and legal equality versus actual equality; women considered as minors or dependents of men; use of "honor" as a mitigating factor in judgments of such crimes; Turkish legal definition of crimes that involve sexual violence against women as "felonies against public decency and family order," while other forms of assault against the person are placed under "felonies against individuals"; classification of women according to their marital or virginity status while in custody; forced virginity testing while in custody; manifestations of controlling women's sexuality other than honor killing: confinement, intimidations, physical abuse, living in constant terror; violation of the right to life; failure of Turkey to uphold CEDAW, which was signed in 1985; classical liberal understanding of human rights as individual rights against the state: public versus private domains.

**Arin, Canan.** (2001). Femicide in the name of honor in Turkey. *Violence Against Women*, 7(7), London: Sage, July, pp. 821-25.

**Keywords:** Hacer: victim of an honor killing in Turkey; 16 years old; ran away from home; police found her and delivered her to her father; locked up in a small room while the male family members decided what to do; despite her father's protests the other male family members decided she must be killed; her 13-year-old brother shot her; because of the mitigating circumstance of "honor" he only served two years and her uncles who denied everything were acquitted; between 1994-1998 in small area of Turkey five girls are known to have been killed by family members in the name of honor; according to the local chief prosecutor these cases occur more often, every 2-3 months; "honor" crimes in the Netherlands; Nazand Begikhani: awarded the third Emma Humphreys Memorial Prize in London, United Kingdom in October 2000; found of Kurdish KWAHK.

**Van Eck, Clementine.** (2003). *Purified by blood: Honour killings amongst Turks in the Netherlands.* Amsterdam: Amsterdam University Press, 303 pp. Appendix 1: "More case studies from the court records" (pp. 223-35), Appendix 2 "Case studied from Bitlis province" (pp. 237-39), Appendix 3 "The Turkish criminal code and honour killing" (pp. 241-44). ISBN 90 5356 491 8.

**Keywords:** anthropological study of 20 cases of honor killing, based on court records, by "Turks in the Netherlands," i.e., "migrants from Turkey, regardless of their ethnicity"; ethnic identity specified in some of the studied cases; two types of honor, *namus* and *şeref*; honor killing located in Turkey's rural areas but has emerged in the cities due to migration since the 1960s and 1970s and to Western Europe (the Netherlands, Belgium, Germany, France, Denmark, and Sweden); more prevalent in Eastern than Western Turkey and more inland than on the coast; honor killing, blood revenge, Turkish jurisprudence, Islam; forms and varieties of killing; funeral; protests against honor killing; planners and accomplices; honor killers, male and female; hired assassins; Dutch jurisprudence; elopement and honor killing; alternatives to honor killing; why an honor killing?

**Eldén, Åsa.** (2003). Summary. Life-and-death honour. Violent stories about reputation, virginity and honour. In Åsa Eldén, *Heder på liv och död: Våldsamma berättelser om rykten, oskuld och heder.* Comprehensive Summaries of Uppsala Dissertations from the Faculty of Social Sciences 128, Uppsala, Sweden: Acta Universitatis Upsaliensis, 106-117. ISSN 0282-7492, ISBN 91-554-5686-3.

**Keywords:** study of reputation, virginity, and honor in the lives of Arab and Kurdish women in Sweden, and their relation with understanding of culture and religion; research based on interviews with ten Arab and Kurdish women (1998 to 2000), and seven Swedish legal cases concerning honor killing (1994 to 2002); author's constructivist and "feminist comprehensive perspective"; understanding violence in its context by seeing connections between culture, violence, and gender; analysis of Fadime Şahindal's speech to the Swedish parliament; research ethics, and "the fear of being branded as a racist."

**Düzkan, Ayse and Filiz Koçali.** (2000). An honor killing: She fled, her throat was cut. In Pinar Ilkkaracan (Ed.), *Women and sexuality in Muslim societies,* Istanbul: Women For Women's Human Rights-New Ways, pp. 381-87. One photograph. Originally appeared in *Pazartesi* (Feminist Newspaper for Women), *13,* April 1996.

**Keywords:** Sevda Gök: 16-year-old victim of an honor killing; murder by her maternal aunt's 14-year-old son, Mehmet; Sevda ran away from home; Mehmet said in way of explanation, "We are Kurds. We don't send girls to school"; class and education: "Only high society Kurds send their girls to school"; rumors that she had a boyfriend; marriage in between relatives is widespread; every girl born is reserved for the son of her paternal uncle unless he does not want her.

**Filkins, Dexter.** (2003). Murder in the name of "honour" a grim fact of life in Turkey. *Toronto Star,* July 14, p. A3. Also appeared in the New York Times, one photograph.

**Keywords:** Şemse Allak: victim of an honor killing in Mardin, Southeastern Turkey; stoned to death by male family members; spent seven months in a coma; buried by a large group of women activists who unconventionally performed Islamic burial rights; her family did not claim the body and none of them attended her funeral.

**Frenning, Anna.** (2004). *Oppression in the name of honour: It's about disobedience.* Report from a series of seminars involving the Turkish women's organisation KA-MER and the Centre for Children and Adolescents in Crisis at Save the Children Sweden. Stockholm: Save the Children Sweden, ISBN 91-7321-145-1, code no: 3166.

**Keywords:** Save the Children Sweden: honor killing or honor crimes have "a cultural background, but not an ethnic or religious background," are a form of homicide, a supreme punishment for breaking the rules, violence connected to honor or chastity ethics in feudal patterns; the question of language use in conversations with girls and their families; Nebahat Akkoç (chairperson of KA-MER): "violence part of being a woman"; feminism limited and marginal;

women subjected to violence are "a long away from the women's movement"; KA-MER's work to combat honor killing; similarities and differences between Sweden and Turkey; integration; social responsibility; earning a living; male power; law; arranged marriages and virginity; connections between honor killing and suicide; psychological help.

**KA-MER**. (2004). The story of Ayşe. In Shahrzad Mojab & Nahla Abdo (Eds.), *Violence in the name of honour: Theoretical and political challenges* (pp. 127-35). Istanbul: İstanbul Bilgi University Press. ISBN 975-6857-98-6.

**Keywords:** The work of KA-MER in preventing the murder of Ayşe in a village of Diyarbakir; the intervention of government and civil organizations; the politics and culture of shame and honor.

**KA-MER**. (2004). Keşke dememek için: Namus adına işlenen cinayetler. "No more if only's": Killings in the name of "Honour" 2004 Report. A. Spangler (Trans.). KA-Mer, Diyarbakır, Contents (p. 4), preface by Nebahat Akkoç (p. 6), introduction (p. 8), Turkish text (pp. 9-99), English text (pp. 101-97).

**Keywords:** honour killing treated as a case of extrajudicial execution; news and analysis of KA-MER's activism against male violence in 2004; information on 31 women who approached KA-MER for protection from killers in 2004; six applications, from abroad, not accepted; analysis of the applications and work carried out; increase in the number of those who act against honor killing; need to act immediately if a woman is threatened; speeches and essays by Nebahat Akkoç; turning women's movements into social movements; honor killing not a Kurdish problem; contact info for women in the East and Southeast of Turkey.

**Kurdish Human Rights Project**. (2003). Action against honour killings. *KHRP Newsline*, *23*, Autumn, p. 19. One photograph.

**Keywords:** Dr. Nazand Bezighani: from KWAHK, visited KHRP's London office as part of ongoing work related to Kurdish women and their rights; KWAHK is currently organizing an art exhibit about Kurdish women's lives.

**Kurdish Human Rights Project**. (2004). KHRP condemns "honour killing" in Turkey. *KHRP Newsline*, *26*, Summer, p. 2.

**Keywords:** condemnation of the honour killing of a fourteen-year-old girl, Nuran Halitogullari; strangled to death by her father and brother following her abduction and rape by a stranger; the perpetrator was arrested; she was strangled afterwards because according to the father and the brother she had soiled the family name; recent amendments to Turkish legislation that entitled convicted murderers who cited honour as the motive to reduced sentences; KHRP participated in June 2004 in a London Metropolitan Police Service briefing about honour killings; KHRP's definition of violence against women: "any act of gender-based violence that results in, or is likely to result in, physical, sexual or psychological harm or suffering to women, including threats of such acts, coercion or arbitrary deprivation of liberty, whether occurring in public or in private life."

**Maris, Cees and Sawitri Saharso**. (2001). Honour killing: A reflection on gender, culture and violence. *The Netherlands Journal of Social Sciences, 37*(1), 2001, pp. 52-73.

**Keywords:** 17-year-old Kurdish Turkish boy shot and injured several people when he tried to kill the boy he claimed had abducted his sister in the town of Veghel, Netherlands; reaction of the Dutch society: most incidents unnoticed; only after the above incident (December 7, 1999) was public debate launched in the Dutch media; story made breaking news on CNN as a school shoot-out whose probable cause was an attempted honour killing; daughter claimed that she did not go on her own accord but was abducted and was engaged to someone else apparently proving that her honour was not in danger; virginity test: proved that she was still a virgin; cultural relativism and tolerance; multiculturalism.

**Mojab, Shahrzad**. (2004). The particularity of "honour" and the universality of "killing": From early warning signs to feminist pedagogy. In Shahrzad Mojab & Nahla Abdo (Eds.), *Violence in the name of honour: Theoretical and political challenges* (pp. 15-37). Istanbul: İstanbul Bilgi University Press. ISBN 975-6857-98-6.

**Keywords:** short- and long-term measures to prevent honor crimes; self-immolation and honor killing in Iraqi Kurdistan; cases of Ayşe (Turkey), Heshu (Britain), and Fadime (Sweden); patriarchy as a regime of exercise of male gender power; legal reform, legalism and legal education; critique of post-structuralism and cultural relativism; racism and anti-feminism; resistance against honor crimes; early warning signs in honor crimes; the centrality of feminist education.

**Mojab, Shahrzad**. (2004). No "safe haven": Violence against women in Iraqi Kurdistan. In Wenona Giles & Jennifer Hyndman (Eds.), *Sites of violence:*

*Gender and conflict zones* (pp. 108-33). Berkeley: University of California Press. ISBN 0-520-23072-8 and 0-520-23791-9 (pbk).

**Keywords:** patriarchy and the complex social organization of the Kurds; honor killing in times of peace; honor killing according to Mullah Mahmûdê Bayezîdî; the freedom of Kurdish women and killing as a means of disciplining; honor killing and the post-WWI nation states; Kurdish nationalism and honor killing; honor killing in the war zone and "zone of genocide" of Iraqi Kurdistan since 1961; the U.S.-led 1991 war against Iraq and the formation of the "safe haven" and the Regional Government of Kurdistan; statistics of assassinations and self-immolation of women; treating honor killing as national tradition; resistance to honor killing: eloping, its politics and political economy; the Kurdish poet Abdullah Goran's poem, "A Tombstone," Yilmaz Güney's film *Yol*; campaigns by Kurdish women's groups; demand for abolishing Iraq's personal status laws; legal reform by the Regional Government of Kurdistan.

**Morgan, David**. (2000). Honour killings in Iraqi Kurdistan. *Kurdistan Report, 30*, Winter, pp. 50-56. One photograph.

**Keywords:** conference organized by the Kurdish women Action Against Honour Killings campaign: held at Priory Community Centre, Acton, London; honour killings in Iraqi Kurdistan; legal action against honour killing: Munira Muftizadeh; Dr. Nazand Begikhani PUK and KDP ambivalent attitude toward political Islamic movement; Dr. Fuad Masum: member of the political bureau of the PUK; Dr. Hoshyar Zebari: Director of the International Relations bureau of the KDP; Dr. Nuri Talabani: Kurdish jurist and head of the Kurdish Organisation for Human Rights; Dr. Mahmud Osman: independent politician: destruction of the social infrastructure; in Turkey, Sanliurfa (close to the Syrian border) is known as the capital of honour killings as the practice has spread throughout the countries because of migration; perpetrators of these crimes do not face prosecution in many countries; in Turkey, perpetrators are charged with murder but claim extreme provocation in order to gain reduced sentences or impunity; Turkey can be held accountable for this due to its international obligations: ECHR, CEDAW, the Optional Protocol to CEDAW, the U.N. CRC, and the U.N. CAT; November 2000: U.N.'s adoption of a Draft Resolution on "Working towards the Elimination of Crimes against Women committed in the Name of Honour."

**Pervizat, Leylâ**. (2003). In the name of honor. Carnegie Council on Ethics and International Affairs, *Human Rights Dialogue*, Violence Against Women,

2(10), Fall, pp. 30-31. One photograph.

**Keywords:** Şemse Allak: victim of an honor killing in Mardin, Southeastern Turkey; stoned to death by male family members; spent seven months in a coma; buried by a large group of women activists who unconventionally performed Islamic burial rights; case received worldwide attention because stoning is rare in Turkey; violence against women in Turkey: honour killings, marital rape, female genital mutilation, nose cutting, bride price, forced marriages, polygamy, and forced virginity testing; failure of state to act to eradicate these problems; state legitimizing these problems by calling them "family problems" or "domestic situations"; public versus private divide; KA-MER: independent women's organization in Diyarbekir; first open meeting inviting representatives from the government, judiciary, media, police force health groups, the community, and other NGOs to discuss ways of eradicating honour killing; strategy of KA-MER: work both on the community level and with government officials to create awareness and eventually eradicate honor killings; honor killing as separate from religious traditions; failure of Turkish judiciary: justification of honour killings on the grounds of tradition, culture, and assault on manhood; citing honour as a mitigating factor or provocation in judgments; failure of human rights activists to see honor killing as a human rights issue, seeing it only as a women's issue and less serious than torture, freedom of expression and extrajudicial killings; patriarchy as an embedded structure; redefinition of the concept of honour; "cultural discourse" in order to educate on the community level as opposed to a human rights framework; males as victims of the concept of masculinity; use of mediation to solve conflicts of honour; human rights framework when dealing with government officials to achieve official recognition that honour killings are a form of extrajudicial execution.

**Pervizat, Leylâ**. (2004). In the name of honour. In Shahrzad Mojab & Nahla Abdo (Eds.), *Violence in the name of honour: Theoretical and political challenges* (pp. 137-41). Istanbul: İstanbul Bilgi University Press. ISBN 975-6857-98-6.

**Keywords:** the stoning of Şemse Allak in Mardin, Turkey; honour as a question of culture and tradition rather than religion; obstacles to the struggle against honour killing; limitations of the legal system, human rights activists, state actors, and society; honour killing and masculinity; honour killing as a means of preventing family and clan feuds; the need to redefine the concept of honour, to change society's discourse, and reform the judiciary.

**Salih, Mehabad**. (2001). Domestic violence, the rights of Kurdish women and Iraqi personal status law. *Kurdistan Report, 31*, Autumn, pp. 82-83.

**Keywords:** Iraqi personal status law; Sharia'; Hanifa School of Jurisprudence; divorce; polygamy; women and Islamic law; domestic violence; male legal advantages; women's organizations and female lawyers' attempts at having women's legal status changed; legal status of honour killing; maternity leave; Islamic parties' opposition to changes in the legal status of women; increase in domestic violence and honour killing; Jalal Talabani, leader of the PUK, makes honour killing illegal on April 2, 2000; penalty for polygamous marriage without a judge's consent is increased; rootedness of patriarchy in the home, the education system and the workplace; women's access to court; the growth of women's rights in Iraqi Kurdistan; the flourishing of Islamic fundamentalist groups due to the conflict between the PUK and the KDP.

**Stock, Anke**. (2002). "Honour" killings: A scourge of society. *KHRP Newsline, 20*, Winter, p. 12.

**Keywords:** stereotype that honour killings only happen only in very traditional Islamic societies; trial of Eren Keskin increased regional and international recognition of gender specific crimes committed against Kurdish women; Kurdish women are at particular risk of sexual violence perpetrated by the state in Turkey; honour killings: perpetrators usually male relatives; take place within the domestic sphere and more likely to be seen as "traditional" punishments; definition: Yasmeen Hasssan: "acts of murder in which a woman is killed for her actual or perceived immoral behaviour, which can include extramarital affairs, choosing her own marriage partner, demanding a divorce..."

**Yirmibesoglu, Vildan**. (2000). Sevda Gök: Killed for honor. In Pinar Ilkkaracan (Ed.), *Women and sexuality in Muslim societies* (pp. 381-91). Istanbul: Women For Women's Human Rights-New Ways.

**Keywords:** Sevda Gök: 16-year-old victim of an honor killing; murder by her maternal aunt's 14-year-old son, Mehmet; Sevda ran away from home; rumors that she had a boyfriend; at the hearing representatives from the Equality-Watch Committee, the Purple Roof (Women's Shelter Foundation) and the Gaziantep Women's Platform attended.

## 2. In the Diaspora
### a. Fadime Şahindal

**Agence France Presse**. (2002, January). Une Kurde de 26 ans victime d'un 'crime d'honneur' en Suède [26-year-old Kurd victim of "honour crime" in Sweden]. *Institut Kurde de Paris, Information and Liaison Bulletin, 202*, p. 67.

**Keywords:** murder of Fadime Şahindal by her father in Uppsala for committing a "crime of honor"; Fadime's 1988 court action against her father and brother; Fadime's campaign against honor killing.

**Älgamo, Kickis Åhré**. (2004). Confronting honour violence: The Swedish police at work. In Shahrzad Mojab & Nahla Abdo (Eds.), *Violence in the name of honour: Theoretical and political challenges* (pp. 203-10). Istanbul: İstanbul Bilgi University Press. ISBN 975-6857-98-6.

**Keywords:** the experience and assignments of a Swedish detective inspector related to honor crimes; the murder of Pela Atroshi, Swedish-Kurdish girl in Dahok, Iraq, in 1999; action taken against the perpetrators; the sheltering of Pela's sister.

**The Economist**. (2002). Immigrants in Sweden and Denmark: The worries and the welcomes. *The Economist*, originally appeared under the title "Help them, or keep them out?" *The Economist*, 31 January 2002.

**Keywords:** debate sparked by the murder of Fadime Sahindal about Sweden's ability to integrate immigrants; Denmark is having the same debate; each government has taken a different approach; Sweden, Social Democratic party: give more money to crisis centres and support groups for young women trying to avoid forced marriage and to leave violent partners; change the minimum age for marriage for all women to 18 as opposed to 15 for immigrants; Denmark, centre-right coalition: curb immigration; making it harder for foreigners to come to Denmark to join their families who are already there.

**Eldén, Åsa**. (2004). Life-and-death honour: Young women's violent stories about reputation, virginity, and honour in a Swedish context. In Shahrzad Mojab & Nahla Abdo (Eds.), *Violence in the name of honour: Theoretical and political challenges* (pp. 91-99). Istanbul: İstanbul Bilgi University Press. ISBN 975-6857-98-6.

**Keywords:** the Swedish debate on honour crimes after the murder of Fadime Şahindal; "a feminist comprehensive perspective" on honour crimes; analysis of Fadime's address to the Swedish parliament; the honour killing of Sara, a Swedish-Iraqi girl; divided femininity as "virgin" versus "whore"; the construction of a contrast between

145

"Swedish whore" and "Arab-Kurdish virgin"; violence as men's control of women's life and death.

**Gamel, Kim**. (2002). Swedes are shocked by slaying of Kurdish woman as her father faces a murder charge. *Turkish Daily News*, Foreign News, January, p. 3.

> **Keywords:** Rahmi Sahindal: father of Fadime Sahindal, faced preliminary charge of murder after he was accused of killing 26-year-old daughter for refusing to agree to an arranged marriage; killed her while she was visiting her sister in Uppsala, Sweden; before the murder, Fadime allegedly endured years of threats and harassment from her father; the author says that the murder "shocked Swedes who take great pride in a long tradition of democracy and tolerance"; Swedish press: Swedish headlines said, "Murdered by her own father"; a lot of space was given to the coverage of the murder in Sweden; flags flew at half staff in Uppsala; Fadime often spoke publicly about her family conflict and social problems facing immigrant women; Fadime said she would marry her Swedish boyfriend instead of returning to Turkey for an arranged marriage; in 1998, Rahmi Sahindal was fined and one of her brothers was put under supervision after a court found them guilty of harassing her; at the trial she testified that she was convinced that both her father and brother were capable of carrying out their death threat if she did not agree to an arranged marriage.

**Hello!** (2002). Victoria of Sweden distressed by murder of young Kurdish woman. *Hello!* February 6, two photographs.

> **Keywords:** Fadime Sahindal: 26 years old; shot for dating a boyfriend of her choice instead of the man chosen by her family; shot at point blank range in front of her mother and younger sister; family had come to Sweden from a village in Turkey 20 years before; her older sister had married according to her family's wishes; father confessed to the killing; told the police he did it in desperation because his daughter had shamed the family; secular memorial service in Uppsala attended by Crown Princess Victoria; coffin carried by female family members and friends.

**Helsingin Sanomat**. (2002). Kurds in Finland ponder implications of "honour killing" in Sweden. *Helsingin Sanomat, International Edition*, January 25. Foreign Section.

> **Keywords:** cousins of Fadime Sahindal, who live in Finland, react to her murder: killing was a surprise to her male cousin who says that he knows Fadime's father and brother very well; the other male cousin

met her brother in Sweden last week and everything seemed fine; speculation that her father has mental health problems; cousin refuses to believe that the only reason for the murder was her relationship with a Swedish man; says that another cousin who lives in Germany is married to a German; says that by speaking about her struggle in public, Fadime hurt her family and made public things that should be kept to the private sphere; the cousin has a Finnish wife; Fatma Yasa: answering calls at the Kurdistan Committee office in Helsinki, Finland about the murder of Sahindal; people do not believe the coverage of the murder in Finnish newspapers; past summer: story in Helsingin Sanomat about an 18-year-old Kurdish girl who left her family to go to a women's shelter after refusing to marry the man that was chosen for her; education and integration: Yasa says that those who are better educated usually adapt better.

**Helsingin Sanomat.** (2002). Murder trial of father of slain Kurdish woman begins in Sweden on Tuesday. *Helisngin Sanomat, International Edition*, March 12, Foreign Section. One photograph.

**Keywords:** trial of Rahmi Sahindal, father of Fadime Sahindal, begins in March in the district court of Uppsala, Sweden; observers see the trial as one of the most high-profile since the murder of the Prime Minister, Olof Palme; defendant confessed to killing his daughter; told police that his daughter had brought shame to the family by dating a Swedish man; sparked debate about the integration of immigrants in Sweden and whether or not it had succeeded or failed; in debate it has been noted that Swedes have also killed their children; Kurds and other immigrants feel that they have been unfairly singled out in the case; problems of Rahmi Sahindal to integrate: illiterate; failed driving test; author says that because he had grown up in a "patriarchal environment" Rahmi Sahindal found it humiliating to seek help for translation from his daughter; 1998: Fadime's father and brother convicted of threatening Fadime with death; killed her with a pistol at her sister's apartment in Uppsala; expressed no remorse according to the author; will probably get life sentence.

**Helsingin Sanomat.** (2004). Kurds in Finland fear racist reaction to Swedish honour killing. *Helsingin Sanomat.* January 24. One photograph.

**Keywords:** fear of Kurdish refugees in Finland of racist backlash after the murder of Fadime Sahindal in Uppsala, Sweden; fell out of favour with her family because she had "fallen in love" with a Swedish man and would not get an arranged marriage; Fadime Sahindal also made Swedish headlines when she filed charges against her father and brother for threats and assault; Kurds living in Finland called shelters in Helsinki because of fears of a backlash; Merja Hakala: head of the Helsinki Red Cross youth centre said that honour killings are unknown in Finland and was sure that Fadime Sahindal's murder was an isolated incident; said that this did not happen more frequently in immigrant families than in Finnish families; Hakala: says that perhaps more religious families are more susceptible to such crimes; dealt with a case in which two Kurdish girls were beaten by their father because of the boys they were seeing; an agreement was reached where the girls would go back home and live according to the wishes of their father until they were 18; Karwan Ahmand: a Kurdish man who has lived in Finland for 15 years; believed one reason for the murder of Sahindal was because she had spoken about the abuse in public and had humiliated her father so he had to defend his honour; also said that Kurds try to maintain their traditional way of life by sending their children to Turkey to be married at 17 or 18 years old.

**Hildebrandt, Johanne**. (2002). "Honour" killing in Sweden silences courageous voice on ethnic integration. January 3. *The Guardian Weekly*.

**Keywords:** Rahmi Sahindal: referred to by the author as an illiterate Kurdish farmer; parents discouraged Fadime to speak to Swedish children at school; when her father found out about her relationship with Patrik Lindesjo, a Swede, he beat them both up; father disowned her; Lindesjo's parents went to her family regardless and proposed for their son; they were turned down; according to the author, she single-handedly started a debate about integration and double standards for immigrants in Sweden; the government, after the murder, promised $170,000 to help girls in similar positions to Fadime; the minimum age for marriage for immigrants will be raised from 15 to 18, the age that applies to Swedish citizens.

**Kay, Jonathan**. (2002). Multiculturalism's latest victim. *National Post*, July 31, p. A16.

**Keywords:** life of Fadime Sahindal; failure of integration in Sweden of her family and father; clash of civilizations; honour killing as an Islamic and tribal cultural phenomenon; racism; failures of multiculturalism.

**Lyall, Sarah**. (2002). Lost in Sweden: A Kurdish daughter is sacrificed. *The New York Times*, July 23, A3. Four photographs.

**Keywords:** murder of Fadime Sahindal: has hardened Swedes' attitudes toward non-Nordic immigrants; unwillingness of Fadime's parents to adapt to Swedish culture; did not learn to speak Swedish; lived with Kurds from the same region in a community in Uppsala; author refers to the community as a clan; 1998 trial against her father and brother for threatening her with death received a lot of media attention and became the subject of a documentary; her brother, Mesud, referred to Fadime as a whore while on trial; after 1998 Fadime agreed not to speak publicly about what she had suffered; Songul, her sister, believes that the media sensationalized the story.

**Lytje, Maren.** (2002). When men kill women (G. Monrad Madsen, Trans.). *Northern Light,* Aalborg University, March.

**Keywords:** clash of civilizations, racism: debate sparked in Scandinavia about problems facing "ethnic women" who struggle between traditional values and asserting their rights in a "modern, democratic and globalized setting" after the death of Fadime Sahindal; clash between "tradition" and "modernity": supposedly fatal outcomes; killed because she had fallen in love with a Swedish man, her father and brother threatened to kill her because she had "stained the family's honour"; Fadime Sahindal exposed her story in the media and gave a speech to the Swedish Riksdag (Parliament); according to the author, Sahindal was the perfect example of the "integrated immigrant" because she was "opposing the traditional norms of her own culture and was trying to assert her democratically secured rights"; Mona Sahlin, the Swedish Minister of Integration, said that integration had failed; suggestion to raise the age limit for marriage of non-Swedish citizens; immigrant associations have been blamed for not doing their job; spokeswomen of ethnic women's networks in Denmark urged people not to cast honour killing as an integration or cultural problem, rather it should be cast as a problem of women's oppression and gender relations; Catarina Kinnvall: Swedish researcher argued that the reason why Fadime Sahindal was killed was because "women's bodies become battlefields in the clash between different patriarchal cultures, or in other words, women's bodies are prime symbols of political structures, be they traditional or modern"; according to the author, Fadime was killed because she was a woman not because she was Kurdish.

**Marklund, Liza.** (2002). OK, there are varying degrees of hell. *Expressen,* April 7, Editorial Page.

**Keywords:** murder of women; domestic violence; separation of honour killing from other murders of women; cultural relativism; racism; seeing the murder of Fadime Sahindal in the name of honour as a result of Kurdish culture as opposed to the fundamental patriarchal power structure in general as is the case in the murders of Swedish women; very little differences in the murder of Fadime Sahindal and the murder of other Swedish women; separation of "honour killings" or murdering one's daughter from the murder of one's wife.

**Reuters**. (2002). Swedes mourn Kurdish victim. *The Toronto Star*, February 5, A13. One photograph.

**Keywords:** Fadime Sahindal: 26-years-old; shot for dating a boyfriend of her choice instead of the man chosen by her family; shot at point blank range in front of her mother and younger sister; family had come to Sweden from a village in Turkey 20 years before; her older sister had married according to her family's wishes; father confessed to the killing; told the police he did it in desperation because his daughter had shamed the family; secular memorial service in Uppsala attended by Crown Princess Victoria; coffin carried by female family members and friends; wanted to be married in the Uppsala Cathedral where her memorial service was held; Kurdish immigrants close to the family said that Sahindal's father never felt comfortable in Sweden.

**Reuters**. (2002). Remembering tragic event. *Metro*, Toronto Edition. February 5, one photograph.

**Keywords:** memorial service for Fadime Sahindal in hometown of Uppsala, Sweden; female family members and friends carry the coffin; Crown Princess Victoria attended the service; 26 years old; shot point blank by her father for dating a boyfriend of her choice instead of the one chosen by her family.

**Soreklî, Shahîn**. (2002). To Fadime. *Kurdish Media: United Kurdish Voice*. February 11.

**Keywords:** honour killing of Fadime Şahindal in Sweden; arranged marriage; Kurdish girls in exile; poetry.

*See also* Poetry

**Truc, Olivier**. (2001). Le meurtre d'une jeune Kurde devise la Suède. *Liberation*, reprinted in *Institut Kurde de Paris, Information and Liaison Bulletin, 198*, January 2001, p. 25.

**Keywords:** honour killing; integration; sexuality.

**Williams, Carol J.** (2002). Price of Freedom, in Blood. March 7, *LA Times.*

**Keywords:** lack of reaction to complaints by Fadime Sahindal that her life was in danger: Swedish police gave her an alarm system when she complained of death threats; politicians told her to make peace with her parents; appeal on television interviews for aid in escaping her father; public versus private space: provokes sympathy among Swedes but not much willingness to get involved in a family matter; after her death, debate about immigrants in Sweden; author refers to Fadime as a "martyr among women who came to the liberal country from patriarchal cultures"; warning to the authorities about not integrating immigrant communities; refers to the Kurds as a clan and Uppsala, Sweden as the "clan stronghold"; lack of comprehensive statistics in Scandinavia to show the extent of honor killings; appear to be infrequent; cultural relativism: ignoring human rights abuses in certain communities because of cultural and religious considerations; Dilsa Demirbag-Sten: Kurdish woman from Turkey who came to Sweden when she was seven: accuses the authorities of arrogance because certain rights and freedoms afforded to Nordic residents, specifically gender equality and protection from forced marriage, are not extended to immigrants; Fadime's brother told authorities that honour killing is part of the Kurdish culture but most Kurds do not agree; Nalin Pekgul: Social Democratic legislator of Kurdish origin cautions against interpreting an act of criminal extremism as typical of fundamentalist immigrants; blames backwardness and illiteracy for creating an atmosphere in which honour killing is possible; Pekgul thought that Fadime's revealing her story in the media only enhanced the danger she was in and tried to intervene on her behalf; women's advocacy groups in Sweden: say that profound contradictions exist between Sweden's commitment to human rights and the tolerance of ethnic traditions; differences in laws for immigrants and Swedish citizens: legal age for marriage in immigrant families is 15 while for Swedish citizens it is 18; national campaign started to prevent forced marriage; Pela Atroshi: 19 year old shot in the head by her uncle on the orders of her father and brother because she refused to marry her cousin when she went to Iraqi Kurdistan; a few months earlier while in Sweden she had been scalded with boiling water; uncle received a one year sentence for the death in Iraq; in Sweden, her father, uncle, and brother were sentenced to 15 years or higher upon their return to Sweden; Sara Mohammad: Iraqi Kurd, changed her name to avoid creating problems for her family when she immigrated to Sweden; says that there are 30-40 women hiding from male relatives in Sweden who have threatened to kill them; founded an organization called Never Forget Pela; accuses Swedes of misguided liberalism, tolerance for practices in immigrant communities that would never be allowed amongst Swedish citizens; lack of respect on the part of Swedish government for people and their human rights in immigrant communities; Mohammad to rename her organization, "Never Forget Pela and Fadime"; holding a memorial gathering on International Women's Day to raise awareness about the dangers facing immigrant women; sent a list of demands for legislative change to Mona Sahlin, minister of Integration; demands include: raising the minimum age for marriage to 18 years old for all women; advisory sessions for new immigrants about cultural differences in gender relations; prohibition of headscarves for women under 16 years old; equal opportunity in all aspects of education including sex education and co-educational sports and field trips.

## b. Heşo/Heshu Yones

**Allen, Vanessa and Pat Clarke**. (2003). Killed by her dad because she snubbed Muslim faith. *The Advertiser*, October 1.

**Keywords:** Abdalla Yones: described as a strict Muslim father; slit his daughter's throat, Heshu Yones, because she was too Westernized and was in a sexual relationship with a non-Muslim; following the murder, Abdalla Younes attempted suicide by slitting his throat and jumping off a third-floor balcony; sentenced to life in prison; first person in Britain to plead guilty to murder in an "honour killing" case; Heshu was beaten for months before the attack; Heshu Yones planned to run away and wrote a letter to her father that mentioned the previous months' beatings; while in hospital recovering from the attempted suicide, Abdalla said that his daughter was murdered by Al-Qaida who broke into his house and who had thrown him off the balcony; asked to be sentenced to death after admitting to the crime; according to this article, Heshu feared that her father might arrange a marriage for her; the judge, Neil Denison described the story as "arising out of irreconcilable cultural differences between traditional Kurdish values and the values of western society"; before the murder, Abdalla Yones received a letter written in Kurdish calling his daughter a slut and saying that she was sleeping with her boyfriend every day, it had distressed him; according to Scotland Yard, there have been 12 honour killings in the past year in Britain in the Islamic, Sikh, and Christian communities.

**Allison, Rebecca**. (2003). Where's the honour in this? *The Guardian*. Reprinted under the title "Where's the honor in Britain's honor killings?" *Taipei Times*, 9 October 2003, p. 9.

**Keywords:** Heshu Yones: 16-year-old student from West London; murdered by her father, Abdalla Yones: slit her throat, stabbed her 11 times because of fears that she was becoming too "Westernized" and may have been in a relationship with a Lebanese Christian student; following the murder, Abdalla Yones attempted suicide; serving a life sentence for the murder; honour killings in other communities: according to Scotland Yard there have been 12 honour killings in the past year in Britain in the Islamic, Sikh, and Christian communities; Metropolitan police: task force to increase understanding and awareness of honour crimes; community silence: police say it is hard to investigate these crimes because the community remains silent on the issue; leading up to the murder, Yones was suffering from physical abuse but it was not reported; members of the Kurdish community allegedly tried to help Abdalla Yones to cover up the crime; honour as an excuse for murder and abuse; cultural relativism as a form of racism and discrimination.

**The Associated Press.** (2003). Kurdish man in London gets life in prison for "honor killing" daughter. *The Salt Lake Tribune.* October 5, one photograph.

**Keywords:** Abdalla Younes (Yones): received life sentence in London for killing his daughter, Heshu Younes (Yones); slit her throat, stabbed her 11 times because of fears that she was becoming too "Westernized" and may have been in a relationship with a Lebanese Christian student; Heshu Yones planned to run away: in a letter addressed to her father she referred to the beatings that had previously been inflicted on her; the judge, Neil Denison, described the story as, "arising out of irreconcilable cultural differences between traditional Kurdish values and the values of western society"; according to Scotland Yard, there have been 12 honour killings in the past year in Britain.

**Asthana, Anushka and Ushma Mistry.** (2003). For families that fear dishonour, there is only one remedy...murder. *The Observer,* October 5.

**Keywords:** Abdalla Yones sentenced to life imprisonment for murdering his daughter, 16-year-old Heshu Yones; authors say that the perpetrator appeared to be calm and without remorse; stabbed Heshu 11 times after receiving an anonymous letter in Kurdish that said that his daughter was behaving like a slut and that she was sleeping with her boyfriend on a daily basis; multiple stab wounds on her back, breast, and chest; marks on her hands and arms showed that she had struggled to defend herself; after the murder, Abdalla Yones attempted suicide by slitting his throat and jumping off a building; Abdalla asked to be executed; before the trial, Yones claimed that his daughter was killed by al-Qaida and they had tried to kill him; people were afraid to come forward; the Independent Women's Organization in Kurdistan reported that since 1992 up to 9,000 women had been killed or had committed suicide because of "shaming" the family.

**Clough, Sue**. (2003). British migrant jailed for killing "wilful" daughter. *The Age*, October 1. Originally appeared in *The Telegraph*, London.

**Keywords:** Abdalla Younes (Yones): received life sentence in London for killing his daughter, Heshu Younes (Yones); slit her throat, stabbed her 11 times because of fears that she was becoming too "Westernized" and may have been in a relationship with a Lebanese Christian student; Heshu Yones planned to run away: in a letter addressed to her father she referred to the beatings that had previously been inflicted on her; the judge, Neil Denison, described the story as, "arising out of irreconcilable cultural differences between traditional Kurdish values and the values of western society"; three days before the murder Abdalla Yones received a letter in Kurdish saying that Heshu was behaving like a prostitute; on a trip to Iraqi Kurdistan, Heshu said she thought that her father wanted to arrange a marriage for her and might have discovered that she had a boyfriend and was not a virgin; the night of the murder, Heshu's mother had gone out and left her with her father; police intend to pursue an investigation into attempts to pervert the course of justice by some of Abdalla's friends who helped him cover up the murder.

**Daily Record**. (2003). Moslem cut daughter's throat "out of honour." *Daily Record*, September 30.

**Keywords:** Abdalla Yones: referred to as a "strict Moslem"; received life sentence in London for killing his daughter, Heshu Younes (Yones); slit her throat, stabbed her 17 times because of fears that she was becoming too "Westernized" and may have been in a relationship with a Lebanese Christian student; Heshu Yones planned to run away: in a letter addressed to her father she referred to the beatings that had previously been inflicted on her; during the trial Abdalla Yones requested the death penalty; Abdalla Yones attempted suicide after the murder by cutting his throat and throwing himself off a third floor balcony; in hospital for several months to recover from the attempted suicide; claimed Islamic extremists had broken in to their flat and murdered Heshu.

**Dodd, Vikram.** (2003). Kurd who slit daughter's throat in "honour killing" is jailed for life. *The Guardian*, September 30.

**Keywords:** Abdalla Younes (Yones): received life sentence in London for killing his daughter, Heshu Younes (Yones); slit her throat, stabbed her 17 times because of fears that she was becoming to "westernized" and may have been in a relationship with a Lebanese Christian student, Samnizam Elkhouri; Heshu Yones planned to run away: in a letter addressed to her father she referred to the beatings that had previously been inflicted on her; during the trial Abdalla Yones requested the death penalty; Abdalla Yones called a strict Muslim in the article; problems adapting to the culture in London; before the murder Abdalla Yones received a letter written in Kurdish calling his daughter a slut; according to Scotland Yard there have been 12 honour killings in the past year in Britain; Sawsan Salim, coordinator of the Kurdistan Refugees Women's Organization said that the Kurdish community condemned such killings; Abdalla Yones attempted suicide after the murder but cutting her through and throwing himself off a third floor balcony; in hospital for several months to recover from the attempted suicide; claimed Al-Qaida had broken in to their flat and murdered Heshu; the judge, Neil Denison described the story as, "arising out of irreconcilable cultural differences"; while on holiday in Iraqi Kurdistan, Abdalla Yones found out that his daughter had a boyfriend and was not a virgin; he pulled a gun on her and threatened to kill her; when she returned home she made plans to run away.

**The Guardian.** (2003). Father kills child for being too westernized. Reprinted in *Taipei Times*, October 1, p. 7. Two photographs.

**Keywords:** Abdalla Younes (Yones): received life sentence in London for killing his daughter, Heshu Younes (Yones); slit her throat, stabbed her 17 times because of fears that she was becoming too "Westernized" and may have been in a relationship with a Lebanese Christian student; Heshu Yones planned to run away: in a letter addressed to her father she referred to the beatings that had previously been inflicted on her; during the trial Abdalla Yones requested the death penalty; Abdalla Yones attempted suicide after the murder by cutting his throat and throwing himself off a third floor balcony; in hospital for several months to recover from the attempted suicide; claimed Al-Qaida had broken in to their flat and murdered Heshu; Abdalla Yones called a strict Muslim in the article; problems adapting to the culture in London; the judge, Neil Denison, described the story as, "arising out of irreconcilable cultural differences between traditional Kurdish values and the values of western society"; before the murder, Abdalla Yones received a letter written in Kurdish calling his daughter a slut and saying that she was sleeping with her boyfriend every day; it had distressed him; according to Scotland Yard, there have been 12 honour killings in the past year in Britain in the Islamic, Sikh, and Christian communities.

**Gupta, Rahila**. (2003). A veil drawn over brutal crimes. *The Guardian*, October 3.

**Keywords:** "focus on 'honour killing' as a special case outside the boundaries of domestic violence risks promoting a racist agenda"; murder being exoticized; clash of civilizations; danger of seeing minority women's struggles as being inspired by British values as opposed to a sense of injustice; killing of women to exert control is not unique to any one class, community, race, or religion; The Metropolitan Police says that there were 12 honour killings in the past year in the Sikh, Christian, and Muslim communities; more that 100 women are killed by their partners in England and Wales every year; cultural relativism; "mature multiculturalism."

**The Job**. (2003). Drive to prevent more honour killings. *The Job*, *36*(914), October 10.

**Keywords:** Heshu Yones' honour killing impetus towards setting up a strategic working group to find ways to prevent honour killings; Abdalla Yones sentenced to life imprisonment; originally pleaded that Al-Qaida broke into his house, murdered his daughter and attacked him; memo sent to all boroughs in January giving advice about how to identify and deal with potential victims of honour crimes.

**Judd, Terri**. (2003). Execute me, pleads Muslim who killed his daughter over her Western lifestyle. *The Independent*, September 30.

**Keywords:** Abdalla Younes (Yones): received life sentence in London for killing his daughter, Heshu Younes (Yones); slit her throat, stabbed her 17 times because of fears that she was becoming too "Westernized" and may have been in a relationship with a Lebanese Christian student, Samnizam Elkhouri; Heshu Yones planned to run away: in a letter addressed to her father she referred to the beatings that had previously been inflicted on her; during the trial, Abdalla Yones requested the death penalty; Abdalla Yones called a strict Muslim in the article; problems adapting to the culture in London; before the murder, Abdalla Yones received a letter written in Kurdish calling his daughter a slut; according to Scotland Yard, there have been 12 honour killings in the past year in Britain; Sawsan Salim, coordinator of the Kurdistan Refugees Women's Organization said that the Kurdish community condemned such killings; Abdalla Yones attempted suicide after the murder by cutting his throat and throwing himself off a third floor balcony; in hospital for several months to recover from the attempted suicide; claimed Al-Qaida had broken in to their flat and murdered Heshu; the judge, Neil Denison, described the story as, "arising out of irreconcilable cultural differences"; while on holiday in Iraqi Kurdistan, Abdalla Yones found out that his daughter had a boyfriend and was not a virgin; he pulled a gun on her and threatened to kill her; when she returned home she made plans to run away.

**Keating, Matt**. (2003). What they said about…Heshu Yones. *The Guardian*, October 2.

> **Keywords:** Yasmin Alibhai-Brown: writer for the *Daily Mail*; said that she understood the panic that parents from certain communities feel from the West's over-sexualized society but no excuse for murder; Abdalla Yones: sentenced to life for the murder of his 16 year old daughter, Heshu; first time in British legal history that a plea of honour killing had been entered; according to Scotland Yard there have been 12 honour killings in the past year in Britain; practice does not have to do with religion; condemned by the Muslim community says writer from *Daily Express*, Hilary Freeman; increase in fanaticism in Britain and France as opposed to Turkey or Iran says Amir Taheri in the *Times*; cultural relativism.

**Kurdish Human Rights Project**. (2003). "Honour killing" father jailed for life. *KHRP Newsline, 24*, Winter, p. 3.

> **Keywords:** Abdalla Younes (Yones): received life sentence in London for killing his daughter, Heshu Younes (Yones); slit her throat, stabbed her 17 times because of fears that she was becoming too "Westernized" and may have been in a relationship with a Lebanese Christian student; marks on the body indicate that she had desperately tried to prevent the attack; following the murder Abdalla Younes attempted suicide and was admitted to the hospital for several months; during the trial he requested the death penalty; honour killings in other communities: according to Scotland Yard, there have been 12 honour killings in the past year in Britain in the Islamic, Sikh, and Christian communities.

**McGowan, Patrick**. (2003). Life for father who cut girl's throat. *Evening Standard*, September 29.

**Keywords:** Abdalla Younes (Yones): received life sentence in London for killing his daughter, Heshu Younes (Yones); slit her throat, multiple stab wounds, wounds to her back, breasts, and chest; fears that she was becoming too "Westernized" and may have been in a relationship with a Lebanese Christian student; marks on the body indicate that she had desperately tried to prevent the attack; following the murder Abdalla Younes attempted suicide and was admitted to the hospital for several months; during the trial he requested the death penalty; Abdalla described as Muslim who wanted his daughter to live a strict Muslim lifestyle.

**Mistry, Ushma**. (2003). Exclusive: My tears for tragic Heshu. *Ealing Times*. Reprinted under the title "Tears for tragic 'honour killin' victim Heshu," *Wanstead Woodford Guardian*, October 2, 2003.

**Keywords:** 20-year-old friend of Heshu Yones speaks about her honour killing; contacted the newspaper via email; murdered by her father, Abdalla Yones; friend thought that her family was protecting her about how Heshu had really been killed; Abdalla jailed for life after pleading guilty to killing his daughter; stabbed her more than 11 times and slit her throat; friend was told that a group of men had broken into the apartment and killed Heshu and tried to kill her father and she did not believe this; Abdalla Yones killed his daughter because she was in a relationship with a Lebanese man and lived a Western lifestyle; friend knew Heshu from Iraq; she believed that the story was a cover-up because she "knew what he [her father] was like."

**The Observer**. (2004). Death before dishonour. *The Observer*, November 21.

**Keywords:** Abdalla Yones: killed his daughter, Heshu Yones by stabbing her 11 times and then slitting her throat; two days earlier he received an anonymous letter at the south London offices of the PUK saying that the community knew that she had a boyfriend and that she was behaving like a prostitute; this article says that he worked there as a volunteer (while others say that it was Heshu who worked there); after being sentenced to life imprisonment, Abdalla Yones said that he was forced to kill Heshu Yones; the judge in the case said the murder arose from irreconcilable cultural differences: "cultural superiority"; most effective campaigners against honour killings are South Asian, Middle Eastern and Kurdish women; honour killings have a lot in common with other domestic violence; honour killing has nothing to do with Islam and is a result of misinterpretations; following Heshu Yones' murder, Commander Baker launched an initiative inside the Metropolitan Police to take honour killings more seriously; honour killing as a matter of human rights.

**Priestley, Mike**. (2003). Culture change Muslims must learn to accept. *Telegraph and Argus*, October 6.

**Keywords:** clash of cultures/civilizations: seen as reason for the honour killing of Heshu Yones according to Mike Priestly; reaction of people outside of the Muslim community: most condemn the crime; reaction of Muslim people: some have condemned the crime; Abdalla Yones murdered his daughter because of her relationship with a Lebanese man he believed to be Christian; the author, Priestly, claims that without condoning the attack it is possible to understand it because of the pain that can be caused to parents if their children select a partner that they feel is unsuitable; the difference between "Western" fathers and "Muslim" fathers is that Western fathers will not use physical violence to show their disapproval.

**Rao, H. S.** (2003). Man jailed for honour killing. *Hindustan Times*, Chandigarh Edition, World Section, September 30, p. 10. One photograph.

**Keywords:** Abdalla Yones: 47-year-old man sentenced to life in jail for the honour killing of his 16-year-old daughter, Heshu Yones; the article says that she had decided to marry a Lebanese Christian; Scotland Yard described the killing as having been brought about by a "clash of cultures" between Yones—a refugee from Iraqi Kurdistan, where such murders are common—and his Westernized daughter; Heshu Yones began a sexual relationship with the Lebanese Christian student; before the murder, Abdalla Yones received a letter written in Kurdish saying that his daughter was "behaving like a prostitute"; letter was sent to the south London offices of PUK, where Heshu Yones was doing volunteer work; Abdalla Yones asked the judge to sentence him to death after the murder.

**Reuters**. (2003). "Westernised," so dad kills girl. *Reuters*, September 30.

**Keywords:** Abdalla Yones: described as a Muslim immigrant; life imprisonment for the honour killing of Heshu Yones, his 16-year-old daughter for being "Westernized" and for having a Lebanese Christian boyfriend, Samanizam Elkouri (Elkhouri); throat cut, wounds to her back, breasts, and chest according to *The Evening Standard*; injuries on her hands and arms show that she had tried to defend herself; after the murder, Abdalla Yones jumped from the balcony and spent four months in hospital; the prosecutor John McGuinness said that Abdalla Yones was a "strict Muslim"; Detective Inspector Bren Hyatt said that Yones attempted to diminish his responsibility in the murder by claiming psychiatric problems to extreme provocation; claimed initially that Al-Qaida broke into his home, killed his daughter and tried to kill him; police found a runaway letter written by Heshu in which she referred to beatings by her father prior to the murder.

**Smith, Rebecca**. (2003). Heshu's boyfriend tells of loss. *Evening Standard*, September 30.

Keywords: Heshu Yones stabbed to death by her father, Abdalla Yones, after he found out that she was not a virgin; Nizam (Samanizam) Elkhouri, 20 years old; Heshu Yones' boyfriend; went to great lengths to hide their relationship; allegedly spoke to Heshu's brother who said he was okay with their relationship; Nizam is Muslim contrary to court and many news reports; his parents did not have a problem with the relationship.

**Sunday Herald**. (2003). No honour for anyone in avoidable killings. *Sunday Herald*, October 19.

Keywords: high-profile honour killings in the UK: Heshu Yones: 16-year-old girl knifed to death by her father, Abdalla; sentenced to life imprisonment; described in the article as a strict Kurdish Muslim who thought his daughter had become too Westernized and was upset about her relationship with a Lebanese Christian; she planned to run away from home.

**Taheri, Amir**. (2003). Don't blame Islam for the lowly status of women. *The Times of London*, October 1.

Keywords: author believes question of "What's wrong with Islam?" will be raised by the murder of Heshu Yones.

**The Telegraph**. (2003). Culture clash led to "honour killing" of teen daughter. *The Telegraph*, September 30.

Keywords: Abdalla Yones: described as a Muslim immigrant; life imprisonment for the honour killing of Heshu Yones, his 16-year-old daughter for being "Westernized" and for having a Lebanese Christian boyfriend; the night of the murder, Heshu's mother went out with her brother and left her alone with her father; Abdalla Yones stabbed Heshu 11 times and slit her throat; before the murder, Abdalla Yones received a letter written in Kurdish saying that his daughter was "behaving like a prostitute"; letter was sent to the south London offices of PUK, where Heshu Yones was doing volunteer work; Abdalla Yones asked the judge to sentence him to death after the murder; he attempted suicide by slitting his own throat and jumping of the third floor balcony; spent four months in hospital; claimed initially that Heshu was murdered by Islamic extremists; also claimed psychological damage at the hands of Saddam Hussein and being the victim of a chemical attack; police found a runaway letter written by Heshu in which she referred to beatings by her father prior to the murder.

**The Western Mail**. (2003). Strict father jailed for killing daughter. *The Western Mail*, September 30.

> **Keywords:** Abdalla Yones: referred to as a "strict Muslim" murdered his daughter, 16-year-old Heshu Yones because she was becoming too Westernized; Heshu beaten for months before the honour killing and planned to run away from home; begged her father to leave her alone; stabbed to death 11 times and bled to death because her throat was cut; Abdalla Yones tried to kill himself after the murder by cutting his throat and jumping 25 feet from a third floor balcony; while in hospital claimed that the murder had been carried out by Al-Qaida; first person in Britain to plead guilty to honour killing; asked the judge to sentence him to death; Heshu left behind a runaway letter referring to beatings that had been carried out before the murder; Neil Denison described the story as, "arising out of irreconcilable cultural differences between traditional Kurdish values and the values of western society."

## C. State Violence

**Boland, Vincent**. (2005). Turkey launches probe into police break-up of rally. *Financial Times*, reprinted in *Institut Kurde de Paris, Information and Liaison Bulletin, 240*, March 2005, p. 19. One photograph.

> **Keywords:** riot police brutalized marchers in the March 8th International Women's Day march in Turkey; the European Union was "shocked" by the use of force; the Turkish foreign minister, Abdullah Gul, ordered an inquiry into the event; the march was unauthorized and a legal one had taken place on Saturday.

**Hilton, Isabel**. (2002). Threatened by their protectors: Turkey's record in Kurdistan is a grim warning to Afghan women. *KHRP Newsline, 18*, Summer, p. 3.

> **Keywords:** the impact of Turkey's record of rape and sexual violence perpetrated by State officials and the lack of punishment for such crimes on Afghan women if Turkey leads the command of the 18-nation U.N. security force in Afghanistan; conclusion based on the

trial of the five women charged for participating and organizing a congress on sexual violence perpetrated by the state of Turkey in June 2000; charged specifically for mentioning the disproportionate amount of sexual violence and rape of Kurdish women; rape as a nationalist tool for destruction of a rival ethnic group; November 2001: conference to mark the International Day Against Violence Against Women; Eren Keskin: lawyer and co-found of the project, *Legal Aid for Women Raped or Sexually Assaulted by State Security Forces*, charged with disseminating "separatist propaganda."

**Kurdish Human Rights Project**. (2001). State violence against women in Turkey and attacks on human rights defenders of victims of sexual violence in custody: A Kurdish Human Rights Project trial observation report. London: Kurdish Human Rights Project. ISBN 1900175 41 X. Written by Margaret Owen with assistance from Tina Devadasan. Foreword by Kerim Yildiz (pp. 1-2), introduction by Margaret Owen (pp. 3-4), text (pp. 5-30), annexes (16 unnumbered pages), three black and white photographs (pp. 13, 14, 29), December.

**Keywords:** systematic sexual violence perpetrated by state officials against women in custody; Congress of 10-11 June 2000, entitled "Against Sexual Violence in Custody"; Legal Aid Project for Women Raped or Sexually Assaulted by State Security Forces; Fatma Karakas, lawyer and founder of the Legal Aid Project; Kamile Cigci, victim of a brutal rape; Fatma Kara, Nahide Kilici, and Zeynep Ovayolu, organizers of the Congress; 1982 Constitution of Turkey; Eren Keskin, defence lawyer in the trial of 19 Congress participants; expelling of Armenians and Greeks from Anatolia; PKK; European Court of Human Rights; rape; sexual harassment; virginity testing; difficulty in proving rape; differences in sentences for the rape of a virgin as opposed to the rape of a non-virgin; honour killings; shame and stigma attached to rape; sexual torture in police custody; post-traumatic stress disorder; tortured three year old child forced to sexually abuse his mother; Asiye Zeybek Guzel, a woman raped in prison who wrote a book entitled İşkencede bir Tecavüz Öyküsü (A Story of Rape Under Torture); Fatma Deniz Polattaş, a women who was allegedly raped in detention at Iskenderun Police Headquarters, was forced under torture to confess to supporting the PKK and who has since been sentenced to a long prison term; GÖÇ-DER, a grass-roots organization which publicises the plight of migrants from Eastern Turkey who come to Istanbul; position of Kurdish migrants in Istanbul; poverty; Kurdish girls exploited as cheap labour in garment sweatshops; destruction of homes in the Southeast; the Peace Mothers Initiative; Peace Train; Saturday Mothers of Istanbul; the "peace mothers" who went to Diyarbakir, then on to Northern Iraq in order to talk to the Kurdish factions still fighting after the cease fire and who, upon returning to Turkey were arrested and sexually harassed whilst detained; village guard system; Dicli Women's Cultural and Arts Centre; high level of depression and suicide among Kurdish women; Women's Rights Enforcement Centre in Istanbul; CEDAW; Beijing Platform for Action; domestic violence; the unwillingness of Kurdish women to complain about domestic abuse to the Turkish police; IHD; Fatma Tokmak, a woman whose two-year-old son, Azat, was tortured in front of her in order to have her confess to supporting the PKK; Professor Fincanci, head of the Forensic Medicine Institute at Istanbul Medical Faculty Hospital, whose findings, in almost all cases, have upheld victims' testimonies, and against whom the Governor of Istanbul lodged a formal complaint to the government; Dr. Ufuk Sezgin, a psychologist working in the trauma faculty of Çapa University; the closing of the only women's shelter in Istanbul due to lack of funds; KA-MER.

**Kurdish Human Rights Project**. (2003). *Trial observation report. The state and sexual violence: Turkish court silences female advocate*. London: KHRP and Bar Human Rights Committee of England and Wales. ISBN 1900175 56 8. Report written by Hugo Norton-Taylor, Kerim Yildiz (Ed.). Table of contents, foreword by Kerim Yildiz and Mark Muller (p. 1), text (pp. 2-17), appendix A, B, and C (CEDAW, p. 23), January.

> **Keywords:** the indictment of Eren Keskin, advocate, Chair of the Istanbul branch of the Human Rights Association and founder of LAPASHRC; charged with inciting "to hatred or hostility on the basis of a distinction between social classes, races, religions, denominations or regions" and insulting the military; Keskin had accused the Turkish army of raping women and sexual harassment; the LAPASHRC cited 157 applications against the government of which 119 were Kurdish women; political interference in the courts.

**Kurdish Human Rights Project**. (2003, December). *Trial observation report. Turkey's shame: Sexual violence without redress–The plight of Kurdish women*. London: KHRP. ISBN 1900175 69 X. Report written by Margaret Owen, Kerim Yildiz, & Suzanne Dowse (Eds.). Table of contents (pp. 5-6), postscript (p. 7), foreword by Kerim Yildiz (p. 9), text (pp. 11-39), appendix A to H (pp. 41) references (pp. 61-63).

> **Keywords:** follow up of KHRP report of 2001 (see Kurdish Human Rights Project); on state violence against women in Turkey; police and army continue to use sexual torture and rape against Kurdish women

in spite of legal and political reforms of 2002.

*See also* Genocide, Gendercide, War Crimes and Crimes Against Humanity

**Oberlé, Thierry**. (2005). Les rates turcs de la marche vers la démocratie. *Le Figaro, 8* reprinted in *Institut Kurde de Paris, Information and Liaison Bulletin, 240,* March 2005, pp. 13, 1 photograph.

**Keywords:** riot police brutalized marchers in the March 8th International Women's Day march in Turkey; the European Union was "shocked" by the use of force; the Turkish foreign minister, Abdullah Gul, ordered an inquiry into the event.

**School of Oriental and African Studies**. (2001). DFID round table to explore issues on violence against women in Iraqi Kurdistan. *School of Oriental and African Studies, University of London*, April 10.

**Keywords:** Iraqi Personal Status Law: derived from the principles of Sharia and based on the Hanifa school of jurisprudence; effects of Islamic law on women; patriarchal interpretation of the law; since 1959 the passing of a few amendments to improve women's position vis-à-vis the law but only so as not to conflict with Islam and Sharia; administration of Kurdish and Central governments: women exposed to domestic violence and deprived from protection that is laid out in various articles of Iraqi law; Second Amendment No. 12 of 1978: most significant reform: broadened the circumstances in which women were able to sue for judicial divorce; result of economic development in the 1970s which required women to play a role in the economic life of Iraq; no article exists that mentions or regulates domestic violence by name; 1991 Kurdish uprising: raised expectations amongst Kurdish women; proposal introduced to parliament by women's organizations to reform Iraqi laws: proposal neglected and rejected completely by MPs representing Islamic parties; victims of domestic violence increased and "honour killings" grew in number post-1991; 2 April 2000: under pressure from women's campaigns, Jalal Talabani passed an order prohibiting the killing or harming of women by their male relatives on the pretext of honour and punishment for the crime would be the same as for manslaughter; also the penalty for polygamy without a judge's permission was increased from one year imprisonment and 100 Iraqi dinar to three years and 10,000 Iraqi dinar; discussion between various political parties is continuing about the polygamy amendment; majority of Kurdish women ignorant of their rights; illiteracy amongst women in villages and small towns; suicide as a means of escaping domestic violence as opposed to going to court; male legislature: majority of judges are male; lack of financial resources to pay legal fees; need for a legal advice centre run by women who are trained as paralegals; establishment of women's shelters in Iraqi Kurdistan: problems and challenges facing their establishment; concept of honour in Kurdish culture; violence against women as officially invisible: public versus private divide; increase in violence against women in Iraqi Kurdistan in the last 10 years due to political and economic problems; the reintroduction of obsolete traditions such as the exchange of girl-brides between families, ransoming of women in blood feuds, increase in the practice of female genital mutilation, and honour killings; compromising with Islamic groups; impact of the destruction of Kurdish villages under the Ba'athist Regime; the abuse of Kurdish women at the hands of Iraqi soldiers; smuggling of women across borders into prostitution; prostitution in order to support families; murder of prostitutes; Islamic groups as a means to fill the social vacuum left by the destruction of the Kurdish social infrastructure; the change from Kurdish to Islamic dress in areas controlled by Islamic groups; Kurdish poetry and music: no restrictions regarding discussing love and the female body; Kurdish poetry as the most erotic in the Middle-East; socio-economic reasons for the rise in honour killings; arranged marriages; low standard of education; desperation of war-widows: prevalence of prostitution; the encouragement of the central government (Baghdad) for male relatives to murder their female relatives if they are involved in prostitution; the killer is only sentenced to three months in prison (new laws); cutting of the noses of women in order to deform their faces as a form of punishment; honour killing in the Kurdish diaspora in Europe; forms of domestic violence in Iraqi Kurdistan: psychological abuse, verbal abuse, jeering and stone throwing, sexual harassment in the workplace, explosion of beauty salons by Islamist groups, female genital mutilation; rise in suicide rates; women as enforcers of the patriarchal structure: abuse at the hands of female in-laws; self-immolation as a means of escape from violence; neglect of Anfal widows by local authorities and NGOs: these women still have no legal status; neglect of female ex-prisoners: imprisoned by the Iraqi authorities for being involved in Kurdish political activities themselves or because one of their family members was; suffered physical, psychological, and sexual torture; many had children after being raped in prison; following their release many committed suicide because they felt there was no place for them in Kurdish society; exploitation of women for a nationalist cause; male ex-prisoners treated as heroes; shelter (*Panahgahe Aram*, peaceful shelter): project initiated in 1999;

women's organizations asked Jalal Talabani for help and received it; since it began, 35 women have been referred to the shelter by the police, the Security Head Quarter and Women's organizations.

**Schubert, Brigitte.** (1996). Kurdische Frauen: Leben und Widerstehen im Krieg [Kurdish women: Living and resisting war]. *Wir Frauen,* Düsseldorf, *3,* pp. 12-14. Z G 20.

**Keywords:** Turkey; state violence; Kurdish women; Kurdistan; violence against women; female guerrillas; Frauenfriedenskonferenz April 1996.

**Serpil.** (1991). Kurdische Frauen: Die Leidtragenden [Kurdish women: Those who suffer]. *Jiyan - Kurdische Frauenzeitschrift,* March, pp. 8-9.

**Keywords:** massacres; racism in Turkey; poison gas in Iraq; state terror; illiteracy among Kurdish women in Turkey; women and the division of labour in Turkish Kurdistan; farming; domestic violence; honor system; torture of women; psychological effects of torture; rape of women as a means of pressuring men to talk; Women's Congress in Istanbul; deaths of women in detention; deportation; secret police; Kurdish women in western Turkey; assimilation; Kurdish women in Germany; generational conflicts between mother and daughter; psychosomatic illnesses among Kurdish women in exile; sexism in German immigration policies; KOMJIN.

**Turkish Daily News.** (1996). NGO's protest against police violence. *Turkish Daily News,* reprinted in *Institut Kurde de Paris, Information and Liaison Bulletin, 134-135,* May/June 1996, p. 141.

**Keywords:** Habitat II; Saturday Mothers; Meryem Göktepe; Hasene Turkoğlu; civil servants' demonstration; KESK; ÖDP; HADEP.

## D. Suicide

**The Economist.** (2005). A woman's place: The theory and the practice. In looking to Europe: A survey of Turkey, *The Economist,* reprinted in *Institut Kurde de Paris, Information and Liaison Bulletin, 240,* March 2005, p. 63.

**Keywords:** Aytekin Sir: professor at Dicle University in Diyarbekir; says that when families move into cities from Eastern Anatolia, suicide rates increase amongst women between the ages of 15-25; he also says that many families claim that girls commit suicide to cover up an honour killing.

**KIC/KSC Publications.** (1992). Virginity test leads to two teenage suicides.

*Kurdish women: The struggle for national liberation and women's rights.* London: KIC/KSC Publications, October, p. 37.

Keywords: after two girls went on a picnic, the principal of their religious training school in Simav forced them to undergo virginity testing; when the test came out negative, the principal made them redo it at a larger hospital; in reaction the girls attempted suicide and one of them died.

**Kurdistan Report**. (1992). Virginity test led two teenage girls to commit suicide. *Kurdistan Report, 10*, July, p. 20.

Keywords: after two girls went on a picnic, the principal of their religious training school in Simav forced them to undergo virginity testing; when the test came out negative, the principal made them redo it at a larger hospital; in reaction the girls attempted suicide and one of them died; in a similar incident, another girl, Ula, killed herself.

**Frantz, Douglas**. (2000). In Turkey's Southeast, suicide rates for women soar. *International Herald Tribune,* reprinted in *Institut Kurde de Paris, Information and Liaison Bulletin, 188,* November 2000, p. 10.

Keywords: suicide; domestic violence; polygamy; women's disproportionate share of work; loneliness; migration; burning of villages; housing problems; collapse of social order; lack of educational opportunities for Kurdish women; population explosion; shanty towns; feudal family structures; importance of virginity.

**Mazhar, Bağlı and Aysan Sev'er**. (2003). Female and male suicide in Batman, Turkey: Poverty, social change, patriarchal oppression and gender links. *Women's Health and Urban Life: An International and Interdisciplinary Journal, II*(1), pp. 60-84.

Keywords: Batman: suicide rate higher for women than for men; study suggests that extreme patriarchal oppression of Batman women may be responsible for their high suicide rate; prevention of female suicides may require the "loosening of the choke" on women in general and young women in particular; female suicide in Batman is more than three times the Turkish general rates; traditional suicide theories ill equipped to explain higher rates of female suicides and new models need to be constructed.

**Pope, Nicole**. (2001). Pauvreté et tribalisme provoquent des suicides dans le Kurdistan de Turquie [Poverty and tribalism cause suicides in Turkish Kurdistan]. *Le Monde,* reprinted in *Institut Kurde de Paris Information and Liaison*

*Bulletin, 190,* January 2001, p. 3.

**Keywords:** poverty; tribalism; suicide by women; Hizbullah; PKK; IHD; women's education; honor; patriarchy.

# GENOCIDE, GENDERCIDE, WAR CRIMES, AND CRIMES AGAINST HUMANITY

## I. GENOCIDE

### A. Anfal Genocide (Iraq)

**Alliance Internationale pour la Justice**. (2003). Open letter to Mrs. Mubarak re *Anfal* disappeared girls, signed by Françoise Brié, August 1.

**Keywords:** *Anfal* and Kurdish women; names of 18 women sold as slave girls in Egypt; request sent to Mrs. Mubarak, president of the National Council of Women, Cairo to investigate the fate of the women.

**BBC**. (2002). Voices from Iraq. *BBC* in *Institut Kurde de Paris, Information and Liaison Bulletin, 213,* December 2002, pp. 34-35.

**Keywords:** Anfal Widow Gulzar Ahmad; Anfal Widows; Jabari Village; Kirkuk; Topzawa; the raping and killing of women in Topzawa camp; Shoresh resettlement camp.

**Bouchet, Françoise**. (1988). Massacres au Kurdistan Irakien [Massacres in Iraqi Kurdistan]. *La Croix,* reprinted in *Institut Kurde de Paris, Information and Liaison Bulletin, 37-38-39,* April-June 1988, p. 7.

**Keywords:** chemical warfare against the Kurds; Iran-Iraq conflict; Genocide Convention of 1948.

**Cypel, Sylvain**. (2003). La campagne Anfal en 1988: le 'génocide des Kurdes' [The Anfal campaign in 1988: the "genocide of the Kurds"]. *Le Monde,* reprinted in *Institut Kurde de Paris, Information and Liaison Bulletin, 216,* March 2003, p. 153.

**Keywords**: genocide; Human Rights Watch; Physicians for Human Rights; Halabja; the chemical bombardment of dozens of villages; Ali Hassan Al-Majid; Saddam Hussein; the arbitrary imprisonment and detention of women, children, and the aged; the destruction of Qala Dizé Village in September 1989.

**Fuad, Tanya**. (1993). The current situation in Kurdistan. *Kurdistan Times, 3,* December, pp. 228-29. ISSN 1057-8668. One black and white photograph (p. 229).

**Keywords:** Iraqi Kurdistan; widows of the Anfal; women in deportation camps; women in prison; PUK; KDP; Kurdish refugees in Turkey.

**Gähwyler, Karl**. (1991). Kurdistan (A. Kamber, Trans.). *Écho Magazine,* reprinted in *Institut Kurde de Paris, Information and Liaison Bulletin, 87-88,* June/July 1992, pp. 6-9.

**Keywords:** Anfal; Halabja; refugees; destruction of Kurdish villages; war widows.

**Galbraith, Peter W**. (1993). Genocide and the Kurdish documents report. *Kurdistan Times, 3,* December, pp. 158-63. ISSN 1057-8668. One black and white photograph (p. 162).

**Keywords:** al-Anfal; documentation of the genocide; photograph of a mother of two sons murdered in the Anfal.

**Goldberg, Jeffrey**. (2002). The great terror. *The New Yorker,* March 25, pp. 52-75. Three black and white photographs (pp. 52, 58-59, 66) and one colour map of Kurdistan (p. 56).

**Keywords:** Kurdish women Jayran Muhammad, Chia Hammassat, and Nasreen Abdel Qadir Muhammad recount the events of 1988 in Halabja; Iran-Iraq War; Bahar Jamal; long-term health effects of poison gas dropped on Kurdish villages; cancer; Goktapa Village; genocide; refugees; Halabja Medical Institute; congenital abnormalities; spermatogenesis; infertility as a result of chemical weapons; biological weapons; sanctions; widows; divorce of infertile women; sterility; depression; woman divorced due to her blindness; Human Rights Watch; al-Anfal; Salma Aziz Baban, an Anfal widow; Topzawa Army Base; starvation; the feeding of the dead to dogs at Nugra Salman; al Qaeda; Ayman al-Zawahiri; Ansar al-Islam; Kurdish fundamentalism; Al Tawhid's initiation of a campaign of acid-throwing against unveiled Kurdish women and the assassination of a Christian politician; deportations of women and children; Shawqat Hamid Muhammad; Arabization of Kirkuk.

**Institut Kurde de Paris**. (1988). Halabja: A martyr town [Special issue]. *Institut Kurde de Paris, Information and Liaison Bulletin,* March, pp. 1-68.

**Keywords:** Halabja; list of villages bombed with chemical weapons by

Iraq.

**Institut Kurde de Paris**. (1988). Special issue on the events in Iraqi Kurdistan. *Institut Kurde de Paris, Information and Liaison Bulletin, 42*, September, pp. 1-180.

> **Keywords:** Halabja; chemical gas; Barjan; destruction of Kurdish villages; Babier; Warmeil; Barhule; Bielijan; Hess; Gudya; Ekmalla; Berchi; Tuka; refugees; public opinion; U.N.; list of destroyed villages; list of gassed villages; European Parliament resolution.

**Minoui, Delphine**. (2002). Le spectre de la mort hante toujours Halabja [The specter of death still haunts Halabja]. *Le Figaro*, reprinted in *Institut Kurde de Paris, Information and Liaison Bulletin, 211*, October 2002, p. 60.

> **Keywords:** Mala Nazif, a survivor of chemical attack, who lost 35 members of her family, recounts the chemical attack on Halabja; chemical weapons used against 281 Kurdish villages between 1987 and 1988; U.N. Inspections; U.N. Food for Oil program; crimes against humanity.

**Mohammed, Zara**. (2003). The forgotten Faylee Kurds of Iraq: A personal account. *KHRP Newsline, 23*, Summer, pp. 2-3. One photograph.

> **Keywords:** part of a large-scale operation by the Iraqi state against Faylee Kurds; Zara Mohammed had her house stormed and was taken along with her family to main security headquarters; put in a room filled with naked women and some children; obvious that they were sexually violated and raped; police officials making jokes about victim's virginity.

**O'Donnell, Lynne**. (2003). Saddam 'made sex slaves' of Kurdish women. *The Scotsman*, August 17.

> **Keywords:** women in *Anfal*; 18 Kurdish women abducted by Iraqi government in 1989; women sent to Egypt; Egyptian government denial.

**Perrin, Jean Pierre**. (2002). Des ONG ont enquêté sur l'épuration ethnique en Irak: 'ma mère a été mangée par les chiens sous mes yeux' [NGOs investigate ethnic cleansing in Iraq: "my mother was eaten by dogs in front of me"]. *Liberation*, reprinted in *Institut Kurde de Paris, Information and Liaison Bulletin, 213*, December 2002, p. 85.

> **Keywords:** Halabja; Kirkuk; NGO AIJ; destruction of villages; Arabization Campaign in Kirkuk region; ethnic minorities in Kirkuk;

collective punishment; ethnic cleansing; Khanain Region; Mandeli Region; 182,000 "disappeared" Kurds; Anfal; women's bodies fed to dogs in the Anfal campaign; detention centres; secret prisons.

**Semo, Marc.** (2003). Sur la trace des disparues de Saddam: De jeunes Kurdes enlevées en 1988 auraient été vendues en Egypte [On the trail of Saddam's disappearances: Young Kurds kidnapped in 1988 would have been sold to Egypt]. *Liberation,* reprinted in *Institut Kurde de Paris, Information and Liaison Bulletin, 220-221,* July/August 2003, p. 90.

**Keywords:** Tchawari Village; Tazkhrmatoo; *Al Anfal;* a document found in the archives of the Kirkuk Security Services reveals that a group of girls aged 14 to 29 were sold to Egyptian intermediaries as prostitutes or cabaret workers; Hassiba Hidayet, a Kurdish girl mentioned in the document; honour; PUK; an elderly Kurdish woman who was imprisoned in Tikrit recounts the loss of 15 of her family members.

**Vidal-Naquet, Pierre.** (2003). La campagne irakienne contre les Kurdes a été une enterprise génocidaire délibérée [The Iraqi campaign against the Kurds was a deliberate genocidal enterprise]. *Le Figaro,* reprinted in *Institut Kurde de Paris, Information and Liaison Bulletin, 215,* February, p. 12.

**Keywords:** genocide; killing of women and children; *al-Anfal;* Human Rights Watch.

**Wykeham, Sakie and Robin Parmelee** (Producers). (1992). *Saddam's killing fields.* Documentary, colour, 60 minutes, PBS WETA-TV (22 June 1993), Frontline, WGBH, Boston, LC Control Number 93517565.

**Keywords:** al-Anfal; widows of Barzan; Kanan Makiya; genocide; genocide survivors; orphans; prostitution; honour; Northern Iraqi "safe haven"; deportations; mass graves; the missing.

## B. Dersim Genocide

**Mönch-Buçak, Yayla.** (1994). Geschlechtsspezifische Auswirkungen der türkischen Kolonialpolitik [Gender-specific effects of Turkish colonial policy]. In Sabine Atasoy, Siamend Hajo, & Felix Weiland (Eds.), *Kurdologie: Studien zu Sprache, Geschichte, Gesellschaft und Politik Kurdistans und der Kurdinnen und Kurden* (pp. 119-35). Berlin: AstA-FÜ. ISBN 3-86093-066-4 (pb).

**Keywords:** Kemalism; Turkish colonialism in Kurdistan; Kemalist Nationalism; Treaty of Lausanne; Dersim Rebellion of 1937/38; killing of women in the Dersim Rebellion; active role of women in the Dersim Rebellion; Sheikh Said; Nuri Dersimi; deportations; genocide

171

and women; female survivors of the Dersim Genocide; forced prostitution among female survivors of the Dersim Genocide; *Elazığ Kız Enstitüsü*; Elazığ Elazığ; Kurdish women's resistance to Turkish education; residential schools; loss of mother language; Turkification of Kurdish women; Kemalist reforms; emigration to Western Europe; Seyit Riza; Kemalist etatism; the post-Kemalist era; women's loss of economic function; military coup of 1971; assimilation; KDP-Turkey; *Doğu Devrimci Kültür Ocakları*; patriarchy.

**Yildirim, Hüseyin.** (2001). *Ema Lenge: Une femme témoigne sur les massacres au Kurditan, Dersim, 1937-1938* [Ema Lenge: A woman testifies about the massacres in Kurditan, Dersim, 1937-1938] (M. Achard and G. Chaupin, Trans.). Paris: L'Harmattan. Foreword by Gérard Chaupin (p. 7), preface by Kendal Nezan (pp. 9-10), prologue: Summer 1982 (pp. 13-19), first part: Galboussane (pp. 23-69), second part: In search of the past (pp. 73-102), third part: Mourad (pp. 105-113), epilogue: Exile (pp. 117-18), annex (Letter from the tribes of Dersim to the League of Nations (1937; pp. 121-124). ISBN 2-7475-1579-6.

**Keywords:** testimonies of a woman about the suppression of the uprising of the Kurds of Dersim by Turkey in 1937-38, considered a genocide by some historians; author, a lawyer, from Dersim was forced into exile in Sweden in 1982.

## C. Gendercide

**Fossum, L. O.** (1918). The war-stricken Kurds. *The Kurdistan Missionary*, *10*(1), pp. 5-6.

**Keywords:** Armenian and Kurdistan overlap each other fully one-half; attention given to war-stricken Armenians and Nestorian Syrians; thousands of innocent Armenians "mostly women and children" have been killed; men were armed and could protect themselves or flee; three years of relief work for the survivors, still many widows, orphans, and sick in great need; with the Kurdish region changing hands from the Ottoman army to the Russian army, the "destruction and massacre of the Kurds" followed; "frightful things, too awful to publish, happened throughout Kurdistan"; eyewitness account of "hundreds of Kurds of military age" led or driven out of the city to be shot or moved down by the sword; over 7,000 were massacred in Sauj Bulagh by the Russian army, and Armenian and Assyrian militias; Kurdish women and girls were "abused in an indescribable manner"; "about 400 were carried away to be abused, and many were sold and resold or traded away for abuse"; villages laid in ruins, and cattle killed.

**Mojab, Shahrzad**. (2003). Kurdish women in the zone of genocide and gendercide. *Al-Raida* (Beirut), *21*(103), Fall (Women and War in the Arab World), pp. 20-25.

**Keywords:** the theorization of "gendercide" and relation to genocide; used here as "mass killing" of both women and men, at times of peace and war in patriarchal culture and in the course of state- and nation-building projects; Marxist-feminist approach; Eastern Anatolia (Armenia, Kurdistan, Mesopotamia, now Northern Iraq, Eastern Turkey) as a "Zone of Genocide" (Mark Leven's concept); Kurdish women in the zone; the 1991 U.S. war against Iraq, and the creation of a "safe haven" in Iraqi Kurdistan; the destruction of the social fabric of life in Iraqi Kurdistan due to the Anfal genocide of 1988, continuing wars, and the mass exodus of the Kurds in the wake of 1991 war; women's resistance to patriarchal violence; the Independent Women's Organization, International Campaign for the Defence of Women's Rights in Iraqi Kurdistan, Women's Union of Kurdistan, and activism in diaspora; legal reform for penalizing honor killing in Iraqi Kurdistan.

## II. WAR CRIMES AND CRIMES AGAINST HUMANITY

**Institut Kurde de Paris**. (2001). A little Kurdish girl bitten to death by the dogs of Turkish gendarmes. *Institut Kurde de Paris, Information and Liaison Bulletin, 194*, May, p. 13.

**Keywords:** Turkish Foundation for Human Rights; Gazal Beru; Meral Beru; military brutality against children.

**Institut Kurde de Paris**. (2003). Some inhabitants of Hakkari province beaten up and dragged through excrement following a search. *Institut Kurde de Paris, Information and Liaison Bulletin, 223*, October, p. 11.

**Keywords:** the Hakkari section of the IHD; Fatma Çetin, a 60-year-old woman beaten by a Special Forces member; children from Hani village whose faces were covered with excrement; village guard system.

**Kurdistan Report**. (1993). Why they call us terrorists. *Kurdistan Report, 16*, October/November, p. 17.

**Keywords:** Gülay Yildirim; Petrol-İş; desecration of killed guerillas; atrocities in Kurdistan; the dragging of naked women through villages; trade unions; NATO; May Day massacre of 1977; 1980 military coup; contra-guerillas; Grey Wolves.

**Le Figaro**. (2002). L'UE condamne Ankara pour traitement inhumain [EU condemns Ankara for inhumane treatment]. *Le Figaro,* reprinted in *Institut Kurde de Paris, Information and Liaison Bulletin, 211,* October, p. 27.

Keywords: Meryeme Algür, a 22-year-old student tortured in detention; European Court.

**Sullivan, Laura**. (1994). DEP trial and visit to Adana. *Kurdistan Report, 19,* September/October, pp. 4-6. Three black and white photographs, pp. 5, 6.

Keywords: DEP; human rights violations; the burning alive of civilians by Turkish forces; refugees in Adana; torture of women by Turkish soldiers; PKK; ARGK; massacre in the village of Zengok; murder of an 80-year-old woman by Turkish soldiers; HADEP.

**Whaley, S**. (1991). A plea from Kurdish women. *Il Foglio de il Paese della Donna, 1-2,* July/August, reprinted in *Women's Studies Abstracts,* 1991-1992, p. 27.

Keywords: the razing of villages in Iraqi Kurdistan; Halabja; deportations from Iraqi Kurdistan; Turkey's killing of about 7,000 Kurds in 1984, the imprisonment of about 10,000 Kurds in Turkey; U.N.; NATO; Rezan Khazan, a Kurdish woman studying in Italy and a representative of the Association of Kurdish Women in Europe of the Iraqi Kurdestan Front answers questions regarding Kurdish women and war.

## A. Disappearance and Destruction of Villages

**Amnesty International**. (1995). *Turkey: Unfulfilled promise of reform.* London: Amnesty International, September.

Keywords: disappearances; extrajudicial executions; harassment; torture; deaths in custody; lawyers; human rights activists; women; journalists; local government representatives; women; minorities.

**Clara-Magazine**. (1999). 3 millions de civils kurdes déplacés [3 million Kurdish civilians displaced]. *Clara-Magazine,* reprinted in *Institut Kurde de Paris, Information and Liaison Bulletin, 168-169,* March/April 1999, p. 96.

Keywords: Leyla Zana; PKK; evacuation of Kurdish villages by the Turkish army; arrests of Kurds; sale of weapons to Turkey by France.

**Human Rights Tribune des Droits Humains**. (1996). The Kurdish situation forced relocation in Turkey's southeastern provinces Kurdish mothers tell their stories. *Human Rights Tribune des Droits Humains, 3*(4),

August/September, pp. 33-34. Reprinted in *Women Living Under Muslim Laws Newssheet*, Vol. IX, *1 & 2*, March and June, 1997, p. 16. One photograph.

**Keywords:** war; Kurds in prison; hunger strike; burned villages; disappearances; killing of journalists; PKK; displaced villagers.

**Institut Kurde de Paris**. (1992). The situation in Turkish Kurdistan [Special issue]. *Institut Kurde de Paris, Information and Liaison Bulletin,* November, 123 pages.

**Keywords:** war; destruction of Kurdish villages; list of Kurdish villages destroyed; assassinations of Kurdish civilians; migration; torture.

**Institut Kurde de Paris**. (1997). Mrs. Mitterrand's letter to the political leaders of the fifteen. *Institut Kurde de Paris, Information and Liaison Bulletin, 152-153*, November-December, p, 7.

**Keywords:** Danielle Mitterrand; destruction of 847 villages in Turkish Kurdistan; assassination of 1,800 intellectuals and peaceful democrats by death squads; Musa Anter; Mehmet Sincar; Leyla Zana.

**Ryan, Nick**. (1997). The disappeared. *Kurdistan Report, 25*, July/August, pp. 29-31.

**Keywords**: IHD; European Court of Human Rights; Amnesty International; PKK; Hasibe Edren (mother of a disappeared son); village guards; HADEP; Selma Tanrıkulu.

**Sutton, Jenny**. (1999). UK women's delegation to the "Saturday Mothers." *Kurdistan Report, 28*, July-September, pp. 47-49.

**Keywords:** the "Saturday Mothers" (Mothers of the Disappeared); ICAD; Lawyers' International Forum for Women's Human Rights; Scottish Socialist Party; international women's solidarity; Peace in Kurdistan Campaign; IHD; Eren Keskin; Emine Ocak (mother of Hasan Ocak); Hanife Yıldız (mother of Mustafa Yıldız); Filiz Karakuş (of the IHD); sexual violence against women in police custody; sexual abuse; women speaking out against rape and sexual torture; the decrease in the stigma of rape and sexual assault due to the number of women who have spoken out against it; HADEP; deaths in detention; torture; EKB; Ayşe Yilmaz (of the EKB); Asiye Güzel (a woman raped in police custody who spoke out against her rape); domestic violence; sexual abuse within the family; statistics of domestic violence.

**Turkish Daily News**. (1994). At least 20 civilians killed in weekend bombing of Kurdish villages. *Turkish Daily News,* reprinted in *Institut Kurde de Paris, Information and Liaison Bulletin, 108*, March 31, pp. 140-141.

**Keywords:** bombing of villages; death of civilians; wounded civilians; Behiye Bengin; Koçaklı; Şırnak; Nafiye Belgin; Eren Bayın; Emine Şengül; food embargo; travel limitations.

**Die Weltwoche.** (1987). Niemand wird es bemerken wenn ich hier sterbe [Nobody will notice when I die here]. *Die Weltwoche,* reprinted in *Institut Kurde de Paris Information and Liaison Bulletin, 29*, August 20, pp. 21-22.

**Keywords:** Pecenk; PKK; Cadiya Belka; Yuvali; a lone woman who remains behind as her village is emptied; massacres of civilians.

## B. Iraq

**Daniel, Sara.** (2002). Tortures, Exécutions Sommaires, Amputations... Amnesty accuse [Torture, summary executions, amputations...Amnesty accuses]. *le nouvel Observateur,* reprinted in *Institut Kurde de Paris Information and Liaison Bulletin, 211*, October 10-16, p. 62.

**Keywords:** torture in Iraq; electric shock; sexual abuse; execution in October 2000 of dozens of women accused of prostitution, but who were actually members of the opposition; Najat Haydar, a doctor who denounced corruption was one of those executed; Um Haydar, another woman killed; amputations; summary executions; NGOs; Amnesty International; amputations of tongues; Fedayin; Human Rights Committee of the U.N.

**Francis, Susan with Andrew Crofts.** (1993). *Nowhere to hide: A mother's ordeal in the killing fields of Iraq and Kurdistan.* London: Weidenfeld and Nicholson. ISBN 0 297 81289 0. List of illustrations (p. vii), map (pp. viii-ix), text (pp. 1-240). 18 black and white photos (unnumbered centre pages).

**Keywords:** domestic violence against women; birth control; fertility; arranged marriages; polygamy; racism; violence by women against women; bride price; women and work; division of labour; poverty; women and education; rape; torture; honour; Halabja; Iran-Iraq War; Gulf War; Allied bombardment of Iraq; al-Anfal; Iraqi Kurdistan; women and war; refugees; immigration; Kurdish uprising against Saddam Hussein; Shi'i uprising against Saddam Hussein; lack of support for uprisings by external powers; health.

**Gearing, Julian.** (1993). The ones left behind. *Kurdistan Report, 13,* February/March, pp. 31-32.

**Keywords:** Gulf War; Iraqi Kurdistan; al-Anfal; widows; orphans; female refugees; the struggles of women to raise families on their own; Kurdistan Reconstruction Organisation; the village of Qushtapa; Halima Barzani; Kurdish Women's Union; rape of Kurdish women by Iraqi soldiers; honour; honour killing; rape as a weapon; torture; women and unemployment; women and agriculture; regional discrimination; female literacy; Ba'th Party policies regarding women; women and poverty; a women's sewing workshop in Kurdistan; literacy classes for women.

**Glass, Charles**. (1992). The great betrayal. In Charles Glass (Ed.), *Money for old rope: Disorderly compositions* (pp. 146-53). London: Pan Books Ltd. ISBN: 0 330 32209 5.

**Keywords:** Karrahanjir; Kirkuk; bombing of Kurdish villages; Arbil; refugees; orphaned children; KDP; PUK; Chamchamal; Mujahideen-e Khalq.

**Glass, Charles**. (1992). Murder by helicopter in Kurdistan. In Charles Glass (Ed.), *Money for old rope: Disorderly compositions* (pp. 154-55). London: Pan Books Ltd. ISBN: 0 330 32209 5.

**Keywords:** Kurdish uprising in Northern Iraq; exodus from Northern Iraq; genocide.

**Karrer, Cristina**. (1998). Sie haben unsere Männer verschleppt [They abducted our men]. *Mosquito,* Bern, *5,* pp. 24-27, Z P 12. An extract from Christina Karrer, Sie haben unsere Männer verschleppt, eFeF Verlah.

**Keywords:** Iraq; war; Kurdish women.

**Omar, Suha**. (1994). Women: Honour, shame and dictatorship. In *Iraq since the Gulf War* (pp. 60-71). Committee Against Repression and for Democratic Rights in Iraq. London: Zed Books. ISBN 1 85649 231 1 (hb), ISBN 1 85649 232 X (pb).

**Keywords:** women's rights; nuclear families; pressures on working women; decrees against women; honour killing; Decision 1110 of the RCC which makes honour killing legal; birth rate; fertility drive and its implications for women; contraception; reproductive rights; General Federation of Iraqi Women; Iraqi Communist Party; official rape; widows' towns of Iraqi Kurdistan; Gushtapa settlements; Barzani widows; honour killings carried out by Barzani widows; PUK; KDP; Kurdish women MPs; Communist Party; Democratic Independent Party of Kurdistan; divorce; inheritance laws; Islamic law.

## C. Massacre

**Bayla, Akgül**. (1992). Turkey: Massacre of Kurdish people continues. *Spare Rib*, October/November, p. 52.

**Keywords:** Kurdish MPs; Leyla Zana; massacres; state terror; PKK; Ôirnak; destruction of villages.

**Institut Kurde de Paris**. (1991). A bloody Christmas in Turkish Kurdistan. *Institut Kurde de Paris, Information and Liaison Bulletin, 80-81*, November-December, pp. 4-5.

**Keywords:** Turkish media; demonstrations; massacres; Leyla Zana; PKK; Kulp; Lice.

**Libération**. (1987, June 23). La traque des Kurdes apres le massacre [The hunt for the Kurds after the massacre]. *Libération*, reprinted in *Institut Kurde de Paris, Information and Liaison Bulletin, 27*, June 1987, p. 11-12.

**Keywords:** Pınarcık; Mardin; Kenan Evren; massacre of Kurdish civilians; Armenian Genocide; PKK.

**Rozsa, Klaus**. (1994). Im Worten kaum zu fassen [Hard to believe in words]. *DAZ*, reprinted in *Institut Kurde de Paris Information and Liaison Bulletin, 113-114*, August/September, pp. 90-92.

**Keywords:** massacre of civilians by the Turkish military; *Özgür Ülke*; Cudi mountains; Silopi; PKK; ERNK; ARGK; resistance by female farmers against the state; murder of men, women, and children; torture; Turkish soldiers' use of the word "Armenian" as an insult; Zakho; presence of Turkish Secret Police in Northern Iraq.

**Der Spiegel**. (1987). Waisen des Universums [Orphans of the universe]. *Der Spiegel*, reprinted in *Institut Kurde de Paris, Information and Liaison Bulletin, 28*, July 29, p. 26.

**Keywords:** Pınarcık; massacre of Kurdish civilians; Kenan Evren; PKK.

## D. Rape

**Alkan, Xane**. (1997). Crimes against Kurdish women. *Kurdistan Report, 25*, July-August, p. 50.

**Keywords:** Xane Alkan (President of KPE); village guard system; statistics of crimes committed by village guards; rape; burning of houses; kidnappings by village guards; Remziye Dinç (raped at gunpoint by Ekrem and Ceyhan Altiner, two village guards); rape of a ten-year-old girl by Süleyman Askan (a village guard); Zeynep Baran; women taking action against their attackers.

**Amnesty International**. (1995). *Turkey: A policy of denial.* London: Amnesty International, February.

**Keywords:** extrajudicial execution; disappearances; death in custody; torture; house destruction; harassment; sexual assault; incommunicado detention; minorities; teachers; politicians; human rights activists; women; lawyers; journalists; trade unionists.

**Amnesty International**. (2003). *Turkey: End sexual violence against women in custody!* London: Amnesty International. AI Index: EUR 44/0006/2003, 44 pages. Also in French, *Halte aux violence sexuelles contre les femmes en détention!*

**Keywords**: state as perpetrator of violence against women; especially at risk: Kurdish women and women holding political beliefs not accepted by government and the military; rape in Turkish and international law; honour and rape in custody; virginity tests; sexual harassment of women lawyers.

*See also* Political Prisoners

**Bejna**. (1993). Geschlecht: Weiblich Herkunft: Kurdin Strafe: Folterung, Vergewaltigung, Tod [Gender: Female Origin: Kurdish Punishment: Torture, rape, death]. *Jiyan - Kurdische Frauenzeitschrift,* December, p. 16.

**Keywords:** arrests of women; rape; murder of women; Şükran Aydin; Newroz Bozkurt; disappearances.

**Celikaslan, Leman**. (1995). Rape victim Leman Celikaslan's letter to the General Secretariat of HADEP (People's Democracy Party). In *Resistance: Women in Kurdistan* (p. 56). London: KIC/KSC Publications.

**Keywords:** Leman Celikaslan: taken into custody during a raid by the anti-terror unit; inhuman treatment, torture; tied to a tree; sexually assaulted; threatened with rape; three men raped her from behind; lost consciousness, bleeding; another man raped her afterward; vomiting; heavy bleeding for several days.

**Cevahir**. (1995). Sexuelle Gewalt als Kriegsstrategie [Sexual violence as a war strategy]. *Wir leben hier. Frauen in der Fremden,* pp. 95-99.

**Keywords:** Turkey; state oppression; rape; genocide; Kurdish women; Kurdistan.

**Graf-Metghalchi, Denise**. (1987). Frauen als Geiseln-frauenspezifische Verfolgung in der Türkei [Women hostage-specific persecution in Turkey]. In Kathrin Moussa-Karlen (Ed.), *Wenn Frauen flüchten* (p. 14). Zürich.

**Keywords:** Turkey; torture; asylum; Kurdish women; violence against women.

**Hamburger Frauen Zeitung**. (1998). Der Kampf von Frauen und Mädchen. *Hamburger Frauen Zeitung, 54*, December/March, pp. 10-13.

**Keywords:** women fighting against rapists; rape in Turkish prisons; rape by village guards; rape by police officers; PKK; YAJK; Women's Army; poverty; Agas; farming; social structure of Kurdistan; Meral Kidir; women and war; torture; Eren Keskin; silence surrounding rape; patriarchy; honour; court cases against rapists; solidarity; FrauenLesben Kurdistan Solidaritäts Komitee.

**Hamburger Frauen Zeitung**. (1998). Der Kampf von Frauen und Mädchen gegen Vergewaltigungen durch Dorfschützer, Militär und Polizei in Kurdistan und der Türkei [The fight of women and girls against rape by village guards, the military and the police in Kurdistan and Turkey.]. *Hamburger Frauen Zeitung, 54,* Hamburg, pp. 10-13, Z G 19.

**Keywords:** Turkey; Kurdistan; rape.

**Institut Kurde de Paris**. (2003). 405 Turkish soldiers in court for the rape and torture of a young Kurdish woman in Mardin. *Institut Kurde de Paris, Information and Liaison Bulletin, 223*, October, p. 7.

**Keywords:** gang rape of a Kurdish woman in detention; Mardin; torture.

**Institut Kurde de Paris**. (2003). Plus de 400 soldats turcs jugés pour viol [More than 400 Turkish soldiers tried for rape]. *Le Figaro*, reprinted in *Institut Kurde de Paris, Information and Liaison Bulletin, 223*, October 12, p. 34.

**Keywords:** gang rape of a Kurdish woman in detention; Mardin; torture.

**Kalkan, Ersin**. (1997). A baby called Negrican. *Kurdistan Report, 25*, July-August, p. 52.

**Keywords:** Remziye Dinç; Negrican (the child born as a result of Remziye's rape); education; language; Ceyhan and Nevzat Altuner (the village guards who raped Remziye when she was 17 years old).

**Keskin, Eren**. (1997). Do not leave Remziye alone. *Kurdistan Report, 25,* July-August, p. 51, originally appeared in *Human Rights Bulletin,* February/March 1997.

> **Keywords:** women's triple burden in Turkey: national, gender, and class-related oppression; Remziye: woman who was raped and could not tell anyone because of the repercussions she would face in her community; gave birth to a child; pressed charges against the rapists; medical examination proved the rape and determined the identity of the father; Fadime: raped around the same time; no evidence; but was pursued; the reason for the difference in the prosecution of the two cases was that Fadime's rape served state ideology whereas Remziye's did not: Fadime was allegedly raped by two men who were part of a religious group whereas Remziye's rapists were village guards.

**Kurdish Human Rights Project**. (1999). Council of Europe condemns Turkey's treatment of Kurds. *KHRP Newsline, 7,* Summer, pp. 1-2. One photograph.

> **Keywords:** Sukran Aydin: raped in custody; 17 years old and a virgin; medically examined: confirmed that hymen had been torn although would not draw any conclusions; case presented in front of the European Court for Human Rights; Turkey ordered to pay compensation to the victim.

**Kurdish Human Rights Project**. (2002). New KHRP Reports. *KHRP Newsline, 17,* Spring, p. 15. One photograph.

> **Keywords:** *State Violence Against Women in Turkey and Attacks on Human Rights defenders of Victims of Sexual Violence in Custody*: new KHRP report based on the delegation sent to observe the trial of five women charged after organizing and participating in a congress on the topic of the report; also examines the wider context of the case and Turkey's international obligations.

**Kurdish Human Rights Project**. (2003). KHRP observes two trials of 410 soldiers and police for rape. *KHRP Newsline, 24,* Winter, pp. 4-5. Two photographs.

> **Keywords:** Sukran Esen: in Mardin (Southeastern Turkey), trails of 405 paramilitary solders indicted for the repeated rape of Sukran Esen in 1993 and 1994; in a separate case, five soldiers were indicted for the rape of Hamidiye Aslan, in March 2002; raped anally with sticks; in the case of Aydin v. Turkey, the European Court ruled for the first time that rape constitutes a form of torture contrary to the European

Convention on Human Rights; a further 40 gendarmerie were indicted bringing the total to 445; in October 2003, a representative of the Ministry of Justice, Professor Dogan Soyaslan, justified the continuation of a law that exonerates rapists from prosecution if they marry the victim after the crime, saying that no one would want to marry a girl that was not a virgin.

**Kurdish Human Rights Project**. (2003). Trial observation of 410 police officers and gendarmes, November 2003. *Kurdish Human Rights Project, Annual Report 2003*, p. 36.

**Keywords:** Sukran Esen: in Mardin (Southeastern Turkey), trails of 405 paramilitary solders indicted for the repeated rape of Sukran Esen in 1993 and 1994; in a separate case, five soldiers were indicted for the rape of Hamidiye Aslan, in March 2002; raped anally with sticks; in the case of Aydin v. Turkey, the European Court ruled for the first time that rape constitutes a form of torture contrary to the European Convention on Human Rights; a further 40 gendarmerie were indicted bringing the total to 445; in October 2003, a representative of the Ministry of Justice, Professor Dogan Soyaslan, justified the continuation of a law that exonerates rapists from prosecution if they marry the victim after the crime, saying that no one would want to marry a girl that was not a virgin.

**Kurdish Human Rights Project**. (2004). KHRP report highlights sexual violence in Turkey to UK Parliament. *KHRP Newsline*, 25, Spring, p. 3.

**Keywords:** *Turkey's Shame: Sexual Violence without Redress—the Plight of Kurdish Women*; Baroness Symons: written response to the report saying that KHRP raises issues of a serious concern, saying that Turkey will surely investigate KHRP's findings even though EU representatives, NGOs, and the Turkish Justice Minister, Cemil Cicek, have expressed concerns of the failure of Turkey to implement reforms on the ground.

**Kurdish Human Rights Project**. (2004). KHRP fact-finding mission in Turkey. *KHRP Newsline*, 25, Spring, p. 5. Two photographs.

**Keywords:** from March 11-19, KHRP fact finding mission assessed the current human and women's rights situation.

**Kurdish Human Rights Project**. (2004). Turkey's shame: sexual violence without redress—the plight of Kurdish women. *KHRP Newsline*, 25, Spring, p. 19. One photograph. Also appears in *Kurdish Human Rights Project, Annual Report, 2003*, p. 40. One photograph.

**Keywords:** details how Kurdish women face a continuing risk of sexual violence by state actors in Turkey; met with Gulbahar Gunduz to talk about her experience of abduction and sexual violence; observed the trials of the 410 Turkish paramilitary police for rape; makes recommendations to the Turkish government and the international community about how to protect women from sexual violence and to ensure that actors cannot act without impunity.

**Milroy, Chris.** (1998). Medicine and torture. *KHRP Newsline, 5,* October-December, p. 7.

**Keywords:** Sukran Aydin: raped in custody; 17 years old and a virgin; medically examined: confirmed that hymen had been torn although would not draw any conclusions; case presented in front of the European Court for Human Rights.

**Project "Legal Aid for Women Raped or Sexually Assaulted by State Security Forces."** (2000). *Sexual violence: perpetrated by the state: a documentation of victim stories.* Istanbul: DOZ Basım-Yayın Ltd. Şti. Introduction (pp. 5-7), stories (pp. 9-139). Publication funded by Raft Foundation, Bergen, Norway; The 21st August Committee, Bergen; Hotel and Restaurant Workers Union, Norway; Red Cross, Bergen.

**Keywords:** stories of 113 women, mostly Kurdish and/or socialist, told between 1995 and 1999; stories collected by "a number of female lawyers" in Turkey; the 113 women were sexually assaulted or raped in custody at police stations, at gendarmeries or during army raids in villages; perpetrators are policemen, soldiers, or village guards; disclosure of stories risked re-arrest and more violence; some victims did not dare to publish their stories; sexual violence a method of warfare; rape and sexual torture under conditions of war as a crime against humanity; Legal Aid for Women Raped or Sexually Assaulted by State Security Forces was launched in summer 1997 to provide victims with medical care, legal aid, and legal action within Turkey and with the European Commission on Human Rights.

**Semo, Marc.** (2003). 405 militaires face à la justice turque [405 soldiers facing Turkish justice](Pierre Mornet, illustrator). *Liberation,* reprinted in *Institut Kurde de Paris, Information and Liaison Bulletin, 224,* November 5, pp. 16-17.

**Keywords:** Şükran Esen, a 22-year-old Kurdish woman gang raped by Turkish soldiers; electric shock; torture; rape in detention; Eren Keskin; the Centre for Victims of Torture and Sexual Abuse created by Eren Keskin; lawyer Reyhan Yalçindağ; the trial of 405 soldiers for gang rape.

183

**Zaman, Amberin**. (1999). U.S. Human Rights Official gets and earful in a "listening tour" of Turkey. *International Herald Tribune,* reprinted in *Institut Kurde de Paris, Information and Liaison Bulletin, 173,* August 4, p. 4.

> **Keywords:** torture of Kurdish girls by the Turkish police; sexual abuse of Kurdish girls by Turkish police; suicide of Kurdish girl who preferred death to more torture; Kurdish girls' commitment to Kurdish struggle; Kurdish girls' support of Abdullah Öcalan.

## E. Torture

**Amnesty International**. (1984). Turkey. *File on Torture* (Amnesty International), 1, May, pp. 1-8, reprinted in *Institut Kurde de Paris, Information and Liaison Bulletin, 7,* July 1984, unnumbered pages.

> **Keywords:** torture; Sema Özgür; Mehdi Zana; 1980 coup; Socialist Party of Turkish Kurdistan; Meryem Sendil Çolako lu; Mamak Military Prison; Nursel Yılmaz; Ayşe Necmiye Bekel; Turkish Communist Party; Kurdish Workers' Party; Progressive Democratic and Cultural Association; hunger strikes by prisoners; Diyarbakir Military Prison; Gülhan Tomak; İskenderun Martial Law Command; torture of girls; torture of elderly women; death in detention; martial law; European Commission of Human Rights; European Convention on Human Rights.

**Amnesty International**. (1997). Testimony: Sexual abuse. *File on Torture,* reprinted in *Institut Kurde de Paris, Information and Liaison Bulletin, 31-32-33,* October-December, p. 22.

> **Keywords:** sexual assault as a form of torture; General Turgut Sunalp; sexual torture; Nilüfer Aydur; torture of students; student protests.

**Amnesty International**. (1997). Testimony: Forced to watch torture of wife. *File on Torture,* reprinted in *Institut Kurde de Paris, Information and Liaison Bulletin, 31-32-33,* October-December, pp. 20-21.

> **Keywords:** psychological torture; use of women and children as a means of torture; Turkish Communist Workers' Party.

**Burrell, Ian**. (1999). Turkey is accused of electric shock torture. *The Independent,* reprinted in *Institut Kurde de Paris, Information and Liaison Bulletin, 166-167,* January-February 19, p. 140.

> **Keywords:** torture; female activist tortured; Medical Foundation in London; United Nations Committee against Torture; Council of Europe's Committee for the Prevention of Torture.

**Erzeren, Ömer**. (1990). *Septemberspuren.* Reinbeck bei Hamburg: Rowohlt Taschenbuch Verlag. ISBN: 3 499 127288 (pb). Foreword (pp. 7-11), black and white photographs (pp. 12-13), text (pp. 14-153).

**Keywords:** Gülten Akkaya; Saadet Akkaya; TİKKO; torture; rape in prison; Münevver Sönmez; self-immolation; Mutu Village; Tunceli; PKK; May Day; TDKP; war; Şırnak; Dev-Yol; Zeynel Abidin Ceylan; Ayşe Pekdemir; Ayşe Kars; TAYAD (Tutuklu ve Hükümlü Aileleri Yardımlaşma Derne i); hunger strikes; Server Kök; Women in Black; *Kaktüs* and *Feminist* (two feminist journals published in Istanbul); Gülnur Savran; Filiz Karakuş; Ayşe Düzkan; women in the PKK; relationship between Turkish feminists and the PKK.

*See also* Feminist and Women's Journalism

**Institut Kurde de Paris**. (2000). The European Human Rights Court awards damages of $3,000 to a young girl tortured in Turkey. *Institut Kurde de Paris, Information and Liaison Bulletin, 181*, April, p. 7.

**Keywords:** Sevtap Veznedaroğlu; forced confessions; torture.

**Institut Kurde de Paris**. (2000). Strasbourg: The European Human Rights Court again condemns Turkey. *Institut Kurde de Paris, Information and Liaison Bulletin, 187*, October, pp. 4-5.

**Keywords:** killing of Zubeyir Akkoç; torture of his widow, Nabahat Akkoç; death squads; European Human Rights Court.

**Institut Kurde de Paris**. (2003). The tragedy of a young Kurdish woman tortured in detention with her son of 2 and a half years, and excluded from her own trial because she only speaks Kurdish. *Institut Kurde de Pari, Information and Liaison Bulletin, 223*, October, pp. 11-12.

**Keywords:** Eren Keskin, Vice President of IHD and founder of the "Project for the legal aid against sexual ill-treatment and torture during detention"; Fatma Toprak, accused under Article 125 of the Penal Code of "links with the PKK"; use of Kurdish in court; use of Kurdish translator in court; Turkish Doctors Union; Istanbul Medical Council; Human Rights Foundation; the detention of children; sexual abuse in detention; torture of a child of two-and-a-half-year-old child; Gebze Prison; the placing of Fatma Toprak's child in the abandoned children's Department in Bahçelievler; Public Prosecutor of Fatih; Assize Court at Beyoğlu; European Court for Human Rights; violation of Article 3 of the European Convention.

*See also* Language

**Institut Kurde de Paris**. (2004). The Netherlands Courts forbid the extradition of a PKK women's leader, demanded by Ankara, on the grounds that Turkey is continuing to violate human rights. *Institut Kurde de Paris, Information and Liaison Bulletin, 236*, November, pp. 9-10.

> **Keywords:** Nusriye Kesbir: former leader of the PKK wanted by Turkey on charges of being responsible for attacks on military objectives; Netherlands refused on the grounds that Turkey violates human rights; she feared torture if she was extradited to Turkey; denies being involved in attacks on military objectives and claims that she was only concerned with "women's questions."

**Institut Kurde de Paris**. (2005). The Hague Appeal Court forbids the extradition of a PKK leader because of the risk of torture in Turkey. *Institut Kurde de Paris, Information and Liaison Bulletin, 238*, January, p. 9.

> **Keywords:** Nusriye Kesbir: former leader of the PKK wanted by Turkey on charges of being responsible for attacks on military objectives; Netherlands refused on the grounds that Turkey violates human rights; she feared torture if she was extradited to Turkey; denies being involved in attacks on military objectives and claims that she was only concerned with "women's questions."

**Kurdish Human Rights Project**. (2003). Abduction and sexual torture of DEHAP executive member. *KHRP Newsline, 22*, Summer, p. 5.

> **Keywords:** Gülbahar Gündüz: executive member of DEHAP; four plainclothes men describing themselves as police officers forced Gündüz into a car; men told her she should not be engaging in political activities because she is a woman and that this would be a lesson to her; claims that one of the men forced his penis into her mouth; previously arrested during March 8 International Women's Day demonstrations in 2003.

**Kurdish Human Rights Project**. (2003). Police officers on trial for torture and ill-treatment of a woman. *KHRP Newsline, 23*, Autumn, pp. 5-6. Two photographs.

> **Keywords:** two police officers from the anti-terror forces are due to stand trial for the torture and ill-treatment of a woman, in the Alsangak area of Izmir, Turkey; woman made a complaints to the Izmir state prosecutor after she was abducted, blindfolded, assaulted, and threatened with death; on the same day she complained she was

threatened by a man in civilian clothes; abducted a second time: blindfolded, interrogated, sexually assaulted, stripped, and threatened with death; received on-going hospital treatment as a result of the assault.

**Kurdish Human Rights Project**. (2004). Sexual violence against DEHAP official. *KHRP Newsline, 25*, Spring, p. 2.

**Keywords:** Afife Mintas: provincial head of DEHAP's women's branch, reportedly kidnapped by plainclothes security force personnel and sexually tortured; received death and rape threats; reminded of the abduction and torture of Gulbahar Gunduz by her abductors.

**Laizer, Sheri**. (1995). Hezal-the Kurdish family as the target of state terror. In *Resistance: Women in Kurdistan* (pp. 25-26). London: KIC/KSC Publications. One photograph.

**Keywords:** women and nationalism: woman as bearers/mothers of the nation; women and education: Hezal had never been to school; politicization of women in nationalist movements.

**Turkish Daily News**. (1994). Claims of 'psychological torture' in Democracy Party case. *Turkish Daily News,* reprinted in *Institut Kurde de Paris, Information and Liaison Bulletin, 113-114,* August/September, p. 134.

**Keywords:** DEP; Leyla Zana; PKK; burning of villages.

**Turkish Daily News**. (1999). Iskenderun police alleged to have tortured and raped teenage girls. *Turkish Daily News,* November 8, reprinted in *Kurdistan Report, 29,* March/April 2000, p. 43.

**Keywords:** torture in police custody; rape in police custody; confessions obtained under torture; families of torture and rape victims; PKK; doctors' cooperation with the authorities; Temin Salmanoğlu; protests in Iskenderun against the arrest of Öcalan; Kürkçüler Prison in Adana; TTB; ATO; torture statistics; the "Manisa Children"; suicide in police custody; cases filed against Turkey in the European Court of Human Rights by women raped in police custody.

## F. Turkey

**Alkan, Xane**. (1996). The Turkish government's dirty war in Kurdistan: Its toll on Kurdish women [Special issue]. *Kurdistan Report, 23,* March-May, pp. 39-40.

**Keywords:** human rights (violations); women and war; women and migration; lack of birth control; women's deaths during childbirth; women political prisoners; self-immolation of Latife Kaya; women hunger strikers; Tomris Özden; CHP; Kemalism.

**Institut Kurde de Paris**. (1997). Turkey refuses to sign the treaty banning anti-personnel mines. *Institut Kurde de Paris, Information and Liaison Bulletin, 152-153*, November/December, pp. 11-12.

Keywords: mines in Mardin; death of 11 women and children due to landmines.

**Marais, M**. (1996, February 8). Les kurdes oubliés [The forgotten Kurds]. *Humanité dimanche*, reprinted in *Institut Kurde de Paris, Information and Liaison Bulletin, 130-131*, January/February 1996, p. 129.

Keywords: physical and cultural genocide; bombardments; imprisonments; torture; Leyla Zana.

## G. Virginity Control

**Kurdistan Report**. (1986). Die kurdische Frau ist heute Praktiken ausgesetzt, die die Würde aller Frauen der Welt verletzen [Kurdish women today are exposed to practices that violate the dignity of all women in the world]. *Kurdistan Report*, December, pp. 16-17.

Keywords: Necla Yüce, a Kurdish woman examined by two male Turkish doctors to determine whether or not she had had sexual relations with her guerrilla husband; Dersim; pressure exerted on Ms. Yüce by the Turkish authorities for her to divorce her husband; Turkish authorities' abuse of Kurdish women's illiteracy; PKK; Turkish colonialism and women; abuse of human rights; women fighting for national liberation; national liberation and women's liberation.

**Kurdistan Report**. (1994). Virginity control on women in Turkey. *Kurdistan Report, 19*, September/October, p. 21.

Keywords: Human Rights Watch Women's Rights Project; virginity control examinations in police custody; custodial rape; laws governing public morality and prostitution; focus on virginity when investigating sex crimes; regulation of female virginity; honour.

# GEOGRAPHY

## I. DIASPORA

**Alinia, Minoo**. (2004). *Spaces of diasporas: Kurdish identities, experiences of otherness and politics of belonging*. Göteborg, Sweden; Göteborg University, Department of Sociology, Göteborg Studies in Sociology, *22*, 354 pages.

**Keywords:** doctoral dissertation based on interviews with 22 Kurdish women and men, first-generation refugees in Gothenburg, Sweden between March 1999 and January 2004; Kurdish women more successful than men in Sweden (show more openness to Swedish society and learn the language faster); men face racism more directly and in more naked form, and experience downward social mobility; women more ambivalent towards Kurdish diasporic community—more at home in the Kurdish community due to the exclusionary Swedish society (they face racism, exclusion, and inferiorisation), and critical of their subordination within the Kurdish community (they enjoy more rights in Sweden than in countries of origin); skeptical towards Kurdish institutions; feminism, as an ideological and political movement, very weak in the Kurdish diaspora; Kurdish political organizations subject the struggle for gender equality to class and national struggles; Kurdish left has paid more attention to gender issues than the nationalists; women more present oriented; there is consensus about gender inequality and women's subordination, explained variously as a product of national oppression, women's aptitudes, or patriarchal relations; the identity of "Kurdish woman" includes resistance against women's subordination within the Kurdish community and imposed national identities.

**Mojab, Shahrzad and Amir Hassanpour**. (2004). Kurdish diaspora. In Ian Skoggard (Ed.), *Encyclopedia of diasporas* (pp. 214-24). Diasporas. Human Relations Area Files, Inc.

**Keywords:** homeland; hostland; Europe

**Wahlbeck, Östen**. (1999). *Kurdish diasporas: A comparative study of Kurdish refugee communities*. Macmillan Press. ISBN 0-333-75011-X (hb). Acknowledgments (p. ix), abbreviations and glossary (p. x), introduction (pp. 1-7), text (pp. 8-190), appendix (pp. 191-195), notes (pp. 196-201), references (pp. 202-214), index (pp. 215-219).

**Keywords:** specific experiences of female refugees; honour, shame;

arranged marriages in England; gender-specific problems; Kurdish women's lack of accessibility to social services and resources; Kurdish associations in Europe; Kurdish women's work in Europe; diasporic consciousness; assimilation difficulties; feelings of alienation; differences between Kurdish refugees in England and Finland.

## A. Australia

**Batrouney, Trevor**. (1995). *Kurdish immigration and settlement in Australia*. Australian Government Publishing Service. ISBN 0 644 34847 X. Foreword by John Nieuwenhuysen, Director, Bureau of Immigration, Multicultural and Population Research, (p. iii), contents (pp. v-vi), list of figures (p. vii), list of tables (p. viii), the author (p. ix), acknowledgements (p. x), list of abbreviations (p. xi), terminology and notes (p. xii), executive summary (pp. xiii-xvii), text (pp. 1-89), maps of Kurdistan (pp. 5-6), appendices (pp. 90-92), references and bibliography (pp. 93-94).

> **Keywords:** gender-specific migration/immigration statistics; refugees; history of Kurdistan; geography of Kurdistan; languages of Kurdistan; religions of Kurdistan; Kurdish national identity; the Kurdish diaspora; human rights issues; torture survivors; denial of language rights to the Kurds; Kurdish Institute of Australia; gender imbalance of Kurdish community in Australia; immigration; age; marriage; arranged marriages; Kurdish fertility rates; women and domestic work; women and familial decision making; tribe and clan membership; religion; settlement in Australia; language; education; gender-specific disparity of educational opportunities; (un)employment; underemployment; access to healthcare; family reunification; domestic violence against women; women and national identity; women's health; isolation; services.

**Hansen, Dominique and Marg Le Sueur**. (1996). Separating mothers and children. *Alternative Law Journal, 21*(5), pp. 203-06.

> **Keywords:** Australian immigration law is gender-discriminatory; Kurdish woman separated from child and held in detention at Villawood; cuts to offshore refugee program mainly affects women and children.

**White, Peter**. (1985). Political comments gagged, visiting musicians claim. *Sydney Morning Herald*, February 8, reprinted in *Institut Kurde de Paris, Information and Liaison Bulletin, 11*, March, p. 21.

> **Keywords:** Melike Demirağ, Turkish-Kurdish group comprised of two women and two men; Ôivan Perwer; exiles; censorship of

criticism in Australia.

**White, Paul J.** (2004). Die Entstehung kurdischer nationaler Identität unter kurdischen Frauen aus der Türkei in Nordwest-Melbourne, Australien [The emergence of Kurdish national identity among Turkish Kurdish women in Northwest Melbourne, Australia]. In Siamend Hajo, Carsten Borck, Eva Savelsberg, & Şükriye Dogan (Eds.), *Gender in Kurdistan und der Diaspora, Kurdologie Series Vol. 6* (pp. 327-45), Münster: UNRAST-Verlag. ISBN 3-89771-014-5 (pb).

**Keywords:** ethnic re-awakening in Turkey; PKK; Kurdish community of Melbourne; the development of national identity among Kurdish women in Melbourne; self-concept of Kurdish women prior to and after emigration; KAV; Alevi, Kurdish, and Turkish identities of women who emigrated from Turkish Kurdistan; Kurdish women's definitions of identity and Kurdishness; women in the diaspora; multiculturalism.

*See also* Urban Life

# B. Canada

**Das, Satya.** (1999). Requiem for a clandestine land. *Dispatches from a Borderless World* (pp. 50-53). NeWest Press, ISBN 1-896300-42-1 (pb).

**Keywords:** Sabah Barzangi; Edmonton; Koya; assimilatory policies of Iraq and Turkey; refugees; Jalal Barzangi; Saddam Hussein; Kurdish Canadians; Regional Government of Kurdistan; United Nations; rape; torture; imprisonment; slavery; Niga Barzangi; Ewar Barzangi; Jwamer Barzangi; poetry; Kurdish publishing; history of the Kurds; Zoroastrianism; Islam; Newroz; chemical weapons attacks against Kurds; Halabja; Kurdish autonomy; women's rights.

**Javed, Nayyar S.** (1993). Refugee women: Intersection of race and gender identities in the mental health setting in a small region of Canada. *Gender Issues and Refugees: Development Implications, 2*, pp. 801-818.

**Keywords:** women refugees; Vietnamese; Kurds; mental health; case studies; gender discrimination; ethnic discrimination; Canada.

**Peralta, Judith B.** (1997). The Kurds in Canada: A question of ethnic identity [Master's thesis]. Carleton University. Text (pp. 1-94), appendix (pp. 95-96), bibliography (p. 97).

**Keywords:** Kurdish-Canadian identities; 11 Kurdish women living in Ottawa, Canada.

**Tahir, Sabah**. (2002). Memoirs of dolma. *Canadian Geographic*, January/February, pp. 31-32.

**Keywords:** Kurdish refugees in Canada; difficulties and challenges facing refugees in the province of Alberta; importance of food in Kurdish culture; advice passed on from generation to generation.

*See also* Food/Cooking

## C. Europe

**Abdulkarim, Amir**. (1998). Les Kurdes irakiens en Europe, nouveaux 'Boat People' [Iraqi Kurds in Europe, new "boat people"]. *Revue Europeénne des Migrations Internationales, 14*(1), pp. 263-276.

**Keywords:** Anna, a 42-year-old woman from Erbil, who fled Kurdistan in 1997 and escaped to Europe; difficulties facing those who seek to reach Europe.

**Ammann, Birgit**. (1997). Ethnische Identität am Beispiel kurdischer Migration in Europe [Ethnic identity using the example of Kurdish migration in Europe]. In Carsten Borck; Eva Savelsberg & Siamend Hajo (Eds.), *Ethnizität, Nationalismus, Religion und Politik in Kurdistan:* Vol. 1 (pp. 217-38). Münster: Lit Verlag. ISBN 3-8258-3420-4.

**Keywords:** Kurdish refugees, immigrants, and migrants in Western Europe; Kurdish organizations in Europe; the meaning of ethnic identity for Kurds; marriage choices facing Kurds in Europe; marriage choices for Kurdish women in Europe; arranged marriages in Europe; Yezidis; language; identity conflicts; religion; citizenship; desire to return; contacts; PKK.

**Gairaud, Michel**. (1995). Militants kurdes devant le consulat d'Allemagne [Kurdish activists in front of the German consulate]. *Les Dernières Nouvelles d'Alsace,* reprinted in *Institut Kurde de Paris, Information and Liaison Bulletin, 124-125,* July/August, p. 103.

**Keywords:** Gülnaz Baghistani; Kurdish community in Strasbourg; ERNK; PKK; Kurdish protests in Paris; Frankfurt; Berlin; London; Moscow and Washington; illegality of PKK in Germany.

**The Guardian**. (1999). Flame and fury as Ocalan seized. *The Guardian,* reprinted in *Institut Kurde de Paris, Information and Liaison Bulletin, 166-167,* January/February 17, pp. 89-90.

**Keywords:** protests in Europe; self-immolation; Abdullah Öcalan;

PKK.

**Sengupta, Kim**. (1999, February 17). Hour by hour, a new Kurd attack. *The Guardian,* reprinted in *Institut Kurde de Paris, Information and Liaison Bulletin, 166-167,* January/February 17, p. 86.

Keywords: Abdullah Öcalan; PKK; Necla Kanteper; self-immolation; Kurdish protests in Europe; ERNK.

**Teimourian, Hazhir**. (1993). The making of Kurdish militants. *The European,* reprinted in *Institut Kurde de Paris, Information and Liaison Bulletin, 100,* July 23, pp. 148-149.

Keywords: Kurds in Europe; NATO; PKK; Turkish policies against the Kurds; Council of Europe; foreign military aid to Turkey; female guerrillas.

**Al-Tschauschli, Samia**. (1994). Frauen in Kurdistan - Kurdinnen im europäischen Exil [Women in Kurdistan - Kurdish women in European exile]. In Susanne Hübel (Ed.), *Frauen auf der Flucht* (pp. 30-34). Terre des Femmes.

Keywords: Europe; immigration; Kurdistan; Kurdish women; migrants; exiles.

## 1. Austria

**Ammerer, Irene and Rozvita Demsar**. (1984). Türkinnen/Kurdinnen in Ottakring, Teil 2: Die Arbeit mit den Kindern [Turkish women/Kurdish women in Ottakring, part 2: Working with the children]. *Frauensolidarität, 2-3,* Vienna, pp. 48-54.

Keywords: women's projects; migrants; Turkish women; Kurdish women; childcare.

**Frauensolidarität**. (1986). Wege aus der Isolation. Türkinnen und Kurdinnen in Ottakring [Ways out of isolation. Turkish and Kurdish women in Ottakring]. *Frauensolidarität, 18,* Vienna, pp. 14-18. Z A 30.

Keywords: Austria; women's projects; female migrants; Turkish women; Kurdish women; learning together.

**Hanser, Judith and Aslıhan Karabiber-Ertuğrul**. (1995). 'Ich bin wie ein Fisch.' Protokoll und Evaluation einer Selbsterfahrungsgruppe mit Frauen aus der Türkei ["I am like a fish." Protocol and evaluation of a self-awareness group with women from Turkey]. In Miteinander Lernen & Birlikte

Öğrenelim (Eds.), *Frauen im Fremdland* (pp. 141-47). Promedia Druck- und Verlagsgesellschaft m.b.H, ISBN 3-900478-94-5.

**Keywords:** heterogeneity of immigrant women from Turkey; Arabic, Turkish, and Kurdish speaking women from Turkey living in Austria; immigrant experiences; migration and identity; marriage and partnership; relations in the nuclear and extended family.

**Hiebinger, Cora and Aurelia Weikert.** (1995). Deutschkurse mit Migrantinnen aus der Türkei - Erfahrungen und Konzepte [German courses with migrant women from Turkey - experiences and concepts]. In Miteinander Lernen/Birlikte Öğrenilim (Eds.), *Frauen im Fremdland* (pp. 99-99). Promedia Druck- und Verlagsgesellschaft m.b.H, ISBN 3-900478-94-5.

**Keywords:** German language courses for immigrant women; importance of gender-specific language courses; Armenian women; Assyrian women; Kurdish women; Turkish women; political differences and conflict between Kurdish and Turkish women in German language classes; role of religion; veiling; political situation in Austria and its effects on foreign women.

*See also* Language

**Kronsteiner, Ruth.** (1995). "Wenn die Worte fehlen, muß der Körper sprechen" Bewältigung und Hintergründe der Arbeitsmigration als psychische Krisel ["If the words are missing, the body has to speak." Dealing with and background to labor migration as a mental crisis]. In Miteinander Lernen & Birlikte Öğrenilim (Eds.), *Frauen im Fremdland* (pp. 154-204). Promedia Druck- und Verlagsgesellschaft m.b.H, ISBN 3-900478-94-5.

**Keywords:** transcultural, feminist social therapy; health; relationship between class and health, between culture and health, between migration and health; ethnocentrism; racism; antisemitism; classism; homophobia; legal situation of foreign women in Austria; xenophobia; motives for migration; socialization; gecekonus; sexuality; gender specific socialization in Anatolian villages; Aramaic, Arabic, Zazaja, Kurmanci, and Rumca (Anatolian Greek) speakers from Turkey; culture shock; depression; hypochondria; hysteria; second generation "foreigners"; psychotherapy with foreign women in Austria.

**Strasser, Sabine and Uschi Daniel.** (1984). Türkinnen/Kurdinnen in Ottakring [Turkish women/Kurds in Ottakring]. *Frauensolidarität*, Vienna, 1, p. 41. Z A 30.

**Keywords:** Austria; female migrants; Turkish women; Kurdish women; women's projects; learning together.

## 2. Belgium

**L'Humanité**. (1993). Bruxelles: 750 Kurdes en grève de la faim [Brussels: 750 Kurds on hunger strike]. *l'Humanité*, reprinted in *Institut Kurde de Paris, Information and Liaison Bulletin, 95-96*, February/March, p. 10.

**Keywords:** Kurds from Turkey protest Turkish repression; hunger strikes; destruction of villages; foreign military aid to Turkey.

## 3. Denmark

**Abeid, G**. (1989). The needs of Kurdish refugee women in Denmark. *Refugee Participation Network, 5*, pp. 20-23, Oxford.

**Keywords:** women refugees, women's status; resettlement; social classes; belief systems; education; Denmark; Turkey.

## 4. France

**Bataller, J. L.** (1993). Des Kurdes en Auvergne [Kurds in Auvergne]. *Campagnes Solidaires*, reprinted in *Institut Kurde de Paris, Information and Liaison Bulletin, 103*, October, p. 142.

**Keywords:** refugees in France; immigration.

**Bordes, Philippe**. (1987). Trois Kurdes a Saint-Luc [Three Kurds in Saint-Luc]. *Le Journal Qotidien Rhone Alpes,* June 17, reprinted in *Institut Kurde de Paris Information and Liaison Bulletin, 27*, June, p. 6.

**Keywords:** female Kurdish refugees; poison gas; chemical weapons used by Baghdad.

**Le Courrier de l'Ouest**. (1993). Mobilisés pour Rojin et contre le gouvernement [Mobilized for Rojin and against the government]. *Le Courrier de l'Ouest*, reprinted in *Institut Kurde de Paris, Information and Liaison Bulletin, 105*, December 14, p. 78.

**Keywords:** Rojin Ayaz; Communist Party of France.

**Le Courrier de l'Ouest**. (1994). La jeune Kurde Rojin Ayaz a retrouvé sa liberté [Young Kurdish Rojin Ayaz has regained her freedom]. *Courrier De l'Ouest*, reprinted in *Institut Kurde de Paris, Information and Liaison Bulletin, 116-117*, November/December 29, p. 221.

**Keywords:** immigration; difficulties facing refugees in France.

**Dernières Nouvelles d'Alsace**. (1994). Des femmes kurdes occupent le consulat d'Allemagne [Kurdish women occupy German consulate]. *Dernières Nouvelles d'Alsaces,* September 30, reprinted in *Institut Kurde de Paris, Information and Liaison Bulletin, 113-114,* August/September, p. 190.

> **Keywords:** Kurdish women in France; protests by Kurdish women against German police brutality towards Kurdish women and children.

**Dernières Nouvelles D'Alsace**. (1994). Les enfants kurdes contre la guerre [Kurdish children against the war]. *Dernières Nouvelles D'Alsace,* April 24, reprinted in *Institut Kurde de Paris, Information and Liaison Bulletin, 109-110,* April/May, p. 111.

> **Keywords:** Kurdish women and children protest.

**L'Humanité**. (1993). La grève de la faim des Kurdes continue [Kurdish hunger strike continues]. *L'Humanité,* February 17, reprinted in *Institut Kurde de Paris, Information and Liaison Bulletin, 95-96,* February/March, p. 46.

> **Keywords:** hunger strikes; silence regarding Turkish oppression of Kurds.

**L'Humanité**. (1994). Trois Kurdes tentent de s'immoler par le feu [Three Kurds attempt to set themselves on fire]. *L'Humanité,* 23 March, reprinted in *Institut Kurde de Paris, Information and Liaison Bulletin, 108,* March, p. 82.

> **Keywords:** self-immolation.

**Institut Kurde de Paris**. (1983). The Women's Workshop. *Institut Kurde de Paris, Information and Liaison Bulletin, 2,* September, p. 5.

> **Keywords:** workshop for Kurdish women in Paris; courses for Kurdish women.

**Institut Kurde de Paris**. (1996). Paris: A photographic exhibition of the Iraqi Kurdish refugees. *Institut Kurde de Paris, Information and Liaison Bulletin, 139-140,* October/November, pp. 9-10.

> **Keywords:** Iraqi Kurdish refugees in France; women's special efforts at adapting to life in France; integration; education in France; Krista Boggs.

**Meyer, Michelle**. (1992). Femmes Kurdes [Kurdish women]. *Questions sur le Moyen-Orient: Le Kurdistan, Ed. Prospective 21,* November, pp. 99-109. ISBN: 2-905871-13-X.

> **Keywords:** interview with a Kurdish girl from Turkey living in France;

PKK; education; identity; an interview with a young Kurdish man from Turkey living in France, about Kurdish women; ERNK; Alevism; Sunnism; Barzani; Talabani; interview with a young Kurdish woman living in France.

**Telegramme de Brest**. (1986). La fête pour Fatma, la Kurde et Thion, la Cambodgienne [The party for Fatma, the Kurd and Thion, the Cambodian]. *Telegramme de Brest,* June 20, reprinted in *Institut Kurde de Paris, Information and Liaison Bulletin, 19*, July, p. 9.

Keywords: Kurdish refugee women in France; literacy programmes for women; women's solidarity.

## 5. Germany

**24 Heures**. (1994). Des Kurdes se transforment en torches humaines sur les autoroutes allemandes [Kurds turn into human torches on German highways]. *24 Heures,* March 23, reprinted in *Institut Kurde de Paris, Information and Liaison Bulletin, 108*, March, p. 82.

Keywords: self-immolation; Newroz; PKK; Kurds in Germany protest against Turkish and German governments.

**Becker, Marcus**. (1991). Diskriminierung kurdischer Frauen im Asylverfahren [Discrimination against Kurdish women in the asylum procedure]. *Jiyan-Kurdische Frauenzeitschrift,* March, p. 10.

Keywords: women and state terror; gynecological examinations of women against their will; virginity testing; rape of women in prison; women's shame about reporting rape or sexual abuse; difficulties facing women who apply for asylum.

**Beinzger, Dagmar, Heidi Kallert, and Christine Kolmer**. (1995). "Frau K., Kurdische Pädagogin in einer anonymen Wohngruppe: "Bei denen sind auch manche, die rückfällig werden"," *"Ich meine, man muß kämpfen können. Gerade als Ausländerin"; Ausländische Mädchen und junge Frauen in Heimen und Wohngruppen* ["Ms. K., Kurdish pedagogue in an anonymous living group": "They also have some who relapse," "I mean, you have to be able to fight. Especially as a foreigner": Foreign girls and young women in homes and residential groups]. IKO - Verlag für Interkulturelle Kommunikation, pp. 112-118. ISBN: 3-88939-603-8 (pb).

Keywords: social work; domestic violence against women; Kurdish woman working with abused Turkish girls in Germany; women's and girls' shelters; honour; sexual abuse of girls; importance of marriage in Turkish community in Germany; importance of bearing children;

difficulties facing Turkish girls who wish to be independent; therapy.

**Bennholdt-Thomsen, Veronika, Andrea Dokter, Gülsun Firat, Brigitte Holzer, and Karin Marciniak**. (1987). Exemplarische Lebensläufe und Gespräche von und mit Frauen [Exemplary résumés and conversations by and with women]. In Dietmar Niermann (Ed.), *Frauen aus der Türkei kommen in die Bundesrepublik: Zum Problem der Hausfrauisierung* (pp. 130-79). Bremen: CON Literaturvertrieb. ISBN: 3-88526-307-6

> **Keywords:** arranged marriage of young girls; fear of loss of virginity prior to marriage; honour; emigration to Austria and Germany; difficult work conditions in Germany; domestic division of labour; the "renting" of daughters as labour to wealthy families; divorce; division of families wrought by emigration; domestic abuse; women's shelters in Germany; alcoholism.

**Le Courrier Picard**. (1994). Des Kurdes se transforment en torches humaines sur les autoroutes allemandes [Kurds turn into human torches on German highways]. *Le Courrier Picard,* March 23, reprinted in *Institut Kurde de Paris, Information and Liaison Bulletin, 108,* March, p. 83.

> **Keywords:** self-immolation; Newroz; PKK.

**Davis, Floyd James and Barbara Sherman Heyl**. (1986). Turkish women and guestworker migration to West Germany. In Rita James Simon & Caroline B. Brettell (Eds.), *International migration: The female experience* (pp. 178-96). Rowman & Allanheld.

> **Keywords:** immigrant women; Germany; family; discrimination; racism; urbanization; patriarchy; immigration policy; marriage; divorce; gender roles.

**Decroix, Christophe**. (1993). Rojine toujours assignée à residence. *L'Humanité,* December 2, reprinted in *Institut Kurde de Paris, Information and Liaison Bulletin,* p. 24.

> **Keywords:** Rojine Ayaz; Kurdish refugee in France; immigration.

**Emma**. (1996). Jihan & Monika gerettet [Jihan & Monika saved]. *Emma,* May/June, pp. 24-25.

> **Keywords:** Jihan Ineid; Monika Ineid; Kurdish-German girls held in Syria by their father against their will; campaign by their classmates to have them returned to Germany; failure of the German authorities to seek the return of the girls (who are German citizen); the German authorities dismissal of the campaign to have them returned to

Germany as "cultural racism."

**Firat, Gülsun**. (1987). Leider weiß ich bis heute noch nicht, wie es weiter gehen soll [Unfortunately, I still don't know how to go on]. In Dietmar Niermann (Ed.), *Frauen aus der Türkei kommen in die Bundesrepublik: Zum Problem der Hausfrauisierung* (pp. 125-128). CON Literaturvertrieb. ISBN: 3-88526-307-6.

**Keywords:** arranged marriages; high birth rate in Turkish Kurdistan; importance of giving birth to a son; pressure exerted on a daughter-in-law by her mother-in-law; emigration to Germany; domestic work; friendships between German, Turkish, and Kurdish women; parental and societal controls placed on Turkish and Kurdish female students in German universities; importance of virginity; importance of beauty; the branding of women who differ from the traditional norms as "whores"; double standards regarding virginity; lack of solidarity among women.

**Franger, Gaby.** (1984). *Wir haben es uns anders vorgestellt: Türkische Frauen in der Bundesrepublik* [We imagined it differently: Turkish women in the Federal Republic]. Fischer Taschenbuch Verlag. ISBN 3-596-23753-X. Introduction (p. 7), text (pp. 9-103), 13 black and white photographs (pp. 12, 27, 34, 49, 57, 63, 70, 77, 81, 90, 92, 96, 98).

**Keywords:** life histories of women from all parts of Turkey who now live in Germany; immigration; racism; education; marriage; domestic abuse; honour; alcoholism; divorce; working conditions in Germany; working conditions in Turkey; poverty; religion; birth control; difficulties in obtaining access to birth control; abortion; childcare; difficulties in obtaining childcare.

**Frauen in der Einen Welt**. (1990). Flucht, Vertreibung, Exil, Asyl. Frauenschicksale im Raum Erlangen, Fürth, Nürnberg, Schwabach [Flight, displacement, exile, asylum. The fate of women in the Erlangen, Fürth, Nuremberg, Schwabach area]. *Frauen in der Einen Welt*, Sonderband 1, ISSN 0937-5845.

**Keywords:** Germany prior to 1945; The Federal Republic of Germany; history; flight; refugees; asylum; Iran; Kurdish women; exile.

**Großer-Kaya, Carina**. (2004). Auf der Suche nach Sicherheit: Der Alltag kurdischer Frauen in Leipzig [In search of security: the everyday life of Kurdish women in Leipzig]. In Siamend Hajo, Carsten Borck, Eva Savelsberg, & Şükriye Dogan (Eds.), *Gender in Kurdistan und der Diaspora, Kurdologie Series Vol. 6* (pp. 287-326), UNRAST-Verlag. ISBN 3-89771-014-5 (pb).

**Keywords:** Kurdish asylum-seekers in Leipzig; PKK; Sunni Kurdish women discriminate against Yezidi Kurdish women in Germany; Alevi Kurdish woman complains of anti-Alevi sentiments expressed by Sunni Kurdish woman; difficulties facing married couples in exile; empowerment of exiled women; physical attacks on refugee Kurdish women by German racists; women in hijab verbally assaulted by German youths; financial difficulties of asylum-seekers in Germany; divisions among the Kurdish exile community on Germany; attacks on foreigners in Rostock and Hoyerswerda.

*See also* Alevism; Sunnism; Yezidism

**Homann-Lanfer, Anni Jülich, Beate Lippmann, Gabriele Niedzwetzki, Schmeißer, J. A. Stüttler, Brigitte Topp, and Dorothee Wolf-Malik.** (1983). *Im Spannungsfeld zweier Kulturen* [In the field of tension between two cultures]. Verlag Modernes Lernen. ISBN 3-8080-0069-4. Foreword by Joachim Baltes (p. 1), table of contents (pp. 2-6), text (pp. 7- 210), bibliography (pp. 211-14).

**Keywords:** social work; statistics; bi-culturalism; socio-political structure of Turkey; economic migrants; family structures in Turkey; religion; Islam; Alevism; gender-specific child-rearing; sex roles for children in Turkey; school system in Turkey; living conditions for immigrants from Turkey in Germany; legal situation of immigrants in Germany; racism in Germany; Kemalism; marriage; honour; rural-urban dichotomy in Turkey; regional differences and marriage choices; regional differences and education; dichotomy of the sexes; leisure activities of women; Qur'an schools in Germany; Islamism; veiling; virginity.

**Institut Kurde de Paris.** (1995). Berlin: Death of a Kurdish woman on a hunger strike. *Institut Kurde de Paris, Information and Liaison Bulletin, 124-125*, July/August, p. 5.

**Keywords:** Turkish prisons; hunger strikes in Turkey; Gülnaz Baghistani; police brutality in Germany; protests in Europe against German policies; attacks against Turkish interests in Germany; IFHR; France Libertés; political prisoners in Turkey; disappearances; Turkish Foundation of Human Rights.

**Karasan-Dirks, Sabine.** (1983). *Die Geschichte Der Fatma Hanim in Köln* [The story of Fatma Hanim in Cologne]. Edition Herodot. ISBN: 3-88694-026-8. Foreword (pp. 2-4), text (pp. 5-189), appendices (pp. 190-200), endnotes (pp.

201-212).

> **Keywords:** Kurdish and Turkish women in Germany; domestic abuse of women in Germany; difficulties in extending residence permits in Germany; women workers in Germany; women from Turkey compare Germany and Turkey; corruption in Turkey; class differences and their importance in Turkey; poor medical care in Turkey; political strife of the pre-military coup era in Turkey; difficulties facing migrants upon return to Turkey; civil war in Turkey between leftists and right-wingers; political divisions between migrants in Germany; women's views of the military coup of 1980.

**Kızılhan, İlhan.** (1995). *Der Sturz Nach Oben: Kurden in Deutschland - Eine psychologische Studie* [The fall to the top: Kurds in Germany - A psychological study]. Medico International. ISBN: 3-923363-19-2. Foreword by Hans Branscheidt (pp. 9-10) introduction (pp. 11-15), text (pp. 17-203), bibliography (pp. 205-211), endnotes (pp. 212-214).

> **Keywords:** history of Kurdistan; geography of Kurdistan; children and war; repression as Turkish state policy; Kurdish children in exile; Kurds in Germany; legal situation of Kurds in Germany; laws regarding asylum; political, every day, and media discourse towards racism; Kurdish children in German schools; special problems of young Kurdish women in Germany; identity in exile; collective memory; health and sickness in migration; psychological effects of oppression.

**Krampfader.** (1997, January 15). Repression nach Soli-Aktionen für Kurdistan [Repression after solos for Kurdistan]. *Krampfader,* p. 32.

> **Keywords:** solidarity; state repression in Germany.

**Kurdish Observer.** (2001). Women marched for peace. *Kurdish Observer,* December 10.

> **Keywords:** 3,000 Kurdish women took part in a march and meeting in Cologne, Germany; Action Platform Against War and Racism; Kurdish Peace Bureau; Gülbahar Aslan; PKK.

**Kurdistan Report.** (1993). 100 Kurdish women on hunger strike. *Kurdistan Report, 16,* October/November, p. 23.

> **Keywords:** hunger strike by Kurdish women in Germany; PWAK in Europe; attempts at encouraging international solidarity for the Kurds; attempts at raising awareness of the plight of the Kurds.

**Libération**. (1994). Allemagne: trois Kurdes tentent de s'immoler par le feu [Germany: Three Kurds attempt to set themselves on fire]. *Libération,* March 23, reprinted in *Institut Kurde de Paris, Information and Liaison Bulletin, 108*, March, p. 83.

**Keywords:** Berivan; Ronahi; PKK; Kurdistan Information Bureau; self-immolation; protest against military sales to Turkey.

**Libération**. (1994). La Colere Suicidaire des Kurdes D'Allemagne [The suicidal wrath of the Kurds of Germany]. *Libération,* March 24, reprinted in *Institut Kurde de Paris, Information and Liaison Bulletin, 108*, March, p. 97.

**Keywords:** self-immolation; death of a young Kurdish woman.

**Linda, Dalal Frau D**. (1995). Alles ist fremd [Everything is strange]. In Ulrike Behnen (Ed.), *In einem Fremdenland: Flüchtlinge und Deutsche erzählen* (pp. 17-32). Unrast. ISBN 3-928300-35-0.

**Keywords:** Yezidi Kurdish women in Germany; illiteracy; poverty; PKK; discrimination against Kurds in Turkey; discrimination against Yezidis by other Kurds and Turks; childbirth; living conditions in Yezidi villages in Turkey; the flight of Yezidis from Turkish Kurdistan; illegality of Kurdish language; lack of schools and electricity in Yezidi villages; labour conditions in Germany; refugees and education in Germany; smuggling of migrants from Germany.

**Louis, Chantal**. (1996). Sengül wird Abgeordnete [Sengül becomes a member of parliament]. *Emma,* May/June, p. 22. Photograph by Bettina Flitner (p. 23).

**Keywords:** Sengul Senol; Köln; Green Party; first Kurdish woman elected to Köln municipal government; Arbeitsgemeinschaft gegen internationale sexuelle und rassistische Ausbeutung; immigration laws and women; difficulties facing non-German women residents in Germany; Dersim; Turkish government's destruction of Dersim; literacy and immigrant women in Germany; Alevis; difficulties facing Alevi Kurdish migrants in Sunni areas; military coup of 1980; importance of education for Alevis.

**Mazoué, Pascal**. (1994). Femmes Kurdes: la réponse politique du Conseil de l'Europe [Kurdish women: the political response of the Council of Europe]. *DNA - Derniers Nouvelles D'Alsace*, October 3, reprinted in *Institut Kurde de Paris, Information and Liaison Bulletin, 115*, October, pp. 6-7.

**Keywords:** march by Kurdish women from Mannheim to Strasbourg; delegation of Kurdish women from Turkey received by the Council of

Europe.

**Meyer-Ingwersen, Johannes**. (1995). Die kurdische Minderheit [The Kurdish minority]. In Cornelia Schmalz-Jacobsen & Georg Hansen (Eds.), *Ethnische Minderheiten in der Bundesrepublik Deutschland: Ein Lexikon* (pp. 310-28). C.H. Beck'sche Verlagsbuchhandlung. ISBN 3 406 39147 8.

**Keywords:** situation in Kurdistan; history of the Kurds; flight of Armenians and Yezidi Kurds to the Caucasus following the Armenian genocide; heterogeneity of the Kurds; development of the Kurdish language; language; religious groups; Alevis; Armenians whose mother language is Kurdish; Yezidis; oppression; PKK; DEP; KDP; PUK; history of the Kurds in Germany; statistics regarding the Kurds in Germany; stateless Kurds from Lebanon living in Germany; economic situation of Kurds in Germany; familial relations; social status of girls in the Kurdish immigrant family; polygamy in Germany; the traditional position of the Kurdish woman; patriarchy; a Kurdish proverb regarding women; changes in the position of women wrought by immigration; economically independent Kurdish women; women's rights and the struggle for national rights; divisions between Kurds in the diaspora; use of the Turkish language by Kurds from Turkey; religious divisions; solidarity between Sunni Turks and Kurds vis-a-vis solidarity between Alevi Turks and Kurds; politicization of Kurds; the length of time Kurdish and Turkish women spend in the kitchen in comparison with German women; music; Newroz; deportation of Kurdish refugees to Turkey; Kurdish organizations in Germany; illegality of the PKK in Germany; *Özgür Ülke; Özgür Gündem*; education.

**Le Nouveau Quotidien**. (1994). Quatre Kurdes s'immolent en Allemagne [Four Kurds set themselves on fire in Germany]. *Le Nouveau Quotidien,* March 25, reprinted in *Institut Kurde de Paris, Information and Liaison Bulletin, 108,* March, p. 105.

**Keywords:** self-immolation.

**Ouest France**. (1995). Mort d'une Kurde gréviste de la faim à Berlin [Death of a Kurdish hunger strike in Berlin.]. *Ouest France,* July 29-30, reprinted in *Institut Kurde de Paris, Information and Liaison Bulletin, 124-125,* July/August, p. 94.

**Keywords:** PKK; illegality of PKK in Germany; attacks on Turkish interests in Germany.

**Pogrom**. (1984). Kurden/Bundesrepublik: 'Wir sind ein eigenständiges

Volk'[Kurds/Federal Republic: "We are an independent people"]. *Pogrom*, *109*, reprinted in *Institut Kurde de Paris, Information and Liaison Bulletin, 8*, September 1984, pp. 3-4.

> **Keywords:** Kurds in Germany; Kurdish women in Germany; isolation; language difficulties; difficulties with Turkish women in Germany; Mizgin; absence of programs for Kurdish women in Germany; psychosomatic illnesses affecting Kurdish women in Germany.

**Potts, Lydia and Brunhilde Prasske**. (1993). *Frauen - Flucht - Asyl: Eine Studie zu Hintergründen, Problemlagen und Hilfen* [Women - flight - asylum: A study on backgrounds, problems and help]. Kleine Verlag. ISBN: 3-89370-158-3. Introduction (pp. 8-10), text (pp. 13-114), bibliography (pp. 115-140), appendix (pp. 143-154).

> **Keywords:** women and asylum; Assyrian women in Turkey; gender-specific oppression of Assyrian women in Turkey; forced marriages; physical torture; psychological torture; torture survivors; gender-specific aspects of torture; sexual torture; social work; family planning; women's health; education for female refugees; rape; statistics.

*See also* Assyrians/Chaldeans

**Le Quotidien**. (1994). Allemagne: des Kurdes tentent de s'immoler [Germany: Kurds attempt to immolate themselves]. *Le Quotidien*, March 23, reprinted in *Institut Kurde de Paris, Information and Liaison Bulletin, 108*, March, p. 83.

> **Keywords:** Newroz; self-immolation.

**Rona, Céline S**. (1992). Ziemlich frei! [Pretty free!]. *Unterschiede, 4*, January, pp. 30-33.

> **Keywords:** Kurdish girls in German schools; racism; national awareness among Kurdish girls in the diaspora; restrictions placed on Kurdish girls by their families; inter-cultural friendships.

**Le Roux, Martina and Lars-Border Keil**. (1999). Unter den drei erschossenen Kurden war auch eine junge Frau [Among the three Kurds who were shot was a young woman]. *Welt am Sonntag*, February 21, reprinted in *Institut Kurde de Paris, Information and Liaison Bulletin, 166-167*, January/February, p. 177.

> **Keywords:** Sema Alp (18); PKK; Israeli Consulate security guards shoot three Kurdish protesters; Kurdish Centre in Berlin.

**Savelsberg, Eva**. (2004). Einblicke in die Vorstellungen kurdischer Jugendlicher zu Ehe und Partnerwahl [Insights into the ideas of Kurdish young people about marriage and choice of partner]. In Siamend Hajo, Carsten Borck, Eva Savelsberg, & Şükriye Dogan (Eds.), *Gender in Kurdistan und der Diaspora, Kurdologie Series Vol. 6* (pp. 255-85). UNRAST-Verlag. ISBN 3-89771-014-5 (pb).

**Keywords:** views of Kurdish youth in the European diaspora regarding marriage; eight Kurdish youths in Berlin (four girls, four boys) explain their ideas about marriage and mate selection; marriage strategies of Kurdish migrants in Germany; Kurdish youths' views of Germans, Turks, Arabs, and Persians; the importance of marrying a partner of the same religion; gender roles and marriage; Kurdish girls' acceptance of gender-specific household roles; Kurdish youths' views of femininity and masculinity; greater social control over Kurdish women in comparison to German women; a Kurdish girl considers not having sex before marriage is a specifically Kurdish practice, though it is the same for all Muslims; the importance of virginity for men and women prior to marriage; German women's inability to be good housewives is contrasted with Kurdish women's abilities as such.

*See also* Marriage

**Schmalz-Jacobsen, Cornelia and Georg Hansen**. (1997). Kurden/Kurdinnen. In *Kleines Lexikon der ethnischen Minderheiten in Deutschland* [pp. 97-100]. C. H. Beck'sche Verlagsbuchhandlung. ISBN 3 406 39292 X.

**Keywords:** origins of Kurds in Germany; statistics regarding Kurds in Germany; religion; language; legal status; political situation in countries of origin; PKK; KDP; cultural life in Germany; new possibilities for Kurdish women in Germany.

**Schröder, Kilian**. (1994). Diaspora politics and change: Kurdish politics in Germany. *Kurdistan Report, 18*, May/June 1994, pp. 12-13.

**Keywords:** self-immolation of Bedriye Taş (Ronahi) and Nilgün Yildirim (Berivan); media coverage of Kurdish politics in Germany; ban on Newroz activities in Germany; "popular racism" in Germany; PKK.

**Sen, Faruk and Andreas Goldberg**. (1994). *Türken in Deutschland: Leben zwischen zwei Kulturen* [Turks in Germany: Living between two cultures]. Beck'sche Reihe Verlagsbuchhandlung. ISBN: 3 406 37465 4. Text (pp. 9-139), bibliography (pp. 140-144), four black and white photos (pp. 52, 84, 130, 139).

**Keywords:** "guest workers" in Germany; attacks against foreigners in Germany; legal situation of foreign residents in Germany; family life in Germany; religion; Islam; veiling; Sunnism; Shi'ism; Alevism; first Kurdish immigrants to Germany; Nestorians; Assyrians; Yezidis; PKK; Kurdish organizations in Germany.

**Şenol, Şengül.** (1992). *Kurden in Deutschland: Fremde unter Fremden* [Kurds in Germany: Strangers among strangers]. Haag + Herchen Verlag. ISBN 3-89228-886-0. Foreword by Jürgen Trittin (pp. 9-11), introduction (pp. 12-14), text (pp. 15-239), map of Kurdistan (p. 27), bibliography (pp. 240-42).

**Keywords:** general history of Kurdistan; history of the Kurds in Germany; difficulties facing Kurds in Turkish classrooms in Turkey and in Germany; economic reasons for migration from Kurdistan; political reasons for migration from Kurdistan; smuggling of migrants to Germany; position of the German government vis-a-vis the Kurds; identity conflicts in emigration; racism in Germany; mother language as human right; the Swedish model; interviews with Kurdish women in Germany; assimilation of Kurds; social work; Kurdish self-help organizations in Germany.

**Stollowsky, Christoph.** (1995). Sie haben keine Angst vor dem Sterben und hungern für ihre tote Freundin [They are not afraid of dying and starve for their dead friend]. *Der Tagesspregel*, July 29, reprinted in *Institut Kurde de Paris, Information and Liaison Bulletin, 124-125*, July/August, pp. 93-94.

**Keywords:** Gülnaz Baghistani; Kurdish Cultural Centre in Berlin (Navca-Kurd); hunger strikes in Germany.

**Straube, Hanne and Karin König.** (1982). *Zuhause bin ich "die aus Deutschland": Ausländerinnen erzählen* [At home I am "those from Germany": Foreign women tell stories]. Otto Maier Verlag. ISBN: 3-473-35225-X. Introduction (pp. 7-8), nine black and white photographs by Hans-Georg Roth (pp. 9, 21, 31, 45, 67, 87, 99, 103, 119).

**Keywords:** Erzincan; village life in Turkish Kurdistan; life in a gecekondu quarter of Istanbul; life in Germany; loss of Kurdish language in Istanbul; racism in Turkey; racism in Germany; tensions between Turks and Kurds in Germany; Alevism; atheism; cultural differences between Germans and non-Germans; domestic work; gender-specific division of labour; military coup of 1980; Koçgir; feudalism; Koçgir Rebellion; migration; childhood in Kurdistan; Kurdish children's fear of the Turkish military; Kurdish holidays; Turkish nationalism in the Turkish school system; beatings administered by teachers to those children who spoke Kurdish;

Atatürk.

**Der Tagesspiegel**. (1995). Kurden trauern friedlich in Berlin [Kurds mourn peacefully in Berlin]. *Der Tagesspiegel*, August 2, reprinted in *Institut Kurde de Paris, Information and Liaison Bulletin, 124-125*, July-August, pp. 112-113.

**Keywords:** Gülnaz Baghistani; hunger strikes; PKK; arrests by German police of PKK supporters; Kurdish demonstrations in Brussels, Strasbourg, and Athens.

**Terre des Femmes**. (1995). Kurdistan - Terre des Femmes protestiert [Kurdistan - Land of Women protestiert]. In *Terre des Femmes Rundbrief, 2*, p. 36. ISSN 09460373.

**Keywords:** legal measures against Kurdish organizations in Germany; protest by Terre des Hommes in support of Kurdish organizations in Germany.

**Yurtdaş, Hatice**. (1995). *Pionierinnen der Arbeitsmigration in Deutschland: Lebensgeschichtliche Analysen von Frauen aus Ost-Anatolien* [Pioneers of labor migration in Germany: Analyzes of the life history of women from Eastern Anatolia]. Lit Verlag. ISBN 3-8258-2925-1. Foreword (pp. 12-13), introduction (pp. 14-21), text (pp. 22-196), bibliography (pp. 197-205).

**Keywords:** life histories of Kurdish women living in Germany; Alevism; Aşiret System; Yezidi Kurds; Nestorians; Ahl-i Haqq Kurds; Shi'i Kurds; Tahtacis; dede system; Kahraman Maraş Massacre; Çorum Massacre; Sivas Massacre; land tenure in Anatolia; health conditions in Turkish Kurdistan; poverty; the giving of young girls to the village Ağas; girls' access to education; working conditions in German factories; abortion; class consciousness and migration; gender identity; marriage; role conflicts in marriage; migration as a catalyst for change in traditional gender roles; female breadwinners; health conditions in the Tunceli (Dersim) region; divorce; women and illiteracy; honour system; shame; Kurdish refugee women from Iran who migrated to Turkey, then Germany; Kurdish single mother in Germany; Armenians in Dersim region; Zaza language.

**Zentrum für Türkeistudien/Türkiye Araştırmalar Merkezi**. (1998). *Das ethnische und religiöse Mosaik der Türkei und seine Reflexionen auf Deutschland* [The ethnic and religious mosaic of Turkey and its reflections on Germany]. Lit Verlag. ISBN: 3-8258-3934-6. Foreword by Enno Vocke, text (pp. 1-190), bibliography (pp. 191-201).

**Keywords:** Kurdish women's organizations in Germany; Alevi Kurds;

Yezidi Kurds; Sunni Kurds; PKK; PSK; YWXK; YJWK; Yezidi beliefs regarding women; Kurdish publishing in Germany; generational differences regarding marriage of Yezidis with non-Yezidis; Alevi publishing in Germany; HEP; SHP; HADEP; DEP; DBP; Kurdische Demokratische Platform; MKM; Jiyona Rewşen; Med-Kom.

## 6. Italy

**Dernières Nouvelles d'Alsace**. (1997). Vague d'immigration clandestine en Italie [Wave of illegal immigration to Italy]. *Dernières Nouvelles D'Alsace,* November 3, reprinted in *Institut Kurde de Paris, Information and Liaison Bulletin, 152-153,* November-December, p. 12.

**Keywords:** Kurdish women refugees; child refugees.

**R. H**. (2002). L'Odyssée des Kurdes du 'Monica' [The 'Monica' Kurdish Odyssey]. *Le Figaro,* March 22, reprinted in *Institut Kurde de Paris, Information and Liaison Bulletin, 204*, March, p. 52.

**Keywords:** 200 Kurdish women refugees, 361 child Kurdish refugees risk lives to reach Italy.

*See also* Displacement, Refugees, and Migration

## 7. Norway

**Rugkåsa, Marianne**. (2004). Die Traditionellen, die Modernen und die Politischen: Politische Ausrichtung und Geschlechterideologie unter kurdischen Migranten in Oslo [The traditional, the modern and the political: Political orientation and gender ideology among Kurdish migrants in Oslo]. In Siamend Hajo, Carsten Borck, Eva Savelsberg, & Şükriye Dogan (Eds.), *Gender in Kurdistan und der Diaspora, Kurdologie Series Vol. 6* (pp. 217-31). UNRAST-Verlag. ISBN 3-89771-014-5 (pb).

**Keywords:** Kurdish groups in Oslo; gender ideologies among Kurdish migrants in Oslo; PKK; Marianne Rugkåsa, the Norwegian, female partner of a "modern" Kurd; sympathy for the PKK among the Norwegian Kurdish community; the division of the Oslo Kurdish community into three groups: traditional, modern, and political; "Traditional" Kurds from the province of Konya in Turkey; Islamic rules; veiling among "traditional" Kurdish women; the importance of a Muslim, as opposed to Kurdish or Turkish identity for "traditional" Kurds from Konya province; the lack of participation of "traditional" Kurdish women in Norwegian society; the "modern" Kurds from the urban middle class; gender roles among the "modern" Kurds; the participation of "modern" Kurdish women and children in Norwegian society; western dress among the "modern" Kurdish women; secular world view of "modern" Kurds; "modern" Kurds' support for political causes and their purchasing of Kurdish books and watching of Medya-TV; politically-oriented Kurds; political activists; atheism among political activists; gender and political activity; Abdullah Öcalan's view of the Kurdish Revolution as a Women's Revolution; honor; shame; control of female sexuality; women as symbols of the unity and purity of a nation; women as national icons; marriage.

*See also* Kurdish Nationalist Movements; Urban Life

## 8. Sweden

**Alinia, Minoo**. (2004). Die Grenzen der Diaspora: Geschlechtsspezifische Einflüsse auf die Bildung nationaler Identität in der kurdischen Diaspora [The limits of the diaspora: Gender-specific influences on the formation of national identity in the Kurdish diaspora]. In Siamend Hajo, Carsten Borck, Eva Savelsberg, & Şükriye Dogan (Eds.), *Gender in Kurdistan und der Diaspora, Kurdologie Series Vol. 6* (pp. 233-53). UNRAST-Verlag. ISBN 3-89771-014-5 (pb).

> **Keywords:** Kurdish national identity in the diaspora; the Kurdish diaspora as an important factor in the development of Kurdish nationalism; identity; identity politics; gender and migration; Sweden; Sara and Soma, two Kurdish women living in Sweden; views of immigrants in Sweden; difficulty in gaining acceptance in Sweden; women's lack of visibility on Kurdish television; Kurdish women's position in Kurdish organizations; exile; assimilation; integration; women who feel equal, but not welcome in Swedish society; diaspora women and the Kurdish movement.

**Baksi, Mahmut**. (1984). The immigrant experience in Sweden. *Merip Reports: Migrant Workers,* May, reprinted in *Institut Kurde de Paris, Information and Liaison Bulletin, 7,* July, unnumbered pages.

> **Keywords:** Kurdish diaspora in Sweden; immigration; massacre of Kurds in Syria; mechanization of farming in Kurdistan; racism in Sweden; women and literacy/illiteracy; social problems of Kurdish women in Sweden; gender gap between levels of personal freedom for Kurdish men and women in Sweden; Kurdish organizations in Sweden; Swedish support for Kurdish publishing.

**The Economist**. (2002). Immigrants in Sweden and Denmark: The worries and the welcomes. *The Economist,* February 2, reprinted in *Institut Kurde de*

*Paris, Information and Liaison Bulletin, 203*, February, p. 6.

**Keywords:** the murder of Fadime Sahindal by her father for "honour crimes"; arranged marriage; Uppsala, Sweden; vigils for Fadime Sahindal; Fadime Sahindal's funeral; integration; Danish immigration policies; Swedish immigration policies; anti-immigrant People's Party in Denmark.

*See also* Diaspora; Honour Killing

**Haglund, Roland**. (1995). Kurdish refugees in a Swedish church. *Kurdistan Times, 4,* November, pp. 180-83, ISSN 1057-8668. Two black and white photographs (pp. 180, 182).

**Keywords:** threat of deportation against two Kurdish families from Iraq; solidarity; Asele Kyrka, the church in Åsele where the families were sheltered; Rojda, the Kurdish girl elected to represent Santa Lucia in the Lucia celebrations.

**Hanson, Margreta**. (1995). Nalin Baksi: The first Kurdish member of a western parliament. *Kurdistan Times, 4*, November, p. 179. ISSN 1057-8668.

**Keywords:** Swedish Social Democratic Party; Turkish Military Coup of 1980.

**Hasanpoor, Jafar**. (2000). Kurdish refugees and nonmarital cohabitation: Attitudes among Iranian Kurds settled in Sweden. *Multiethnica, 26-27*, pp. 20-27.

**Keywords:** non-marital cohabitation; refugees; family units; cultural changes; honour killings; integration into Swedish society; tradition; Komele; virginity; abuse of women; patriarchal forms of family life.

*See also* Family and Home

**Kurdish Institute of Brussels**. (1994). A Kurdish woman in the Swedish parliament. *Kurdish Institute of Brussels Quarterly Newsletter, 20*, September, p. 5.

**Keywords:** election of Nalîn Baksi, Kurdish-Swedish of the Social Democratic Party as member of the Swedish parliament; Nalîn was born in Kherza, near Batman in Turkey.

**Turkish Daily News**. (1996). Swedish PM admits blunder over Kurdish expulsions. *Turkish Daily News,* January, reprinted in *Institut Kurde de Paris, Information and Liaison Bulletin, 130-131,* January-February, p. 59.

Keywords: deportation of Kurdish women and children from Sweden; splitting up of families due to deportations.

## 9. Switzerland

**Hilty, Anne-Lise**. (1994). Keine Rechte ohne Kampf [No rights without a fight]. *Mosquito,* Bern, *4*, p. 3, Z P 12.

Keywords: Turkish women; Kurdish women; Switzerland; asylum; female guerrillas.

**Karrer, Cristina, Regula Turtschi, and Maritza Le Breton Baumgartner**. (1996). *Entscheiden im Abseits. Frauen in der Migration* [Decide on the sidelines. Women in Migration]. Ein Buch des FIZ, Zürich, Limmat. ISBN 3-85791-278-2.

Keywords: Switzerland; trade in women; migration; Kurdistan; female migrants; labour migrants; trade in marriage; prostitution tourism; women's projects; land in transformation.

## 10. United Kingdom

**The Guardian**. (1987). Judge gives Kurds a new hope of staying. *The Guardian,* May 18, reprinted in *Institut Kurde de Paris, Information and Liaison Bulletin, 26,* May, p. 13.

Keywords: immigration; refugees; attempted suicide by Kurdish woman and her son.

**The Guardian**. (2002). I would do it again. *The Guardian,* February 18.

Keywords: Nejla Coskun; self-immolation; PKK.

**Hadley, Christopher**. (1994). All my Kurdish friends have been tortured, but they cannot crush us. *Kurdistan Report, 18,* May/June, pp. 23-24.

Keywords: popularity of the PKK with Kurdish students in Turkey; Dicle University; PKK; Hezil Ozcan, a Kurdish woman refugee in England; assimilatory policies of the Turkish education system; anti-education policies of the PKK; torture; Kurdish studies at the School of Oriental and African Studies; contra-guerrilla/ Hizbollah.

**The Kurdish Community Centre** (1997). *Annual Report 1996-1997*. The Kurdish Community Centre, London.

Keywords: childcare issue; projects for health care, women and the elderly; the Medical Foundation for the Care of Victims of Torture;

women's health problems; domestic violence; marriage breakdown; psychological disorders; HIV; AIDS; birth control; monogamy; polygyny; gender conflict between staff; the need for support of disadvantaged women of the Kurdish community in London.

**Kurdistan Report**. (1994). Go and see for yourself who the real terrorists are! *Kurdistan Report, 17,* February/March, pp. 22-24.

**Keywords:** interviews with hunger strikers; female hunger striker's message to women of the world; calls for solidarity; PKK; Kurdish girls speak about their identity and their reasons for going on a hunger strike; Halk Evi in London.

**Kurdistan Report**. (2001). Support Zaide Asan! *Kurdistan Report, 31,* Autumn, p. 81.

**Keywords:** Zaide Asan; torture; threat of deportation; Kurdish Community Centre in Haringey; Ilisu Dam Campaign; Freedom for Kurdistan, Freedom for Öcalan Campaign; National Coalition of Anti-Deportation Campaigns.

**Kurdistan Report**. (1991). "I want to go back to my country soon..." *Kurdistan Report, 5,* October, pp. 28-29. Also appeared in *Kurdish women: The struggle for national liberation and women's rights.* London: KIC/KSC Publications, pp. 39-40.

**Keywords:** Teresa Allan interviews Gülsin, a Kurdish refugee in London; London's Kurdistan Workers Association; village of Der Sim in Northern Kurdistan; language laws of Turkey; education; harassment by security forces; supposed lack of arranged marriages in Kurdish culture; difficulties facing refugees in Britain; deportations of Kurdish villagers; 1989 Newroz celebrations; Kurdish community of London; tensions between Turkish and Kurdish communities in London.

**Kurdistan Workers Association**. (1996). *Annual Report 1995-1996.* Kurdistan Workers Association and Community Center, London.

**Keywords:** gender conflict between staff at the Kurdistan Workers' Association; patriarchal nature of traditional Kurdish society; creche/nursery project.

**Steiner, Susie and Stewart Tendler**. (1999). My sister was fearless and passionate about our cause. *The Times,* February 17, reprinted in *Institut Kurde de Paris, Information and Liaison Bulletin, 166-167,* January-February, pp. 119-

120.

**Keywords:** Necla Kanteper; self-immolation; Gülsen Kanteper; Kadirye Kanteper; Kurds in Northern Cyprus; PKK; Kurds in England; refugees; asylum.

**Uğuriş, Tijen.** (2001). *Diaspora and citizenship: Kurdish women in London* [Paper presentation]. The East London Refugee Conference: Crossing Borders and Boundaries. Organized by Social Action for Health, June 25.

**Keywords:** diaspora; citizenship; Kurdish women from Turkey living in London; identity; gender; ethnicity; class; status; sexuality; ability; age/generation; Alevi Kurds; Zaza community; Sunnis; Yezidis; homophobia in the exiled Kurdish community; Asylum and Immigration Appeals Act of 1993; access to services in London; racism; class exploitation; heterogeneity of the diasporic social space occupied by Kurdish women.

**Uğuriş, Tijen.** (2004). Landschaften der Diaspora: Kurdische Frauen in London [Landscapes of the diaspora: Kurdish women in London]. In Siamend Hajo, Carsten Borck, Eva Savelsberg, & Şukriye Dogan (Eds.), *Gender in Kurdistan und der Diaspora, Kurdologie Series Vol. 6*, (pp. 15-31). UNRAST-Verlag. ISBN 3-89771-014-5 (pb).

**Keywords:** Kurdish refugees in London; psychological trauma; separation from families; multiculturalism; British colonialism; ethnicity; Alevism; Sunnism; citizenship; European Union.

*See also* Alevism; Sunnism; Urban Life

**Wahlbeck, Östen.** (1998). Community work and exile politics: Kurdish refugee associations in London. *Journal of Refugee Studies, 11*(3), pp. 215-30.

**Keywords:** Kurdistan Workers Association; Kurdish community of North London; Alevi refugees; British immigration policies; exploitation of Kurdish labour in British sweatshops; solidarity among refugees; an interview with a Kurdish woman refugee from Iran.

# D. Japan

**Ozawa, Harumi.** (2003). Kurds fight for status, monitor war. *The Daily Yomiuri,* April 3, reprinted in *Institut Kurde de Paris, Information and Liaison Bulletin, 217*, April, p. 17.

**Keywords:** Kurdish refugees from Turkey in Japan; Meryem Kosal, a Kurdish woman who, along with her family, was denied refugee status in Japan; the detention of asylum seekers by the Japanese authorities; Japan's failure to recognize Kurdish asylum seekers from Turkey; Kurdish refugees in Japan watch developments in Kurdistan.

*See also* Displacement, Refugees, and Migration

## E. U.S.A.

**American Kurdish Information Network and the Human Rights Alliance** (Eds.). (1998). *The fast for peace in Kurdistan and the freedom of Leyla Zana.* AKIN. ISBN 0-9658604-9-3. Preface by Kani Xulam (pp. 1-2), letter asking for the nomination of Leyla Zana for the 1997 Nobel Peace Prize by John Edward Porter (pp. 3-4), text (pp. 7-153), acknowledgments (p. 154), 11 photographs (nine black and white, unnumbered center pages, two color photographs, front and back covers).

**Keywords:** Leyla Zana; Mehdi Zana; HEP; human rights; KNC; Kathryn Cameron Porter; Kani Xulam; Amed Kozlu; Ferda Beyrikan; Linnaea Melcarek; Dara Rizgari; Bob Filner; Esteban Torres; Benjamin Gilman; Lee Hamilton; Patrick Leahy; Maurice D. Hinchey; John Edward Porter; Elizabeth Furse; Steve Horn; Neil Abercrombie; Steny Hoyer; Frank Pallone; Brad Sherman; Edward Kennedy; Elie Wiesel; Jose Ramos-Horta; Dario Fo; France Rame; jailed Kurdish parliamentarians; Jack Healy; Bill Callahan; Quixote Center; Bianca Jagger; Sezgin Tanrıkulu; Elena Bonner; Jennifer Harbury; East Timor Action Network; Guatemalan Human Rights Commission/USA; Friends Committee on National Legislation; First Congregational United Church of Christ; Canadian Labour Congress; Tom Ver Ploeg; Eziz Bawermend; Parliament of Kurdistan in Exile; Svend J. Robinson; Dr. Mahmut Osman; Burhan Elturan; President Clinton.

**The Cyprus Weekly.** (1987). Dr. Saeedpour: A Kurd with a cause. *The Cyprus Weekly,* May 15-21, reprinted in *Institut Kurde de Paris, Information and Liaison Bulletin, 27,* June, p. 21.

**Keywords:** Vera Saeedpour; American Hellenic Association; situation of Kurds in Turkey.

**Gamk.** (1997). Le Sort de Leyla Zana Evoque Devant le Congres Americain. *Gamk,* November 21, reprinted in *Institut Kurde de Paris, Information and Liaison Bulletin, 152-153,* November-December, pp. 63-64.

**Keywords:** Leyla Zana; KDP; PUK; President Clinton; Saddam Hussein; Halabja.

**Howe, Marvine**. (1986). Kurdish culture finds Brooklyn home. *The New York Times,* March 23, reprinted in *Institut Kurde de Paris, Information and Liaison Bulletin, 17*, March, p. 89.

Keywords: Vera Beaudin Saeedpour; Hommayoun Saeedpour; Kurdish library; Kurdish Program; Cultural Survival Inc.

**İmset, İsmet G**. (1994). US Congress prepares to send letter of concern to Çiller. *Turkish Daily News,* September 24, reprinted in *Institut Kurde de Paris, Information and Liaison Bulletin, 113-114,* August-September, p. 174.

Keywords: U.S. Congress; DEP; Bundestag; Commission on Security and Cooperation in Europe; U.S. Committee on Foreign Affairs.

**Institut Kurde de Paris**. (1997). Washington: Congress the fate of Leyla Zana and the Kurdish question are raised. *Institut Kurde de Paris, Information and Liaison Bulletin, 152-153*, November-December, pp, 7-8.

Keywords: Steny Hoyer; President Clinton; Leyla Zana; Helsinki Commission; NATO; Democratic Party of Kurdistan; PUK; Congress Helsinki Watch Commission; Turkey's use of napalm and fragmentation bombs; Eşber Yağmurdereli; Mrs. Elisabeth Purse; Assyrian minority; Iraqi national congress; Halabja.

**Institut Kurde de Paris**. (1997). American congressmen launch a campaign for the release of the Kurdish M.P. Leyla Zana. *Institut Kurde de Paris, Information and Liaison Bulletin, 148-149,* July-August, pp. 5-6.

Keywords: Leyla Zana; American Congress Representatives; State Security Court; Helsinki Commission of the House of Representatives.

**Institut Kurde de Paris**. (1998). A meeting between Leyla Zana and the American under-secretary of state. *Institut Kurde de Paris, Information and Liaison Bulletin, 154-155,* January- February, pp. 9-10.

Keywords: John Shattuck, Leyla Zana; Leyla Zana's nomination for the Nobel Peace Prize; U.S. sale of helicopters to Turkey; systematic torture; obstacles to freedom of expression; American delegation to Turkey; Senator Porter; European Parliament resolution calling for the release of Leyla Zana; United Nations' Commission on Human Rights.

**Institut Kurde de Paris**. (1999). Evidence by Kurdish lawyer Rojbin Tuğan before lawyers committee for human rights, New York. *Institut Kurde de Paris, Information and Liaison Bulletin, 166-167,* January-February, pp. 10-11.

Keywords: Rojbin Tuğan; Hakkari; Köprücük.

**Mathews, Ann**. (1991). Keeping Kurdish in America. *Kurdish Life*, *1*, Fall, pp. 8-10.

**Keywords:** Kurdish women in the United States: Muntaha Zana; Chiman Zebari; Herro Mustafa; national identity; Kurdish politics in the Middle East.

**McGrov, Mary.** (1997). Human rights may be coming. *International Herald Tribune*, December 1, reprinted in *Institut Kurde de Paris, Information and Liaison Bulletin, 152-153*, November-December, pp. 99-100.

**Keywords:** Robert F. Kennedy Foundation for Human Rights; Leyla Zana; Şenal Sarıhan; Sezgin Tanrıkulu.

**Turkish Daily News.** (1994). US Law Group criticizes DEP case. *Turkish Daily News*, August 11, reprinted in *Institut Kurde de Paris, Information and Liaison Bulletin, 113-114*, August-September, p.36.

**Keywords:** International Human Rights Law Group; DEP.

**Turkish Daily News.** (1997). US Congressman plan to push for release of Zana. *Turkish Daily News*, July 27, reprinted in *Institut Kurde de Paris, Information and Liaison Bulletin, 148-149*, July-August, p. 78.

**Keywords:** Leyla Zana; AKIN; U.S. House of Representatives.

**Turkish Daily News.** (1997). Zana's lawyers will receive Kennedy Award. *Turkish Daily News*, November 21, reprinted in *Institut Kurde de Paris, Information and Liaison Bulletin, 152-153*, November-December, p. 65.

**Keywords:** DEP; Leyla Zana; 1997 Robert F. Kennedy Human Rights Award; Şenal Sarıhan; Sezgin Tanr2kulu; Diyarbakir Human Rights Foundation; 1995 Sakharov Peace Prize.

**Turkish Daily News.** (1997). Zana's lawyer shocks pro-Kurdish congressional crowd. *Turkish Daily News*, November 22, reprinted in *Institut Kurde de Paris, Information and Liaison Bulletin, 152-153*, November-December, p. 66.

**Keywords:** Leyla Zana; Robert F. Kennedy; Human Rights Awards; PKK; Şenal Sarıhan; Sezgin Tanrıkulu; Diyarbakir Human Rights Foundation.

**U.S. State Department.** (1989). Country report on human rights practices for 1988. *US Government Printing Office, Washington*, reprinted in *Institut Kurde de Paris, Information and Liaison Bulletin, 49-50-51*, April-May-June 1989, pp. 1-14.

**Keywords:** Turkey; Iran; torture; political killing; disappearance; arbitrary arrests; detention; exile; denial of fair public trial; freedom of speech and the press; freedom of peaceful assembly; freedom of religion; freedom of movement; discrimination based on race, sex, religion, language, and social status.

## II. KURDISTAN

### A. General

**Alberti, Fulvia**. (1992). Kurdistan: Le combat des femmes [Kurdistan: The struggle of women]. *femina,* September 20, reprinted in *Institut Kurde de Paris, Information and Liaison Bulletin, 89-90,* August/September, pp. 84-86.

**Keywords:** pre-Islamic Kurdish women rulers; Kurdish proverbs about women; women's work; widows of Barzan; Kurdish women deputies; female guerrillas; KSP.

**Alberti, Fulvia**. (1994). Kurdistan: Un Peuple en Otage [Kurdistan: A people hostage]. *femina,* March, pp. 15-17, reprinted in *Institut Kurde de Paris, Information and Liaison Bulletin, 108,* March, pp. 3-5.

**Keywords:** embargo; war; Turkish bombing of PKK bases; U.N.; typhoid; malaria; diarrhea; health problems facing pregnant women; anaemia; female doctors; Islamists; Iranian funding of Islamists; Zhinan; women's education; first women's magazine in Kurdistan; female prisoners; Hero Khan Talabani; bombing of Kurdistan by Turkey and Iran; Iraqi agents in Kurdistan; Assyrian Christians; KDP; PUK; discrimination against Christians; refugees; emigration.

**Brooks, Geraldine**. (1993). For Kurds, at least, "safe area" designation provides protection. *The Wall Street,* May 21, reprinted in *Institut Kurde de Paris, Information and Liaison Bulletin, 97-98,* April/May, pp. 74-75.

**Keywords:** Operation Provide Comfort; Arabization policies of Saddam Hussein; Teacher Training Institute for Girls; Talabani; Christians in Iraqi Kurdistan; economic difficulties; war widows; Zhinan Women's Union of Kurdistan; Anfal; Halabja.

**Cafler, Caroline**. (1991). J'ai été infirmière dans un camp kurde [I was a nurse in a Kurdish camp]. *Cosmopolitan,* November, reprinted in *Institut Kurde de Paris, Information and Liaison Bulletin, 80-81,* November/December 1991, pp. 12-17.

**Keywords:** health conditions; refugees; refugee camps; typhoid.

**Cerha, Birgit**. (1991). Und wieder einmal erwach Kurdistan zu neuem Leben [And once again Kurdistan is awakening to new life]. *Der Bund,* November 2, reprinted in *Institut Kurde de Paris, Information and Liaison Bulletin, 80-81,* November/December, pp. 40-41.

**Keywords:** Caritas; Saddam Hussein; women refugees; Halabja; Qala Disa.

**Fontaine, Guillaume and Olivier Touron**. (2000). Voyage dans L'Irak Interdit [Travel to Iraq forbidden]. *VSD,* 1168, January 13-19, reprinted in *Institut Kurde de Paris, Information and Liaison Bulletin, 178,* January, pp. 48- 53.

**Keywords:** female soldiers; PDK; PUK; PKK; Islamists; autonomous region of Iraq; smuggling; tradition which prevents widows from working; Organization of Independent Women; honour; prostitution; repudiation of women; mutilation of women; murder of women; women refugees; suicide; self-immolation.

**Institut Kurde de Paris**. (1999). Irbil: A new government is formed. *Institut Kurde de Paris, Information and Liaison Bulletin, 176-177,* November/December, pp. 6-7.

**Keywords:** Kurdish parliament in Irbil; KDP; Barzani; Nazanin Mohamed Wasu; Nesrin Berwari.

**KIC/KSC Publications**. (1995). *Resistance: Women in Kurdistan.* London: KIC/KSC Publications. 26 photographs, one colour, 25 black and white (front and back covers, unnumbered front page and pp. 1, 5, 6, 9, 11, 12, 13, 14, 19, 25, 28, 29, 31, 33, 39, 41, 43, 49, 50).

**Keywords:** Leyla Zana; Kani Xulam; prison; death threats; torture; self-immolation in exile; disappearance of political prisoners; mothers of the disappeared; violence against the press; destruction of Kurdish villages in Turkey; life of Kurdish women; resistance of Kurdish women; contra-guerrillas; women and the trade-union movement; Adela Khanum; Turkish colonialism and the oppression of women in Kurdistan; position of Kurdish women; Kurdish International Women's Conference; Abdullah Öcalan.

**Kutschera, Chris**. (1993). L'espoir du peuple kurde [The hope of the Kurdish people]. *Je Bouquine,* February, reprinted in *Institut Kurde de Paris, Information and Liaison Bulletin, 95-96,* February/March, pp. 31-39.

**Keywords:** Halabja; Iran-Iraq War; Kaladiza; lack of veiling among Kurdish women; chemical bombardment of Halabja; orphans; widows; education.

**Leukefeld, Karin**. (1996). Die Frauen von Kurdistan [The women of Kurdistan]. In Karin Leukefeld (Ed.), *"Solange noch ein Weg ist..."*: *Die Kurden zwischen Verfolgung und Widerstand* (pp. 208-227). Göttingen: Verlag Die Werkstatt. ISBN 3-89533-161-9. Photographs by Sebastian Bolesch and Ralf Maro, five black and white photographs (pp. 209, 219, 225, 227).

> **Keywords:** clan structure of the Kurds; preference of male children as opposed to female children; bride price; arranged marriages; honour; honour killings; Dersim Rebellion of 1938/39; Alevi Kurdish women; Alevi Kurdish women's dress; Alevi Kurdish women's equal position; polygamy; *Mem o Zin*; Musa Beg Kiõani; colonialism; PKK; International Women's Day; KDP; PUK; women's peace march from Suleymania to Erbil; TAJK; rape; torture; Anfâl; female lawyers; female artists; female journalists; female guerillas; Independent Women's Union of Kurdistan; Kurdish proverbs about women; Women's Union of the PUK; women workers; KOMJIN; YAJK; Kurdistan Parliament in Exile; Helin Delal; sexuality; Komala; KP-Iran.

**Middle East Intelligence Bulletin**. (2001). Interview: Nasreen Mustafa Sideek. *Middle East Intelligence Bulletin, 3*(7), reprinted in *Institut Kurde de Paris, Information and Liaison Bulletin, 196-197*, July/August 2001, pp. 88-89.

> **Keywords:** Nasreen Mustafa Sideek, Minister of Reconstruction and Development, Kurdistan Regional Government; United Nations High Commission for Refugees; United Nations Center for Human Settlements.

**Physicians For Human Rights**. (1993). Scientific team uncovers crimes against humanity in Iraqi Kurdistan. *Physicians for Human Rights Record,* Winter, reprinted in *Institut Kurde de Paris, Information and Liaison Bulletin, 97-98*, April/May 1993, p. 91.

> **Keywords:** Anfal Campaign; Koreme; Middle East Watch; murder of 180,000 people; collective camps for women and elderly; Birjinni; relocation camps.

**Roberts, Gwynne.** (1992). A silent Holocaust of the Kurds. *The Independent,* January 11, reprinted in *Institut Kurde de Paris, Information and Liaison Bulletin, 82,* January, p. 12.

> **Keywords:** Anfal; starvation; women and children survivors and victims of war.

**Wilson, Ruth**. (1988). Kurdistan: A nation severed by borders. *Connexions,*

*26*, pp. 16-18.

**Keywords:** Ottoman rule; Kurdish uprisings; NATO; U.S. foreign policy; Russian occupation of Iran; British occupation of Iran; Arabization policy of Syria; effects of war on women; Republic of Mahabad; Komala; KDP; PUK; imprisonment; torture; assassination; rape; solidarity among minorities in Iraq.

## B. Armenia and Azerbaijan

**Abramian, Jackline**. (1992). Jarjaris–a Kurdish village in Armenia. *Kurdistan Report, 11*, September, pp. 21-22.

**Keywords:** Jarjaris Village; Yezidism; Kurdish women in Armenia; domestic work; domestic culture; dress; food; Rooja Mazala (Day of the Graves) feast held on the second Thursday in June; Yezidi women's mourning rituals.

*See also* Customs and Beliefs; Yezidism

## C. Iran

**Dubois, Christian**. (1983). Kurdes: guerre à Khomeiny [Kurds: War in Khomeini]. *L'Express,* July 29, pp. 64-69, reprinted in *Institut Kurde de Paris, Information and Liaison Bulletin, 2*, September, unnumbered pages.

**Keywords:** lack of veiling among Kurdish women; Khomeini; Barzani.

**Ingold, Jean-Luc**. (1988). Téhéran, cité-fantôme. *L'Hebdo Suisse,* April 14, reprinted in *Institut Kurde de Paris, Information and Liaison Bulletin, 37-38-39*, April-June, p. 11.

**Keywords:** PUK; Halabja; Iraqi Kurdish refugees in Iran.

**Iranian Women Students' Federation (U.S.A.)**. (1987). Kurdish women: Their lives and struggles. In Miranda Davies (Ed.), *Third World - Second Sex: Vol. 2* (pp. 87-89). London: Zed Books.

**Keywords:** civil war in Iran; Kurdish opposition to the Islamic Republic: the movement for autonomy; women and social class; women's work; marriage; cities and villages; feudalism; tribalism; domestic violence; refugees; female guerillas.

**Kordi, Gohar**. (1991). *Iranian Odyssey.* London: Serpent's Tail. Text (pp. 1-141).

**Keywords:** author born in a small Kurdish village; moved to Tehran with family; mother-daughter relations; girls in Iranian society; health; blindness; smallpox; marriage of children; gender roles; Newroz; poverty; education; student activism; rural-urban migration; poverty; Amirabad Prison; torture; Shah Mohammed Reza; the White Revolution.

**Kurdistan Komitee Frankfurt.** (1986). Frauen, Islam und Islamische Unterdrückung [Women, Islam and Islamic oppression]. *Kurdistan Info, 4,* June, pp. 7-8.

**Keywords:** women living under Islamic law; women living under capitalism; women living under the Shah; women and work; housework; factory work; women and childcare; women's role in the overthrow of the Shah; Khomeini's position regarding women; blood money; veiling; Islamic dress; women demanding secularism.

**Kurdistan Komitee Frankfurt.** (1986). Frauen [Women]. *Kurdistan Info, 4,* June, p. 7.

**Keywords:** women's participation in political life in Iranian Kurdistan; female guerrillas; literacy courses for women; courses in hygiene and childcare; Islamic law.

**Outwrite.** (1987). Under pressure but resisting: Three refugees describe the Kurdish struggle in Iran. *Outwrite,* May, reprinted in *Institut Kurde de Paris, Information and Liaison Bulletin, 26,* May, p. 15.

**Keywords:** Iranian Kurdish women in exile; Shah Reza Pahlavi; Ayatollah Khomeini; Islamic Republic; civil war; KDPI; Komala; political prisoners in Turkey; Pamuk Yıldız; torture; Dev Yol.

**Revolutionary Worker.** (1980). Interview with Sheik Ezzedin Hosseini, a respected leader of the Kurdish People. *Revolutionary Worker,* July 11, pp. S2, S6.

**Keywords:** Komoleh; Khomeini; Sheik Ezzedin Hosseini; U.S. policy; Tudeh Party; KDP; Pasdaran; Kurdistan; Savak.

**Revolutionary Worker.** (1980). The Kurds: A history of oppression and revolutionary struggle. *Revolutionary Worker,* July 11, pp. S4-S5.

**Keywords:** refugees; the Shah; tradition of resistance; U.S. support for the Shah; Kurdish Republic; SAVAK; uprising against the Shah; peasant revolts; Islamic Republic; peasant movement; feudalism; Marxist-Leninist organizations.

**Women's Commission of the Iranian Students Association**. (1984). Kurdish women: Their lives and struggles. *Women and Struggle in Iran, 3,* Summer, pp. 14-15. Four photographs.

> **Keywords:** civil war in Iran; Kurdish opposition to the Islamic Republic: the movement for autonomy; women and social class; women's work; marriage; cities and villages; feudalism; tribalism; domestic violence; refugees; female guerillas.

## D. Iraq

**Alberti, Fulvia**. (1992). Kurdistan le combat des femmes [Kurdistan the fight of women]. *Femina,* September 20, pp. 84-86.

> **Keywords:** pre-Islamic Kurdish women who governed; tradition; women's work; village of Barzan; widows of Barzan; female parliamentarians; importance of virginity for marriage; female khans; KSP; economic conditions in Iraqi Kurdistan; women warriors.

**Babakhan, Ali**. (1994). *Les Kurdes d'Irak* [Iraqi Kurds]. Lebanon: Dépôt légal. ISBN: 2-9508641-0-4. Introduction (pp. 9-18), text (pp. 19-338), maps (pp. 339-45), index (pp. 346-47), table of contents (pp. 348-51).

> **Keywords:** natural resources of Iraqi Kurdistan; the Kurds under the monarchy; the Kurds under the Republic; revolts; Fayli Kurds; Luristan; Kurdish dialects; political history of Fayli Kurds in Iraq; Fayli Kurds and the Iraqi National Movement; Fayli Kurds and the Iraqi Economy; Deportation; Ba'th Party; Ba'thization of the Kurds; policies of Arabization; internal deportation; PDK; Talabani; Saddam Hussein; Iran-Iraq War; Iraqi legislation; deportation camps; divorce; inheritance laws; Islamic law.

**Chahal, Nahla**. (2000). Saddam Hussein renvoie les femmes dans leurs foyers [Saddam Hussein sends women back to their homes]. *Courrier International, 506,* July 13-19, reprinted in *Institut Kurde de Paris, Information and Liaison Bulletin, 184-185,* July/August, p. 39.

> **Keywords:** new restrictions on Iraqi women; economic effects of sanctions; presence of women in public space; honor killings made legal.

**Cobbett, Deborah**. (1986). Women in Iraq. In CARDRI (Committee Against Repression and for Democratic Rights in Iraq), *Saddam's Iraq: Revolution or reaction?* (pp. 120-35). London: Zed Books. ISBN: 0-86232-333-9 ISBN 0-86232-334-7 (pb).

**Keywords:** traditional customs and attitudes; historical background; women organizing; The General Federation of Iraqi Women; torture of women; disappearances; Aida Yasin; Laila Yusuf; Ramzia al-Shaybani; Firyal Abbas; Nidhal al-Jawahiri; Shadha al-Barak; Samirah Jawad al-Musawi; Laila 'Abd al-Baki; Badria Dakhil Allawi; Raja Majid Muhammad; Amina al-Sadr/Bint al-Huda; Sinobar Mahmud; Amina Sour; Amirah Audisho; Baghilah Ali Ahmed; thallium; Dr. Salwa al-Bahrani; Najia Hatim al-Rikabi; Iraqi Communist Party; sexual torture against women; women's participation in uprisings in Iraqi Kurdistan; Union of Iraqi Women; Union of Women of the Iraqi Republic-Mujahidin; the Iraqi Women's League; League of Muslim Women; Arab Women's Union; World Federation of Democratic Women; International Committee for the Release of Detained and Disappeared Women in Iraq; legal changes; war widows; Personal Status Law; monetary incentives given to Arab men who marry Kurdish women; destruction of Kurdish villages; deportation of Kurds to Southern Iraq; women and education; women in the workforce; women and health; effects of the war against Iran.

**Dutch Ministry of External Affairs.** (2001). The summary of the report issued Dutch Ministry of Foreign Affairs: Country report North-Iraq. *Dutch Ministry of Foreign Affairs,* April 11, reprinted in *Institut Kurde de Paris, Information and Liaison Bulletin, 194,* May, pp. 84-87.

**Keywords:** refugees; forced return of Kurdish refugees to Northern Iraq; refugee policies of European countries; European Council; deportation policies of European countries; questions of honor.

**GEO.** (1990). Saddam Hussein hat uns das Leben zur Hölle gemacht [Saddam Hussein made our lives hell]. *GEO,* December, reprinted in *Institut Kurde de Paris, Information and Liaison Bulletin, 69,* December 1990, p. 15.

**Keywords:** Halabja; widows; KDP; PUK; PASOK; Saddam Hussein.

**Hansen, Henny Harald.** (1961). *Daughters of Allah: Among Muslim women in Kurdistan* (Reginald Spink, Trans.). London: George Allen & Unwin. Introduction (pp. 7-9), list of illustrations and maps (p. 13), maps (pp. 14-15), text (pp. 17-190), index (p. 191), photographs (13 unnumbered, black and white photographs). Reviews: C. J. Edmonds in *Journal of Royal Central Asian Society,* Vol. 48, Part II, pp. 185-86.

**Keywords:** accounts of travels and residence of the author, an anthropologist, member of a Danish archeological expedition working on "salvage archeology" in Iraqi Kurdistan in 1957; Dokan Dam; Zab River; Tell Shemshara; Topzawah; Tawfiq Wahbi; Sulaimaniyah;

clothing, jewelry and make-up; women's lives from birth to wedding and death; polygamous families; domestic chores such as cooking and washing; ignorance about childcare; women's education; farming; health; infant mortality; mourning rituals; religion; illiteracy; segregation of the sexes; veiling; superstitions.

**Institut Kurde de Paris**. (2000). Iraq: According to Amnesty repression is massive and systematic. *Institut Kurde de Paris, Information and Liaison Bulletin, 178*, January, pp. 5-6.

**Keywords:** torture; arbitrary arrests and detention; death sentence; rape; disappearances; arbitrary executions; forcible expulsion of non-Arab citizens.

**Institut Kurde de Paris**. (2001). An interview with Nasreen Berwari, Minister of Reconstruction and Development. *Institut Kurde de Paris, Information and Liaison Bulletin, 189-199*, September/October, pp. 15-18.

**Keywords:** Nasreen M. Sideek; Kurdistan Regional Government; KDP; U.N. Resolution 986; NGOs; oil-for-food program; displaced people; destruction of villages; gender component of workforce; female engineers, computer operators, technicians and administration staff; unemployment; mass emigration; reconstruction of villages; Anfal.

**Iraq Today**. (1978). Emancipation of Kurdish women under self-rule. *Iraq Today, III*(66), June 1-15, pp. 20-21. Three photographs.

**Keywords:** women in the Kurdish Autonomous Area, Iraq; new nurseries and kindergartens; participation of women in the Legislative Council of the Autonomous Area.

**Laizer, Sheri**. (1995). Amina: Government by rape and execution. In *Resistance: Women in Kurdistan* (pp. 30-31). London: KIC/KSC Publications. One photograph.

**Keywords:** rape and torture in Kirkuk, Abu Ghraib prisons in Iraq; illegitimate children.

**Laizer, Sheri**. (1996). Kurdish women: Identity and purpose. In Sheri Laizer (Ed.), *Martyrs, Traitors and Patriots* (pp. 161-92). London: Zed Books.

**Keywords:** *Anfal*; honour killings; widows of Barzan; Halabja; torture; refugees; guerilla movements; war; rape.

**Middle East Watch and Physicians for Human Rights.** (1992). *Unquiet*

224

*graves: The search for the disappeared in Iraqi Kurdistan.* U.S.A.: Human Rights Watch and Physicians for Human Rights. ISBN: 1-56432-057-X (hb). Map (unnumbered page), acknowledgements (p. i), introduction (pp. 1-3), text (pp. 5-41), illustrations (pp. 15, 18, 24).

> **Keywords:** Ali Hassan al-Majid; Saddam Hussein; Kurdish Autonomous Region; al-Anfal; history of the Kurds; Arabization programme; Assyrians; Chaldeans; Iran-Iraq War; Operation Desert Storm; PUK; safe haven; exhumations; secret police records; political prisoners; torture; execution; Gula Karin Ahmed; Minnesota Protocol II (Model Protocol for Disinterment and Analysis of Skeletal Remains).

**Middle East Watch and Physicians for Human Rights**. (1993). *The Anfal campaign in Iraqi Kurdistan: The destruction of Koreme.* U.S.A.: Human Rights Watch and Physicians for Human Rights. ISBN: 0-300-05757-1. Acknowledgements (pp. ix-x), introduction (pp. 1-9), map (p. 11), text (pp. 12- 106), plan of villages at Koreme (p. 14), map (p. 21), Birjinni village plan (p. 33), illustration (p. 48), Koreme graves plan (p. 53), 10 black and white photographs by Susan Meiselas and Mercedes Doretti (pp. 55-62), map (p. 57), graph (p. 70), references cited (p. 107), Convention on the Prevention and Punishment of the Crime of Genocide (pp. 109-112), Memorandum: The Elements of Crimes Against Humanity Applied to the Destruction of Koreme (pp. 113-116).

> **Keywords:** Koreme; Anfal Campaign; refugees; chemical weapons attack on Birjinni; detention and disappearance; forced relocation; dead infant girls; prayer over the dead at Koreme.

**Miller, Judith**. (1993). Iraq accused: A case of genocide. *The New York Times Magazine,* Janaury 3, reprinted in *Institut Kurde de Paris, Information and Liaison Bulletin, 94,* January, pp. 1-9.

> **Keywords:** Anfal; genocide; genocide case; Koreme; mass graves; Middle East Watch; Mergatoo; widows; American complicity in Iraqi military buildup; deforesting of Kurdish land; Baath Party; PUK; uprising against Saddam Hussein.

**Morgan, David**. (2000). Kurdish women take action against honour killings. *Women for Socialism, 4,* October, pp. 6-7.

> **Keywords:** discrimination; oppression; patriarchal society; honour killings; male-dominated tradition; feudalism; London campaign to raise awareness of honour killings in Kurdistan; Kurdish Cultural Centre Women's Group (London); Kurdistan Refugee Women's

Group (London); Kurdish Women's Organization (London); Worker-Communist Party of Iraq; Talabani; PUK: International Women's Day; feudal family relations; shame; dishonour; low status of women; KDP; Islamic movement in Iraqi Kurdistan; Kurdish women's groups.

**Nezan, Kendal.** (2001). Fragile printemps kurde en Irak [The Kurds: A fragile spring]. *Le Monde Diplomatique,* reprinted in *Institut Kurde de Paris, Information and Liaison Bulletin, 196-197,* July/August 2001, pp. 135-37.

**Keywords:** U.N.; KDP; PUK; Assyrians; Chaldeans; Yezidis; health; education; Kurdish renaissance; media; Turkmen; honour killings.

**Nezan, Kendal.** (2001). The Kurds: A fragile spring (Wendy Kristianasen, Trans.). *Le Monde Diplomatique/ The Guardian Weekly,* August, reprinted in *Institut Kurde de Paris, Information and Liaison Bulletin, 196-197,* July/August, pp. 138-39.

**Keywords:** U.N.; KDP; PUK; Assyrians; Chaldeans; Yezidis; health; education; Kurdish renaissance; media; Turkmen; honour killings.

**Nezan, Kendal.** (2001). Demokratie in Zeiten des Embargos [Democracy in times of embargo](E Peinelt, Trans.). *Le Monde Diplomatique/ die tageszeitung/WoZ,* reprinted in *Institut Kurde de Paris, Information and Liaison Bulletin, 196-197,* July/August 2001, pp. 138-139.

**Keywords:** U.N.; KDP; PUK; Assyrians; Chaldeans; Yezidis; health; education; Kurdish renaissance; media; Turkmen; honour killings.

**Off Our Backs.** (1994). Kurdish women murdered. *Off Our Backs, 7,* July, p. 3.

**Keywords:** honour killings; government complicity in the killing of women.

**Olms, Ellen.** (1988). Der 'heimliche' Völkermord [The secret genocide]. *Pogrom,* reprinted in *Institut Kurde de Paris, Information and Liaison Bulletin, 40-41,* July/August 1988, pp. 20-23.

**Keywords:** Halabja; Saddam Hussein; Iran-Iraq War; chemical weapons; PUK; Khomeini; Ba'ath Party; KDP; destruction of Kurdish villages in Iraqi Kurdistan; foreign support for the Ba'ath regime; NATO; German sales of chemicals to Iraq.

**Philip, Bruno.** (2003). Le Kurdistan, laboratoire d'une 'exception démocratique.' [Kurdistan, laboratory of a 'democratic exception'] *Le Monde,* April 17, reprinted in *Institut Kurde de Paris, Information and Liaison Bulletin, 217,*

April, p. 95.

Keywords: Halam Mansour, editor of the women's section of weekly *Hawlati* (*Aolati*) in Sulemani, Iraqi Kurdistan; no democracy for women (Iraqi Kurdistan); women as "prisoners of tradition."

**Physicians for Human Rights**. (1988). Medical team finds evidence of Iraqi use of chemical weapons on Kurds [Press release]. *Physicians for Human Rights*, October 22, reprinted in *Institut Kurde de Paris, Information and Liaison Bulletin, 43-44-45*, October-December, pp. 50-53.

Keywords: chemical weapons; Turkish authorities' denial of doctors' access to refugee camps.

**Pisik, Betsy**. (2000, December 25). Suffering of war opens way to a brighter future for Kurds. *Washington Times*, December 25, reprinted in *Institut Kurde de Paris, Information and Liaison Bulletin, 189*, December, pp. 79-80.

Keywords: refugees; returnees; women's work.

**Pointon, Claire**. (1993). The mother of all tragedies. *The Times Magazine*, March 13, reprinted in *Institut Kurde de Paris, Information and Liaison Bulletin, 95-96*, February/March, pp. 8-9.

Keywords: Kurdish women and war; women's work; widows; economic difficulties of widows; Qushtepe widows; sanctions; Iraqi embargo on the North; Barzani widows; Anfal; tribalism; changes in woman's status due to Anfal; honour killings; chemical weapons.

**Pope, Hugh**. (2002). The transformation of Iraqi Kurdistan. *Wall Street Journal*, February 12, reprinted in *Institut Kurde de Paris, Information and Liaison Bulletin, 203*, February, pp. 31-32.

Keywords: reconstruction of Iraqi Kurdistan; interview with Ms. Nasreen Mustafa Sadeek, Minister of Reconstruction.

**Struchtemeier, Thea A**. (1994). Fluchtursachen von Frauen aus Nord-und Südkurdistan-ein Überblick [Causes of flight of women from North and South Kurdistan–an overview]. In Susanne Hübel (Ed.), *Frauen auf der Flucht* (pp. 35-37). Tübingen: Terre des Femmes.

Keywords: flight; Kurdistan; Kurdish women.

**Thornton, Lesley**. (1993). Into the Kurdish mountains. *The Independent on Sunday*, July 11, reprinted in *Institut Kurde de Paris, Information and Liaison Bulletin, 100*, July, pp. 88-90.

**Keywords:** Kurdish Minister of Tourism Kafia Sulaiman; landmines; Saddam Hussein; Yezidis; KDP; Halabja; U.N.; effects of sanctions; UNESCO; women's clothes; Anfal; Mines Action Group; refugees; Anfal widows; malaria.

**The Times**. (1988). Baghdad accused of torturing children. *The Times,* March 13, reprinted in *Institut Kurde de Paris, Information and Liaison Bulletin, 34-35-36*, January-March, p. 11.

**Keywords:** U.N. Human Rights Commission; Amnesty International; Sulaimaniya; student protests; torture and killing of children.

**Wilson, Ruth.** (1987). "For us there will still be war." Kurdish women in Iraq. *Outwrite,* January, reprinted in *Institut Kurde de Paris, Information and Liaison Bulletin, 23*, February, p. 12.

**Keywords:** Saddam Hussein; Iran-Iraq war; health conditions for Kurdish women; raping of women by Iraqi soldiers; prohibition of contraceptives; reproductive rights; abortion; polygamy; war widows; government incentives for marrying war widows; KDP; PUK; cooperation with Iran; Kurdish refugee camps in Iran.

## E. Syria

**Baban, Eliassi**. (2000). Syrian Kurds deprived of their citizenships. *Kurdish Media,* February 9, reprinted in *Institut Kurde de Paris, Information and Liaison Bulletin, 179*, February, pp. 21-22.

**Keywords:** citizenship rights; restrictions on non-citizen Kurds in Syria.

**Deonna, Laurence**. (1996). *Syrians: A Travelogue 1992-1994* (C. Snow, Trans.). Pueblo, Colorado: Passeggiata Press. ISBN 1-57889-041-1 (c), 1-57889-040-3 (pb). The original French-language edition published by Editions Zoé, Carouge-Genève (Switzerland) 1995. Introduction (pp. ix-x), text (pp. 1-110), map (p. vi), 31 black and white photographs (pp. v, 2, 5, 10-11, 14, 17, 18-19, 23, 29, 30, 32-33, 34-35, 39, 40-41, 47, 48-49, 54, 55, 59, 65, 66-67, 72-73, 78, 89, 94, 95, 99, 100, 103, 106, 107, 110, 112-113), 15 colour photographs (unnumbered centre pages).

**Keywords:** honour killings in Hasakah; religious communities of Syrian Kurdistan; Jewish community of Qamishli.

**Glass, Charles.** (1992). There is no sea in Baghdad. In Charles Glass (Ed.), *Money for old rope: Disorderly compositions* (pp. 103-107). London: Pan Book. ISBN: 0 330 32209 5.

**Keywords:** Qamishli; Iraqi Kurdish refugees in Syria; torture; Halabja; chemical weapons; Yezidis; Mizgeft; Tel Tamar; Yezidis of Sinjar; summary executions; sexual abuse of prisoners; threat of rape as a form of torture.

*See also* State Violence; War Crimes and Crimes Against Humanity

## F. Turkey

**Ergil, Doğu.** (2001). Aspects of the Kurdish problem in Turkey. In Debbie Lovatt (Ed.), *Turkey since 1970: Politics, economics and society* (pp. 161-93). Hampshire and New York: Palgrave. ISBN: 0-333-75378-X.

**Keywords:** history; citizenship; nationalism; poverty; education; population exchanges with Greece; tribalism; PKK; 1980 coup; Öcalan; Marxism; HADEP; Leyla Zana; DEP; HEP; danger of female role models; torture; deaths in custody; disappearances in custody.

**Erzeren, Ömer.** (1997). *Der lange Abschied von Atatürk* [The long farewell to Ataturk]. Berlin, ID Verlag. ISBN 3-89408-069-8. Foreword (pp. 7-9), text (pp. 12-175), bibliography (p. 176), editorial note (p. 177).

**Keywords:** Leyla Zana; Bahçeköy; torture; DEP; MHP; Alevis; Gazi Mahalle Uprising; Sivas Massacre; Pir Sultan Abdal; *Özgür Gündem*; solidarity movements; *Yeni Ülke*; *2000e Doğru*; PKK; Manisa; ÖDP; trade unionists.

*See also* Leyla Zana

**van Gelder, Pauline**. (2005). Political-social movements: Ethnic and minority–Turkey. In Suad Joseph (General Editor), *Encyclopedia of women and Islamic cultures: Vol. II. Family, Law and Politics* (pp. 579-81). Leiden: Brill.

**Keywords:** citizenship in the Turkish Republic based on Turkish ethnonationalism, and the use of women as a "barometer of Turkish modernization"; Turkification through forced assimilation and mass deportation: the 1920s-1930s Kurdish resistance movements, male dominated with ethnic and religious elements, violently suppressed; the state sponsored modernization of state and gender relations had little impact on Kurdish women's lives; the rise of a Kurdish nationalist movement led by PKK in 1984 with a guerrilla force of 20% females, and stress on the "woman question"; two decades of war and destruction reinforced patriarchy due to the increased cooperation between Turkish military and Kurdish tribal leaders against the PKK; increased gender violence, both by the state and the family, under conditions of war; no state rehabilitation for women after the end of war in 1999; the rise of Kurdish feminist and women's journalism; the rise of feminist critique of official constructions of Turkish identity and women's "liberation."

**Lennox, Gina**. (2001). *Fire, snow and honey. Essays: Voices from Kurdistan.* Sydney, Australia: Halstead Press. Foreword by Danielle Mitterrand.

**Keywords:** four women from Alevi villages in Turkey; women and war; Kurdish and Armenian conflicts; Dersim genocide; Alevism and relations with Christians and Sunni Muslims; women's lives in rural areas; superstitions; first television in 1986; patriarchal relations in Kurdish society; gender division of labor in villages; female education; virginity, marriage, women, and PKK, village guards; denial of Kurdish rights in Turkey; feminism and nationalism; Kurdish women in Australia.

**Thieck, Jean Pierre (Michel Farrère)**. (1992). *Passion d'Orient.* Paris: Éditions Karthala. ISBN 2-86537-386-X. Jean Copans (Ed.). Introduction by Gilles Kepel (pp. 5-9), text (pp. 13-226), bibliography (p. 227), index (pp. 229-38).

**Keywords:** intellectuals in Turkey; women's emancipation; transvestites' hunger strike; cinema in Turkey; Islamism; Kurdish separatism; assimilation; Islamist writers in Turkey; PKK; killing of civilians; government policies in Tunceli (Dersim) region; emigration from Tunceli; difficulties people from Tunceli have in finding employment in Turkey due to their reputation of being communists; patriarchal oppression; veiled feminists; Kemalism; hyper-Occidentalism; censorship; Antioch; heterodoxies; secularism.

**Toronto Sun**. (1995). Turks get tough. *The Toronto Sun*, April 18, p. 36. One photograph.

**Keywords:** Tunceli; PKK; Turkish army; female guerillas; Bingöl; Ôemdin Sakık; Blond Mazlum.

**Turkey Newsletter**. (1989). Women and Kurdistan. *Turkey Newsletter,* May, reprinted in *Institut Kurde de Paris, Information and Liaison Bulletin, 49-50-51,* April-June, p. 55.

**Keywords:** municipal elections; Islamist gains; Turkified Kurds; state support for Islamists; Kurdish feminism; veiling; peasant women; importance of children; women tribal leaders; patriarchy; women and tribal conflicts; abuse; Musa Anter; Newroz.

**Turkish Daily News**. (1997). November: A month when Turkey lobbied in vain to become a full member of the EU. *Turkish Daily News,* December 1, reprinted in *Institut Kurde de Paris, Information and Liaison Bulletin, 152-153*, November/December, pp. 96-97.

> **Keywords:** Kurdish women plaintiffs in European Court of Human Rights; destruction of Kurdish homes by security forces.

**Verlag Medico International**. (1995). *Spurensuche: Ergebnisse der Fact-Finding-Missions nach Kurdistan, Newroz 1995* [Searching for traces: Results of the fact-finding missions to Kurdistan, Newroz 1995.]. Frankfurt am Main: Verlag Medico International. ISBN 3-923363-22-2 (pb). Foreword by Hans Branscheidt (pp. 6-7), text (pp. 8-230) map of Kurdistan (p. 13), map of Tunceli (p. 36), two maps of Turkey (pp. 39), map of deforestation in Turkish Kurdistan (p. 40), two maps of climate (p. 44), black and white photos (pp. 14, 15, 22, 23, 29, 37, 38, 42, 43, 45, 47, 55, 56, 57, 63, 70, 79, 80, 81, 91, 96, 97, 116, 117, 121, 123, 132, 133, 138, 139, 144, 156, 157, 165, 174, 175, 186, 187, 194, 201, 202, 203, 214, 215, 216, 222, 227).

> **Keywords:** war; health; children; migration; refugees; shanty towns; political status of Kurdistan; Newroz Delegation from Canada; Newroz Delegation from Germany; Svend Robinson; media censorship; attacks on the press; PKK; Alevi Kurds; Kurdish Alevis; burning of forests; deforestation; *Özgür Ülke*; DEP; IHD; HADEP; destruction of villages; destruction of the environment; chemical weapons; Dersim; torture; political prisoners; education; Kontra-Guerilla; sexual abuse of women; landmines.

# HEALTH AND MEDICINE

**Ahlberg, Nora**. (2000). *"No five fingers are alike": What exiled Kurdish women in therapy told me*. Oslo: Solum Forlag, 2000. ISBN: 82-560-1266-8.

> **Keywords:** Kurdish women in Norway; trauma; post-traumatic stress; violation of gender; violations of inter-generation obligations; honor; violation of human rights; legacy of despair; Islamic law; "morally corrupt" women; lesbianism; Islamization of prison life; gender mobility; torture; virginity; rape; depression.

*See also* Norway

**Bannwarth, Dominique**. (1994). Sage-femme au Kurdistan. *L'Alsace,* November 16, reprinted in *Institut Kurde de Paris, Information and Liaison Bulletin,*

*116-117*, November-December, p. 47.

**Keywords:** Médicale Internationale; health conditions among Kurdish women; law prohibiting contraception for women with less than five children; reproductive rights.

**Berivan** (Ed., Trans.). (1992). Die auswirkungen des Golfkrieges auf die Psyche der Frauen und Kinder in Irakisch-Kurdistan [The impact of the Gulf War on the psyche of women and children in Iraqi Kurdistan]. *Jiyan,* February, p. 8.

**Keywords:** Gulf War; health conditions of the Iraqi people following the Gulf War; psychological effects of war on women and children; cholera; typhoid; economic hardship facing women after the Gulf War.

*See also* War Crimes and Crimes Against Humanity

**Cindoglu, Dilek and Ibrahim Sirkeci**. (2001). Variables that explain variation in prenatal care in Turkey; social class, education and ethnicity revisited. *Journal of Biosocial Science*, 33(2), pp. 261-270.

**Keywords:** prenatal care among Kurdish women; socio-economic status of Kurdish women in Turkey; education among Kurdish women; ethnicity in Turkey; fertility and family planning; contraceptives.

**The Economist**. (2002). Turkey and its Kurds: A turn for the worse. *The Economist,* February 2, reprinted in *Institut Kurde de Paris, Information and Liaison Bulletin, 203*, February, pp. 5-6.

**Keywords:** HADEP; Mersin; PKK; ethnic groups of Turkey; Viranşehir; a health clinic with Kurdish-speaking nurses who teach Kurdish peasant women about contraceptives.

**England, Rhiannon, Kathy Doughty, Sevtap Genec, and Zeynep Putkeli**. (2003). Working with refugees: Health education and communication issues in a child health clinic. *Health Education Journal, 62*(4), December, pp. 359-368.

**Keywords:** views of Kurdish and Turkish female refugees in North London, United Kingdom about child feeding issues and communication with health professionals in a children's health clinic; maternal anxiety about diet, feeding and behaviour; cultural issues around nutrition and diet; social isolation and relationships; concerns about communication with health professionals; difference in family structures; feudal versus nuclear; forming relationships with neighbours of different cultural backgrounds in order to compensate; husbands not helping with food production and organization of mealtimes; cultural differences; lack of access to advocates in the community.

**Kansu, Funda.** (1999). Needs assessment of the health requirements of Turkish and Kurdish migrant women in London. *Women's Global Network on Reproductive Rights Newsletter, 66-67*, pp. 12-16. One photograph.

**Keywords:** abridged version of a report called "Assessing the health needs of Turkish and Kurdish speaking women in Hackney"; estimated that the Turkish and Kurdish community in London live mainly in Hackney; conditions in the country of origin relates closely to current health status of the women; aims of the study: assess the health needs of the women; inform the women of existing services; investigate ways of improving service by eliciting views from the women; improve communication between users and providers of services; areas which need further research: health needs of Turkish and Kurdish speaking sex workers, lesbians, women who have had abortions, and disabled women; key health problems suffered: depression, headaches, aches and pains, gynecological problems, sexually transmitted diseases, problems with family planning services, unwanted pregnancies, domestic violence, asthma and respiratory problems, gastric problems, and sexual child abuse; migrant women have settled better than refugee or asylum seeking women.

**Khanum, Saeeda.** (1991). Inside Iraq. *New Statesman and Society, 4*(152), May 24, pp. 12-16.

**Keywords:** sanctions; refugees; Iraqi Red Crescent; health conditions; malnutrition; cholera; typhoid; tuberculosis; kwashiorkor; gastroenteritis; disease; contaminated water; failed rebellions; Rutba; Karbala; Al Zubair; Baghdad; Kirkuk; Erbil; Ba'ath Party; Saddam Hussein.

**Koc, Ismet.** (2000). Determinants of contraceptive use and method choice in Turkey. *Journal of Biosocial Science, 32*, pp. 329-42.

**Keywords:** study on the use and method of contraceptives in Turkey; Kurdish couples have the lowest proportion of contraceptive use but have the highest proportion of modern contraceptive use; couples with three children have the highest proportion of contraceptive use, have the highest proportion of modern contraceptive use; couples living in the East have the lowest proportion of modern contraceptive

233

use; couples living in the West have the highest proportion of contraceptive use; a Kurdish wife or a Kurdish husband in mixed couples decreases the probability of contraceptive use.

**O'Shea, Maria**. (2001). Medic, mystic or magic? Women's health choices in a Kurdish city. In Shahrzad Mojab (Ed.), *Women of a non-state nation: The Kurds* (pp. 161-79). Costa Mesa: Mazda Publishers.

> **Keywords:** Sine (Sanandaj); women doctors; Sufism; history; mystics; folk illnesses; amulets; charms; evil eye; djinn; do' anûs; do'a; minaÍbîn; kitêb temaşa kirdin; kitêb bînîn; fâl; contraception; abortion; sterilization; importance of male children; ziyaret.

# HISTORY

**Alakom, Rohat**. (2001). Kurdish women in Constantinople at the beginning of the twentieth century. In Shahrzad Mojab (Ed.), *Women of a non-state nation: The Kurds* (pp. 53-70). Costa Mesa: Mazda Publishers.

> **Keywords:** Kurdish nationalism; Kürd Kadınları Teali Cemiyeti; Sheref Khan Bidlisi; Kara Fatma; Aynur Mısıroğlu; Turkish nationalism; Sureyya Bedir Khan; Kadınlar Dünyası; relations with Greeks, Armenians, and Albanians; Fato Nalî; Delal Xanim; Rojî Kurd; Jîn; Emîne Xanim; Adviye Xanim; Belki Xanim; Edîbe Xanim; Zeynep Xanim; Halîdîye Xanim; Nazlî Xanim; Hîdayet Xanim.

**Jaba, Alexandre**. (1998). Le château de Dimdim [Dimdim castle]. In *Le Kurdistan* (pp. 182-86), text chosen and presented by Chris Kutschera. Lausanne, Suisse: Editions Favre. ISBN 2-8289-0534-9.

> **Keywords:** story written by Mahmoud-Effendi (Mahmud) Bayazîdî, collected and translated by Alexandre Jaba in the late 1850s; the story of the siege of the Kurdish fortress of Dimdim in 1610 by the army of the Iranian king Shah Abbas (1588-1626); Abdal Khan's decision to surrender after three months of resisting the siege; Geuher Xanum, the Khan's mother, opposed surrender, and wanted women to arm, and together with men open the fortress and attack the enemy; resistance began and the fortress was conquered by the Iranians; young women committed suicide by taking poison.

**Mojab, Shahrzad**. (2001). Women and nationalism in the Kurdish Republic of 1946. In Shahrzad Mojab (Ed.) *Women of a non-state nation: The Kurds* (pp. 71-91). Costa Mesa: Mazda Publishers.

**Keywords:** male politics; the KDP; the Society for the Revival of Kurdistan (Komeley J. K.); popular magazine Nîştman (homeland); Kurdish nationalist poetry; Heyran Xanimi Dunbli'; Mahabad; Haji Qadiri Koyi; the Women's Party; the elopement (redūkewtin); feminist consciousness.

van Bruinessen, Martin. (1993). Matriarchy in Kurdistan? Women rulers in Kurdish history. *International Journal of Kurdish Studies* (U.S.), *6*(1&2), pp. 25-39. One black and white photograph (p. 30).

**Keywords:** matriarchy; women rulers; social stratification; gender equality; Kurdish court culture; Ottoman rule; Evliya Çelebi; Adela Khanum; Qara Fatima Khanum; women warriors; Yezidi women; Mayan Khatun; Musa Anter; F. Karahan; Yilmaz Güney; peshmerga; PKK; reprint of *The Illustrated London News*.

van Bruinessen, Martin. (2000). Von Adela Khanum zu Leyla Zana: Weibliche Führungspersonen in der kurdischen Geschichte [From Adela Khanum to Leyla Zana: Female Leaders in Kurdish History]. In Eva Savelsberg, Siamend Hajo, & Carsten Borck (Eds.) *Kurdologie: Kurdische Frauen und das Bild der kurdischen Frau* (pp. 9-32). Lit Verlag.

**Keywords:** Adela Khanum; Halabja; Kara Fatima Khanum; Yezidis; Mayan Khatun; Kurdish folktales; Zambilfirosh; F. Karahan; Musa Anter; Yilmaz Güney; women in the nationalist movement; cult status of Margaret (first female guerilla in Iraqi Kurdistan); PKK; ARGK; Kesire Yıldırım; Abdullah Öcalan; Leyla Zana; HEP.

van Bruinessen, Martin. (2001). From Adela Khanum to Leyla Zana: Women as Political leaders in Kurdish History. In Shahrzad Mojab (Ed.) *Women of a non-state nation: The Kurds* (pp. 95-112). Costa Mesa: Mazda Publishers.

**Keywords:** Adela Khanum; Halabja; Kara Fatima Khanum; Yezidis; Mayan Khatun; Kurdish folktales; Zambilfirosh; F. Karahan; Musa Anter; Yilmaz Güney; women in the nationalist movement; cult status of Margaret (first female guerilla in Iraqi Kurdistan); PKK; ARGK; Kesire Yıldırım; Abdullah Öcalan; Leyla Zana; HEP.

# LANGUAGE

AFP. (2002). L'etat turc se mobilise contre les prénoms kurdes [The Turkish state mobilizes against Kurdish first names]. *AFP,* June 7, reprinted in *Institut*

*Kurde de Paris, Information and Liaison Bulletin, 207,* June, p. 26.

**Keywords:** Kurdish names prohibited by the Turkish state; KADEK; PKK; the forbidden women's names: Berivan; Rojin; Rohjan.

**Frauen in der Einen Welt**. (1994). Wer bist Du, das oder das dort? [Who are you, that or that there?]. *Frauen in der Einen Welt* (pp. 49-73). Verlag für Interkulturelle Kommunikation, *2*, R 4.

**Keywords:** Turkey; language; cultural identity; Kurdistan; female identity.

**Haig, Geoffrey**. (2004). Das Genussystem in der kurdischen Sprache: Strukturelle und soziolinguistische Aspekte [The pleasure system in the Kurdish language: structural and sociolinguistic aspects]. In Siamend Hajo, Carsten Borck, Eva Savelsberg, & Şükriye Dogan (Eds.), *Gender in Kurdistan und der Diaspora, Kurdologie Series Vol. 6* (pp. 33-58). UNRAST-Verlag. ISBN 3-89771-014-5 (pb).

**Keywords:** grammatical gender in Kurmanji dialect of Kurdish; Kurmanji is different from two-gender system, and is of the type "common gender" theorized by linguist Greville Corbett.

**Hassanpour, Amir**. (2001). The (re)production of patriarchy in the Kurdish language. In Shahrzad Mojab (Ed.), *Women of a non-state nation: The Kurds* (pp. 227-63). Costa Mesa: Mazda Publishers.

**Keywords:** grammatical and social gender in Kurdish; unequal and hierarchical gender relations in language; dominance and difference; study of the exercise of male gender power based on a corpus of lexical resources of Sorani Kurdish in both written and oral traditions; androcentrism of the lexicon and semantic fields of Kurdish; patriarchal language in Kurdish culture (*Kurdewarî*) and Kurdish nationalism (*Kurdayetî*); resistance to patriarchy in tribal and feudal societies; modernist forms of resistance; language as a site for the reproduction of patriarchy; theory of ideology more adequate than discourse theory.

**Institut Kurde de Paris**. (2002). Diyarbekir: Kurdish first names on trial. *Institut Kurde de Paris, Information and Liaison Bulletin, 204,* March, pp. 5-6.

**Keywords:** based on a circular from the Ministry of Interior, the gendarmerie of Dicle ordered seven Kurdish families to Turkify the first names of 23 of their children; the Kurdish names were detected through screening of Registry Office records from 1985 to 2001, such as female names Berivan (milkmaid), Rojhat (Dawn), and Zelal (Clear).

**Kurdish Observer.** (2000). Kurdish interpretation at supreme court proceedings. *Kurdish Observer,* November 10, reprinted in *Institute Kurde de Paris Information and Liaison Bulletin, 188,* November, p. 33.

Keywords: Naciye Sevuk; Ali Adir; Güllü Çelik; Yemiş Altıntaş; Emine Kiyaçiçek; Fatma Sevuk; PKK.

**Schweizerisches Arbeiterhilfswerk SAH/Oeuvre suisse d'entraide ouvrière OSEO/Soccorso Operaio Svizzero SOS.** (1996). *Lesen und Schreiben für kurdische Frauen/ Xwendin û Nivîsandin ji bo Jinên Kurd* [Reading and writing for Kurdish women]. Schweizerisches Arbeiterhilfswerk SAH/Oeuvre suisse d'entraide ouvrière OSEO/Soccorso Operaio Svizzero SOS.

Keywords: language course for Kurdish women; literacy; Kurmancî.

**Schweizerisches Arbeiterhilfswerk SAH/Oeuvre suisse d'entraide ouvrière OSEO/Soccorso Operaio Svizzero SOS.** (1996). *"Wenn ich ein Vogel wäre, könnte ich ohne Ausweis fligen". Kalender zur Evaluation der Alphabetisierungs-, Deutsch- und Sozialinformationskurse für kurdische und türkische Frauen* ["If I were a bird, I could fly without an ID." Calendar for the evaluation of literacy, German and social information courses for Kurdish and Turkish women]. Schweizerisches Arbeiterhilfswerk SAH/Oeuvre suisse d'entraide ouvrière OSEO/Soccorso Operaio Svizzero SOS.

Keywords: literacy programs for Kurdish women; German course for Kurdish women; social information courses for Kurdish women.

**Schweizerisches Arbeiterhilfswerk SAH/Oeuvre suisse d'entraide ouvrière OSEO/Soccorso Operaio Svizzero SOS.** (1996). *Die eigene Sprache finden. Partizipative Evaluation der Alphabetisierungs-, Deutsch- und Sozialinformationskurse für kurdische und türkische Frauen* [Find your own language. Participatory evaluation of literacy, German and social information courses for Kurdish and Turkish women]. Schweizerisches Arbeiterhilfswerk SAH/Oeuvre suisse d'entraide ouvrière OSEO/Soccorso Operaio Svizzero SOS.

Keywords: literacy programs for Kurdish women; German course for Kurdish women; social information courses for Kurdish women.

**Seibert, Thomas.** (2002). Turkish state mobilizes against Kurdish names. *AFP,* June 4, reprinted in *Institut Kurde de Paris, Information and Liaison Bulletin, 207,* June, pp. 12-13.

Keywords: Kurdish names prohibited by the Turkish state; KADEK; PKK; the forbidden women's names: Berivan; Rojin; Rohjan.

*See also* Political Parties; War and Peace–Turkey

**Der Spiegel**. (1982). Die Kurden sprechen nicht mehr [The Kurds don't speak anymore]. *Der Spiegel, 28*, reprinted in *Institut Kurde de Paris Information and Liaison Bulletin,* September 1983, unnumbered pages.

Keywords: trial against 14,000 Kurds; hunger strikes; General Evren; language difficulties; illegality of speaking Kurdish; percentage of Kurds who cannot speak Turkish; PKK; Marxism; Kurdish women flee for fear of rape.

*See also* Rape

**Turkish Daily News**. (2002). Film on Turkish-Kurdish language divide is a hit in Turkey. *Turkish Daily News,* January 4, reprinted in *Institut Kurde de Paris, Information and Liaison Bulletin, 202,* January, pp. 18-19.

Keywords: Hejar, a 5-year-old Kurdish girl depicted in the film *Büyük Adam, Küçük Aşk* (Big Man, Small Love); Kurdish university students demand to study Kurdish on campus; Handan İpekçi, the writer and director of the movie; Antalya Film Festival.

*See also* Film

# LAW

## I. FREEDOM OF THE PRESS

**Arslanoğlu, Necmiye**. (1994). Being a journalist is enough to be tortured. *Kurdistan Report, 18,* May/June, p. 27. Also appeared in *Resistance: Women in Kurdistan.* London: KIC/KSC Publications, 1995, p. 12, one photograph.

Keywords: Necmiye Arslanoğlu writes about her torture in detention; *Özgür Gündem*; Diyarbekir office; detained; "physically mistreated, insulted, and threatened with death"; beaten to extract confession of association with PKK.

**Avşar, Behçet**. (1994). *Özgür Gündem,* the voice of the Kurdish people, closed down. *Kurdistan Report, 17,* February/March, pp. 15-16. One black and white photograph (p. 15).

Keywords: closure of *Özgür Gündem*; attacks on journalists; Welat Newspaper; Zagros Publishing House; HEP; DEP.

**Bowcott, Owen**. (2002). Dead but still in the dock. *The Guardian,* April 13, reprinted in *Institut Kurde de Paris, Information and Liaison Bulletin, 205,* April, pp. 35-36.

> **Keywords:** Ayşe Nur Zarakolu; PEN; ethnic minorities in Turkey; Belge Publishing House.

**Ersöz, Gurbetelli**. (1994). 27 March rubbish dump. *Kurdistan Report, 18,* May/June, p. 5.

> **Keywords:** *Özgür Gündem;* methane explosion at a garbage dump in Ümraniye which resulted in 40 deaths; Ersöz's views on the Turkish elections of 6 April 1994; boycott of elections.

**Ersöz, Gurbetelli**. (1994). This trial is a ghastly black stain on Turkey's democracy: Extract from Gurbetelli Ersöz's defence which will be published in full by the Friends of *Özgür Gündem* in October. *Kurdistan Report, 19,* September/October, pp. 13-14.

> **Keywords:** *Özgür Gündem;* the rape of a Kurdish woman by police; the betrayal of the ethics of journalism by the Turkish press; Campaign Against War; DEP; Ayşe Nur Zarakolu; PKK; attacks on the press; the tapping of journalists' phones.

**Gopsill, Tim**. (1994). The worst country in the world for the persecution of journalists. *Kurdistan Report, 18,* May/June, pp. 25-26.

> **Keywords:** Necmiye Arslanoğlu; *Özgür Gündem;* PKK; Gurbetelli Ersöz; imprisonment of journalists; *Özgür Ülke;* torture of journalists; Mehtap Gürbüz; disappearances; attacks on paper boys; DEP; village guards.

**Human Rights Tribune des Droits Humains**. (1996). Freedom of association and expression challenged NGO forum harassed by Turkish police. *Human Rights Tribune des Droits Humains, 3*(4), August/September, pp. 29-30.

> **Keywords:** NGOs; IHD; displacement of Kurdish villagers; forced evacuation of villages; depopulation policies; hunger strikes; human rights violations; police brutality; KESK; Mothers and Relatives of the Disappeared.

**Institut Kurde de Paris**. (2002). Death of Ayşe Nur Zarakolu Zarakolu, Turkey's "mother courage." *Institut Kurde de Paris, Information and Liaison Bulletin, 203,* February, pp. 7-8.

**Keywords:** Ayşe Nur Zarakoglu; Belge Publishing House; publisher of the first book on the Armenian Genocide in Turkey; International Association of Publisher's Freedom Prize in 1998.

**International PEN: Writers in Prison Committee**. (2002). Case list-July to December 2001. *Institut Kurde de Paris, Information and Liaison Bulletin, 204*, March, pp. 96-104.

**Keywords:** *Turkey*: Zeynel Abidin Kızılyaprak; Article 8; *Özgür Bakış;* The Freedom of Expression Case; FoX 2000 pamphlet containing 60 articles in breach of Articles 7 and 8 of the Anti-Terror Law and Article 312 of the Penal Code; political prisoner Nevin Berktaş, who wrote a book based on her prison experiences called *The Cells*; Elif Camyar, publisher; type F prisons; Yazgül Güder Öztürk, reporter for Kurtuluş; Asiye Güzel Zeybek, editor-in-chief of *Atılım,* raped in detention; Mukkades Çelik, a publisher on trial for Asiye Güzel Zeybek's book *Rape Under Torture,* and for a book about her husband who was killed: *Our Çakır. The Life of a Revolutionary;* Neşe Düzel, columnist for *Radikal,* charged for an article on Alevis; Gülcan Kaya, editor of MEM Publishing House; Ruken Keskin, publisher on trial; Songül Keskin, editor at Avesta Publishing House; Nahide Kılıç, publisher and editor of the Women Workers' Union Bulletin; the conference "Against Sexual Harassment and Rape in Custody" (2000); Emine Şenlikoğlu, writer; Ayşe Nur Zarakolu; Hatice Ruken Kılıç; Lütfiye Uluk; Sefagül Keskin; Gülay Göktürk; Sakine Dönmez; Ayşe Düzkan; Sevil Eroy; Semra Somersan; Suzan Samancı; Panel Discussion "Women in Life. Women on 8 March" in Diyarbakir; Ayşe Oyman; HADEP; *Yeni Gündem;* Songül Özkan; *Iran*: Tahmineh Milani, film director and screen writer charged for her film "The Hidden Half"; Shahla Sherkat, publisher and editor of the feminist monthly *Zanan* magazine; Narghues Mohammadi, journalist with the now-banned weekly *Peyam Hajar.*

**Jégo, Marie**. (2002). Aysé Nur Zarakolu. *Le Monde,* February 12, reprinted in *Institut Kurde de Paris, Information and Liaison Bulletin, 203*, February, p. 65.

**Keywords:** Ayşe Nur Zarakolu.

**Kurdistan Report**. (1994). Over 400 attend Friends of *Özgür Gündem* launch. *Kurdistan Report, 18,* May/June 1994, p. 29

**Keywords:** Release Gurbetelli Ersöz campaign; *Özgür Gündem.*

**The Observer**. (1993). Kurdish woman awarded journalism prize. *The Observer,* July 4, reprinted in *The Kurdistan Review,* October, p. 9.

**Keywords:** Bayan Rahman, winner of the 1993 Farzad Bazoft Memorial Prize.

**Özgür Gündem**. (1994). We wrote the truth and they killed us. We refused to stop and now they want to close us down. *Kurdistan Report, 17,* February/March, pp. 17-18. One black and white photograph (p. 17).

**Keywords:** murder of journalists; murder of distributors, news vendors, paperboys, and office staff; abductions; disappearances; arrests of journalists; torture of journalists; confiscations of issues; court cases against *Özgür Gündem.*

**PEN**. (2003). If not now, when? PEN stages Turkey campaign. Centre to Centre: Newsletter of the Writers in Prison Committee of International PEN, September, reprinted in *Institut Kurde de Paris, Information and Liaison Bulletin, 223,* October, p. 3.

**Keywords:** Leyla Zana; PEN; book banning and court proceedings; censorship in Turkey.

**PEN**. (2002). In Memoriam: Ayse Nur Zarakolu. Centre to Centre: Newsletter of the Writers in Prison Committee of International Pen, January, reprinted in *Institut Kurde de Paris, Information and Liaison Bulletin, 207,* June, p. 90.

**Keywords:** Ayşe Nur Zarakolu; the posthumous court case against Zarakolu for having published a book by the Syrian author Huseyin Turhali, *The Song of Liberty;* Belge Publishing House.

**Ryan, Marie**. (1994). It's important that we tell the truth about what's happening here. *Kurdistan Report, 18,* May/June, pp. 28-29.

**Keywords:** *Özgür Gündem;* Gurbetelli Ersöz; difficulties facing lawyers who defend political prisoners; PKK.

**Zortian, Natacha**. (2002). La Turquie perd sa Mère Courage. *France Arménie, 219,* February, reprinted in *Institut Kurde de Paris, Information and Liaison Bulletin, 203,* February, p. 96.

**Keywords:** Ayché Nour Zarakolu (Ayşe Nur Zarakolu), founder of the Human Rights Association of Turkey; Yves Ternon; Jean-Claude Kebadjian; Armenian Genocide; Jean-Paul Bret.

## II. HUMAN RIGHTS

**Addès, Marcel**. (2002). L'État s'essaie aux droits de l'homme. Turquie:

répression, torture... et impunité en 2001. *Courrier ACAT, 224*, April, reprinted in *Institut Kurde de Paris, Information and Liaison Bulletin, 205*, April, pp. 76-77.

Keywords: HADEP; Eren Keskin; torture of Fehime Ete; torture; freedom of expression.

**Amin, Rizgar and Kerim Yildiz.** (1996). The internal conflict and human rights abuses in Iraqi Kurdistan: Report of KHRP delegations to Iraqi Kurdistan June 1995 and December 1995. London: Kurdish Human Rights Project (KHRP). ISBN: 1 900175 06 1. Map of Iraqi Kurdistan (unnumbered front page), introduction (pp. 1-4), text (pp. 5-33), appendix index (unnumbered centre page), note to the appendixes (p. 35), appendixes (pp. 36-95).

Keywords: IMIK; KCP; KDP; PUK; Naranj Rasul Mohammed, a four-year-old Kurdish girl killed by a cluster bomb dropped from a Turkish airplane during an incursion; atrocities committed by the Turkish military in Iraqi Kurdistan; refugees from Turkish Kurdistan in Iraqi Kurdistan; Kurdistan Human Rights Organisation in Suleymania; Kurdistan Watch in Erbil; increase in prostitution in Iraqi Kurdistan; high and increasing rates of depression and suicide among women and young people; high rate of homicide of women due to post-traumatic stress disorder and schizophrenia; education; poverty; health conditions; sanitary conditions; al-Anfal; internal conflict.

**Amnesty International.** (1995). *Iraq: Human rights abuses in Iraqi Kurdistan since 1991*. February 28, Map of Iraqi Kurdistan (unnumbered front page), glossary (unnumbered front page), introduction (pp. 2-6), text (pp. 7-135), appendix (pp. 136-40).

Keywords: human rights abuses by the Kurdish Administration: methods of torture include threats of sexual torture; victims have included women; KDP abuses of human rights; PUK abuses of human rights; IMIK abuses of human rights; torture of women in Qala Cholan prison; killing of civilian demonstrators by the KDP.

**Aydar, Evin.** (1992). I'm part of my people. I'm firmly grounded in reality and I have nothing to lose. *Kurdish women: The struggle for national liberation and women's rights.* London: KIC/KSC Publications, October, pp. 9-14. Two photographs.

Keywords: Evin Aydar; chairperson of the IHD in Siirt; received death threats; interview with Radio Duisburg (Germany) during the 1991 Gulf War; highly educated; first woman ever elected a chairperson in Kurdistan; high illiteracy rate amongst Kurdish women and oppression by Kurdish men.

**Biegala, Éric.** (2002). Gardée à vue [In custody]. *Le Figaro,* March 12, reprinted in *Institut Kurde de Paris, Information and Liaison Bulletin, 204*, March, pp. 27-28.

Keywords: Eren Keskin, president of IHD-Istanbul; human rights; women's rights; Kurdish women clients of Eren Keskin; assassinations of human rights advocates.

**Butler, Daren.** (1997). Rights group makes new criticism of Turkish record. *Reuters World Report,* December 5, reprinted in *Institut Kurde de Paris, Information and Liaison Bulletin, 152-153*, November-December, p. 107.

Keywords: Human Rights Watch; torture; restrictions on free expression; death in detention; police abuse; Prime Minister Mesut Yilmaz; Leyla Zana; village guard system; PKK.

**Butler, Daren.** (1997). Turquie- Les violations des droits de l'homme persisteraient. *Reuters,* December 5, reprinted in *Institut Kurde de Paris, Information and Liaison Bulletin, 152-153*, November-December, p. 108.

Keywords: Human Rights Watch; torture; restrictions on free expression; death in detention; police abuse; Prime Minister Mesut Yilmaz; Leyla Zana; European Commission; Akin Birdal.

**Ergenc, Erdinç and Zafer F. Yörük.** (1995). Human rights conference generates heated debate. *Turkish Daily News,* November 21, reprinted in *Institut Kurde de Paris, Information and Liaison Bulletin, 128-129,* November-December, pp. 58-60.

Keywords: International Helsinki Federation for Human Rights; suspension of human rights for state security; PKK; virginity control; virginity tests of schoolgirls.

**Institut Kurde de Paris.** (1996). A new balance sheet of human rights violations. *Institut Kurde de Paris, Information and Liaison Bulletin, 136-137,* July-August, pp. 10-11.

Keywords: statistics of human rights violations in Turkey; arrests of women and children; evacuation of villages; disappearances; summary executions; deaths under torture; State Security Courts; military courts; trials of journalists and writers; banning of newspapers and magazines.

**Institut Kurde de Paris.** (2000). Assessment of violations of human rights in Istanbul during March 2000. *Institut Kurde de Paris, Information and Liaison Bulletin, 181*, April, p. 7.

**Keywords:** gender specific statistics of human rights violations.

**Kinesis.** (1996). Human rights abuses in Turkey raised at Habitat II. *Kinesis,* p. 7.

**Keywords:** human rights abuses; NGOs; U.N.; Habitat II; Mothers of the Disappeared.

**Spieler, Michele.** (1996, March 15). Frau zu sein macht es noch schwerer, sagte die Kurdin [Being a woman makes it even more difficult, said the Kurd]. *Emanzipation: Feministische Zeitschrift für Kritische Frauen,* pp. 4-7

**Keywords:** solidarity between Swiss women and human rights activists in Turkey; Nuray Şen; MKM; women and war; women's resistance to oppression; attacks on human rights activists; murder of human rights activists; disappearances; torture; PKK; massacres in Kurdish villages; Swiss press coverage of human rights violations in Turkish Kurdistan; destruction of Kurdish villages; Turkish military's harassment of Kurdish women; sexual abuse and rape of female prisoners; shame and stigma surrounding rape; murder of raped Kurdish women by their fathers; rape as societal institution; abuse of women by their husbands; fear of reporting abuse to the authorities; importance of virginity; written permission required from husband for woman to work; virginity tests; slum quarters of Western Turkey.

*See also* Rape; Switzerland

**Turkish Daily News.** (1994). Önen: Human rights in Turkey are bleak... not a hopeful picture at all. *Turkish Daily News,* December 10, reprinted in *Institut Kurde de Paris, Information and Liaison Bulletin, 116-117*, November-December, pp. 129-130.

**Keywords:** burning of villages; jailed academics; Anti-Terror Law; Human Rights Foundation in Turkey; torture; DEP; criminal trial procedure law; laws in Turkey.

**Turkish Daily News.** (1995). Human rights report 1994. *Turkish Daily News,* October 26, reprinted in *Institut Kurde de Paris, Information and Liaison Bulletin, 126-127*, September-October, pp. 214-218.

**Keywords:** torture; sexual abuse of female prisoners; rape of female prisoners; torture of women and children; deaths in detention; Zeynel Bilgen; Cemile Sanık; disappearances; press; jailed journalists; banning of the Green Party; HEP; HADEP; Leyla Zana.

**Turkish Probe**. (1995). Human rights diary. *Turkish Probe,* November 17, reprinted in *Institut Kurde de Paris, Information and Liaison Bulletin, 128-129,* November-December, p. 47.

Keywords: retrial of Leyla Zana and İsmail Beşikçi; HADEP; Ayşe Nur Zarakolu.

**Whitman, Lois and Tom Froncek**. (1989). *Paying the price: Freedom of expression in Turkey.* U.S.A.: Helsinki Watch Committee. Introduction (pp.1-9), text (pp. 11-128), appendix A (selected articles from the Turkish Penal Code; pp. 129-134), appendix B (journalists in prison; pp. 135-136), appendix C (list of confiscated/banned publications; pp.1-39), appendix D (books confiscated from SOL and ONUR Publishing Houses on 18 February 1988; two pages, unnumbered), sources (unnumbered, one page).

Keywords: restrictions on press freedom; government harassment of political journals; freedom of expression in television and radio; Turkish Writers' Union; legal framework; film censorship board; Asya Film Company; censorship of music; freedom of association; military coup of 1980; Physicians for the Prevention of Nuclear War; Turkish-Greek Friendship Association; Turkish PEN Club; role of the United States and Western Europe; SOL and ONUR Publishing House; PKK; SHP; DISK; Women's Organization for Democracy; The Association of Women in Democratic Struggle; solidarity projects organized by women.

**Whitman, Lois and Lori Laber**. (1987). *State of flux: Human rights in Turkey.* New York/Washington: Helsinki Watch Committee. Introduction (pp. 1-7), text (pp. 9-143), appendices (pp. 145-57), sources (p. 159).

Keywords: human rights violations; Turkish Peace Association; trade unions; the DISK trial; torture; political prisoners; amnesty; prison conditions; hunger strikes; Association of Families of Detainees and Convicts; prison visits; Diyarbakir Prison; death sentences; destruction of ethnic identity; guerrilla attacks in the Southeast; village guard system; abuse of civilian population; forced migration; Kurdish refugees; the role of the United States and Western Europe; Human Rights Association; PKK; SHP; Dersim Genocide survivors; government amnesty of 1950s; Kurdish refugees in Canada.

**Wölte, Sonja**. (1997). *Human rights violations against women during war and conflict* (Report of a roundtable discussion parallel to the U.N. Commission on Human Rights). Geneva, WILPF. April 1, 35 pages. Women's International

League for Peace and Freedom, Geneva.

**Keywords:** war; conflict; human rights violations; politics of peace; rebuilding; violence against women; rape; Kurdistan; Ilknur Sen.

**YAJK.** (1996). *Informationsmappe über Leben und Befreiungskampf der Kurdischen Frauen* [Information folder about the life and liberation struggle of Kurdish women]. Vienna: Vereinigung Kurdischer Frauen in Österreich. 19 pages.

**Keywords:** Turkey; human rights violations; torture; Kurdish women; Kurdistan; Sheri Laizer; women and minorities; short biography of Leyla Zana; YAJK.

## III. WOMEN'S RIGHTS

**AFP.** (2004). Les femmes kurdes pour le maintien du Code de la famille, les chiites contre [Kurdish women for maintaining the Family Code, the Shiites against]. *AFP*, January 21, *Institut Kurde de Paris, Information and Liaison Bulletin, 226*, January, p. 57.

**Keywords:** 1959 Family Code; PUK; KDP; Kurdistan Women's Union; Kurdish women protest abrogation of 1959 Family Code; in Najaf, Shi'a women protest in favour of the abrogation of the 1959 Family Code.

**Arin, Canan.** (1997). *The legal status of women in Turkey*. Women for Women's Human Rights Reports No. 1. Istanbul: Women for Women's Human Rights and Women Living Under Muslim Laws. ISBN 975-7014-01-X. Preface by Pınar İlkkaracan (p. 6), introduction (p. 7), text (pp. 8-42), black and white photographs (pp. 3, 9, 11, 14, 15, 16, 19, 21, 32, 36, 37, 38, 41).

**Keywords:** legal status; family life; dowry; marriage contracts; separation; divorce; desertion; rape; polygamy; fornication; custody; women's sexual freedom; abortion; homosexuality; violence against sex-workers; economic independence; inheritance; the rights of daughters; the rights of female children who work.

**Ertürk, Yakin.** (1995). Rural women and modernization in Southeastern Anatolia. In Sirin Tekeli (Ed.), *Women in modern Turkish society, a reader* (pp. 141-52). London: Zed Books.

**Keywords:** institutional integration of Kurdish women; many women over 30 years of age in Southeastern Anatolia do not speak Turkish, the official language; many married by religious law which is not recognized under the Turkish legal system; many are not registered with the central population bureau so officially they do not exist;

246

program of modernization and institutional integration leads to increasing marginalization and vulnerability within an unfamiliar institutional order; leaves them dependent on local power structures; to overcome the drawbacks of modernization directly linked to the process of pluralist democracy; grassroots participation; nationalism and feminism: nationalist struggle overriding feminist or women's struggle.

**Institut Kurde de Paris**. (2001). Reform of the civil code: Official end of male supremacy. *Institut Kurde de Paris, Information and Liaison Bulletin, 200-201,* November-December, p. 10.

Keywords: women's rights in Turkey; marriage; Turkish civil code.

**Institut Kurde de Paris**. (2004). Suleimaniah: The Kurdish women demonstrate to protest against the decision to abrogate the 1959 Family Code. *Institut Kurde de Paris, Information and Liaison Bulletin, 226,* January, p. 7.

Keywords: Kurdistan Women's Union; women protest abrogation of 1959 Family Code in Suleimaniah; Kafia Suleiman, president of the Kurdistan Women's Union; Rakhshan Zangala, president of the Kurdistan Women's League, close to the Communist Party; SCIRI; Paul Bremer; Provisional Coalition Authority; Kurdistan Parliament passes resolution to ignore abrogation of Family Law, and reaffirms that "in Kurdistan, women would enjoy equality with men."

**Kurdish Human Rights Project and Kurdish Women's Project**. (2004). *Charter for the rights and freedoms of women in the Kurdish regions and diaspora.* London: Kurdish Human Rights Project and Kurdish Women's Project. June, ISBN 1-900175-71-1. Acknowledgments (p. 4), table of contents (p. 1), foreword (p. 7-9), Kurdish women's charter (English text, pp. 11-14), Kurmanji Kurdish text (pp. 13-17), Sorani Kurdish text (pp. 19-21), Arabic text (pp. 23-25).

Keywords: charter of rights initiated by Kurdish women in exile, drafted as a collective effort including Kurdish Human Rights Project; for use by Kurdish citizens, legislators, national and international organizations.

**McDonald, Susan**. (2001). Kurdish women and self-determination: A feminist approach to international law. In Shahrzad Mojab (Ed.), *Women of a non-state nation: The Kurds* (pp. 135-57). Costa Mesa: Mazda Publishers.

Keywords: Persian Gulf War; international law; secession; self-government; Sara Akan; Patriotic Women's Association; KDP; PUK;

PKK; Kesire Yıldırım; human rights abuses; Shaykh Said movement; Dersim Rebellion; destruction of the Kurdish Republic of Mahabad; Halabja; chemical weapons; nationalism.

**New York Times**. (2002). Women's rights in Turkey. *The New York Times,* June 20, reprinted in *International Herald Tribune,* reprinted in *Institut Kurde de Paris, Information and Liaison Bulletin, 207,* June, p. 64.

**Keywords:** women's rights in Turkey; change in law makes school officials no longer authorized to test girls for virginity; recent laws which overturned the supremacy of men in marriage; recent laws which allow women threatened with violence to get orders of protection; Islam; rural traditions; Turkey's Health Minister announced that students in nursing and other health schools should be expelled if they were sexually active; polygamous marriages in Turkish Kurdistan (10% of women in southeast and east); virginity tests; women compelled to renounce their legal inheritance in favour of their brothers; women forced to marry their rapists to salvage the reputation of their families; honour killing; shelters for battered women and those threatened with honour killing; girls' education; girls' higher dropout rate.

**Salih, Mehabad**. (2001). Domestic violence, the rights of Kurdish women and Iraqi Personal Status Law. *Kurdistan Report, 31,* autumn, pp. 82-83.

**Keywords:** Mehabad Salih: female lawyer, working mainly in family law; firsthand experience of the inadequacies and failure of Iraqi law to protect women; inadequacy of legal provisions to end violence and oppression of women; influence of Sharia law as interpreted within a patriarchal framework; Iraqi Personal Status Law No. 188 of 1959 and amendments: changes cannot "breach Islamic norms"; life under the Kurdish administration at central and local levels: women exposed to various kinds of domestic violence and deprived of the minimal protection stated in certain articles of Iraqi law; nationalism and feminism: 1991 uprising in Iraqi Kurdistan raised expectations of women that their position would improve; proposal put forward to Kurdish Parliament to amend certain articles of Iraqi laws generally neglected or vigorously opposed by representatives of the Islamic parties; witnessed the increase in victims of domestic violence and honour killing; under pressure from the campaigning of Kurdish women, Jalal Talabani, leader of the PUK passed an order on April 2, 2000 prohibiting the killing or harming of women by male relatives in the name of honour; penalty for polygamy increased from one year imprisonment and 100 Iraqi dinars to three years and 10,000 Iraqi dinars; legal loopholes; ignorance of rights; illiteracy; women influenced by patriarchal structures; suicide from the stress of being a woman; keeping of "secrets" to protect family honour; absence of centres or organizations to help Kurdish women know their rights; dominance of males in the legal profession: patriarchal structure; financial constraints of legal proceedings; need for legal centres run by women trained in the law; legal training programs.

**Yildiz, Kerim.** (2005). Enforcing the charter for the rights and freedoms of women in the Kurdish regions and diaspora. *Kurdish Human Rights Project* and *Kurdish Women's Project.*

**Keywords:** charter to urge the elimination of all forms of discrimination against Kurdish women and to promote participation of Kurdish women in social, political, economic, and educational spheres of life; aimed at Kurdish women and Kurdish women's organizations; introduction to the international mechanisms currently available to enforce the principles of the charter; descriptions of each article in the charter in practice and guidance as to their application; condemnation and elimination of legal discrimination against Kurdish women; condemnation of the discrimination of Kurdish women in political and public life in Kurdish society; right to vote, to participate in decision making bodies, right to participation in non-governmental organizations and associations; elimination of discrimination of Kurdish women in the private sphere of the family and marriage; control of their own sexuality, health, and fertility; elimination of the discrimination against Kurdish women in the workplace; definition of the term "violence against women" as "any act of gender-based violence that results in, or is likely to result in, physical, sexual or psychological harm or suffering to women, including threats of such acts, coercion or arbitrary deprivation of liberty, whether occurring in public or in private life"; efforts to combat all forms of sexual exploitation and trafficking of women and girls; elimination of discrimination against Kurdish women and girls in the fields of education and healthcare; right to compensation, for example, the Anfal widows; right to free legal advice; description of enforcement mechanisms: U.N. enforcement mechanisms; charter-based bodies; treaty-based bodies; European Court of Human Rights.

# LITERATURE

**Wolfensberger, Ruth.** (1998). *Wo die Himmelsrichtungen aufeinanderprallen:*

*Ethnologische Aspekte neuerer kurdischer Literatur.* IKO-Verlag für Interkulturelle Kommunikation. ISBN 3-88939-457-4. Foreword (pp. 4-5), text (pp. 6-127), bibliography (pp. 128-34), eight maps (pp. 135-41), glossary (pp. 142-43), notes regarding Kurdish phonetics (p. 144).

**Keywords:** writing culture; literature as ethnographical source; Kurdish men and women; Kurdish literature; oral literature; written literature; exile literature; ethnology; Emine Sevgi Özdamar; folklore; women breaking with tradition to discuss rape, torture, and sexual abuse; the threat posed to the Turkish state by Kurdish women as bearers of the Kurdish culture; Kurdish proverbs regarding women; women's organizations; politicization of women; veiling; veiling and Kurdish women in Iran; religion; women and migration.

**Uzun, Mehmed.** (1995). Separation is such a grief. *Kurdistan Times, 4,* November, pp. 196-205. ISSN 1057-8668.

**Keywords:** the importance of Mehmed Uzun's grandmother as a symbol of his childhood; the close relationship between the author's mother and his grandmother; Zaza dialect; the telling of tales, epics, and stories by the author's grandmother; exile; Kurdish exile in Damascus; the author's rediscovery of his native tongue in Sweden.

# I. BIOGRAPHICAL MATERIAL

**Bagdas, Sabir.** (2001). They speak first of the lioness, then of the lion (H. Bagdas, Trans.). In Gina Lennox (Ed.), *Fire, snow and honey. Essays: Voices from Kurdistan. Life stories, poems, short fiction and fables contributed by people from Kurdistan* (pp. 435-45). Halstead Press. Foreword by Danielle Mitterrand. One photograph.

**Keywords:** born around 1900 in Bozhuyuk village, near Sivas in Alevi family; Alevi culture; land relations and the *agha*, landlord; women clothing in Kurdish tribes; weddings; saving victims of Armenian Genocide; the Turkish Republic and Turkification; forced and arranged marriage; husband's second wife; re-marrying; living as a co-wife again; atheism of the husband; suppression of the Kurdish language; moving to Australia in 1977; support of PKK.

*See also* Australia; Diaspora–Turkey; Genocide

**Fatah, Mahabad.** (2001). Always a sun behind the clouds. In Gina Lennox (Ed.), *Fire, snow and honey. Essays: Voices from Kurdistan. Life stories, poems, short fiction and fables contributed by people from Kurdistan* (pp. 257-76). Halstead Press.

Foreword by Danielle Mitterrand. One photograph.

**Keywords:** life story of Mahabad, growing up in Sulaimani, in the course of the Kurdish autonomist war in Iraq; anti-government activities of students; gender relations in family and society; marrying a peshmarga; life in the city with peshmarga husband in the mountains; visiting in the mountains; pregnancy and giving birth to a daughter; female circumcision; chemical bombing in September 1987; Iraq's invasion of Kuwait in 1990; the March 1991 uprising and the escaping of Kurds to the mountains and Iran; immigrating to Australia.

**Heval, Ruken.** (2001). An apple does not fall far from the tree. In Gina Lennox (Ed.), *Fire, snow and honey. Essays: Voices from Kurdistan. Life stories, poems, short fiction and fables contributed by people from Kurdistan* (pp. 495-50). Halstead Press. Foreword by Danielle Mitterrand. One photograph.

**Keywords:** born in Izmit, and growing up in Istanbul; parents from the village Kiği, in Bingöl; grandmother's memories of the Dersim uprising and massacre; memories of great-grandmother, a strong woman; gender relations in the family; sister's resistance to arranged marriage; going to coeducational schools; suppression of the Kurdish language and music; honor killing; dangerous words "democracy" and "freedom": the fascist National Party in schools; the emergence of PKK, and female guerrillas; living the double life as a Turkish girl and a Kurdish Alevi girl; the impact of Leyla Zana; moving to Australia in 1995; Med-TV; support of PKK.

*See also* Australia; Diaspora–Turkey

**Kaya, Devrim.** (1998). *Meine Einzige Schuld ist, als Kurdin Geboren zu Sein: Eine junge Frau auf der Flucht vor türkischer Folter und deutscher Justiz* [My only fault is being born a Kurdish woman: A young woman fleeing Turkish torture and German justice]. Günter Wallraf (Ed.). Campus Verlag. ISBN 3-593-36065-9. Foreword (pp. 9-10), text (pp. 11-304).

**Keywords:** importance accorded to the birth of male children; honour; the history of the oppression of Kurds; education system in Turkey; difficulties facing Kurdish children in Turkish schools; PKK; torture; sexual abuse of female detainees in Turkish prisons; *Özgür Ülke;* Dersim Prison; hunger strike of PKK prisoners; political prisoners; emptied villages; flight to Germany; racism in Germany; difficulties in obtaining political asylum in Germany; women's solidarity; blood feuds and their effects on women; domestic abuse; torture; sexual abuse; rape; psychological scars of torture; kidnapping of children by the PKK; the PKK's killing of suspected traitors; PKK activities in Germany; hunger strikes in Turkish prisons; hunger strikes by Kurdish women in Germany; Amnesty International; difficulties in obtaining asylum in Germany; arranged marriages; women and inter-marriage between Sunnis and Alevis; racism in Germany; women activists in the PKK; destruction of Kurdish villages by the Turkish army; difficulties facing Kurdish refugees in Istanbul.

**Kurdistan Times**. (1995). A brief biography of Dr. Pary Karadaghi. *Kurdistan Times, 4,* November, pp. 44-47. ISSN 1057-8668. Three black and white photographs (pp. 46-47).

> **Keywords:** early years of Dr. Pary Karadaghi; educational achievements of Dr. Karadaghi; Kurdish Human Rights Watch; chemical bombardment of Iraqi Kurds; persecution of Dr. Karadaghi by Iraqi agents; Dr. Karadaghi's life in exile in Romania, France and in the U.S.; Kurdish American Medical Association.

*See also* U.S.A.

**Qazi, Fariba**. (2001). The eye can see but the hand is short. In Gina Lennox (Ed.), *Fire, snow and honey. Essays: Voices from Kurdistan. Life stories, poems, short fiction and fables contributed by people from Kurdistan* (pp. 575-87). Halstead Press. Foreword by Danielle Mitterrand.

> **Keywords:** born in Mahabad when Qazi Mohammad, president of the Kurdish Republic of 1946, was hung in 1947; the formation and fall of the Kurdish Republic; growing up in the family of the Qazis, four sisters and five brothers, with seven college educated; two sisters are writers and one lecturer; education in Persian; grandmother source of inspiration for the play *Mother of a Nation*; grandmother and mother's stories; working as first-aid assistant in Mahabad hospital; protesting the mistreatment of the poor; attraction to communism and the Organization of People's Fedayee Guerrillas; the Iranian army offensive against Mahabad; organizing first aid teams during the war; disdain for war; marrying a member of the OPFG; restrictions imposed by husband's family; the killing of a friend and eight other girls by the Islamic regime; arrested and jailed with three-year-old son in Mahabad; women political prisoners in Mahabad; moving to Australia; Australia freer for women; women's freedom still restricted by husband; divorce.

*See also* Australia; Communism and Socialism; Iran

**Razaghi, Mary**. (2001). From drops of rain the river flows. In Gina Lennox

(Ed.), *Fire, snow and honey. Essays: Voices from Kurdistan. Life stories, poems, short fiction and fables contributed by people from Kurdistan* (pp. 591-664). Halstead Press. Foreword by Danielle Mitterrand.

**Keywords:** living as a teenager in the 1970s in Saghez, Iranian Kurdistan in a family of four sisters and four brothers; gender relations in the family; the changing attitudes of mother-in-laws; a gentle, democratic husband and father; schooling in Persian; reading Kurdish books secretly; admiration for Qazi Mohammad and Mustafa Barzani; wishing to be a doctor serving the poor people; first girl in Saghez to be admitted to medical school; living in girls' dormitory; relations with men limited; gender differences in medical school; arranged marriages common; revolutionary student activism; evolving from a nationalist into an internationalist by joining the Organization of People's Fedayee Guerrillas; conflict between Kurdish nationalism and communism; the experience of the Iranian revolution of 1978-79; the Kurdish autonomist movement; jailed in Tabriz with other female students; three women executed; purged from the university but readmitted and graduated in 1985; medical practice under conditions of poverty and poor resources; treating chemical bomb victims from Iraq; pregnancy complications; little trace of FGM; Shakeri, a communist doctor, and a model human being; married in 1989, moved to Australia; Islamic codes of gender relations; a case of honor killing defended by sister; mentality rather than Islam limits the Kurdish woman's desire to change her status; women forced into staying in abusive relations by tradition and lack of economic resources; the complexity of change in Kurdish society.

*See also* Communism and Socialism; Iran

**Rowandozi, Maryam.** (2001). A fortress of no tomorrows (A. Walid, Trans.). In Gina Lennox (Ed.), *Fire, snow and honey. Essays: Voices from Kurdistan. Life stories, poems, short fiction and fables contributed by people from Kurdistan* (pp. 307-35). Halstead Press. Foreword by Danielle Mitterrand. Two photographs.

**Keywords:** growing up in a family of six daughters and two sons in the context of the Kurdish autonomist war of the 1960s in the town of Rowandoz; the trauma of Republican Guard attack on the home to arrest father; going to school; gender relations; honor killing and the limitations of the 2000 PUK legal action against it; Saddam's use of feudal lords against the Kurdish autonomist movement; the wars of 1970s, destruction, and displacement; Kurdish collaborators *Jash*; in-fighting among Kurdish political parties; marrying cousin Aso, student and member of Kurdistan Socialist Party; working as the first woman announcer on the clandestine radio; women in KSP as compared with those in Komala and PKK; giving birth under conditions of war; joining the PUK; the Anfal genocide and chemical bombing; the 1991 war, displacement, politics under the Kurdish Regional Government; civil war; moving to Australia; Kurdish women freer in Australia.

**Soltani, Mariam**. (2001). See the mother, know the girl. A life story based on interviews with Mariam Sultani. In Gina Lennox (Ed.), *Fire, snow and honey. Essays: Voices from Kurdistan. Life stories, poems, short fiction and fables contributed by people from Kurdistan* (pp. 605-615). Halstead Press. Foreword by Danielle Mitterrand. One photograph.

**Keywords:** born in in Eastern (Iranian) Kurdistan; mother left abusive husband while she was six years old; growing up with mother and one brother and sister; the 1979 revolution and the formation of the Islamic state; Kurdish resistance and the peshmarga; restrictions on women listening to music; arranged marriage with an Iraqi Kurd; virginity; wedding night as rape; persecution of husband and his escape to Turkey; forced to join husband; failing to get passport for baby daughter; smuggling daughter to Turkey; Iraqi Kurds escaping to Iran during the Anfal genocide; moving to Australia.

*See also* Australia; Iran

**Steimel, Regina**. (2004). Autobiographisches Schreiben als Selbstdarstellung: *Henna-Mond* von Fatma B [Autobiographical writing as self-expression: Henna moon by Fatma B]. In Siamend Hajo, Carsten Borck, Eva Savelsberg, & Şükriye Dogan (Eds.), *Gender in Kurdistan und der Diaspora, Kurdologie Series Vol. 6* (pp. 107-48). UNRAST-Verlag. ISBN 3-89771-014-5 (pb).

**Keywords:** German media's perceptions of girls and women from patriarchal migrant families; Kurdish and Turkish women in Germany; literature of female migrants in Germany; literature by second and third generation "migrant" women in Germany; Fatma B., a Kurdish woman from Turkey who writes an autobiography; psychology; self-image; gender roles in Kurdish families; the lack of support for a female's education; traditional Kurdish married life; arranged marriage.

*See also* Germany

## II. NOVELS AND SHORT STORIES

**Aalam, Haleh**. (1996-1997). *La femme kurde selon le roman de Ali Mohammad*

*Afghani: Şowhar-e Âhu Xânom* [The Kurdish woman according to the novel by Ali Mohammad Afghani: Şowhar-e Âhu Xânom], [Doctoral dissertation, Université Paris III, La Sorbonne Nouvelle. Institurt d'Etudes Iraniennes].

**Keywords:** women in Al Mohammad Afghani's Persian novel *Şowhar-e Âhu Xânom* "The Husband of Ahu Khanom"; Kurdish family in Kermanshah in the years 1926-41; women in Mahmud Dowlat Abadi's Persian novel *Keleyder*; socio-economic structure of Kurdistan (nomadism, social relations, economic structure of the village, the family); Kurdish women (choice of spouse, marriage, economic role, repudiation, rights and duties of women in nomadism).

**Baker, Shain.** (2001). Aunty Zeho. In Gina Lennox (Ed.), *Fire, snow and honey. Essays: Voices from Kurdistan. Life stories, poems, short fiction and fables contributed by people from Kurdistan* (pp. 493-94). Halstead Press. Foreword by Danielle Mitterrand.

**Keywords:** elderly women called "Aunty" in Kurdistan; rural to urban migration in Kurdistan (Syria); disdain for urban life: women cover faces, and all are imprisoned in flats like birds in cages, and speak a different language.

*See also* Syria

**Bilbasar, Kemal.** (1976). *Gemmo* (E. B. Rey & M Fitzpatrick, Trans.). Peter Owen. ISBN: 0 7206 0424 9 (hb). Translator's foreword (pp. 5-10), notes on pronunciation (p. 11), text (pp. 13-223).

**Keywords:** bride price; anti-Alevi racism; Zazas; Dersim; feudalism; blood feuds; Kayig Tribe; Shiite-Sunni rivalry; Sheikh Said; Sorik Agha.

**Kemal, Yaşar.** (1983). The baby (T. Kemal, Trans.). *Anatolian Tales.* Writers and Readers Publishing Cooperative Society Ltd., pp. 108-136.

**Keywords:** poverty; rural life; health conditions; Kurdish girls.

**Kemal, Yaşar.** (1983). A dirty story (T. Kemal, Trans.). *Anatolian Tales.* Writers and Readers Publishing Cooperative Society Ltd., pp. 7-35.

**Keywords:** Çukurova; sale of women; prostitution; honor; feudalism.

**Kerruish, Jessie Douglas.** (1932). *The girl from Kurdistan.* Wright & Brown. Prologue (pp. 5-11), text (pp. 13-288). Also published in London and New York: Hodder and Stoughton, 1918. 349 pages.

**Keywords:** ethnic groups of Kurdistan; Armenians of Kurdistan; Jews of Kurdistan; Europeans of Kurdistan; Cossacks; Yezd; Kerman; Isfahan; orphans; servants; Teheran; Kerbala; Shi'ites; Queen Victoria; Bakhtiaris; Lurs; Mingrelians; Seyyids; Mollahs; eunuchs; Zoroastrians; conversion of Christians to Islam.

**Kurdistan Report**. (2000). Roads to happiness: A female Kurdish writer. *Kurdistan Report, 30*, Winter, pp. 87-88.

**Keywords:** Sima Semend; Kurdish women's writing; female characters struggling against sexual discrimination and repressive social traditions in the stories of Sima Semend; Sima Semend's combining of national problems with feminine elements; heroines in the writing of Sima Semend.

**Laird, Elizabeth**. (1991). *Kiss the dust*. London: Mammoth. ISBN 0 7497 0857 3 (pb). Text: pp. 1-279. *Reviews*: Elizabeth MacCallum, "Kurdish family's struggle a fresh and compelling tale," in *The Globe and Mail*, 1 June 1991; Geoffrey Trease, "In search of sanctuary," in *Times Educational Supplement*, 14 June 1991.

**Keywords:** Iraqi Kurdistan; inter-communal relationships; Iran-Iraq War; extrajudicial killings; peshmergas; gender roles; urban-rural dichotomy; bombing of Kurdish villages; Iranian Kurdistan; refugee camps; asylum; immigration; life in the diaspora; assimilation; education; veiling.

**Mansour, Ahlam**. (1995). Pont (I. Darwish, Trans.). In *Nouvelles Kurdes* (pp. 99-108), Paris: Éditions L'Harmattan, ISBN 2-7384-3856-3.

**Keywords:** veiling; Délère, the female protagonist of the story, and her constant sadness; children; the River Tigris; Iraqi Kurdistan.

**Qazi, Mariam**. (2001). Buried alive (F. Qazi, Trans.). In Gina Lennox (Ed.), *Fire, snow and honey. Essays: Voices from Kurdistan. Life stories, poems, short fiction and fables contributed by people from Kurdistan* (pp. 588-603). Halstead. Foreword by Danielle Mitterrand.

**Keywords:** translation of story by a Kurdish writer from Iranian Kurdistan.

**Qizildjî, Hassan**. (1992). Le talisman d'Amina-Khan [Amina-Khan's talisman] (A. Decemme, Trans.). In Halkawt Hakim (Ed.), *Les Kurde par-delà l'exode*. Paris: Editions L'Harmattan, p. 255-62.

**Keywords:** life in an Iranian Kurdish village; woman amulet maker; culture and political economy of amulet making.

**Samanci, Suzan**. (1997). *Die Hêlîn roch nach Baumharz* [The Hêlîn smelled of tree sap]. Ararat Verlag. ISBN 3-9520545-8-5. 137 pages.

**Keywords:** literature; Kurdistan; novel.

**Yıldız, Bekir**. (1990). Resho Agha. In Fahir Öz (Ed.), *An Anthology of Modern Turkish Short Stories* (pp. 266-72). Bibliotheca Islamica. ISBN: 0-88297-021-6 (cloth), 0-88297-022-4 (paper).

**Keywords:** honor killing; feudalism; elopement; family honor.

## III. ORAL TRADITION

**Allison, Christine F**. (2000). Volksdichtung und Phantasie: Die Darstellung von Frauen in der kurdischen mündlichen Überlieferung (pp. 33-50). In Eva Savelsberg, Siamend Hajo, & Carsten Borck (Eds.), *Kurdologie: Kurdische Frauen und das Bild der kurdischen Frau*. Lit Verlag.

**Keywords:** folklore; literacy; proverbs; dengbêj; stranbêj; çîrokbêj; gender-specific genres of folklore; female composers; female singers; women's roles in passing on oral tradition; Mem û Zîn; Strana Folklorî; Yezidis.

**Allison, Christine F**. (2001). *The Yezidi oral tradition in Iraqi Kurdistan*. Richmond, Surrey, UK: Curzon Press. ISBN 0-7007-1397-2.

**Keywords:** Yazidis of Iraqi Kurdistan; war, love, and death in Yezidi oral tradition (text of stories and songs); (arranged) marriage: endogamy and polygamy; wedding; family history; women and performance of song "*stran*"; gender and audience; women's lament "*şîn*"; the widow's lament; genre and gender; manliness "*mêrxasî*" or "*mêranî*" (bravery, generosity); romantic love; love and marriage in Kurdistan and in the Yezidi community; elopement; adultery; love stories and songs; portrayal of women; Mayan Khatun; *namûs*, "honor"; honor killing; status of women in Yezidi society; intermarriage with Christians and Muslims; limited access to Yezidi women interviewees; women's body; women *peshmargas*; women of Gosh Tepe.

*See also* Yezidism

**Allison, Christine F**. (2001). Folklore and fantasy: The Presentation of women in Kurdish oral tradition. In Shahrzad Mojab (Ed.) *Women of a non-state nation: The Kurds* (pp. 181-94). Costa Mesa: Mazda Publishers.

**Keywords:** folklore; literacy; proverbs; dengbêj; stranbêj; çîrokbêj;

gender-specific genres of folklore; female composers; female singers; women's roles in passing on oral tradition; Mem û Zîn; Strana Folklorî; Yezidis.

**Anonymous**. (1945). Sinemkhan. *Le Jour Nouveau: Quotidien kurde*, Troisième Année, *56*, September 10, p. 2.

> **Keywords:** author arrives late at night in a Kurdish village on Euphrates; village owned by a former chief of Hamidiya cavalry; story of a Kurdish girl, Sinemkhan, a refugee in the village, told by the agha's son.

**Sabar, Yona**. (1982). *The folk literature of the Kurdistani Jews: An anthology* (Y. Sabar, Trans.). Yale University Press. ISBN 0-300-02698-6. Preface (p. xi), introduction by Yona Sabar (pp. xiii-xl), note on the English translation (p. xli), text (pp. 3-223), glossary (pp. 225-28), selected bibliography (pp. 229-32), general index (pp. 233-43), scriptural references (pp. 244-45), Rabbinic references (p. 246), tale types, motifs and IFA numbers (pp. 247-50), eight black and white photographs, unnumbered center pages.

> **Keywords:** history of the Kurdish Jews/Jewish Kurds; religions and sects of Kurdistan; marriage; major Jewish centers of Kurdistan; occupations; economic conditions; Jewish travelers to Kurdistan; religiosity, or lack thereof, among the Jews of Kurdistan; popular religion; literature of the Kurdistani Jews; proverbs; proverbs about wives and women; women's lamentations; nursery rhymes; folk songs.

*See also* Jews

## IV. POETRY

**Marie, Alana**. (n.d.). Poetry and the Kurdish woman. *Kurdish Journal*, *2*(1), October, pp. 20-22.

> **Keywords:** poetry; Kurdish women.

**Boskany, Abbas**. (2001). Leyla Zana. In Gina Lennox (Ed.), *Fire, snow and honey. Essays: Voices from Kurdistan. Life stories, poems, short fiction and fables contributed by people from Kurdistan* (p. 382). Halstead Press. Foreword by Danielle Mitterrand.

> **Keywords:** poem wondering how Zana had "the courage to search for love amidst the lurid canine fangs," and witnessing Zana's "immortality" and the poet's "wrathfulness."

**Hanson, Margreta.** (1997). My home in Kurdistan. *Kurdistan Times,* 2(1), November, pp. 124-127. ISSN 1057-8668.

Keywords: poem about Kurdistan; Saddam Hussein; destructions of Kurdish villages; chemical bombing of Kurdistan; Kurdish refugees in Turkish camps.

**Husseini, Jheela.** (2001). "Flag" and "Good news" (K. Avin & G. Muhamad, Trans.). In Gina Lennox (Ed.), *Fire, snow and honey. Essays: Voices from Kurdistan. Life stories, poems, short fiction and fables contributed by people from Kurdistan* (pp. 591 & 604). Halstead Press. Foreword by Danielle Mitterrand.

Keywords: translation of poetry by Kurdish poet from Iranian Kurdistan.

# V. TRAVEL LITERATURE

## A. Middle Eastern Travellers

**'Abd-er-Razzâq Isfahâni in Bittner, Maximilian.** (1896). Der Kurdengau Uschnûje und die Stadt Urûmije. Reiseschilderungen eines Persers, im Originaltexte herausgegeben, übersetzt und erläutert [The Kurdengau Uschnûje and the city of Urûmije. Travel descriptions of a Persian, edited, translated and explained in the original text]. *Sitzunsberichte der Philosophisch - Historischen Classe* (pp. 1-97). Kaiserlichen Akademie der Wissenschaften, Bd. 133, Abh. 3.

Keywords: 'Abd-er-Razzâq Isfahâni travels in Urumiya and Şino (Uschnûje) in early nineteenth century; male-female relations in Uschnûje; abduction, elopement and *doytane*; bride-price; abortion; custody of children; Kurdish-Armenian feast; mixed dancing.

**Çelebi, Evliya.** (1848). *Seyahatname* [Book of Travels]. See also Dankoff, Robert and Sooyong Kim (translation and commentary; 2010). *An Ottoman traveller: Selections from the Book of Travels of Evliya Çelebi.* Eland; as well as Dankoff, Robert (Ed. and Trans.; 1990). *Evliya Çelebi in Bitlis: The relevant section of the Seyahatname* [Book of Travels]. Vol. 2 of Book of Travels: Land and people of the Ottoman empire in the seventeenth century: A Corpus of Partial Editions, Klaus Kreiser (Ed.). Leiden: E.J. Brill.

Keywords: seventeenth century Ottoman empire; Kurdistan; rural-urban women; gender relations; customs and culture; Orient/Occident; morality; Muslims; women's beauty; food, language, and clothing.

## B. Western Traveler

**Begikhani, Nazand**. (2000). Das Bild der kurdischen Frau in der orientalistischen Literatur des neunzehnten Jahrhunderts [The image of the Kurdish woman in nineteenth century Orientalist literature]. In Eva Savelsberg, Siamend Hajo, & Carsten Borck (Eds.) *Kurdologie: Kurdische Frauen und das Bild der kurdischen Frau* (pp. 51-75). Lit Verlag.

> **Keywords:** Orientalism; European travellers in Kurdistan; stereotypes of Kurdish women; nomadism; semi-nomadism.

**Galleti, Mirella**. (2001). Western images of women's role in Kurdish society. In Shahrzad Mojab (Ed.), *Women of a non-state nation: The Kurds* (pp. 209-25). Costa Mesa: Mazda Publishers.

> **Keywords:** European travellers' chauvinism; Assyro-Chaldeans; Jews; Ida Pfeiffer; Cristina Trivulzio di Belgiojoso; Madame Chantre; Lucy Garnett; Isabella L. Bird; Chanun Sultan; physical attributes of Kurdish women; absence of the harem in Kurdish society; absence of polygamy; Armenians; women's education; Kara-Jatana; Kara-Fatma; Kurdish Amazons; Adela Khanum; Jaf Tribe; Hafsa Khan; Sheikh Mahmud; Kurdish customs; Margaret of Kurdistan (Joan of Arc of Kurdistan); Assyrians; Barzani; Ba'thi policies regarding Kurdish women; Layla Qassem; Halima Khan; chemical weapons; destruction of Kurdish villages; increase in prostitution; PUK; KDP; Turkish state's policies of assimilation; Turkish colonization of Kurdistan; PKK; Leyla Zana; DEP; women in the guerilla movement.

**Graham-Brown, Sarah**. (1988). *Images of women*. Quartet Books Ltd. ISBN 0-7043-2541-1. Acknowledgments (pp. vii-ix), chronology (pp. x-xi), introduction (pp. 1-35), text and photographs (pp. 36-238), afterword (pp. 239-51), notes (pp. 252-59), bibliography (pp. 260-65), photographic credits (pp. 266-68), index (pp. 269-274). 210 black and white photographs.

> **Keywords:** Kurdish woman entertainer; Faqa Marif; Kurdish woman who dressed and lived as a man; anthropology; political and economic change; national revival and the role of women; European photographers; power structures; patriarchy; seclusion; segregation; marriage and family life; mothers; children; clothing; working women; women in the public eye; education; campaigning women.

**Mabro, Judy**. (1991). *Western travellers' perceptions of Middle Eastern women*. I.B. Tauris & Co. Ltd. ISBN 1-85043-097-7 (hb). Preface (pp. ix-x), introduction (pp. 1-27), text (pp. 28-264), references (pp. 265-67), sources (pp. 268-75).

**Keywords:** Eurocentrism; Orientalism; Haissa Khatoon; female Kurdish leader; Lady Adela; Ardalan; Halabja; physical attributes of Kurdish women; ethnic groups of Kurdistan; veiling; pilgrims; sexuality; polygamy; honour; shame; European misogyny; European racism.

**Soane, Ely Bannister.** (1912). *To Mesopotamia and Kurdistan in disguise: With historical notices of the Kurdish tribes and the Chaldeans of Kurdistan.* London: John Murray Adela Khanum of Halabja. Extract from *To Mesopotamia and Kurdistan in disguise in resistance: women in Kurdistan.* London: KIC/KSC Publications, 1995, pp. 35-37.

**Keywords:** Adela Khanum (Lady Justice): rare power and position in patriarchal culture; Jaf tribe (Sulaimaniya); skilled in the use of weaponry; governing in the absence of her husband; president of a court of justice that she instituted; made Halabja an important town.

**Tejel, Jodi.** (2000). L'exotisme et les recits de voyage francais au Kurdistan [Exoticism and French travel stories in Kurdistan]. *The Journal of Kurdish Studies*, Volume III, pp. 93-105.

**Keywords:** tribal women; women's work; religion (Islam, Yezidism); European contact with the Kurds; European stereotypes of Kurds.

## A. WOMEN TRAVELERS

**Bird, Christiane.** (2004). *A thousand sighs, a thousand revolts. Journeys in Kurdistan.* New York, Ballantine Books, The Random House Publishing Group, map (p. 2), ISBN 0-345-46892-9 and 0-345-46939-9 (pbk.). 18 photos, including six of women. Reviews: by Shahrzad Mojab in *Middle East Journal*, *59*(1), Winter 2005, pp. 146-48.

**Keywords:** author's travel to Kurdistan in Iraq (spring 2002), Iran and Turkey (fall 2003); Dohuk Writers' Union with nine women members not attending meeting; Kurdish women demand for equality.

**Bird, Isabella [Lucy].** (1988). *Journeys in Persia and Kurdistan, Volume I.* Virago Press. (Original work published 1891 by John Murray). ISBN: 1-85381-055-X. New introduction by Pat Barr (pp. v-xiii), maps (pp. xiv-xv), preface by Isabella L. Bishop (pp. xvii-xx), list of illustrations (pp. xxi), glossary (pp. xiii-viv), text (pp. 1-381), 14 illustrations (pp. 19, to face p. 78, 82, 159, 167, 237, 318, 326, to face p. 351, 362, 366, to face p. 368, 372, to face p. 378). Volume II, London: John Murray, 1891, reprint London: Virago Press, 1989. Introduction by Shusha Guppy (pp. vii- xvi), text (pp. 1-396), appendix A (p. 397), appendix B (pp. 398-99), 21 black and white illustrations (frontpiece and pp. 8, 10, 19, 23, 29, 30, 37, 110, 114, 153, 208, 264, 273, 297, 310, 315, 338, 339, 372).

**Keywords:** *Vol. I:* British woman traveler in Kurdistan, Iran in 1890; ethnic groups of Kurdistan; religions of Kurdistan; religious practices of various groups within Kurdistan; sectarian differences; Muslims; Armenians; Babis; Assyrians; Jews; Bakhtiari Lurs; Persians; Turks; food; commerce; health conditions; medicine; government; harems; clothing of Kurdish women; physical attributes of Kurdish women; domestic life of Kurdish women; *Vol. II:* women's dress; Armenian women of Kurdistan; Turks of Kurdistan; popular religion among the Armenians of Kurdistan; Assyrian Christians of Kurdistan; Jews of Kurdistan; Bakhtiyari attitudes towards women; segregation of the sexes among the Bakhtiyaris; childbirth; women doctors of Kala Kuh; the passing of medical traditions from grandmother to granddaughter; women's role as healers; women's jewelry; blood feuds; love potions used by women; rivalry among co-wives; mourning rituals of women; health conditions; the absence of veiling among Bakhtiyari women; men's treatment of their wives.

**Bishop, Isabella L.** (1891, May). The shadow of the Kurd. *The Contemporary Review.* LIX, Part I, pp. 642-54; Part II, June 1891, pp. 819-35.

**Keywords:** *Part I:* Armenian peasant women; "Armenian Question"; "Nestorian Question"; Chaldeans; Nestorians; Assyrians; poverty; Armenians; comparisons between the situation for Christians in Ottoman and Iranian Kurdistan; oppression of Armenians by the Kurds and the government; *Part II:* Kurdish attacks on Syrian and Armenian peasantry; Kurdish-Christian relations; description of Kurdish women; Kurds of the vilayets of Van and Bitlis; kidnaping of Armenian women by Kurdish men.

**Braidwood, Linda.** (1953). *Digging beyond the Tigris: An American woman archeologist's story of life on a "dig" in the Kurdish hills of Iraq.* Henry Schuman, Inc. Contents (pp. (v-vii), illustrations (list, pp. vii-viii), introduction (pp. ix-xii), text (pp. 3-296). Photographs numbered 48-50: Kurdish wedding. Chapter 23: "A Kurdish wedding and a cherry spree" (pp. 252-60). Also published by Abellard-Schuman, London and New York, 1959.

**Keywords:** American village archeologist; excavations at Barda Balka, Jarmo, Karim Shahir, and Palegawra, Iraqi Kurdistan; description of wedding at Kanisard village.

*See also* Marriage

**Frachon, Renee [Renée] Irana**. (1963). *Quand j'etais au Kurdistan* (When I was in Kurdistan). Editions Marocaines et Internationales. April 25, 46 pages.

**Keywords:** travel in Erzurum, Bayazid, Van, Khoy, Urmaia, Rawandiz, Mosul; ruined Armenian church women in Kurdish society; non-veiling and women's freedom in Kurdish tribes and nomads; women's dress in tribes; sexual division of labor in tribes; tribal wedding; discussions with a Kurdish tribal leader.

**Institut Kurde de Paris**. (1989, May). Mrs. Mitterrand in Kurdistan [Special issue]. *Institut Kurde de Paris, Information and Liaison Bulletin,* ISSN 0761 1285.

**Keywords:** Danielle Mitterrand; refugees; Turkish reactions to Mitterrand's visit.

**Lagard, Dorothée**. (1996). Kurdistan, voyage à travers une terre fantôme [Kurdistan, journey through a ghost land. *Terre Sauvage, 105*, April, pp. 86-100. Photographs by Daniele Pellegrini. 22 photographs (pp. 86, 87, 88, 89, 90, 91, 92, 93, 94, 95, 96, 97, 98, 99, 100), map (p. 100).

**Keywords:** veiling among the Kurdish women of Hakkari; black headscarves worn by Kurdish women in the villages of Hakkari; religion; PKK; the killing of civilians (including women and children) in Pinarcik in 1987 by the PKK; women carpet weavers; women grinding wheat using traditional methods; the fame of Kurdish women's poetry; women composing love songs; Halabja; marriage rites; women baking bread; the "relative" freedom of Kurdish women vis-a-vis Arab and Persian women; Iraqi Kurdish refugees in Turkey.

**Pfeiffer, Ida**. (1852). *A woman's journey round the world from Vienna to Brazil, Chili, Tahiti, Hindostan, Persia and Asia Minor.* Unabridged translation, Office of the National Illustrated Library, 1852.

**Keywords:** Austrian woman traveler to Brazil, Asia, Russia, Greece; travel to Mossul, Ravandus, Sauh-Bulok, Oromia, Tabriz, Armenia, Georgia; Kurdish village women; women at Ravandus; children's tyrannizing of women; teaching women how to mend their clothes; sexual division of labor; eating and washing; village women freer than urban women and with "better state of morals"; male and female costume; women non-veiled; Christian family and church in Sauh-Bulok; the bazaar; common people; village of Mahomed-Jur; quarrel with travel guide; supported by village women; Lake Oromia; Christian missionaries in Oromia: Mr. and Mrs. Wright.

**Pfeiffer, Ida** . (1988). *A lady's voyage around the world: A selected translation from*

263

*the German of Ida Pfeiffer* (P. Sinnett, Trans.). Century Hutchinson Ltd. (Originally published in 1855). ISBN 0-7126-2427-9. Introduction (pp. v-vi), introduction to this edition by Maria Aitken (pp. vii-xii), contents (pp. xiii-xv), bibliography of introduction (p. xvi), text (pp. 3-272).

**Keywords:** Austrian woman traveler to Brazil, Asia, Russia, Greece; travel to Mossul, Ravandus, Sauh-Bulok, Oromia, Tabriz, Armenia, Georgia; Kurdish village women; women at Ravandus; children's tyrannizing of women; teaching women how to mend their clothes; sexual division of labor; eating and washing; village women freer than urban women and with "better state of morals"; male and female costume; women non-veiled; Christian family and church in Sauh-Bulok; the bazaar; common people; village of Mahomed-Jur; quarrel with travel guide; supported by village women; Lake Oromia; Christian missionaries in Oromia: Mr. and Mrs. Wright.

**Rich, Veuve.** (1972). Fragment of a journal from Baghdad to Sulimania. In Cladius James Rich (Ed.), *Narrative of a residence in Koordistan, Volume 1* (pp. 331-75).

**Keywords:** killing of woman by former husband; the harem of the Baban Pasha; Adela Khanum, wife of the Baban Pasha; small-pox and vaccination.

**Selby, Bettina. (1993).** *Beyond Ararat: A journey through Eastern Turkey*. Abacus. ISBN 0 349 10508 1 (pb). List of illustrations (p. vii), acknowledgments (p. viii), map (pp. x-xi), text (pp. 1-211), 16 black and white photographs (unnumbered centre pages).

**Keywords:** PKK; veiling; Marxism; Atatürk; women's work; Kurdish women's account of the Armenian Genocide; Assyrian Christians; Armenians; Assyrian attitudes towards Kurdish uprising/PKK.

**Stark, Freya.** (1959). *Riding to the Tigris*. London: John Murray. Photographs: Yezidi women in Iraqi Kurdistan; Kurdish women south of Van; Soma women weavers.

**Keywords:** Turkish military and civil officials (*memur*s) and their wives in Hakkiari province, Turkey; tribal women weavers; unveiled Kurdish women; Armenian women; Mrs. (Isabella L. Bird) Bishop's travels in the region.

**Thornhill, Teresa.** (1997). *Sweet tea with cardamom. A journey through Iraqi Kurdistan*. Pandora. ISBN 0 04 440984 2 (pb). Author's note (p. ix), acknowledgments (p. xi), prologue (pp. xii -xv), map of Kurdistan (pp. xvi-

xvii), chronology (pp. xviii- xxi), text (pp. 3-210), epilogue (pp. 211-17). Reviews: Aziz, Barbara Nimri. *MESA Bulletin*, *1*(33), 1999, p. 133.

**Keywords:** author, British barrister and linguist, travels to the "safe haven" region in Iraqi Kurdistan, 1993 in the company of British women, Christine, Jill, and Lillian, and Kurdish woman Shireen, member of Iraq's Communist Party; British officer on Kurdish women; women and men in Anfal genocide; visiting the Kurdish parliament, and women members Nahla Mohammed and Galawesh [Galawezh] Abdul Jabbar; Anfal Widows' Association; shari'a, the Islamic family code still in place, except for Assyrian Christians; reforming the law; women peshmargas; mullahs in the parliament; women political prisoners; the Communist Party and its League of Iraqi Women; Arab and Kurdish women peshmargas; meeting two more women MPs; Union of Kurdish Women, Arbil and Sulaymaniya branches; Qushtapa and Sumud, collective towns for Anfal widows; women in post-Anfal Safe Haven; shame, honor, and rape; honor killing of daughter; the story of a nurse, Jwan; class and Kurdish politics; the story of Nazaneen and Sirwa; impact of U.N. sanctions; chemical weapons; developments after the trip; clashes between the Islamic Movement in Kurdistan and PUK; civil war between KDP and PUK in May 1994; 300 women march five days and nights from Sylaymaniyah to Arbil protesting the civil war; division of Iraqi Kurdistan into two zones, administered by KDP and PUK.

## B. MEN TRAVELERS

**Binder, Henry**. (1887). *Au Kurdistan en Mésopotamie et en Perse* [In Kurdistan in Mesopotamia and Persia]. Mission scientifique de Ministère de l'instruction publique. Paris: Maison Quantin.

**Keywords:** Armenia and Kurdistan (Ottoman Turkey); Armenian women; Jewish; Kurdish women–unveiled, nomadic; women of Luristan.

**Braquet, Emmanuel**. (1976). *Dans le brasier kurde* [In the Kurdish blaze]. Vaulx-en-Velin, France: Imprimerie F.O.T., pp. 277, p. 279, map, 21 photographs of women. Chapitre VII: "Une histoire de femme...," (pp. 141-49).

**Keywords:** author travels to the region of Iraqi Kurdistan held by Kurdish autonomists during the 1974 war; travel to the Kurdish regions of Iran and Turkey; interviewing Zakkia Hakki, lawyer and head of the KDP's Federation of Kurdish Women; Federation has 70,000 members out of a population of 1,300,000 women; questioning these figures in a society with 70% illiteracy; this movement is different, according to Zakkia, from the Western women's liberation; the 1958 Iraqi revolution allowed women to organize; Kurdish women freer than Arab women; after 1961, women responsible for family affairs in the absence of men fighting in the mountains; same as women in Europe in 1918; comparing Kurdish women's movement with Europe; poverty and lack of education in Kurdistan; infant mortality 50% and life span is 45 years; contraception not an issue; history of Kurdish women's armed struggle; Khadam Kay [Qedem Xêr] around 1900; 300 women have demanded to become peshmargas, though refused by Mustapha Barzani, the leader; Margarette Georges, Assyrian-Kurdish peshmarga; Iraqi government preparation for chemical war and purchase of 50,000 gas masks; defeat of the autonomist movement in March 1975.

**Coan, Rev. Frederick G.** (1939). *Yesterdays in Persia and Kurdistan*. Claremont, California, Saunders Studio Press. Foreword by R. E. Speer. Illustrations, maps.

**Keywords:** Travel in Iranian Kurdistan; American Presbyterian missionary work; Sheikh Baba of Saujbulak; relative freedom of Kurdish women; women not veiling.

**Edmonds, C. J.** (1949). The travels of Arthur MacMurrough Kavanagh in Kurdistan and Luristan in 1850. *JRCAS*, Vol. XXXVI, Parts 3 & 4, July-October, pp. 267-279.

**Keywords:** Urmiya; Mar Gabriel; Ardishai; Sulduz Plain; Nestorians; the beauty of Kurdish women.

**Harris, Walter B.** (1895). Wanderings in Persian Kurdistan. *Blackwood's Magazine, 158*, November, pp. 736-753.

**Keywords:** Lake Urumiyah; Saujbulak; physical attributes of the Kurds; Kurdish dress; domestic life; polygamy; Shah's rule in Persian Kurdistan; dance; the freedom allowed Kurdish women; moral standards; death penalty for adultery.

**Jaubert, Chevalier Amedée Emilien Probe.** (1821). *Voyage en Arménie et en Perse* [Travel to Armenia and Persia]. Ducrocq. Reprinted in Leipzig, 1822; Weimar 1822.

**Keywords:** geography of Kurdistan (Ottoman Turkey); customs: tribal and nomadic life; treatment of strangers; marriage and wedding, Kurdish and Iranian; love in marriage; Armenian women; Yazidis.

**Kurdish Life**. (1996). Kurdish women in history. *Kurdish Life*, *17*, Winter, pp. 11-12.

**Keywords:** "brief vignettes" about Kurdish women mostly from travellers: Plutarch, Evliya Çelebi, E. B. Barker, *The Illustrated London News*, Ff. Millingen, E. B. Soane, W. R. Hay, and C. J. Edmonds.

*See also* History

**Morier, James**. *The Adventures of Hajji Baba of Ispahan* (C. Cyrus LeRoy Baldridge, Illustrator). Random House Inc., New York MCMXXXVII. (Chapter XXVI: The History of the Beautiful Zeenab, the Curdish Slave" pp. 113-129).

**Keywords:** Kurdistan; the Shah of Persia; Yazidi Kurds (Curds); the giving of a Yazidi Kurdish girl to the Shah's harem; a Kurdish girl's longing to belong to the Shah's harem as a means of escaping poverty; the migration of Kurds from Turkish territory into Persian territory; Kermanshah.

**Müller-Simonis, P**. (1892). *Relation des missions scientifique de MM. H. Hyvernat et P. Müller-Simonis (1888-1889) du Caucase au Golfe Persique a travers l'Arménie, le Kurdistan et la Mésopotamie* [Relation of the scientific missions of MM. H. Hyvernat and P. Müller-Simonis (1888-1889) from the Caucasus to the Persian Gulf through Armenia, Kurdistan and Mesopotamia]. Map of Armenia and Kurdistan (face p. 628), illustrations: Christian women of Ourmiah; Armenian women of Van; girls school in Mosul; Paris.

**Keywords:** Ourmia, Van, Akhlat, Bidlis, Siird, Jazira, Mosul; Kurdish women: inferiority vs husband and her superiority as "maîtresse de maison"; semi-nomadic women, courage and participation in work; temporary marriage in Iran; Armenians; Nestorians.

**Rich, Cladius James**. (1972). *Narrative of a residence in Koordistan, and on the site of ancient Nineveh; with journal of a voyage down the Tigris to Baghdad and an account of a visit to Shirauz and Persepolis*. Veuve Rich (Ed.). London: James Duncan Paternoster Row. Vol. I: Contents (pp. iii-vi), directions for maps, plans, and plates (p. vii), notice respecting maps (pp. ix-x), preface (pp. xi-xiii), brief notice of the life of Mr. Rich (pp. xv-xxxiii), residence in Koordistan, pp. 1-327), appendix I-VI (pp. 331-98), map of route from Bagdad to Sulaimania, Sinna, Nineveh and Mosul, Plate "A Marriage, Coordish women dancing" (facing p. 282). Vol. II: Residence in Koordistan, (pp. iii-176), letters (177-290), appendix I-IX (pp. 293-410), Plate "A Yezid [Yazidi] man and woman from Sinjah [Sinjar]" (facing p. 85). Reprinted by Gregg International Publishers Limited, UK, 1972, ISBN 0 576 03466 1 and 0 576 03468 3.

**Keywords:** women of Jaf tribe; clothing and lack of veil; wedding and women's dancing in Sulaymania; Kurdish women compared with Arab, Persian, and Turkish women; "lower class" women unveiled; absence of veil and "real propriety"; the *harem* of the Baban prince; slave women; Yezidi women; Mrs. Rich; Yezidis, Nestorians.

**Soane, Ely Bannister**. (1912). *To Mesopotamia and Kurdistan in disguise with historical notices of the Kurdish tribes and the Chaldeans of Kurdistan*. Boston: Small, Maynard and Company Publishers. Prefatory note (p. v-vi), contents (p. vii), list of illustrations (p. ix), text (p.1-403), appendix: Kurdish tribes (pp. 405-07) and bibliography (pp. 409-10), foldout map of Mesopotamia and Kurdistan (facing p. 410), index (pp. 411-21). Second Edition, London: John Murray, 1926. Additions to the first edition: "E. B. Soane– A Memoir" by Sir Arnold T. Wilson (pp. ix-xvii) and "Bibliography of published works by E. B. Soane (p. xviii), 11 photographs.

**Keywords:** status of women in Kurdistan; their freedom; Adela Khanum of Halabja – her position as ruler, appearance, dress, reception and sons; life in Halabja; women and breadmaking in Sulaimania; Gulchin, a young Sulaimania woman; costume.

**Valle, Pietro della**. (1989). *The pilgrim: The travels of Pietro della Valle* (translated, abridged and introduced by George Bull. Translation based on *Viaggi di Pietro della Valle Il Pellegrino Descritti da lui medesimo*, 1843). London: Hutchinson. ISBN 0-09-174189-0.

**Keywords:** travels in 1617 (Iranian Kurdistan); geography of Kurdistan; Kurdish dress and language; women, unveiled and socializing with strangers.

# POLITICS

## I. ARMED STRUGGLE

**Agiri, Sirin**. (1991). Confident path in Kurdistan. *Kurdistan Report*, *5*, October, pp. 8-9. Two photographs.

**Keywords:** young female guerillas in the ARGK; 19 young women in the training camp; Berivan: 14 years old; Azimi and two nieces: left university to join armed struggle; distrust of traditional Kurdish parties.

**Greaves, Alan**. (1992). "Our struggle is for all of humanity, not just for the Kurdish people," *Kurdistan Report, 11*, September, p. 7. One photograph. Also appeared in *Kurdish Women: The struggle for national liberation and women's rights*. London: KIC/KSC Publications, October, pp. 36-37.

**Keywords:** Beritan, a female guerrilla with the PKK; torture; oppression; assimilated parents of Beritan; Botan; Cudi Mountain; the PKK's position on the participation of women in the armed struggle; women's position in traditional Kurdish society; the attraction of the PKK for women; gender relations in the PKK camps; Provisional War Government in Botan-Behdinan; semi-feudalism and women.

**Harding, Luke**. (2003). Time for revenge. *The Guardian*, February 28.

**Keywords:** training camp for Peshmerga Force for Women; instruction in "arts of war"; aged 18-48; run by the PUK; founded in 1996; Sirwa Ismael: 27-year-old commander; 500 women soldiers under her command; before 1991, Kurdish women played an active role in the resistance: cook, build camps, take care of the wounded, carry munitions and messages; revenge: torture; threats of rape; sexual torture; fighting with Ansar al-Islam, a Kurdish Islamist group; women heavily involved in fighting; see fight with Ansar al-Islam as a battle against Islamic fundamentalism, giving the example of not allowing girls to go to school; a few of the female fighters have small children but the majority are single or widowed; the unit offers six months' paid maternity leave.

**Hepburn, Bo**. (1992). It's our duty to help rebels. *The Toronto Star*, November 8, reprinted in *Institut Kurde de Paris, Information and Liaison Bulletin, 91-92*, October-November, pp. 83-84.

**Keywords:** Hezal Hessen; women and war; women's support for the PKK; Cizre; attacks on civilians.

**Howard, Michael**. (2002). Revenge spurs women's army. *The Guardian*, November 26.

**Keywords:** Peshmerga Force for Women: Sulaymaniyah, Iraq; run by the PUK; 20 women; learn to attack, ambush, and sabotage; established six years prior; now has 300 fighters; Shams Mahmoud: commander of the force; before the 1991 Kurdish uprising, female peshmerga only accompanied their husbands on their missions in order to cook, build camps, take care of the wounded, and carry munitions and messages; has already fought against Ansar al-Islam, a Kurdish Islamist group.

**Kinaci, Zeynep**. (1997). Total resistance in the struggle for our freedom. *Kurdistan Report, 25,* July-August, p. 53.

**Keywords:** excerpts from a letter by suicide bomber Zeynep Kinaci, addressed to PKK president Abdullah Öcalan; Mamureki tribe; PKK; ARGK; the arming of women by the PKK.

**Kurdistan-Info**. (1987) Frauen!? Ein Gespräch mit Vier Frauen-Peschmerga [Women!? A conversation with four women peshmerga]. *Kurdistan-Info, 5,* II D 84, pp. 1-8.

**Keywords:** guerrilla movement; interview; Iran; Kurdish women; the position of women; female guerrillas.

**Kurdistan Report**. (1991). "We fight for a free Kurdistan and the liberation of Kurdish women": Interview with Medya, a member of the YJWK. *Kurdistan Report, 5,* October, pp. 9-11. Also appeared in *Kurdish Women: The struggle for national liberation and women's rights.* London: KIC/KSC Publications, 1992, pp. 31-35. One photograph.

**Keywords:** YJWK; colonization and women's liberation; PKK; women prisoners; traditional role of women in Kurdish society; women's agricultural work; the effect the PKK has had on Kurdish men's ideas of women's roles in the national liberation struggle; martyred women; the Turkish government's campaign against female guerrillas, in which they were branded "bitches and prostitutes"; initial trepidation felt by many Kurdish men about allowing their daughters to join the guerrillas; the manner in which women's participation in the guerrilla forces has inspired and influenced other women, and has changed the ways men view women; ERNK; Abdullah Öcalan's views concerning women' rights; Kurdish women in Europe; Kurdish women and International Women's Day; women's participation in uprisings.

**Kurdistan Report**. (1993). We salute the courage and determination of the young Kurdish fighters who died in the struggle for an independent and free Kurdistan! *Kurdistan Report, 13,* February/March, p. 8.

**Keywords:** obituary for Beritan, martyred Kurdish guerilla; PKK; KDP/PUK attacks on PKK.

**Laizer, Sheri**. (1991). Confident Kurdistan. *Kurdish Life, 1,* Fall, pp. 6-7.

**Keywords:** guerilla training camps of ARGK and PAK in Iraqi Kurdistan; women guerillas in PKK.

**Metro**. (2003). Les Kurdes prêtes au combat [The Kurds ready for battle]. *Metro*, January 15, reprinted in *Institut Kurde de Paris, Information and Liaison Bulletin, 214*, January, p. 55. One photograph.

**Keywords:** 500 female peshmergas ("those who face death, guerrillas"), members of PUK; getting ready for war near Sulaimaniya.

**Montalbano, William D**. (1993). No longer a step behind in Turkey. *Los Angeles Times*, November 13, pp. A1, A8-10.

**Keywords:** Prime Minister Tansu Ciller and the changes that have been introduced to improve the situation of women by her coming to power; Kurdish areas in the Southeast of Turkey have changed the least; Kurdish female guerillas.

**Wolf, Judith**. (2004). Aspekte des Geschlechterverhältnisses in der Guerilla der PKK/KADEK unter besonderer Berücksichtigung des Ehrbegriffs [Aspects of gender relations in the guerrillas of the PKK / KADEK with special consideration of the concept of honor]. In Siamend Hajo, Carsten Borck, Eva Savelsberg, & Şükriye Dogan (Eds.), *Gender in Kurdistan und der Diaspora, Kurdologie Series Vol. 6* (pp. 183-216). Münster: UNRAST-Verlag. ISBN 3-89771-014-5 (pb).

**Keywords:** images of women; gender discourse; PKK; KADEK; Komala; the organization of women in party and guerrilla structures; TAJK; YJWK; ARGK; ERNK; PJKK; PJA; HPG; Abdullah Öcalan's views on the feminist movement in Europe; gender ideology of the PKK/KADEK and PJA; tribalism; patrilineage; the concept and definitions of honor; Medya, a Kurdish guerrilla from Syria; Pervîn, a Kurdish guerrilla from a northern Kurdistan village; Berfîn, a Kurdish guerrilla who grew up in France; Rojda, a former guerrilla who grew up in an assimilated, Kemalist family in Western Turkey; women's health problems while fighting guerrilla warfare; sexist Turkish propaganda against female guerrillas; two female Syrian guerrillas accused of having had sexual relations who were sent back to their homes; Zinarîn, a Kurdish guerrilla who complained of the patriarchal attitudes of the male guerrillas and of the female guerrillas who collaborated with them; matriarchy.

## II. KURDISH NATIONALIST MOVEMENTS

**Ahmetbeyzade, Cihan**. (2000). Kurdish nationalism in Turkey and the role of peasant Kurdish women. In Tamar Mayer (Ed.), *Gender ironies of nationalism* (pp. 186-209). London and New York: Routledge. Map (p. 186), references (pp. 207-209).

**Keywords:** Kurdish nationalism; killing of Kurds; burning of villages; sexual intimidation; the "new Turkish woman"; Turkish nationalism; misrepresentation and marginalization of Kurdish women by Turkish feminists; peasant households; family; tribal loyalties; Kurdish identity; proletarianization; class-consciousness; rural-urban migration; resistance; Ottoman era; PKK; education; health; village guards; women's work; gender roles; peasant mothers and wives; women's support for the PKK; female guerillas; female suicide bombers; Deniz Kandiyoti; feudal system; patriarchal familial authority; critique of Turkish feminism; patriarchal household; Lale Yalcin-Heckmann; İsmail Beşikci; İHD; HKD; Jiyan Kurt Kadin Kultur Evi; Kurt Kadınları Dayanisma Vakfı; democratic patriarchy; difference; citizenship.

**Eftekhari, Aumecolsoum.** (1984). *La situation de la femme kurde au Kurdistan iranien (Moukrian)* [The situation of Kurdish women in Iranian Kurdistan (Moukrian); Master's thesis]. Nanterre, France, Université Paris X. October, 117 pages, bibliography (p. 112-117).

**Keywords:** review of literature on Kurdish women; village and nomad women; Mukri Kurdistan; Iran; socioeconomic situation; marriage; divorce; education; nationalist movement.

**Fischer-Tahir, Andrea.** (2000). Nationalismus und Frauenbewegung in Irakisch-Kurdistan. In Eva Savelsberg, Siamend Hajo, & Carsten Borck (Eds.), *Kurdologie: Kurdische Frauen und das Bild der kurdischen Frau* (pp. 157-77). Münster: Lit Verlag.

**Keywords:** women's policies of the Ba'th Party; 1968 coup; modernization; literacy campaigns; education; literacy campaigns as a means of integrating women into the Ba'thi system; Iraqi Communist Party; KDP; women's participation in the workforce; unions; Kurdish women academics; women in the Iraqi army; female parliamentarians; Iraqi Women's League; Progressive National Front; female guerrillas; Nidâl al-Mar'a; Komala-i Âfretân le Kurdistân; Yekêti-i Âfretân-i Kurdistân; lack of veiling among Kurdish women; European travellers to Kurdistan; European stereotypes of Kurdish women; Qâra Fâtima; Âdila Xânum; linguistic constructions of women; comparisons of Kurdish dialects/languages; Fayili Kurds; Zakîya Isma'il Haqqî; jin-ba-jin (woman for woman exchange); divorce; jin-ba-xwên (woman for blood exchange); bride price; Yekêti-i Jinân-i Kurdistân; PUK; collective towns; refugees; shame; honour; sexuality; Tawâr; martyrs; sexual abuse/rape of prisoners; palamar kirdn; torture; 1991 uprising; Leila Qâsim.

**Fuad, Tanya**. (1995). National liberation, women's liberation. *Freedom Review*. September-October, pp. 31-33.

**Keywords:** Gulf War; peshmerga; civil war; refugees in Turkey; Northern Iraq; women's political organizations; Bahia Khan; women parliamentarians in Northern Iraq; dress codes; women's work; widows.

**Ignatieff, Michael** (Director). (1994). *Dreaming a nation: The Kurds*. Part 2 of video documentary, *Blood and Belonging*. 58 minutes, color.

**Keywords:** Kurdish nationalism in Iraq, Iran, and Turkey; author's visit to Kurdistan (Iraq and Turkey), Kemalism; guerrilla movements; female guerrillas; Marxism.

**Klein, Janet**. (2001). En-gendering nationalism: The 'woman question' in Kurdish nationalist discourse of the late Ottoman period. In Shahrzad Mojab (Ed.), *Women of a non-state nation: The Kurds* (pp. 25-51). Costa Mesa: Mazda Publishers.

**Keywords:** Jîn; Kurdish Ottoman press; Ottoman Committee of Union and Progress; Kürd Teavün ve Terakki Gazetesi; Young Turk Revolution; Rojî Kurd; Hetawî Kurd; Kürd Kadınları Teâli Cemiyeti; Kürdistan Teâli Cemiyeti; 'Eziz Yamulkî; 'Abdurrahim Rahmi Zapsu; Abdullah Cevdet; Memduh Selîm Beg; religion; education.

**Kurdistan Focus**. (1994). We will ensure many women are selected to stand for parliament. *Kurdistan Focus, 10*, July, pp. 8-9.

**Keywords:** Fadhil Merani, the Regional Commander of the Kurdistan Front in Dohuk Province and member of the Political Bureau of the KDP; improvements in the political position of women; KDP; first woman member of the Central Committee of the KDP elected in 1960; Assyrians; Turkomans; Barzani.

**Kurdistan Report**. (1992). We take our strength from our people, which is becoming ever freer, from the fact that we are in the right and from our organized resistance. *Kurdistan Report, 6*, February, pp. 21-23.

**Keywords:** Sara Akan, representative of the YKD; Özgür Halk; exploitation of women's labour; difficulties facing urban and rural Kurdish women; women and capitalism; the buying and selling of women; women's sexual identities; women and education; women's (lack of) access to healthcare; women and reproduction; importance of giving birth to male offspring; assimilation of Kurdish women in Turkish cities; male-female relations within the home; sexist proverbs regarding women; mothers of martyrs; women fighters/guerrillas; female revolutionaries; women and solidarity movements.

**Kurdistan Report**. (1992). Kurdish women: The struggle for national identity and women's rights. *Kurdistan Report, 10,* July, pp. 20-21.

**Keywords:** an interview with the YKD management committee member Aynur Gurbuz; Ebru Karaibrahimoğlu, reporter with the newspaper Yeni Ülke; nation; class; gender; assimilated Kurdish women; women fighting against colonial and patriarchal oppression; differences between Kurdish women living in Turkish cities and Kurdish women living in Kurdistan; women reclaiming their ethnic identity; International Women's Day; women's health problems in the shanty-towns; Newroz massacres.

**Kurdistan Report**. (1993). Europe-wide demonstrations of Kurdish women and children. *Kurdistan Report, 14,* April/May, pp. 15-16.

**Keywords:** Ermine Turan; death squads in Turkey; Contra-guerrillas/Hezbullah; women and girls murdered during Newroz celebrations in 1992: Bedriye Gümüş; Zeynep Uysal; Nebahat Kakus; Hediye Sağic; Fakiye Yılmaz; Nahiye Yılmaz; Belkız Yumak; Birsen Özcan; Safiye Kalay; Hezar Özen; Zeynep Ören; Birsen Kaya; Women shot during Newroz celebrations in 1992: Semire Acar; Aliye Er; Hediye Ayten; Ayten Bağcin; Fatma Kaçmaz; deaths in police custody; Bişeng Anık; Şefika Tosun; Ayşe Balim; Hanım Tunç; Dudu Şahin; Ayten Öztürk; Naciye Özen; Nurcan Öztabak; Mayre Ayçiçek; Bendi Özdemir; Hatun Korkmaz; Devrim Berktay; rape in custody; Menice Kırtay; electric shock torture; Gülay Tan; Hayal Gül; Halise Sincar; Nazmiye Ermiş; Birgün Yeken; Melek Bora; Dilek Demir; Fatma Can; Hatun Kara; Bahriye Çeviren; burning of villages and homes; Taibet Kaya; Leyla Kırtay; Feyziye Aydın; Mina Beyazıt; Nuran Avcı; Vesile Artunç; Azize Öner; Rukiye Tatlı; Ebide Tatlı; Cahide Kaya; Afife Alan; Nazlı Top.

**Kurdistan Report**. (1993). Women occupy city council in Diyarbakir. *Kurdistan Report, 16,* October/November, p. 21.

**Keywords:** women protest against lack of running water.

**Kurdistan Report**. (1993). IHD and DEP women demand resignation. *Kurdistan Report, 16,* October/November, p. 21.

**Keywords:** women protest against the rape of Şükran Aydin; sexual harassment by state forces.

**Kurdistan Report**. (1993). Kurdish women occupy Reuter news agency in London. *Kurdistan Report, 16*, October/November, p. 21.

**Keywords:** women protest against the murder of *Özgür Gündem* correspondent Ferhat Tepe; women protest against the abduction of *Özgür Gündem* journalist Aysel Malkaç; women protest against the silence of the international public.

*See also* Freedom of the Press; United Kingdom

**Kurdistan Report**. (2000). Without freedom all else is impossible. *Kurdistan Report, 29*, March/April, pp. 82-83.

**Keywords:** Abdullah Öcalan's message to Kurdish and Turkish women; Öcalan's views on the self-immolation of girls in support of the Kurdish cause; Öalan's views on women's sexuality, traditional marriage, and honour.

**Kurdistan Report**. (2000). Women are the fighters for peace: Interview with Peace Mothers' Initiative in Turkey. *Kurdistan Report, 29*, March/April, pp. 84-86. Three black and white photographs (p. 85).

**Keywords:** Kurdish mothers and peace; mothers of guerrillas; mothers of soldiers; women organizing for peace; women's activism; women's organizations; women's publication of a bi-monthly journal; women's march for peace; women demanding democracy; village guards; special teams; armed gangs; mafia; heroin trafficking; feudalism; patriarchal domination; illiteracy; attempts at dialogue with Turkish mothers.

**Mönch-Buçak, Yayla**. (1997). Kurdish women in the struggle for Kurdistan (N. Jameson, Trans.). *Kurdistan Report, 25*, July/August, pp. 54-55.

**Keywords:** women in Kurdish clan society; elder women's position in clan courts; women's integration into the political life of clans; Islamization of Kurdistan and its effects of the position of women; Turkish colonisation and the decline of the position of Kurdish women; mechanisation of farming; urbanisation of Kurdish society and the decline in women's status; women and voting; women and illiteracy; the change in women's roles through repression, resistance and the liberation struggle; PKK's influence on the role of women; Kurdish women's armed units; Komala; the participation of Kurdish women in HEP, DEP, and HADEP; Leyla Zana; gender statistics of HADEP candidates; KPE; Kurdish National Assembly (1993/94); IHD; radicalization of Kurdish women; the Mothers of the

Disappeared; the Peace Train; Zeynep Kinaci, who carried out the first suicide attack.

**Öcalan, Abdullah**. (1994). Women are our greatest source of strength. *Kurdistan Report, 18*, May/June, p. 37. Also appears in *Resistance: Women in Kurdistan*. London: KIC/KSC Publications, 1995, pp. 50-51. One photograph.

**Keywords:** Öcalan's address to the International Kurdish Women's Conference on March 8, 1994; women and liberation; women's strength; the historical oppression and exploitation of the female gender; women's participation in the armed struggle; Newroz; female heroes of the Kurdish movement; Zekiye Alkan.

**Schubert, Brigitte and Beate Rudolph**. (1996). Kurdische Frauen. Überleben und Widerstehen im Krieg [Kurdish women. Survive and Resist in War]. *Terre des Femmes,* Tübingen, *2*, pp. 23-26. Z G 20.

**Keywords:** Turkey; war; resistance; Kurdistan.

**Struchtemeier, Thea A**. (1992). Kurdish women in the political and military struggle. *Kurdistan Report, 7*, March, pp. 11-12. Also appeared in *Kurdish women: The struggle for national liberation and women's rights*. London: KIC/KSC Publications, October, pp. 25-30. Four photographs.

**Keywords:** women's levels of self-awareness/emancipation; Kurdish women in Turkey and Northwest Kurdistan; politicization of Kurdish women; Sevtap Yokuş, a female Kurdish lawyer who works at Diyarbakir University and in the women's commission of the Human Rights Association; socio-economist Sara Akan of the YKD; Leyla Zana; women in the HEP; SHP; struggles of women during Zonguldak miners' strike; struggles of women during the hunger strike in Paşabahçe Prison; İHD; the double oppression of Kurdish women; PKK; changes in gender relations; religion and the oppression of women; rural women and oppression; feudalism and women; Kurdish women and girls in the armed struggle; Ayfer Turhalli, a 15-year-old guerrilla killed by the Turkish army; Asiye Turhalli, mother of Ayfer Turhalli; Kurdish women in the Turkish cities; politicization of the mothers of martyred guerrillas; Yeni Ülke; YKD.

**Wedel, Heidi**. (2000). Frauenbewegung und Nationalbewegung-ein Widerspruch? Gefahren und Chancen am Beispiel der Türkei und Kurdistans [Women's movement and national movement - a contradiction? Dangers and opportunities using the example of Turkey and Kurdistan]. In Eva Savelsberg, Siamend Hajo, & Carsten Borck (Eds.), *Kurdologie: Kurdische Frauen* *und das Bild der kurdischen Frau* (pp. 105-27). Münster: Lit Verlag.

**Keywords:** nationalist movements; women's reproductive role; women as symbols of ethnic/national differences; women as participants in national, economic, and political struggles; Kemalism; modernization; secularism; populism; Islamism; marriage; polygamy; national, economic, and gender oppression of Kurdish women; bride price; wife-exchange; elopement; assimilation; GAP; ÇATOM; NGOs; dissent and cooperation between Turkish feminists and women and the Kurdish movement; PKK; sexuality; İstanbul Women's Platform; Pazartesi); Ayşe Düzkan; Women's Peace Initiative; Habitat II; Women's Initiative Against Rape in War; Legal Aid Project for Women Sexually Abused and Raped in Prison; Roja; Jujin; sexism; racism; class discrimination; confessionalism; multiple identities of women; Kurdish feminists; emancipation of women; national liberation.

**Woodson, LeRoy Jr.** (1975). The Kurds of Iraq risk their lives daily in a desperate struggle for self-determination: 'We who face death.' *National Geographic, 147*(3), March, pp. 364-387. 19 colour photographs (pp. 365, 366, 368, 370, 371, 372, 373, 374, 375, 376, 377, 378, 379, 380, 381, 382-383, 384, 385, 387), two maps (p. 368).

**Keywords:** Kurdish guerrillas in Iraq; General Mulla Mustafa Barzani; effects of war on women and children; Kurdish women's work; Zakia Haqui, head of the Kurdistan Women's Federation; women's participation in the war effort; the Kurdistan Women's Federation's education of village women; Kurdish appeals for United Nations' intervention; Kurdish women's dress; Iraqi Kurdish refugees in Iran.

*See also* Feminist and Women's Movements

## III. POLITICAL PARTIES

**Demir, Ahmet Turan**. (2001). HADEP (Peoples Democracy Party) 4th Annual Congress Opening Speech of Chairman Ahmet Turan Demir. *Kurdistan Report, 31*, Autumn, pp. 25-29.

**Keywords:** women's rights; discrimination against women; oppression of women; violence against women; HADEP's policies regarding the eradication of discrimination against women.

**Le Figaro**. (1994). Procès des deputés kurde: un verdict lourd de consequences. *Le Figaro,* December 7, reprinted in *Institut Kurde de Paris, Information and Liaison Bulletin, 116-117*, November/December, p. 112.

**Keywords:** trial against Kurdish parliamentarians in Turkey.

**İmset, İsmet G**. (1993). DEP, a failing mission. *Turkish Daily News,* December 15, reprinted in *Institut Kurde de Paris, Information and Liaison Bulletin, 105,* December, p. 79.

**Keywords:** death squads; DEP; PKK; ÖZDEP; HEP; Leyla Zana.

**İmset, İsmet G**. (1994). Lifting immunity: A trial case faces Parliament. *Turkish Daily News,* March 2.

**Keywords:** State Security Court; Welfare Party; True Path Party; Sheikh Sait rebellion; DEP; Social Democrat People's Party; PKK; assassination attempts; Article 125 of the Turkish Penal Code; Newroz; attacks on DEP; Nationalist Movement Party; military coercion of Kurdish villagers; DEP withdrawal from elections.

**Institut Kurde de Paris**. (1991). Ankara: The irruption of Kurds causes an upheaval in parliament. *Institut Kurde de Paris, Information and Liaison Bulletin, 80-81,* November/December, p. 6.

**Keywords:** Kurdish nationalism; Leyla Zana; SHP.

**Institut Kurde de Paris**. (2001). 37 Persons in the HADEP offices of Izmir taken in for questioning and 3 deaths during clashes in Silvan. *Institut Kurde de Paris, Information and Liaison Bulletin, 189-199,* September/October, p. 14.

**Keywords:** HADEP; PKK; youth branch of HADEP; female guerilla killed.

**Libération**. (1994). Procès des six députés kurdes sous haute surveillance à Ankara [Trial of the six Kurdish deputies under close surveillance in Ankara]. *Libération,* August 4, reprinted in *Institut Kurde de Paris, Information and Liaison Bulletin, 113-114,* August/September, p.17.

**Keywords:** DEP; PKK.

**Libération**. (1996). Critique kurde à l'Union douanière turco-européenne [Kurdish criticism of the Turkish-European Customs Union.]. *Liberation,* January 18, reprinted in *Institut Kurde de Paris, Information and Liaison Bulletin, 130-131,* January/February, p. 67.

**Keywords:** Leyla Zana; Sacharov Prize; PKK; Danielle Mitterrand; Turkish customs union with Europe.

**Le Nouveau Quotidien**. (1994). Procès houleux en Turquie. *Le Nouveau*

*Quotidien,* August 4, reprinted in *Institut Kurde de Paris, Information and Liaison Bulletin, 113-114*, August/September, p. 17.

Keywords: trial against Kurdish parliamentarians.

**Pailler, Aline**. (1994). Le courage des députés kurdes. *l'Humanité,* December 17, reprinted in *Institut Kurde de Paris, Information and Liaison Bulletin, 116-117,* November/December, p. 176.

Keywords: Leyla Zana.

**Paris Match**. (1994). Ségolène Royal Defend Six Deputés Kurdes [Ségolène Royal defend six Kurdish deputies]. *Paris Match,* August 4, reprinted in *Institut Kurde de Paris, Information and Liaison Bulletin, 113-114*, August/September, p.18.

Keywords: Leyla Zana.

**Pope, Nicole**. (1994). Ankara marque sa volonté de répression lors de la reprise du procès de députés kurdes [Ankara shows its will for repression when the trial of Kurdish deputies resumes]. *Le Monde,* September 8, reprinted in *Institut Kurde de Paris, Information and Liaison Bulletin, 113-114,* August/September, p. 131.

Keywords: PKK; State Security Court tribunal.

**Pope, Nicole**. (1994). Cinq députés kurdes ont été condamnés à quinze ans de prison [Five Kurdish MPs were sentenced to fifteen years in prison]. *Le Monde,* December 10, reprinted in *Institut Kurde de Paris, Information and Liaison Bulletin, 116-117,* November/December, p. 135.

Keywords: Leyla Zana; prison sentences of Kurdish parliamentarians.

**Tan, Erdal**. (1994). A l'heure de la condamnation des députés kurdes [At the time of the condemnation of Kurdish deputies]. *Rouge,* December 22, reprinted in *Institut Kurde de Paris, Information and Liaison Bulletin, 116-117,* November/December, pp. 195-197.

Keywords: DEP; Leyla Zana; PKK.

**Turkish Daily News**. (1994). Pro-Kurdish deputies in court today to face treason charge. *Turkish Daily News,* August 3, reprinted in *Institut Kurde de Paris, Information and Liaison Bulletin, 113-114*, August/September, p. 9.

Keywords: DEP; PKK; Kurdish parliamentarians' loss of diplomatic immunity; death penalty.

**Turkish Daily News**. (1994). Treason case against ex-DEP deputies begins. *Turkish Daily News,* August 4, reprinted in *Institut Kurde de Paris, Information and Liaison Bulletin, 113-114,* August/September, pp. 14-15.

**Keywords:** DEP; Leyla Zana; article 125 of the penal code; HADEP.

**Turkish Daily News**. (1994). DEP treason trial continues at Ankara DGM. *Turkish Daily News,* August 5, reprinted in *Institut Kurde de Paris, Information and Liaison Bulletin, 113-114,* August/September, p. 19.

**Keywords:** DEP; State Security Court; Leyla Zana; PKK.

**Turkish Daily News**. (1994). DGM continues DEP trial hearings. *Turkish Daily News,* reprinted in *Institut Kurde de Paris, Information and Liaison Bulletin, 115,* October 8, p. 41.

**Keywords:** Leyla zana; DEP; Ankara State Security Court.

**Turkish Daily News**. (1994). DEP trial continues. *Turkish Daily News,* August 6, reprinted in *Institut Kurde de Paris, Information and Liaison Bulletin, 113-114,* August/September, pp. 22-23.

**Keywords:** Leyla Zana; HEP; DEP; PKK; ÖZDEP.

**Turkish Daily News**. (1994). DEP trial continues at Ankara DGM. *Turkish Daily News,* August 9, reprinted in *Institut Kurde de Paris, Information and Liaison Bulletin, 113-114,* August/September, pp. 29-30.

**Keywords:** DEP; Turkish penal code; HEP; PKK; ÖZDEP.

**Turkish Daily News**. (1994). Former Democracy Party deputies speak freely at trial. *Turkish Daily News,* August 9, reprinted in *Institut Kurde de Paris, Information and Liaison Bulletin, 113-114,* August/September, pp. 32-33.

**Keywords:** Leyla Zana; DEP; Article 125; SHP.

**Turkish Daily News**. (1994). French observers call for release of Kurdish deputies. *Turkish Daily News,* December 8, reprinted in *Institut Kurde de Paris, Information and Liaison Bulletin, 116-117,* November/December, p. 114.

**Keywords:** European Parliament; Leyla Zana.

**Turkish Daily News**. (1994). Court sentences pro-Kurdish politicians. *Turkish Daily News,* December 9, reprinted in *Institut Kurde de Paris, Information and Liaison Bulletin, 116-117,* November/December, pp. 119-120.

**Keywords:** Leyla Zana; PKK; difficulties facing lawyers and defence.

**Turkish Daily News**. (1994). Foreigners pledge demonstrations against sentences. *Turkish Daily News,* December 9, reprinted in *Institut Kurde de Paris, Information and Liaison Bulletin, 116-117,* November/December, p. 120.

Keywords: DEP; International Human Rights Federation; PKK; demonstrations in Europe; French Socialist Party.

**Turkish Daily News**. (1995). Appeals court to decide on DEP case Thursday. *Turkish Daily News,* October 24, reprinted in *Institut Kurde de Paris, Information and Liaison Bulletin, 126-127,* September/October, p. 197.

Keywords: Leyla Zana; DEP; Anti-Terror Law.

**Turkish Daily News**. (2000). Turkey creates unnecessary problems for itself. *Turkish Daily News,* March 1, reprinted in *Institut Kurde de Paris, Information and Liaison Bulletin, 180,* March 2000, p. 2.

Keywords: DEP; Leyla Zana; European Union.

**Van Gent, Werner**. (1994). Kurdenprozess: Gradmesser für die Demokratie [Kurdish process: Yardstick for democracy]. *Tages-Anzeiger,* September 8, reprinted in *Institut Kurde de Paris, Information and Liaison Bulletin, 113-114,* August/September, p. 131.

Keywords: DEP.

**La Vie Ouvrière**. (1994). Les Kurdes encore menaces [Kurds still threatened]. *La Vie Ouvrière,* December 16-22, reprinted in *Institut Kurde de Paris, Information and Liaison Bulletin, 116-117,* November/December, p. 170.

Keywords: Kurdish parliamentarians.

**White, Paul**. (2000). *Primitive rebels or revolutionary modernizers? The Kurdish national movement in Turkey.* London & New York: Zed Books. ISBN 1 85649 821 2. Preface (pp. vii-xi), text (pp. 1-219), appendices (pp. 220-27), bibliography (pp. 228-50), index (pp. 251-58), maps (pp. 15, 43).

Keywords: PKK; Öcalan; national consciousness; origins of the Kurds; economy; religion; Kurdish religious and ethnic divisions; Sunnism; Sufism; Nurcu Movement; Fazilet Partisi; Alevi Kurds; Dailam and the Dailamites; Kizilbash; Zazas; Ottoman Empire; Sheikh Ubaydallah rebellions; Koçkiri Rebellion; Sheikh Said Rebellion; Ararat Uprising; Dersim Rebellion; nomadism; GAP; Kurdish proletariat; Marxism; class struggle; Özal; abduction of children; Leyla Zana; Amberin Zaman.

**Yılmaz, Sinan.** (1996). DEP deputies to take their case to European Human Rights Commission. *Turkish Daily News,* January 9, reprinted in *Institut Kurde de Paris, Information and Liaison Bulletin, 130-131,* January/February, p. 34.

**Keywords:** DEP; Leyla Zana; MHP; violations of European Human Rights Agreement; DGM; PKK; İHD.

**Yılmaz, Sinan.** (1994). Trial of DEP deputies begins amid international attention. *Turkish Daily News,* August 2, reprinted in *Institut Kurde de Paris, Information and Liaison Bulletin, 113-114,* August/September, pp. 7-8.

**Keywords:** Leyla Zana; PKK; DEP.

## A. KOMALA, Society of Revolutionary Toilers of Iranian Kurdistan (Komełey Şorrişgêrrî Zehmetkêşanî Kurdistanî Êran)

**Saba, Mariam.** (1997). Mother Bahi-ya: Symbol of revolutionary mothers. *Iranian Outlook* [Communist Party of Iran, London], *1,* May, p. 9. Six photographs.

**Keywords:** Bahiya, from the village of Almaneh in Iranian Kurdistan, mother of Foad Mostfa Soltani, a founder of Komala, the Revolutionary Organization of Toilers of Kurdistan; she lost five sons (Amjad, Amin, Hossein, Foad, Majed) members of Komala; supported revolutionary struggle; visited military camps of Komala; died in exile in Uppsala, Sweden.

**The Worker's Advocate.** (1988). Kurdistan - 9 years of revolutionary struggle. *The Workers Advocate,* March 1, pp. 9-10.

**Keywords:** Komala; Iran; KDP; MLP; Shah Reza Pahlavi; Ayatollah Khomeini; revolution; Fedayeen; Sanandaj.

**The Worker's Advocate.** (1988). A March 8 - International Working Women's Day: Salute the communist women of Iran! *The Workers Advocate,* March 1, p. 8.

**Keywords:** Communist Party of Iran; Women's Day; Khomeini; Kurdistan; Komala; working conditions; forced marriage; Islamic Law.

## B. Kurdistan Workers' Party (Partiya Karkerên Kurdistan)

**Border, Jake.** (1992). Orphan guerillas: Lonely struggle of Kurdish freedom fighters. *Soldier of Fortune,* October, pp. 38-43, 80. Six photographs, one map.

**Keywords:** PKK; Turkish incursions/bombing of Northern Iraq; Northern Iraqi "Safe Haven"; child guerillas; Abdullah Öcalan; Leyla

Zana; Bekaa Valley; Diyarbakir; Cizre; KDP; Zakho; Marxism; female guerillas.

**Kattein, Martin**. (1994). Frauen im kurdischen Befreiungskampf [Women in the Kurdish liberation struggle]. *Xanthippe,* June, pp. 19-22.

**Keywords:** Turkish Kurdistan; DEP; Newroz; murder of DEP parliamentary candidates; IHD; PKK; Patriotic Women's Union; International Women's Day; effects of the uprising on women's freedoms; changes in gender roles due to the uprising; revolutionary marriages; Turkish propaganda against revolutionary marriages; female guerrillas; female commanders in the guerrilla armies; religion; effects of the uprising on religious belief; veiling/covering; Öcalan; women's roles in the preservation of Kurdish culture and language; state policy of birth control; burning of Kurdish villages; women's attitudes towards the guerrillas; destruction of houses by the Turkish army; village guard system; poverty; aerial bombardment of Kurdish villages by the Turkish state; Hizbullah; children; education policies of the Turkish state; self-organization of the Kurdish people; solidarity; Kurdistan solidarity movement in Germany; internationalism.

**Krampfader**. (1994). Die Befreiung Kurdistans hängt von der Befreiung der Frau ab [The liberation of Kurdistan depends on the liberation of women]. *Krampfader, 3*, pp. 28-32.

**Keywords:** PKK; banning of the PKK in Germany; killing of a Kurdish youth by a German police officer; sentencing of Kurds who occupied the Turkish Embassy in Germany; German complicity in Turkish war on Kurds; women and war; women's demonstrations; women's organization in Diyarbakir; Berivan; Serhildan; changes in the status of Kurdish women; *Ez Kurdim - ich bin Kurdin;* situation of women in Kurdistan; women's assistance for the PKK; Women's Prison in Diyarbakir; conditions for female prisoners; Emine Turan; Hizb-i Kontra; Zeynep Uysal; Nebahat Kakus; Hediye Sagic; Fakiye Yilmaz; Nahiye Yılmaz; Belkis Yumak; Birsen Özcan; Safiye Kalay; Hezar Özen; Zeynep Ören; Birsen Kaya; rape; murder of women and girls; arrest of women; Menice Kırtay; S. Akdağ; Taibet Kaya; Leyla Kırtay; Feyziye Aydın; Nuran Avcı; Çiğdem Esmer; Rahşan Demirel; self-immolation; female guerrillas; Kurdish women's choices; national struggle as gender struggle; Free Women's Movement of Kurdistan; women's hunger strikes; First International Women's Conference of Kurdistan (Köln, March 1994); socialism; solidarity/lack of solidarity between European women and Kurdish women; sale of chemical weapons to Turkey; Halabja; history of the Kurds.

283

**KurdishMedia.com**. (2001). Secret rape and execution of 20 PKK guerrillas in Bingol. *KurdishMedia.com,* July 17, reprinted in *Institut Kurde de Paris, Information and Liaison Bulletin, 196-197,* July/August, p. 46.

**Keywords:** rape; summary execution.

**Kurdistan Report**. (1993). Women from Kurdistan, Palestine, Tamil Eelam, Latin America, Pakistan, Ireland and Britain celebrate International Women's Day. *Kurdistan Report, 14,* April/May 1993, pp. 38. Four photographs.

**Keywords:** evening of music, dance, and speakers organized by the YJWK.

**Laizer, Sheri**. (1995). Nermin and the guerrillas. In *Resistance: Women in Kurdistan* (pp. 27-29). London: KIC/KSC Publications. Three photographs.

**Keywords:** female PKK guerillas: Bahar (pseudonym): training camp Bekaa valley, Lebanon for 15 months; hundreds of other girls and women in the training camps; equal treatment to men; no discrimination against women; family: constraints placed upon young women to marry and have children instead of studying or joining the resistance; honour: dying for the nation; return to traditional gender relations after winning the nationalist struggle; PKK, national struggle: instilling self-worth in women; poem: *Karnveli Hill—How I love these mountains*: protecting the honour/virginity of the Kurdish mountains; mountains as the mother's womb.

**Middle East Times**. (1992). Mountain life prepares female Kurd guerillas. *Middle East Times, X*(17), April 21-27, p. 16.

**Keywords:** female guerillas; Northern Iraq; Turkey; Abdullah Öcalan; PKK; Turkish bombing raids.

**Özgenç, Kayhan**. (1998). Verführte Mädchen. *Focus,* November 16, reprinted in *Institut Kurde de Paris, Information and Liaison Bulletin, 164-165,* November/December, p. 66-67.

**Keywords**: child guerillas; female guerillas; PKK; kidnapping of children; recruitment of Kurdish girls in Germany.

**Patriotic Women's Association of Kurdistan (UK)**. (1993). *Kurdistan Report, 13,* February/March, pp. 42. Also appeared in *Kurdistan Report, 14,* April/May 1993, pp. 39. Also appeared in *Kurdistan Report, 15,* July/August 1993, pp. 39.

**Keywords:** women and nationalism; women's role in the Kurdish national struggle; women's equality in the national struggle; 40% of ARGK (armed wing of PKK) are made up of young women; women's participation in demonstrations, hunger strikes, and other forms of protest; YJWK was formed in 1987; aim: to educate Kurdish women about their rights; raise political consciousness; eradicate illiteracy and ignorance about Kurdish history and Turkish oppression; use of Kurdish women in national struggle; struggle to combat the influence of "semi-feudal tribal society"; branches in most European countries and in Kurdistan; aim to encourage interest of other women's groups in the history and culture of Kurdistan; publication of booklets about the Kurdish struggle, history and culture; organization of events on March 8th, International Women's Day.

**Solina, Carla**. (1996). *Der Weg in die Berge: Eine Frau bei der kurdischen Befreiungsbewegung* [The way to the mountains: A woman in the Kurdish liberation movement]. Hamburg: Edition Nautilus Verlag Lutz Schulenburg. ISBN 3-89401-271-4. Text (pp. 10-347), regions of Kurdistan (pp. 348-49), maps (pp. 349-51), glossary of abbreviations to do with Kurdish parties and political organizations (pp. 352-53), glossary (pp. 354-65), bibliography (pp. 366-67), 51 black and white photographs (cover, pp. 8, 50, 51, 96, 97, 98, 99, 134, 135, 136, 137, 158, 159, 184, 185, 206, 234, 235, 236, 237, 238, 239, 240, 241, 242, 243, 292, 293, 294, 295, 320).

**Keywords:** Abdullah Öcalan; tribe; Massoud Barzani; İsmail Beşikçi; female guerillas; PKK; ARGK; KDP; Conta-guerillas; Dersim Genocide; Kurdish folk dance; destruction of villages; embargo; U.N. Resolution #661; ERNK; women's army; İHD; Kemalism; position of Kurdish women; refugee women; difficulties facing Kurdish women in the guerillas and in society; hopes of Kurdish women; progress made by Kurdish women; feudalism and Kurdish women.

**Stein, Gottfried**. (1994). *Endkampf um Kurdistan?: Die PKK, die Türkei und Deutschland* [Final battle for Kurdistan ?: The PKK, Turkey, and Germany]. München: Verlag Bonn Aktuell. ISBN: 3-87959-510-0 (hb). Foreword (pp. 7-8), text (pp. 10-213), abbreviations glossary (pp. 215-16) index (pp. 217-20), maps (pp. 21, 116), 17 black and white photographs (pp. 44, 45, 55, 68, 88, 105, 111, 163, 175, 178).

**Keywords:** history of PKK; guerilla war; Abdullah Öcalan; Özgür Gündem; DEP; KURD-HA; Berxwedan; Serxwebun; ERNK; YJWK; Ronahi; Berivan; self-immolation; German weapons sales to Turkey; PKK activities in Germany; FEYKA-Kurdistan; HEP; HRK; HUNERKOM; İHD; KDP; PDK-Iraq; PSK; PUK; SHP; TEVGER; YKWK; YXK.

**Turkish Daily News**. (1994). 'PKK militant' dies mysteriously at the Adapazarı Police Department. *Turkish Daily News,* September 16, reprinted in *Institut Kurde de Paris, Information and Liaison Bulletin, 113-114,* August/September, p. 158.

Keywords: Nuriye Özgüroğlu; PKK; death of a 17-year-old girl in police custody.

## IV. POLITICAL PRISONERS

### A. Leyla Zana

**Aachener Volkszeitung**. (1995). Ich glaube, daß Leyla Zana als Heldin in die Geschichte eingehen wird [I believe Leyla Zana will go down in history as a heroine]. *Aachener Volkszeitung,* September 1, reprinted in *Institut Kurde de Paris, Information and Liaison Bulletin, 126-127,* September/October, pp. 7-8.

Keywords: interview with Danielle Mitterrand about Leyla Zana.

**Agence France Presse**. (1997). Un ex-deputé kurde refuse une remise en liberté pour raison de santé. *AFP,* March 2, reprinted in *Institut Kurde de Paris, Information and Liaison Bulletin, 152-153,* November/December, p. 95.

Keywords: Leyla Zana; PKK; President Clinton; Eşber Yağmurdereli; Feridun Yazar; health problems of Leyla Zana.

**Agence France Presse**. (2001). Turkey cited for unfair trial of Kurdish deputy Leyla Zana. *AFP,* July 17, reprinted in *Institut Kurde de Paris, Information and Liaison Bulletin, 196-197,* July/August, pp. 28-29.

Keywords: Leyla Zana; European Court of Human Rights; PKK; DEP.

**Agence France Presse**. (1996). Requête de Leyla Zana contre la Turquie devant la Commission européenne des droits de l'Homme [Leyla Zana's application against Turkey before the European Commission of Human Rights]. *AFP,* January, reprinted in *Institut Kurde de Paris, Information and Liaison Bulletin, 130-131,* January/February, p. 69.

Keywords: Leyla Zana; Sakharov Prize; case against Turkey at the European Human Rights Commission; PKK; Article 6 of the European Human Rights Commission.

**Agence France Presse**. (1995). Les députés kurdes ont été condamnés pour leurs Arelations avec le PKK. *AFP,* January, reprinted in *Institut Kurde de Paris, Information and Liaison Bulletin, 118-119,* January/February, p. 31.

**Keywords:** PKK; imprisoned parliamentarians; Leyla Zana.

**Amnesty International**. (1993). Turkey: Human rights violations against women activists. *Kurdistan Report, 15*, July/August, p. 37.

**Keywords:** Leyla Zana: named in a leaflet threatening death: "Muslims, we swear in the name of Allah that the whore Leyla Zana will be slaughtered in the name of Allah," signed by the "Islamic Holy War-B (First of Islam)"; but threats have been attributed to Turkish security forces.

**Arif, Parween N**. (1997). Turkey's state terrorism against the Kurdish people in Turkey: Leyla Zana, a woman to emulate. *Kurdistan Times,* 2(1), November, pp. 74-78. ISSN 1057-8668.

**Keywords:** Leyla Zana; Leyla Zana early life; politicization of Leyla Zana; the torture of Leyla Zana; SHP; media campaign against Leyla Zana; al-Anfal.

**Amalric, Jacques**. (1994). La politique de la carotte [The carrot policy]. *Libération,* December 20, reprinted in *Institut Kurde de Paris, Information and Liaison Bulletin, 116-117*, November/December, p. 186.

**Keywords:** Leyla Zana; European Customs Union with Turkey.

**American Kurdish Information Network.** (1997). *Free Leyla Zana!* American Kurdish Information Networkand Human Rights Alliance (Eds.), Washington DC: AKIN. ISBN 0-9658604-5-0. Preface by Dr. Jose Ramos-Horta (pp. 1-3), preface by Kathryn Cameron Porter (pp. 5-6), preface by Lord Eric Avebury (pp. 7-9), acknowledgements (pp. 201-202). Two black and white photographs, two colour photographs (front and back cover and pp. 93, 94).

**Keywords:** Leyla Zana; HEP; U.S. Congress; Ahmet Turk; Helsinki Commission of the United States Congress; prison; Sakharov Freedom Award; European Parliament; women parliamentarians; Danielle Mitterrand; trialof Leyla Zana; indictment of Leyla Zana; defense of Leyla Zana; Hatip Dicle; PKK; SHP; DEP: Orhan Doğan; Sırrı Sakık; Nizamettin Toğuç; Mehmet Sincar; Naif Gunes; Mahmut Alinak; Abdullah Öcalan.

**Balci, Kemal**. (1994). Parliament to lift immunity of Mezarci & DEP MPs. *Turkish Daily News*, March 1.

**Keywords:** DEP; RP; Leyla Zana; Ahmet Türk; Mahmut Alinak; Orhan Doğan; Hatip Dicle; Sirri Sakik; Selim Sadak; Hasan Mezarci.

**Baydar, Yavuz**. (1995). Reports indicate Leyla Zana closer to Nobel Peace Prize. *Turkish Daily News,* September 27, reprinted in *Institut Kurde de Paris, Information and Liaison Bulletin, 126-127,* September/October, p. 106.

**Keywords:** Leyla Zana; Nobel Peace Prize; DEP; PKK.

**Bertrand, Marie-Noëlle**. (2004). La femme du jour Leyla Zana [Woman of the day, Leyla Zana]. *L'Humanité,* April 22, reprinted in *Institut Kurde de Paris, Information and Liaison Bulletin, 229,* April, pp. 81. One photograph (Leyla Zana).

**Keywords:** Leyla Zana: barely had any school; father forced her to stop after one and a half years of primary school; arranged marriage to her cousin, Mehdi Zana; Mehdi Zana: beginning of marriage, sexist; believed political life was not for women; when he goes to prison Leyla become active in politics; gets arrested; tortured, raped; when she gets out becomes a journalist; in 1991 because Mehdi cannot run for office, Leyla is elected deputy of Diyarbekir; goes all over the world to speak about hardships of Kurdish people; when she gets back in 1994 she is arrested; patriarchy in Kurdish culture.

**Le Bien Public**. (1996). Remise quelque peu embarrassée du Prix Sakharov à Leyla Zana [Leyla Zana somewhat embarrassed presentation of the Sakharov Prize]. *Le Bien Public,* January 18, reprinted in *Institut Kurde de Paris, Information and Liaison Bulletin, 130-131,* January/February, p. 67.

**Keywords:** Leyla Zana; Sakharov Prize; Mehdi Zana; Turkish Customs Union with Europe; Danielle Mitterrand.

**Campiotti, Alain**. (1994). La Turquie joue ses relations avec l'Europe devant sa Haute Cour [Turkey plays its relations with Europe in front of its High Court]. *Le Nouveau Quotidien,* reprinted in *Institut Kurde de Paris, Information and Liaison Bulletin, 115,* October 7, pp. 27-28.

**Keywords:** Leyla Zana; PKK; trial of Kurdish deputies.

**Droits humains**. (1997). Pour la libération de Leyla Zana. *Droits humains, 43,* March/April, reprinted in *Institut Kurde de Paris, Information and Liaison Bulletin, 144-145,* March/April 1997, p. 6.

**Keywords:** Leyla Zana; mobilization of European parliamentarians for the freedom of Leyla Zana; Mehdi Zana; Danielle Mitterrand.

**Ebadi, Chirine and Danielle Mitterrand**. (2004). Courage, chère Leyla Zana [Courage, dear Leyla Zana]. *Le Monde,* March 11, reprinted in *Institut Kurde de Paris, Information and Liaison Bulletin, 228,* March, p. 43.

**Keywords:** letter to Leyla Zana written by Chirine Ebadi, Iranian lawyer and 2003 Noble Laureate; and Danielle Mitterrand admiring her courage to resist and confirming their support.

**Erzeren, Ömer.** (1991). Die Hexe und Heldin von Diyarbakır. *Wochenzeitung "Woz,"* November 29, reprinted in *Institut Kurde de Paris, Information and Liaison Bulletin, 80-81*, November/December, pp. 51-53.

**Keywords:** Leyla Zana; SHP; death penalty; PKK; HEP.

**Faits & Arguments sur l'Union Européenne.** (1995). Le prix Sakharov à Leila Zana [The Sakharov Prize to Leila Zana]. *Faits & Arguments Sur l'Union Européenne, 35*, November/December, reprinted in *Institut Kurde de Paris Information and Liaison Bulletin, 128-129*, November/December, p. 82.

**Keywords:** Leyla Zana; Sakharov Prize; European Parliament.

**Faits & Arguments sur l'Union Européenne.** (1998). Turquie: libérer Leyla Zana [Turkey: Free Leyla Zana]. *Faits & Arguments sur l'union européenne, 52*, September/October, reprinted in *Institut Kurde de Paris, Information and Liaison Bulletin, 162-163*, September/October, p. 78.

**Keywords:** Leyla Zana; European Parliament; HADEP.

**Faits & Arguments sur l'Union Européenne.** (1999). Libérer Leyla Zana [Free Leyla Zana]. *Faits & Arguments sur l'union européenne,* January/February, reprinted in *Institut Kurde de Paris, Information and Liaison Bulletin, 166-167*, January/February, p. 202.

**Keywords:** Leyla Zana; Mehdi Zana; European initiative to free Leyla Zana; Danielle Mitterrand; European Parliament; 1995 Prize for Freedom of Spirit.

**Le Floc'Hmoan, Annick.** (1996). le crime d'être née kurde [The crime of being born Kurdish]. *Elle,* February 5, reprinted in *Institut Kurde de Paris, Information and Liaison Bulletin, 130-131*, January/February, p. 120.

**Keywords:** Leyla Zana; Sakharov Prize; Mehdi Zana; Danielle Mitterrand.

**Le Floc'Hmoan, Annick.** (1996). Leyla Zana au nom de tous les siens. *Elle,* September 2, reprinted in *Institut Kurde de Paris, Information and Liaison Bulletin, 138*, September, pp. 13-15.

**Keywords:** Leyla Zana; Nobel Peace Prize nomination; military coup; Mehdi Zana; life of Leyla Zana; life in prison; Sakharov Prize.

**Gamk**. (2000). Andras Barsony et Daniel Cohn-Bendit rendent visite a Leyla Zana en Prison [Andras Barsony and Daniel Cohn-Bendit visit Leyla Zana in prison]. *Gamk,* April 6, reprinted in *Institut Kurde de Paris, information and Liaison Bulletin, 181*, April, p. 12.

**Keywords:** Leyla Zana; DEP; HEP.

**Gamk**. (1994). Le Conseil de l'Europe fait une nouvelle tentative pour aider les députés kurdes emprisonnés [Council of Europe makes another attempt to help jailed Kurdish MPs]. *Gamk,* September 2, reprinted in *Institut Kurde de Paris, Information and Liaison Bulletin, 113-114*, August/September, p. 110.

**Keywords:** DEP; PKK; Council of Europe.

**Gamk**. (1997, December 8-9). Leyla Zana refuse sa libération pour raison de santé [Leyla Zana refuses her release for health reasons]. *Gamk,* reprinted in *Institut Kurde de Paris, Information and Liaison Bulletin, 152-153*, November/December 1997, p.113.

**Keywords:** Leyla Zana; European Summit of December 12-13 in Luxembourg; Eşber Yağmurdereli.

**Gamk**. (1998). Leyla Zana À Nouveau Proposée Pour Le Prix Nobel de la Paix [Leyla Zana nominated again for Nobel Peace Prize]. *Gamk,* February 13, reprinted in *Institut Kurde de Paris, Information and Liaison Bulletin, 154-155*, January/February, p. 126.

**Keywords:** Leyla Zana; John Porter; Nobel Peace Prize.

**Gautier, Florence**. (1996). Ne les oublions pas: Le silence tue [Let's not forget them: Silence kills]. *Le Travail, 1105*, March/April reprinted in *Institut Kurde de Paris, Information and Liaison Bulletin, 134-135*, May/June, pp. 2-3.

**Keywords:** Leyla Zana; Kendal Nezan; Institut Kurde de Paris; American and German military support for Turkey; Sakharov Prize; International Aix-la-Chapelle Peace Prize; Nobel Peace Prize.

**Halisdemir, Orya Sultan**. (1995). EP leftists signal "delay" vote, after Zana gets Prize. *Turkish Daily News,* November 11, reprinted in *Institut Kurde de Paris, Information and Liaison Bulletin, 128-129*, November/December, p. 41.

**Keywords:** Leyla Zana; European Parliament; customs-union agreement; Sakharov Prize; Anti-Terrorism Law; criminal code.

**Hervé, Florence**. (1997). Ein Tag im Gefängnis für Leyla Zana [A day in prison for Leyla Zana]. *Wir Frauen,* Düsseldorf, *1*, p. 20, Z G 20.

**Keywords:** Turkey; Kurdish women; political prisoners; Leyla Zana.

**de La Horie, Marine**. (1995). Parce qu'elle avait parlé des Kurdes...prison jusqu'en 2005 pour la députée turque [Because she had spoken of the Kurds...prison until 2005 for the Turkish MP]. *Elle*, November 13, reprinted in *Institut Kurde de Paris, Information and Liaison Bulletin, 128-129*, November/December, p. 35.

**Keywords:** Leyla Zana; Nobel Peace Prize nomination; Leyla Zana made honorary citizen of Rome.

**L'Humanité**. (1995). René Piquet a rencontré Leila Zana à la prison d'Ankara [René Piquet met Leila Zana at Ankara prison]. *L'Humanité*, December 6, reprinted in *Institut Kurde de Paris, Information and Liaison Bulletin, 128-129*, November/December, p. 88.

**Keywords:** Leyla Zana; European Parliament delegation; René Piquet; human rights in Turkey.

**L'Humanité**. (1994). La FIDH dénonce la dictature turque [FIDH denounces the Turkish dictatorship]. *L'Humanité*, December 16, reprinted in *Institut Kurde de Paris, Information and Liaison Bulletin, 116-117*, November/December, p. 168.

**Keywords:** International Human Rights Federation; Leyla Zana.

**L'Humanité**. (1995). Visite à une démocrate emprisonnée [Visit to imprisoned Democrat]. *L'Humanité*, May 5, reprinted in *Institut Kurde de Paris, Information and Liaison Bulletin, 122-123*, May/June, p. 27.

**Keywords:** Sylvie Jan; International Democratic Federation of Women; Leyla Zana.

**L'Humanité**. (1996). Prix Sakharov à Leyla Zana [Sakharov Prize to Leyla Zana]. *L'Humanité*, January 18, reprinted in *Institut Kurde de Paris, Information and Liaison Bulletin, 130-131*, January/February, p. 68.

**Keywords:** Leyla Zana; Sakharov Prize; Mehdi Zana; Danielle Mitterrand.

**humanité Dimanche**. (1994). 15 ans de prison pour Leila Zana, deputee kurde [15 years in prison for Leila Zana, Kurdish deputy.]. *humanité dimanche*, December 15, reprinted in *Institut Kurde de Paris, Information and Liaison Bulletin, 116-117*, November/December, p. 155.

**Keywords**: Leyla Zana.

İmset, İsmet G. (1994). Democracy Party moves against Dicle, *Turkish Daily News,* February 22, reprinted in *Institut Kurde de Paris, Information and Liaison Bulletin, 106-107,* January/February, pp. 195-198.

Keywords: DEP; Leyla Zana; assassination attempt on Leyla Zana; PKK.

Institut Kurde de Paris. (1994). The Kurdish deputies: Prisoners of conscience [Special issue]. *Institut Kurde de Paris, Information and Liaison Bulletin,* September.

Keywords: DEP; Leyla Zana; Kurdish parliamentarians.

Institut Kurde de Paris. (1995). Leyla Zana awarded the European Parliament's Sakharov Prize. *Institut Kurde de Paris, Information and Liaison Bulletin, 128-129,* November/December, pp. 5-6.

Keywords: Leyla Zana; Sakharov Prize.

Institut Kurde de Paris. (1996). The Rose Prize for Human Rights of the Danish Labour Movement awarded to Leyla Zana was handed over on February 13th in Copenhagen by the Danish Prime Minister. *Institut Kurde de Paris, Information and Liaison Bulletin, 130-131,* January/February, p. 9.

Keywords: The International Rose Prize; Leyla Zana; crime of opinion; democratic struggle.

Institut Kurde de Paris. (1996). The European Commission refers to the case of Leyla Zana and her colleagues of the Party for Democracy to the European Human Rights Court. *Institut Kurde de Paris: Information and Liaison Bulletin, 136-137,* July/August, pp. 9-10.

Keywords: European Commission; Leyla Zana; Kurdish Members of Parliament; International Federation for Human Rights.

Institut Kurde de Paris. (1997). Leyla Zana refuses to be freed on health grounds. *Institut Kurde de Paris, Information and Liaison Bulletin, 152-153,* November/December, pp. 10-11.

Keywords: Leyla Zana; Article 399 of the penal code procedure (CUMUK); Amnesty International; U.N. Working Group on arbitrary detention; Articles 10 and 11 of the Universal Declaration of Human Rights; Fraueniative; Deanielle Mitterrand; CILDEKT; Madame Ilse Ridder-Melchers.

Institut Kurde de Paris. (1998). Leyla Zana, H. Dicle, A. Birdal and F. Yazar receive further sentences. *Institut Kurde de Paris, Information and Liaison Bulletin, 162-163*, September/October, pp. 5-8.

Keywords: Leyla Zana; European Parliament; Sakharov Prize; HADEP; Newroz; HEP; DEP; State Security Court; *Ülkede Gündem*; Eva Juhmke.

**Institut Kurde de Paris**. (1999). Mr. Koh, American Under-Secretary for Human Rights, visited Leyla Zana and Akin Birdal in the Ankara central prison. *Institut Kurde de Paris, Information and Liaison Bulletin, 173*, August, p. 3.

Keywords: Leyla Zana; DEP; Turkish press attacks against Mr. Koh and America for criticizing Turkey's human rights record.

**Institut Kurde de Paris**. (2000). Ankara refused Daniel Cohn-Bendit Permission to Visit Leyla Zana. *Institut Kurde de Paris, information and Liaison Bulletin, 179*, February, p. 12.

Keywords: Parliamentary Mixed Commission; Leyla Zana.

**Institut Kurde de Paris**. (2000). Claudia Roth's visit to Leyla Zana. *Institut Kurde de Paris, Information and Liaison Bulletin, 188*, November, p. 8.

Keywords: Leyla Zana; Claudia Roth; Parliamentary Human Rights Commission.

**Institut Kurde de Paris**. (2002). Council of Europe General Secretary calls for retrial of Leyla Zana and colleagues. *Institut Kurde de Paris, Information and Liaison Bulletin, 202*, January, pp. 3-4.

Keywords: Leyla Zana; DEP; Council of Europe's General Secretary Walter Schwimmer called on Turkey to free all the Kurdish parliamentarians; Zana has refused to be released with other colleagues remaining in jail.

**Institut Kurde de Paris**. (2002). A call for the liberation of imprisoned Kurdish M.P.s. *Institut Kurde de Paris, Information and Liaison Bulletin, 203*, February, pp. 2-3.

Keywords: France Libertés; Leyla Zana; Agir pour un Monde Solidaire; ACAT; Amnesty International; Le Mouvement de la Paix; European Human Rights Court.

**Institut Kurde de Paris**. (2002). Turkish politicians debate "Politicisation of PKK," while Kurdish M.P.s remain jailed for "Thought Crimes." *Institut Kurde de Paris, Information and Liaison Bulletin, 203*, February, p. 12.

**Keywords:** Leyla Zana; DEP; PKK.

**Institut Kurde de Paris**. (2002). The Parliamentary Assembly of the Council of Europe Criticises Turkey for failing to apply European legal decisions and demands a retrial for the Kurdish former Members of Parliament. *Institut Kurde de Paris, Information and Liaison Bulletin, 210*, September, pp. 6-7.

**Keywords:** Legal and Human Rights Commission of the Council of Europe; Leyla Zana.

**Institut Kurde de Paris**. (2002). Strasbourg: The European Human Rights Court finds Turkey guilty in the case of the banning of the DEP Party. *Institut Kurde de Paris, Information and Liaison Bulletin, 213*, December, pp.3-4.

**Keywords:** Leyla Zana; DEP; European Human Rights Court.

**Institut Kurde de Paris**. (2003). Paris: The NGOs denounce the irregularities in the trial of Leyla Zana and her colleagues and call for an equitable and impartial trial. *Institut Kurde de Paris, Information and Liaison Bulletin, 218-219*, May/June, pp. 5-7.

**Keywords:** FIDH; *Femmes Solidaires* (Women's Solidarity); *France-Libertés*; CILDEKT; the Paris Kurdish Institute; Leyla Zana; European Human Rights Court; DEP; PKK; State Security Court; 12 September 1980 coup d'état; European Parliament; European Council in Thessoloniki.

**Institut Kurde de Paris**. (2003). Fifth Hearing of the re-trial of Leyla Zana and her colleagues: The observers denounce a "parody of justice." *Institut Kurde de Paris, Information and Liaison Bulletin, 220-221*, July/August, pp. 5-7.

**Keywords:** Leyla Zana; DEP; State Security Court; Dr. Özden Özdemir; inter-tribal conflicts; PKK; Metina and Zirka Tribes; Turkish Human Rights Association; International Federation for Human Rights; a petition to free Leyla Zana started by the MRAP; signatories of the MRAP petition; European Parliament United Left Group.

**Institut Kurde de Paris**. (2003). Ankara: The interminable retrial of the Kurdish members of parliament. *Institut Kurde de Paris, Information and Liaison Bulletin, 218-219*, May/June, pp. 3-5.

**Keywords:** Leyla Zana; DEP; State Security Court; Article 6 of the European Convention on Human Rights; Dorken Tribe; village guard system; Anti-Terrorist Law; Susurluk.

**Institut Kurde de Paris**. (2003). Leyla Zana and her three colleagues will be retried by the State Security Court. *Institut Kurde de Paris, Information and Liaison Bulletin, 215*, February, p. 1.

Keywords: Leyla Zana; Ankara State Security Court; DEP; 1995 Sakharov Prize; European Human Rights Court.

**Institut Kurde de Paris**. (2003). Zana's retrial: The Turkish State Security Court refuses to free the Kurdish ex-M.P.s on bail and postpones the next hearing to 25 April. *Institut Kurde de Paris, Information and Liaison Bulletin, 216*, March, p. 5.

Keywords: Leyla Zana; DEP; human rights; democratisation; the European United Left Group; European Parliament.

**Institut Kurde de Paris**. (2003). Ankara: The second hearing of the Kurdish members of parliament's retrial: Renewed refusal of release and cacophony in the evidence. *Institut Kurde de Paris, Information and Liaison Bulletin, 217*, April, pp. 5-6.

Keywords: Leyla Zana; DEP; PKK; Babat Tribe; HADEP; European Parliament observers; Danielle Mitterrand; Kendal Nezan; the film by Kudret Güneş, *Leyla Zana, the Cry of a Gagged Voice*.

**Institut Kurde de Paris**. (2003). Seventh hearing of the Kurdish M.P.s retrial: They were manhandled while being transported to the court room, at a time when the European Union was expressing its indignation at the conduct of the trial. *Institut Kurde de Paris, Information and Liaison Bulletin, 222*, September, pp. 4-5.

Keywords: DEP; Leyla Zana; European Parliament; State Security Court.

**Institut Kurde de Paris**. (2003). Leyla Zana and her colleagues denounce the horse trading between Turkey and the European Union, revealed by the Turkish press, of which they are the pawns. *Institut Kurde de Paris, Information and Liaison Bulletin, 223*, October, p. 4.

Keywords: Leyla Zana; KADEK; PKK; DEP; *Hürriyet;* DGM.

**Institut Kurde de Paris**. (2003). Leyla Zana and her colleagues apply again to the European Human Rights Court to denounce the partiality of the Turkish courts. *Institut Kurde de Paris, Information and Liaison Bulletin, 224*, November, pp. 6-7.

Keywords: DEP; Leyla Zana; European Human Rights Court;

Khadija Boucart, Deputy Mayor of Paris responsible for Integration of non-E.U. foreign residents, ask the Mayor of Paris to intervene with the Turkish authorities on Leyla Zana's behalf and to grant her honorary citizenship of Paris.

**Institut Kurde de Paris**. (2004). The European Court's verdict: Leyla Zana and her colleagues did not have a fair trial. *Institut Kurde de Paris, Information and Liaison Bulletin, 196*, July/August, pp. 1-3.

**Keywords:** Leyla Zana; European Court; Sakharov Peace Prize; DEP.

**Institut Kurde de Paris**. (2004). Read in the Turkish press: "Prodi and Zana on the Same Day!" *Institut Kurde de Paris, Information and Liaison Bulletin, 226*, January, pp. 14-15.

**Keywords:** Leyla Zana's retrial; DEP; Roman Prodi, president of the European Commission; democratisation package; Turkish-European Union Parliamentary Commission.

**Institut Kurde de Paris.** (2004). The trial of the Kurdish Members of Parliament: Leyla Zana and her colleagues refuse to attend the hearings. *Institut Kurde de Paris, Information and Liaison Bulletin, 228*, March, pp. 9-10.

**Keywords:** Leyla Zana; DEP; PKK; State Security Court; retrial of the MPs; Sakharov Prize.

**Institut Kurde de Paris**. (2004). The Ankara State Security Court has again found the Sakharov Prizewinner, Leyla Zana, and her colleagues guilty: Consternation of the human rights defenders. *Institut Kurde de Paris, Information and Liaison Bulletin, 229*, April, pp. 1-3.

**Keywords:** Leyla Zana: open letter to Shirin Ebadi, 2003 Nobel Peace Prize winner, and to Danielle Mitterrand, president of *France-libertés* and of the CILDEKT, expressing pessimism about her retrial that she saw as a "show piece" to advance the Turkish government's foreign policy; women's solidarity.

**Institut Kurde de Paris**. (2004). Leyla Zana and her three colleagues released on 9 June after more than ten years in Ankara prison, tour Kurdistan. *Institut Kurde de Paris, Information and Liaison Bulletin, 231*, June, pp. 6-9.

**Keywords:** Leyla Zana: released from prison on June 9, 2004.

International Committee for the Liberation of Imprisoned Kurdish Deputies in Turkey. (1995). Campagne turque contre l'attribution du Prix Nobel de la Paix à la parlementaire kurde Leyla Zana (Press release) [Turkish campaign against awarding the Nobel Peace Prize to Kurdish parliamentarian Leyla Zana]. *Gamk*, reprinted in *Institut Kurde de Paris, Information and Liaison Bulletin, 126-127*, September/October, p. 153.

**Keywords:** Leyla Zana; Nobel Peace Prize; Atatürk Peace Prize; Nelson Mandela; Sakharov Peace Prize.

**Jallabert, Claire**. (1996). Leyla Zana: La faute d'être Kurde. *Le Pelerin Magazine*, March 1, reprinted in *Institut Kurde de Paris, Information and Liaison Bulletin, 132-133*, March/April, p. 1.

**Keywords:** Leyla Zana; Mehdi Zana.

**Jan, Sylvie**. (2003, July 2). "J'ai assisté au procès de Leyla Zana" ["I attended Leyla Zana's trial"]. *L'Humanité*, reprinted in *Institut Kurde de Paris, Information and Liaison Bulletin, 220-221,* July/August 2003, pp. 1-2.

**Keywords:** Sylvie Jan, former president of the International Federation of Women represents the French Communist Party as an observer of Leyla Zana's trial; retrial of Leyla Zana, Orhan Doğan, Hatip Dicle, and Selim Sadak; PKK; State Security Court; Akin Birdal; Eren Keskin; Yavuz Önen, President of the Human Rights Foundation in Turkey; Leyla Zana's daughter Rüken; democratization.

**Jégo, Marie**. (2003, October 11). La Turquie change, sauf pour les Kurdes. *Le Monde*, reprinted in *Institut Kurde de Paris, Information and Liaison Bulletin, 223*, October 2003, p. 38.

**Keywords:** Leyla Zana; PKK; DGK; Recep Tayyip Erdoğan; reforms regarding cultural liberties of the Kurds in Turkey.

**Journal de Genève**. (1995, November 10). Prix Sakharov à Leyla Zana [Sakharov Prize to Leyla Zana]. *Journal de Genève*, reprinted in *Institut Kurde de Paris, Information and Liaison Bulletin, 128-129*, November/December 1995, p. 28.

**Keywords:** Leyla Zana; Sakharov Prize.

**Karadaghi, Pary**. (1995, November). Portrait of a brave woman Leyla Zana. *Kurdistan Times, 4*, pp. 39-43, ISSN 1057-8668. One black and white photograph (p. 39).

**Keywords:** early life of Leyla Zana; Mehdi Zana; self-education of Leyla Zana; Leyla Zana's role in promoting a women's organization; Yeni Ülke; Leyla Zana's electoral campaign and subsequent election; KHRW; Kurdish refugees in the Washington Metropolitan area; Leyla

Zana's nomination for the Nobel Peace Prize; 4th U.N. Conference on Women; Union de Femme Francaise.

**Karlsson, Helena**. (2003). Politics, gender, and genre—The Kurds and "the West": Writings from prison by Leyla Zana. *Journal of Women's History, 15*(3), Autumn, pp. 158-160.

**Keywords:** review of the memoirs of Leyla Zana, *Writings from Prison*; nationalism in conflict with feminism; Kurdish nationalist struggle overtaking feminist struggle; Zana calls herself a feminist.

**KIC/KSC Publications**. (1995). Appendix 1: From oppression to resistance: A portrait of Leyla Zana. In *Resistance: Women in Kurdistan*. London: KIC/KSC Publications, pp. 52-53.

**Keywords:** Leyla Zana: women and nationalism, female nationalists; history: barely had any school; father forced her to stop after one and a half years of primary school; arranged marriage to her cousin, Mehdi Zana; Mehdi Zana: beginning of marriage, sexist; believed political life was not for women; when he goes to prison Leyla become active in politics; gets arrested; tortured, raped; when she gets out becomes a journalist; in 1991 because Mehdi cannot run for office, Leyla is elected deputy of Diyarbekir; goes all over the world to speak about hardships of Kurdish people; when she gets back in 1994 she is arrested.

**KIC/KSC Publications**. (1995). Women parliamentarians support Leyla Zana. In *Resistance: Women in Kurdistan*. London: KIC/KSC Publications, p. 53.

**Keywords:** fourth Annual Parliamentary session of the OSCE, held in Ottawa, Canada, July 4-8, 1995; petition handed out by Green Member of Finnish Parliament, Tuija Maaret Pykalainen, which called for the immediate release of Leyla Zana from prison; signed by nearly all the women delegates present at the caucus.

**Kinzer, Stephen**. (1997). As Turkey bends on pardon, activist says she'll refuse it. *Herald International Tribune,* December 8, reprinted in *Institut Kurde de Paris, Information and Liaison Bulletin, 152-153*, November/December, p. 114.

**Keywords:** Prime Minister Mesut Yilmaz; Leyla Zana; President Clinton; Eşber Yağmurdereli; Justice Minister Oltan Süngürlü; Nobel Peace Prize nomination.

**Kinzer, Stephen**. (2000). EU-Turkey relations hit a new snag over visit to

Kurdish prisoner. *International Herald Tribune,* February 21, reprinted in *Institut Kurde de Paris, Information and Liaison Bulletin, 179,* February, p. 68.

**Keywords:** European Union; Leyla Zana; Abdullah Öcalan; Wadie Jwaideh's book confiscated.

**Kouyoumdjian, J. N.** (1995). La guerre contre le Aséparatisme' kurde. *France Armenie,* October, reprinted in *Institut Kurde de Paris, Information and Liaison Bulletin, 126-127,* September/October, p. 123.

**Keywords:** Leyla Zana; DEP; PKK; torture; Armenian Genocide; European Community.

**Kravetz, Marc.** (1994). Petits arrangements avec la mort et la vie. *Le Magazine de Libération,* reprinted in *Institut Kurde de Paris, Information and Liaison Bulletin, 116-117,* November/December, p. 174.

**Keywords:** Leyla Zana.

**Kurdistan Report.** (1992). Meeting on the Kurdish question and human rights: Extracts of speeches made on March 1 at the Halkevi. *Kurdistan Report, 8,* April, pp. 6-11.

**Keywords:** extracts from a speech by Leyla Zana; HEP; ANAP policies towards HEP; SHP; human rights; Kemalism; military coup of 1980; Turkish policies regarding the use of Kurdish; PKK; Turkish policies towards the press; NATO; U.N.

**Kurdistan Report.** (1996). Leyla Zana [Special issue]. *Kurdistan Report, 23,* March/May, pp. 33-34.

**Keywords:** letter by Leyla Zana to the European Parliament in response to receiving the Sakharov Prize; HEP; DEP; Article 8 of the Anti-Terror Law; burning of villages; orphans; widows.

**Kutschera, Chris.** (1993). A silent scream. *The Middle East,* reprinted in *Institut Kurde de Paris, Information and Liaison Bulletin, 103,* October, pp. 143-145.

**Keywords:** Leyla Zana; arranged marriage; torture; Mehdi Zana; Socialist Party of Kurdistan; patriarchy; education; Communist Party of Turkey; tradition; women's work; importance of boy children for Kurds; prison life; DEP; SHP.

**La lettre de Femmes d'europe.** (1996). Le Prix Sakharov [The Sakharov Prize]. *La lettre de Femmes d'europe,* Veronique Houdart-Blazy (Ed.), *58,* March,

p. 3.

**Keywords:** European Parliament; Sakharov Prize; Leyla Zana; Mehdi Zana; Danielle Mitterrand.

**Libération and AFP**. (2003). Quatre ex-députés kurdes rejugés en Turquie [Four former Kurdish deputies retried in Turkey.]. *Libération,* March 20, reprinted in *Institut Kurde de Paris, Information and Liaison Bulletin, 216,* March, pp. 177-178.

**Keywords:** retrial of Leyla Zana on charges of ties with PKK.

**Libération**. (1994). Six députés kurdes en procès à Ankara [Six Kurdish deputies on trial in Ankara]. *Libération,* August 9, reprinted in *Institut Kurde de Paris, Information and Liaison Bulletin, 113-114,* August/September, p. 20.

**Keywords:** Leyla Zana; DEP; PKK.

**La Liberté**. (1994). Six députés kurdes répondent de leurs opinions en justice [Six Kurdish MPs answer for their opinions in court]. *La Liberté,* August 4, reprinted in *Institut Kurde de Paris, Information and Liaison Bulletin, 113-114,* August/September, p. 17.

**Keywords**: DEP; PKK.

**Lorieux, Claude**. (1994). Quinze ans de prison pour cinq députés kurdes [Fifteen years in prison for five Kurdish deputies]. *Le Figaro,* December 9, reprinted in *Institut Kurde de Paris, Information and Liaison Bulletin, 116-117,* November/December, p. 125.

**Keywords:** prison sentences for Kurdish parliamentarians; Leyla Zana; DEP; HEP; deaths due to war.

**Martinet, Marie-Michèle**. (2004). Ankara intraitable avec les Kurdes. *Le Figaro,* April 22, reprinted in *Institut Kurde de Paris, Information and Liaison Bulletin, 229,* April, pp. 80. One photograph (Leyla Zana).

**Keywords:** Leyla Zana: open letter to Shirin Ebadi, 2003 Nobel Peace Prize winner, expressing pessimism about her retrial that she is seen as a "show piece" to advance the Turkish government's foreign policy; women's solidarity.

**Matthews, Owen**. (2003). Justice in the dock: A high-profile trial in Ankara becomes a litmus test for Turkey's aspirations to join the EU. *Newsweek,* December 8, reprinted in *Institut Kurde de Paris, Information and Liaison Bulletin, 225,* December, pp. 16-77.

**Keywords:** Leyla Zana; AK Party; PKK; Kemalism; Ayşe Handan İpekçi, a Turkish filmmaker put on trial for "denigrating the security forces."

**Mercier, Sophie**. (2003). Libérez Leyla Zana [Free Leyla Zana]. *Clara Magazine,* May, reprinted in *Institut Kurde de Paris, Information and Liaison Bulletin, 218-219,* May/June, p. 55.

**Keywords:** Leyla Zana; *Femmes Solidaires; Clara Magazine*; European Human Rights Court; Turkey's candidacy for the European Union; reforms regarding the use of Kurdish in Turkey; democratization; Leyla Zana's children Ronay and Rüken.

**Le Meridional**. (1993). Amnesty International - Les femmes en action. *Le Meridional,* March 25, reprinted in *Institut Kurde de Paris, Information and Liaison Bulletin, 95-96,* February/March, p. 26.

**Keywords:** Leyla Zana; campaign to collect signatures for her release.

**Mitterrand, Danielle**. (1994). We must never again leave millions of men, women and children at the mercy of the Turkish army. *The European,* February, reprinted in *Kurdistan Report, 18,* May/June, p. 3

**Keywords:** incommunicado detentions of Kurdish members of parliament; Kurdish asylum-seekers in Europe; state terror; destruction of Kurdish towns by Turkey; Leyla Zana; Mehdi Zana; lack of freedom of expression in Turkey; PKK.

**Mitterrand, Danielle**. (1994). Kurdish leaders on trial for treason in Turkey: Danielle Mitterrand's letter to Layla Zana. *Kurdish Affairs,* September, *1*(2), reprinted in *Institut Kurde de Paris, Information and Liaison Bulletin, 113-114,* August/September, p. 125.

**Keywords:** Leyla Zana; the press in Turkey.

**Morgan, David**. (2001). Ann Clwyd becomes first British MP to meet Leyla Zana. *Kurdistan Report, 31,* Autumn, p. 78.

**Keywords:** peace in Kurdistan campaign; Ann Clwyd; Leyla Zana; attempt by Bianca Jagger to meet with Leyla Zana; Estella Schmid; Parliamentary Human Rights Committee; European Court of Human Rights; DEP; visit by Leyla Zana's daughter; Leyla Zana's views on the Terrorism Act in Britain; Leyla Zana's views on women's special role in fostering dialogue; Sally Eberhard; Kurdish Human Rights Project; Nilufer Koç of the Women's Peace Bureau in Germany; PKK; KNC.

301

**Mugny, Patrice**. (1994). Seront-ils condamnés à mort pour délit d'opinion? [Will they be sentenced to death for a crime of opinion?]. *Le Courrier,* September 7, reprinted in *Institut Kurde de Paris, Information and Liaison Bulletin, 113-114*, August-September, p. 124.

**Keywords:** Leyla Zana; Reporters sans frontières; European Parliament; Swiss Parliament; PKK.

**Neue Zürcher Zeitung**. (1995). Wirbel um Leyla Zana und den Sacharow-Preis [There is a stir about Leyla Zana and the Sakharov Prize]. *Neue Zürcher Zeitung,* December 1, reprinted in *Institut Kurde de Paris, Information and Liaison Bulletin, 128-129*, November/December, p. 86.

**Keywords:** Leyla Zana; Sakharov Prize; European Parliament; Mehdi Zana; destruction of Kurdish villages; deaths in the war; PKK.

**Neue Zürcher Zeitung**. (1996). Leyla Zana dankt fur den Sacharow-Preis [Leyla Zana thanks for the Sakharov Prize]. *Neue Zürcher Zeitung (Internationale Ausgabe),* January 18, reprinted in *Institut Kurde de Paris, Information and Liaison Bulletin, 130-131*, January/February, pp. 64-65.

**Keywords:** Leyla Zana; Sakharov Prize; elected Kurdish representatives.

**Nezan, Kendal**. (1994). Procès politique à Ankara [Political trial in Ankara]. *Le Monde,* September 7, reprinted in *Institut Kurde de Paris, Information and Liaison Bulletin, 113-114*, August/September, p. 123.

**Keywords:** Kurdish parliamentarians; PKK; Council of Europe.

**Niemeier, Harald**. (1992). Kurdischer Bürgermeister: Nach Besuch in Spandau wieder in Haft [Kurdish Mayor: After visiting Spandau, arrested again]. *Spandauer Volksblatt,* February 22, reprinted in *Institut Kurde de Paris, Information and Liaison Bulletin, 83-84*, February/March, p. 78.

**Keywords:** Mehdi Zana; Leyla Zana; Aso Agace; Hinbun.

**Nord Éclair**. (1996). Une militante kurde honorée par le Parlement européen [Kurdish activist honored by European Parliament]. *Nord Eclair,* January 18, reprinted in *Institut Kurde de Paris, Information and Liaison Bulletin, 130-131*, January/February, p. 67.

**Keywords:** Leyla Zana; Mehdi Zana; PKK; Sakharov Prize; deaths due to war; Danielle Mitterrand.

**Ouest France**. (1996). Leyla Zana, prix Nobel de la paix? [Leyla Zana, Nobel

Peace Prize Laureate?]. *Ouest-France,* February 8, reprinted in *Institut Kurde de Paris, Information and Liaison Bulletin, 130-131,* January/February, p. 128.

Keywords: Leyla Zana; DEP; Mehdi Zana; PKK; Sakharov Prize; Danish Human Rights Prize.

Parlement Européen. (1997). Intervention de Aline Pailler Pour la libération de Leyla Zana [Intervention of Aline Pailler for the release of Leyla Zana]. *Parlement Europeen, documents de séance,* March 13, reprinted in *Institut Kurde de Paris, Information and Liaison Bulletin, 144-145,* March/April, pp. 53-54.

Keywords: resolution for the freedom of Leyla Zana.

Parlement Européen. (2004). Droits de l'Homme, Remise du Prix Sakharov à Leyla Zana [Human rights, presentation of the Sakharov Prize to Leyla Zana]. *Le point de la session,* October 13-14, reprinted in *Institut Kurde de Paris, Information and Liaison Bulletin, 235,* October, p. 59.

Keywords: Leyla Zana: received the Sakharov Prize in person that she won in 1995 for being the first woman elected to the Turkish Parliament.

Le Pennec, Elsa. (2004). Avec Leila Zana, la pasionaria kurde libérée [With Leila Zana, to liberated Kurds]. *L'Hebdo,* July 8, reprinted in *Institut Kurde de Paris, Information and Liaison Bulletin, 232,* July, pp. 36-37. Three photographs (Leyla Zana).

Keywords: Leyla Zana: barely had any school; father forced her to stop after one and a half years of primary school; arranged marriage to her cousin, Mehdi Zana; Mehdi Zana: beginning of marriage, sexist; believed political life was not for women; when he goes to prison Leyla become active in politics; gets arrested; tortured, raped; when she gets out becomes a journalist; in 1991 because Mehdi cannot run for office, Leyla is elected deputy of Diyarbekir; goes all over the world to speak about hardships of Kurdish people; when she gets back in 1994 she is arrested; patriarchy in Kurdish culture.

Peterson, Scott. (2000). Is Turkey fed up with Europe? *Christian Science Monitor,* April 10, reprinted in *Institut Kurde de Paris, information and Liaison Bulletin, 181,* April, pp. 22-23.

Keywords: candidacy for European Union; Leyla Zana; Sakharov Peace Prize.

Le Peuple Breton. (1995). La député kurde Leyla Zana obtient le Prix

Sakharov des Droits de l'Homme [Kurdish MP Leyla Zana wins Sakharov Prize for Human Rights.]. *Le Peuple Breton, 384*, December, reprinted in *Institut Kurde de Paris, Information and Liaison Bulletin, 128-129*, November/December, p. 85.

**Keywords:** Leyla Zana; Sakharov Prize.

**Pope, Hugh.** (1995). Kurdish MPs freed for 'sake of Europe.' *Independent,* October 26, reprinted in *Institut Kurde de Paris, Information and Liaison Bulletin, 126-127*, September/October, p. 196.

**Keywords:** Nobel Peace Prize; Leyla Zana; PKK; Kurdish parliamentarians.

**Le Populaire du Centre**. (1996). En pensant à Leyla... [Thinking of Leyla]. *Le Populaire du Centre,* October 18, reprinted in *Institut Kurde de Paris, Information and Liaison Bulletin, 139-140*, October/November, p.103.

**Keywords:** Leyla Zana; Audiovisual Festival of Cultural Minorities in Europe.

**Le Progres**. (1993). Amnesty International: le cas de Leyla Zana [Amnesty International: The case of Leyla Zana]. *Le Progres,* May 12, reprinted in *Institut Kurde de Paris, Information and Liaison Bulletin, 97-98*, April/May, p. 61.

**Keywords:** Leyla Zana, HEP; Islami Cihad-B death threats against Leyla Zana.

**Reuters**. (1997). Turquie - La Cour européene denonce la détention de 6 Kurdes [Turkey - The European Court denounces the detention of six Kurds.]. *Reuters,* November 26, reprinted in *Institut Kurde de Paris, Information and Liaison Bulletin, 152-153*, November/December, p.80.

**Keywords:** Leyla Zana; European Court decision in favor of jailed Kurdish ex-parliamentarians.

**Ripoche, Bruno.** (2005). Zana la Kurde soutient le dossier turc. *Ouest France,* December 15, reprinted in *Institut Kurde de Paris, Information and Liaison Bulletin, 237*, December, p. 65.

**Keywords:** *Les femmes kurdes de Turqie*: a book of photographs about Leyla Zana and Kurdish women in Turkey by Elsa Le Pennec and Pierre-Yves Ginet (a photojournalist) with a preface by Danielle Mitterrand.

**Rollnick, Roman.** (1996). Turkey's Kurdish MP who pens her protest from jail. *The European,* January11-17, p. 11.

**Keywords:** Leyla Zana; PKK; International Women's Conference in Beijing; Gro Harlem; Claudia Roth; Pauline Green; Sakharov Prize; Tansu Çiller; Diyarbakir; Mehdi Zana; Nusret Demiral; Amnesty International; Feridun Yazar; İlnur Çevik; Süleyman Demirel; war; prison.

**Savelsberg, Eva.** (2000). Die Chance versäumt? Ein politisches Porträt der kurdischen Abgeordneten Leyla Zana [Missed the chance? A political portrait of the Kurdish MP Leyla Zana]. In Eva Savelsberg, Siamend Hajo, & Carsten Borck (Eds.), *Kurdologie: Kurdische Frauen und das Bild der kurdischen Frau* (pp. 179-97). Münster: Lit Verlag.

**Keywords:** Leyla Zana; European Union; Baxca; Silvan; Mehdi Zana; military coup of 1980; HEP; SHP; democracy; equality; national liberation; PKK; DEP; CILDEKT; AKIN; Özgür Politika; Öcalan.

**Schumann, Gerd.** (1995). Die Todesmutige Kurdin. *Emma,* July/August 1995, p. 20. One photograph by Leon Maresch (p. 21)

**Keywords:** Leyla Zana; arranged marriage to Mehdi Zana; education of Leyla Zana; torture of Leyla Zana; Leyla Zana's election to parliament.

**Schumann, Gerd.** (1994). Leyla Zana - Kurdin im türkischen Parlament [Leyla Zana - Kurdish woman in the Turkish parliament]. *Wir Frauen, 2*, pp. 20-21.

**Keywords:** Leyla Zana; NATO; Newroz; death penalty; DEP; women and Islam; poverty; arranged marriages; forced marriage; military coup of 1980; Diyarbakir; Mehdi Zana; war; human rights abuses.

**Le Soir de Bruxelles.** (1994). Députés kurdes de Turquie: verdict en décembre [Kurdish MPs from Turkey: verdict in December]. *Le Soir de Bruxelles,* November 25, reprinted in *Institut Kurde de Paris, Information and Liaison Bulletin, 116-117,* November/December, p. 77.

**Keywords:** DEP; Leyla Zana; PKK.

**Sylvie, Jan.** (1995). Leyla Zana - Zu Besuch im Gefängnis [Leyla Zana - A visit to the prison]. *Wir Frauen, 3,* Düsseldorf, p. 18, Z G 20.

**Keywords:** Turkey; human rights violations; female activists; Kurdish women.

305

**Tribune Pour L'Europe**. (1996). Leyla ZANA, Prix Sakharov 1995 [Leyla Zana, 1995 Sakharov Prize]. *Tribune Pour L'Europe, 1-F*, January, reprinted in *Institut Kurde de Paris, Information and Liaison Bulletin, 130-131*, January/February, p. 1.

 **Keywords:** Leyla Zana; Sakharov Prize.

**Turkish Daily News**. (1997). European Parliament to focus on DEP case. *Turkish Daily News*, March 6, reprinted in *Institut Kurde de Paris, Information and Liaison Bulletin, 144-145*, March/April, pp. 34-35.

 **Keywords:** DEP; Leyla Zana; European Parliament.

**Turkish Daily News**. (1995). Nurettin Nurkan: Zana does not merit Nobel. *Turkish Daily News*, September 28, reprinted in *Institut Kurde de Paris, Information and Liaison Bulletin, 126-127*, September/October, p. 112.

 **Keywords:** Leyla Zana; Nobel Peace Prize; DEP; PKK.

**Turkish Daily News**. (1995). Turkey accused of lobbying against Zana for Nobel. *Turkish Daily News*, October 11, reprinted in *Institut Kurde de Paris, Information and Liaison Bulletin, 126-127*, September/October, p. 151.

 **Keywords:** Leyla Zana; Kurdish Institute in Paris; PKK.

**Turkish Daily News**. (1995). Zana not permitted to attend award ceremony. *Turkish Daily News*, November 29, reprinted in *Institut Kurde de Paris, Information and Liaison Bulletin, 128-129*, November/December, p. 79.

 **Keywords:** Leyla Zana; DEP; Sakharov Prize.

**Turkish Daily News**. (1996). Zana's Sakharov Prize will be given to her husband. *Turkish Daily News*, January 13, reprinted in *Institut Kurde de Paris Information and Liaison Bulletin, 130-131*, January/February, p. 47.

 **Keywords:** Leyla Zana; Mehdi Zana; Sakharov Prive; DEP; Turkish penal code; Anti-Terrorism Law.

**Turkish Daily News**. (1996). Zana's Sakharov Prize to be handed to her husband. *Turkish Daily News*, January 17, reprinted in *Institut Kurde de Paris, Information and Liaison Bulletin, 130-131*, January/February, p. 58.

 **Keywords:** Leyla Zana; Mehdi Zana; Sakharov Prize; DEP; European Parliament.

**Turkish Daily News**. (1996). Zana's husband accepts Sakharov Human Rights Prize on her behalf. *Turkish Daily News,* January 18, reprinted in *Institut*

*Kurde de Paris, Information and Liaison Bulletin, 130-131*, January/February, p. 66.

Keywords: Leyla Zana; Mehdi Zana; Sakharov Prize; European Parliament; Danielle Mitterrand; customs union with Europe.

Turkish Daily News. (1997). HADEP protests imprisonment of former pro-Kurdish deputies. *Turkish Daily News*, March 3, reprinted in *Institut Kurde de Paris, Information and Liaison Bulletin, 144-145*, March/April, pp. 17-18.

Keywords: HADEP; DEP; Leyla Zana; protests; political assassinations; PKK.

Turkish Daily News. (1997). Turkey-EU JPC kicks off with angry exchange. *Turkish Daily News*, April 16, reprinted in *Institut Kurde de Paris, Information and Liaison Bulletin, 144-145*, March/April, pp. 244-245.

Keywords: Turkey-European Union Joint Parliamentary Commission; Leyla Zana; women's rights in Turkey; Kurdish rights in Turkey; PKK.

Turkish Daily News. (1997). Zana rejects a Yağmurdereli-type special amnesty. *Turkish Daily News*, December 3, reprinted in *Institut Kurde de Paris, Information and Liaison Bulletin, 152-153*, November/December, pp. 104-105.

Keywords: President Clinton; Prime Minister Mesut Yilmaz; Eşber Yağmurdereli; Democracy Party; fast to free Leyla Zana in Washington; PKK; 1996 Sakharov Prize.

Turkish Daily News. (2002). Turkey's refusal to release Zana angers EU parliament. *Turkish Daily News*, December 18, reprinted in *Institut Kurde de Paris, Information and Liaison Bulletin, 213*, December, p. 70.

Keywords: Leyla Zana; EU Parliament; Sakharov Prize.

Turkish Probe. (1995). Zana says her Nobel candidature condemns Turkey. *Turkish Probe*, October 20, reprinted in *Institut Kurde de Paris, Information and Liaison Bulletin, 126-127*, September/October, p. 186.

Keywords: Leyla Zana; DEP; Nobel Peace Prize; PKK.

Turkish Probe. (1995). Loading meanings on Zana's prize. *Turkish Probe*, November 17, reprinted in *Institut Kurde de Paris, Information and Liaison Bulletin, 128-129*, November/December, p. 49.

Keywords: Leyla Zana; Sakharov Prize; Nobel Peace Prize; PKK; article eight; European Customs Union.

**Ülke, Yeni.** (1992). The first Kurdish woman elected to Parliament. In *Kurdish Women: The struggle for national liberation and women's rights,* October, pp. 15-16. London: KIC/KSC Publications.

**Keywords:** Leyla Zana: interview with Turkish weekly; women and nationalism; national identity overtaking that of being a woman; national aspirations before the aspirations of women.

**La Vie Ouvrière.** (1995). Une députée kurde toujours en prison [A Kurdish MP still in prison]. *La Vie Ouvrière,* February 10-16, reprinted in *Institut Kurde de Paris, Information and Liaison Bulletin, 118-119,* January/February, p. 203.

**Keywords:** Union of French Women; International Democratic Federation of Women; protests in Paris for Leyla Zana.

**Wir Frauen.** (1997). Der Fall von Leyla Zana vor dem Europäischen Gerichtshof [The case of Leyla Zana before the European Court of Justice]. *Wir Frauen,* Düsseldorf.

**Keywords:** European Parliament; court; Kurdish women.

**Women of Europe Newsletter.** (1996). Sakharov Prize to Former Kurdish MP. *Women of Europe Newsletter, 58,* March, Veronique Houdart-Blazy (Ed.), p. 3, ISSN 1025-871X.

**Keywords:** European Parliament; Sakharov Prize; Leyla Zana; Mehdi Zana; Danielle Mitterrand.

**Xulam, Kani.** (1995). My friend Leyla. In *Resistance: Women in Kurdistan.* London: KIC/KSC Publications, pp. 2-3.

**Keywords:** women and family; women and nationalism; life of Leyla Zana; organized the wives of the Kurdish political prisoners for a sit-in in Kurdish cafés to compel Kurdish men to address the plight of the Kurds.

**Xulam, Kani.** (1994). My friend Leyla. *Kurdistan Report, 18,* May/June, p. 4

**Keywords:** Leyla Zana; 1980 military coup d'etat; U.S. policies regarding Turkey; PKK.

**Yılmaz, Sinan.** (1995). 1994 proves to be critical for DEP. *Turkish Daily News,* Janaury 25, reprinted in *Institut Kurde de Paris, Information and Liaison Bulletin, 118-119,* January/February, pp. 111-114.

**Keywords:** DEP; PKK; State Security Court; constitutional court;

Leyla Zana; Kurdish parliamentarians.

**Zana, Leyla**. (1994). Desperate Kurdish cry of protest rises from prison cell: This letter by Leyla Zana was smuggled out of Ankara jail. *The Times,* September 7, reprinted in *Kurdistan Report, 19,* September/October, pp. 1-2; reprinted in *Institut Kurde de Paris, Information and Liaison Bulletin, 113-114,* August/September, p. 121.

> **Keywords:** Tansu Çiller; Süleyman Demirel; Leyla Zana; letter smuggled out of prison.

**Zana, Leyla**. (1995). "Der Preis der Freiheit" - Brief aus dem Gefängnis ["The price of freedom" - letter from prison]. *Wir Frauen,* Düsseldorf, 1, pp. 8-9. Z G 20.

> **Keywords:** Turkey; human rights violations; state violence; Kurdish women; women activists; prisoners.

**Zana, Leyla**. (1995). *Écrits de prison* [Writings from prison] (K. Nezan, Trans.). Paris: des femmes Antoinette Fouque. ISBN: 2-7210-0460-3 (pb). Preface by Claudia Roth (pp. 9-13), text (pp. 15-115).

> **Keywords:** SHP; DEP; HEP; MIT; Taslima Nasreen; Mustafa Kemal Atatürk; Council of Europe; evacuation of Kurdish villages; Kemalism; history of Kurdistan; Danielle Mitterrand; Ségolène Royal; Ruken Zana; Ronay Zana; Kendal Nezan; Antionette Fougue; Alliance of Women for Democracy; Pauline Green; Socialist Group of the European Parliament; Sylvie Jan; International Democratic Federation of Women; Peking Conference; Prix International de la Paix d'Aix-la-Chapelle; Gro Harlem; CHP; International Committee for the Liberation of Kurdish Deputies imprisoned in Turkey.

**Zana, Leyla**. (1995). Editorial: Press statement by Leyla Zana. *Kurdistan Review, VII,* October, pp. 1-2, 4.

> **Keywords:** Zana's candidacy for Nobel Peace Prize; criticism of Turkey's policy on the Kurds; call for solidarity with the Kurds.

**Zana, Leyla**. (1996). *Eine Kurdin meldet sich zu Wort.* Briefe und Schriften aus dem Gefängnis [A Kurdish woman speaks up. Letters and writings from prison]. Dötlingen: Montage Verlag. ISBN 3-932315-00-6. 127 pages. Foreword by Claudia Roth. Black and white photos by Leon Maresch.

> **Keywords:** Turkey; independence movement; Kurdish women; Kurdistan; female guerrillas; political prisoners.

**Zana, Leyla**. (1996). Leyla Zana: Letter to the European Parliament in response to receiving the Sakharov Prize for freedom of thought from Ankara prison, 17 January [Special issue]. *Kurdistan Report*, *23*, March-May, pp. 33-34. One photograph.

Keywords: Leyla Zana: "Before all else, I am a mother"; women as bearers/mothers of the nation.

**Zana, Leyla**. (1999). *Writings from prison* (K. Nezan, H. Lutzky, Trans.). Watertown, Massachusetts: Blue Crane Books. ISBN 1-886434-08-5 (pb). Foreword by Elena Bonner (pp. vii-ix), foreword by Betty Williams (pp. xi-xii), letter nominating Leyla Zana for the Nobel Peace Prize by Senator John Edward Porter, (pp. xiii-xiv), letter from French President François Mitterrand (pp. xv-xvi), preface to the French edition by Claudia Roth (pp. Xvii-xxi), about Leyla Zana (pp. xxiii-xxvii), text (pp. 1-89), appendices (pp. 91-111), bibliography (pp.112-14), map (p. 115).

Keywords: Leyla Zana; DEP; patriarchy; IHD; Diyarbakir; Raftos Prize for Human Rights; Bruno Kreisky Peace Prize; Aix-la-Chapelle International Peace Prize; the Rose Prize; the Sakharov Prize for Freedom of Thought; Nobel Peace Prize; Woman of the Year Prize; HADEP; HEP; SHP; DEP; PEN Women Writers' Committee; death penalty; exile; imprisonment.

**Zana, Leyla**. (1999). Letter from Leyla Zana to Mrs. Yilmaz, wife of the former Turkish Prime Minister, Mesut Yilmaz (American Kurdish Information Network, Trans.), *Kurdistan Report, 28*, July-September, p. 50.

Keywords: Leyla Zana; Berna Yilmaz; PKK; the Turkish media's portrayal of Leyla Zana; PKK; war; the Mothers of the Disappeared; police brutality against the Mothers of the Disappeared.

**Zana, Leyla**. (2000). Lettre de Leyla Zana au Premier ministre turc [Letter from Leyla Zana to the Turkish Prime Minister] (B. Ravenel, Trans). *Il Manifesto. Confluences Méditerranée*, *34*, March 31, pp. 127-29.

Keywords: letter of March 31, 2000 rejecting President B. Ecevit's claim about Zana's refusal to be released on humanitarian grounds.

**Zinsen, Joachim**. (1995). Ein kurdisches Schicksal [A Kurdish fate]. *Aachener Nachrichten, 203*, September 1, reprinted in *Institut Kurde de Paris, Information and Liaison Bulletin, 126-127*, September/October, pp. 7-8.

Keywords: Leyla Zana; military government in Turkey; DEP; PKK.

## B. Other Political Prisoners

**Action for Kurdish Women**. (1994). Atrocities committed by the Turkish State against Kurdish women. *Kurdistan Report, 18*, May/June, p. 50 (back cover of journal), three photographs.

> **Keywords:** women's participation in the Kurdish national struggle; Leyla Zana, Aysel Malkac, Gurbetelli Ersoz; Ozgur Gundem: actions against employees; suggestions for actions to take in solidarity with these female victims of Turkish oppression of the Kurds.

**Akdemir, Musa**. (1996). La grève jusqu'à la mort des détenus turcs [The strike until the death of Turkish detainees]. *Libération*, July 22, reprinted in *Institut Kurde de Paris, Information and Liaison Bulletin, 136-137*, July/August, p. 91.

> **Keywords:** hunger strikes; leftists; DHKP-C; Dev Sol; prison conditions; PKK; Association of Prisoners' Parents; women hunger strikers.

**Altınoğlu, Garbis**. (2001). *A portrait of a terrorist state: A summary of the ordeal of political captives in Turkish prisons*, Leeds: CL. ISBN 0-9540410-0-3. List of abbreviations/glossary (pp. 6-7), introduction (pp. 8-10), text (pp. 11-220), select bibliography (pp. 221-24), list of Kurdish children murdered between July 1989 and April 2000 (pp. 188-96), photographs (front page, pp. 28, 29, 30, 36, 53, 91, 121).

> **Keywords:** Dilan; Berivan; Ulucanlar Prison Massacre (1999); type F prisons; Asiye Güden; Necla Çomak; Ayten Yıldırım; Özgür Kılıç; Gönül Aslan; Mürüvvet Küçük; A. Arzu Torun; Hülya Turunç; Nuray Özçelik; Makbule Akdeniz; Feryal Demiran; Sibel Özcan; sexual assault of female prisoners; rape of female prisoners; PKK; IMF; history of Turkey; TKP; annexation of Hatay; MHP; NATO; ANAP; Öcalan; Armenian Genocide; Maraş Massacre of December 22-6, 1978; İHD; torture; 1980 coup d'état; Kenan Evren; Kontrgerilla; the disappeared; OTAK; ASALA; Grey Wolves; Susrluk; murdered Kurdish children; forced virginity exams; mothers of the disappeared, Saturday Mothers; honour.

**Amnesty International**. (1987). Deaths in custody. *File on Torture*. September. Reprinted in *Institut Kurde de Paris, Information and Liaison Bulletin, 31-32-33*, October-December, pp. 12-13.

> **Keywords:** SHP; Esma Bayram; torture; Diyarbakir Prison; deaths in custody.

**Amnesty International**. (1997). Deaths in custody. *File on Torture.* November. Reprinted in *Institut Kurde de Paris, Information and Liaison Bulletin, 31-32-33*, October-December, pp. 18-19.

Keywords: SHP; Esma Bayram; Diyarbakir Prison; deaths in custody; torture of women and children.

**Amnesty International**. (1997). The colours of their clothes: parliamentary deputies serve 15 years' imprisonment for expressions of Kurdish political identity. *Amnesty International.* December. Reprinted in *Institut Kurde de Paris, Information and Liaison Bulletin, 152-153*, November/December, pp. 94-95.

Keywords: Leyla Zana; wearing of red, yellow, and green clothes as an act of treason; United Nations Working Group on Arbitrary Detention; Articles 10 and 11 of the Universal Declaration of Human Rights; torture of DEP members; political murder of DEP members; bombings of DEP members; disappearances of DEP members; death threats against Leyla Zana; attempts made on Leyla Zana's life.

**Associated Press**. (2000). Women activists detained in Turkey. *Associated Press,* September, reprinted in *Institut Kurde de Paris, Information and Liaison Bulletin, 186*, September, p. 58.

Keywords: Turkish and Kurdish women activists; protest against war and rape and harassment in prison; beating of demonstrators; Leman Yurtsever; torture; conditions in prison.

**Bejna**. (1991). Der Widerstand in Kurdistan geht weiter [The resistance in Kurdistan continues]. *Jiyan-Kurdische Frauenzeitschrift,* October, p. 8.

Keywords: Newroz; self-immolation; Zekiye Alkan; mothers of political detainees' hunger strike; censorship in Turkey; deportations; HEP; Kontra-guerillas; PKK; NATO.

**Berger, Géraldine**. (1994). Le Procès de Six Députés Kurdes [The trial of six Kurdish deputies]. *Témoignage Chretien,* September 2, reprinted in *Institut Kurde de Paris, Information and Liaison Bulletin, 113-114*, August/September, pp. 111-112.

Keywords: Kurdish parliamentarians; 1982 Constitution; forced assimilation of Kurds; Leyla Zana; PKK; DEP.

**Le Bien Public**. (1996). Remise quelque peu embarrassée du Prix Sakharov à Leyla Zana [Somewhat embarrassed presentation of the Sakharov Prize to Leyla Zana.]. *Le Bien Public,* January 18, reprinted in *Institut Kurde de Paris, Information and Liaison Bulletin, 130-131*, January/February, p. 67.

**Keywords:** Leyla Zana; Sakharov Prize; Mehdi Zana; Turkish Customs Union with Europe; Danielle Mitterrand.

**Bird, Maryann and Andrew Finkel.** (2002). What will Turkey tolerate? *Time, Institut Kurde de Paris, Information and Liaison Bulletin, 203*, February 25, p. 98-99.

**Keywords:** Hülya Şimşek; the death of 44 hunger strikers; DHKP-C; prison conditions in Turkey; type F prisons.

**Birler, Hayri.** (1995). Will Zana get Nobel Institute OK for Peace Prize bid? *Turkish Daily News,* September 13, reprinted in *Institut Kurde de Paris, Information and Liaison Bulletin, 126-127*, September/October, p. 35.

**Keywords:** Leyla Zana; Nobel Peace Prize; DEP; PKK.

**Bouge l'Europe.** (2000). Contrat de Khalife [Caliph Contract]. *Bouge l'Europe,* May-June, reprinted in *Institut Kurde de Paris, Information and Liaison Bulletin, 182*, May, p. 111.

**Keywords:** candidacy for European Union; human rights; democratization; Leyla Zana; earthquake victims; International March of Women in Europe; feminist movement; civil society; public service.

**Cesbron, Anne.** (1999). Une femme kurde [A Kurdish woman]. *Clara-Magazine,* December, reprinted in *Institut Kurde de Paris, Information and Liaison Bulletin, 176-177*, November-December, p. 141.

**Keywords:** Sibel Ceylan, Femmes Solidaires; female political prisoners in Turkey.

**Çevik, İlnur.** (1994). Does Zana regard herself as one of us? *Turkish Daily News,* September 9, reprinted in *Institut Kurde de Paris, Information and Liaison Bulletin, 113-114*, August/September, p. 136.

**Keywords:** DEP; Leyla Zana.

**Çevik, İlnur.** (1995). If Leyla Zana gets Nobel Peace Prize. *Turkish Daily News,* September 27, reprinted in *Institut Kurde de Paris, Information and Liaison Bulletin, 126-127*, September/October, p. 106.

**Keywords:** Leyla Zana; Nobel Peace Prize; DEP.

**Çevik, İlnur.** (1995). Leyla who? *Turkish Daily News,* October 14, reprinted in *Institut Kurde de Paris, Information and Liaison Bulletin, 126-127*, September/October, p. 164.

313

**Keywords:** Leyla Zana; DEP; Nobel Peace Prize.

**Çevik, İlnur**. (1995). Sakharov prize instead of the Nobel for Peace. *Turkish Daily News,* November 11, reprinted in *Institut Kurde de Paris, Information and Liaison Bulletin, 128-129,* November/December, p. 39.

**Keywords:** Leyla Zana; PKK; Nobel Peace Prize; Sakharov Prize; European Parliament; Anti-Terrorism Law; freedom of expression; European Customs Union.

**Clara-Magazine**. (1995). Leyla Zana Une année d'interventions solidaires [Leyla Zana: A year of solidarity interventions]. *Clara-Magazine, 36,* December, reprinted in *Institut Kurde de Paris, Information and Liaison Bulletin, 128-129,* November/December, p. 83.

**Keywords:** Leyla Zana; protests for Leyla Zana in Paris.

**Couturier, Kelly**. (1994). Kurdish lawmakers sentenced by Turkey. *International Herald Tribune,* December 9, reprinted in *Institut Kurde de Paris, Information and Liaison Bulletin, 116-117,* November/December, p. 128.

**Keywords:** Leyla Zana; Democracy Party; PKK.

**Çulpan, Hande and Sinem Sakaoğlu**. (1996). Fast to death: Families join inmates on hunger strike. *Turkish Daily News,* July 19, reprinted in *Institut Kurde de Paris, Information and Liaison Bulletin, 136-137,* July/August, pp. 83-85.

**Keywords:** hunger strikes; ÖDP; Justice Minister Ôevket Kazan; women in prison; mothers of prisoners; children of prisoners.

**Edmunds, Lynne**. (1995). The life and resistance of Kurdish women. In *Resistance: Women in Kurdistan,* p. 14. London: KIC/KSC Publications. One photograph.

**Keywords:** first-ever London seminar held at the SOAS on Kurdish women's contribution to the resistance of the Kurds against the Turkish state; Nulifer Koç: contributor to *Ozgur Ulke;* arrested without being charged when interpreting for a German human rights team; blindfolded, striped, threatened with rape, prodded repeatedly; tortured; international pressure forced her release; Mizgin Sen: Free Women's Association of Kurdistan; spoke of bravery of Kurdish women in Iraqi and Turkish Kurdistan who joined the resistance even with risk of being raped; ostracized from family after being arrested and raped in the name of family honour.

**The European**. (1994). Jail for Kurd MPs 'lenient.' *The European,* December

16, reprinted in *Institut Kurde de Paris, Information and Liaison Bulletin, 116-117*, November/December, p. 168.

**Keywords:** Democracy Party; PKK.

**Gundogdu, Mustafa**. (2002). We have lost our "brave mother": Human rights activist, publisher and KHRP applicant to the European Court Aysenur Zarakolu Dies in Turkey. *KHRP Newsline, 17*, Spring pp. 12. One photograph.

**Keywords:** Aysenur Zarakolu: died of cancer on February 28, 2002; women and nationalism; women as mothers of a nation: Zarakolu seen as "brave mother"; coffin carried to her grave by Kurdish women.

**Gurbetelli Ersoz's Defence**. (1995). An impassioned plea for free speech in Turkey. In *Resistance: Women in Kurdistan*. London: KIC/KSC Publications, pp. 7-9. One photograph.

**Keywords:** Nezaht Ozen: reporter with *Ozgur Gundem*; reported that a Kurdish woman had been raped at the police station and had medical documentation to prove it; Ozen was imprisoned; Ayse Zarakolu: owner of Belgé publishing house; imprisoned.

**L'Humanité**. (1994). Pour la libération des députés kurdes menacés de mort [For the release of Kurdish deputies threatened with death.]. *L'Humanité*, December 5, reprinted in *Institut Kurde de Paris, Information and Liaison Bulletin, 116-117*, November/December, p. 112.

**Keywords:** Leyla Zana; petition to free Kurdish parliamentarians.

**L'Humanité**. (1994). Procès des députés kurdes: verdict jeudi [Trial of Kurdish deputies: Verdict Thursday]. *L'Humanité*, December 7, reprinted in *Institut Kurde de Paris, Information and Liaison Bulletin, 116-117*, November/December, p. 113.

**Keywords:** trial against Kurdish parliamentarians.

**Human Rights Watch**. (1997). The women's rights project. *Human Rights Watch world report 1998. Events of 1997*. New York: Human Rights Watch, December.

**Keywords:** Sukran Aydin: in September 1997, European Court of Human Rights found that Aydin, a Kurdish woman from Southeastern Turkey, was subjected to torture when she was raped by guards who detained her in June 1993; judgment seen as an exception to the general inattention to custodial abuse of females around the world.

315

**Human Rights Watch**. (1997). Turkey: Human rights developments. *Human Rights Watch world report 1998. Events of 1997.* New York: Human Rights Watch, December.

Keywords: European Court of Human Rights ruling in September 1997: (Sukran Aydin) a Kurdish woman was raped and tortured by the Turkey gendarmerie in 1993.

**Institut Kurde de Paris**. (2001). The first "police blunder" in one of the type F prisons - as the hunger strike claims its 26th victim. *Institut Kurde de Paris, Information and Liaison Bulletin, 195,* June, p. 9.

Keywords: hunger strikes; type F prisons; torture; Zehra Kulaksiz.

**Institut Kurde de Paris**. (2002). Death of another two hunger strikers. *Institut Kurde de Paris, Information and Liaison Bulletin, 208-209,* July/August, pp. 10-11.

Keywords: hunger strike; Semra Başyiğit, 24-year-old hunger striker dies from her hunger strike; DHKP-C, Marxist Leninist; type F prisons; Fatma Bilgin, a 30-year-old hunger striker dies.

**Institut Kurde de Paris**. (2002). The 57th victim of the hunger strike. *Institut Kurde de Paris, Information and Liaison Bulletin, 210,* p.8, September.

Keywords: Hamide Öztürk, a 32-year-old woman dies as a result of her hunger strike; DHKP-C; prison conditions in Turkey.

**Institut Kurde de Paris**. (2002). Two members of HADEP sentenced to 45 months jail. *Institut Kurde de Paris, Information and Liaison Bulletin, 210,* September, pp. 7-8.

Keywords: HADEP; Necla Yıldırım sentenced "for helping a terrorist organisation"; PKK.

**International Association for Human Rights of the Kurds**. (2002). Wave of arrests against HAK-PAR members in Diyarbakir/Turkey press statement IMK e.V. Reprinted in *Institut Kurde de Paris, Information and Liaison Bulletin, 207,* June, p.56.

Keywords: HAK-PAR; Evin Sitki, founding party member of HAK-PAR is arrested.

**Keskin, Eren**. (1998). Women in prison (N. Jameson, Trans.). *Kurdistan Report, 27,* September-November. p. 38.

Keywords: İHD; Tunceli Laws; State Security Sourts; torture; sexual abuse; sexual torture; political prisoners; PKK; sexual harassment; hunger-strikes; self-immolation; media.

**KIC/KSC Publications**. (1995). Appendix 2: Necmiye's story, the same for all Kurds. In *Resistance: Women in Kurdistan*. London: KIC/KSC Publications, pp. 54.

> **Keywords:** Necmiye Arslanogu: journalist; in prison for the fourth time; being tortured; charged with treason; at 20 years old went to work for *Ozgur Gundem* in November 1993 and was arrested on her first assignment visiting a village that was burnt out by the Turkish security forces; traveling with a human rights delegation from London, UK; threatened with death by a police commanding officer; currently charged with belonging to an illegal terrorist organization (PKK); Gurbetelli Ersoz: editor-in-chief, *Ozgur Gundem*, in prison.

**KIC/KSC Publications**. (1995). Appendix 3: Humiliation, torture, rape. In *Resistance: Women in Kurdistan*. London: KIC/KSC Publications, pp. 55.

> **Keywords:** *Terre des femmes*: human rights organization based in Bochum, Germany; criticism of report published by German Foreign Minister, Kinkel, "Status Report 1995," that had nothing to say about the status of women in Turkey despite documented human rights abuses; according to this organization women in prisons are subjected to humiliation, torture, and rape; Selma B. suffered attempted rape after imprisonment with a baton, started bleeding heavily; report by Amnesty International saying all women are sexually assaulted when they are tortured: men fondle their breasts and finger their genitals; imprisonment of women in Turkey represents a gender-specific form of human rights violations; Germany's overlooking of Turkish human rights violations because of Germany's relationship with Turkey; Bisenk Anik: 16 years old; arrested, raped, and shot after a Newroz celebration; Merice Kirtay: pregnant; raped and murdered; Fadime Guler: 12 years old; raped in the custody of Agri security forces; Seher Yanarer: 12 years old; "displayed" naked by security forces in her village; Sukran Aydin: raped in front of her mother by security forces; Turkish soldiers raping dead female guerillas.

**KIC/KSC Publications**. (1995). Virginity control on women in Turkey. In *Resistance: Women in Kurdistan*. London: KIC/KSC Publications, p. 57. Also appeared in *Info-Turk*, July 1994.

> **Keywords:** July 1993 mission to Turkey; report, *A Matter of Power: State Control of Women's Virginity in Turkey,* found that police are forcing female political detainees and other prisoners to undergo virginity

testing to determine whether or not their hymens are intact; also undergone by women in hospitals, state dormitory residences, and women applying for government jobs; state officials also participate in virginity tests instigated by private individuals; police argue that such testing is a necessary precaution against "custodial abuse"; women report that the examinations are often degrading and painful; in most instances force is used to insert a speculum or hand into the vagina; in some cases the test is a form of punishment; with other suspects police defend the practice as legitimate under laws governing public morality and prostitution; arbitrary arrests of women to undergo virginity testing; virginity testing large part of sexual assault investigations; in Turkey, gynecological examinations are only legal when a prosecutor or judge orders one to test for sexual assault and not virginity; equation of female virginity with family honour.

**KIC/KSC Publications**. (1995). Turkey: Freedom of expression under siege. In *Resistance: Women in Kurdistan*. London: KIC/KSC Publications, pp. 59. Excerpt from PEN, *Newsletter of the Writers in Prison Committee on International Pen*, July 1995.

**Keywords:** Eren Keskin: lawyer and human rights activist; imprisoned for her article, "The world is in debt to the Kurdish people," published in *Ozgur Gundem* in June 1993; sentenced to two years imprisonment; also has six-month sentence for her book, *International Kurdish Conference*; victim of violence; attempt to abduct her; Aysel Malkaç: 22-year-old journalist for *Ozgur Gundem;* disappeared, might be dead.

**Koç, Nulifer**. (1995). My interrogation and torture by the Turkish authorities. In *Resistance: Women in Kurdistan*. London: KIC/KSC Publications, pp. 15-17.

**Keywords:** Nulifer Koç: contributor to *Ozgur Ulke;* arrested without being charged when interpreting for a German human rights team; blindfolded, striped, threatened with rape, prodded repeatedly; tortured; international pressure forced her release; underwent a virginity test to protect against being raped by soldiers while in custody; called a "Kurdish whore."

**Kurdish Human Rights Project**. (2001). Women on trial: KHRP conducts trial observation in Istanbul. *KHRP Newsline, 14*, Summer/Autumn, p. 5. One photograph.

**Keywords:** five women charged under Article 312 (2) of the Turkish Penal Code and Article 8 (1) of the Anti-Terror Law before the State Security Court; KHRP delegation went to observe the trial headed by

Margaret Owen, a human rights lawyer and an international advocate of women's rights; 11 June 2000: congress, *Against Sexual Violence in Custody*, organized by NGOs, held to address sexual violence perpetrated by state officials against women in custody; focused on the information gathered by the project, *Legal Aid for Women Raped or Sexually Assaulted by State Security Forces*; the congress resulted in two state investigations against 19 of the speakers including victims and their lawyers: Fatma Karakas: lawyer and founder of the *Legal Aid for Women* project; Kamile Cigci: rape victim; Fatma Kara, Nahide Kilic, Zuenep Ovayolu: amongst the organizers of the congress; the people arrested spoke specifically of sexual violence and rape in the Kurdish regions in Turkey so allegedly expressed "propaganda against the State's indivisibility"; women and nationalism; Turkey: party to the Convention against Torture, the Convention on the Elimination of all forms of Discrimination against women and the European Convention on Human Rights; adopted the U.N. General Assembly Declaration on the Protection of Human Rights Defenders; in contradiction with the Turkish 1982 Constitution which states: "No protection shall be given to thoughts and opinions that run counter to Turkish national interests..."

**Kurdish Human Rights Project**. (2002). Interim admissibility ruling on torture case: Nuray SEN v Turkey (41478/98) (torture). *KHRP Newsline, 18*, Summer, pp. 8.

> **Keywords:** Nuray Sen: director of the Mesopotamia Cultural Centre in Istanbul, which focuses on the culture of the Kurds and other ethnic groups living in Mesopotamia; when traveling to Diyarbekir, Sen was arrested along with nine colleagues; while in custody she claims she was subjected to torture, sexual abuse, and threats of rape; stripped; no access to lawyers or family; the European Court ruled that Sen did not bring her allegations to the attention of National authorities or logde an appeal therefore her complaint to the court was inadmissible.

**Kurdish Human Rights Project**. (2002). KHRP observes the trial of Eren Keskin. *KHRP Newsline, 20*, Winter, p. 4.

> **Keywords:** Eren Keskin: lawyer charged related to a speech given at a meeting in Cologne, Germany entitled, "Are Women's Rights Human Rights," talking about sexual violence perpetrated by the State.

**Kurdish Human Rights Project**. (003). Trial observation report: The State and sexual violence-Turkish court silences female advocate. *KHRP Newsline, 21*, Spring, p. 18. One photograph. Also appears in *Kurdish Human Rights*

*Project, Annual Report 2003*, p. 39. One photograph.

**Keywords:** report on the 2002 fact finding delegation to Turkey to observe the trial of Eren Keskin, charged with "insulting the military"; by highlighting sexual violence and rape perpetrated by army officials.

**Kurdish Observer**. (2000). HADEP women commission members detained. *Kurdish Observer*, February 29.

**Keywords:** HADEP Van Women Commission; detention of members.

**Kutschera, Chris**. (2001). Death before dishonour? *The Middle East*, reprinted in *Institut Kurde de Paris, Information and Liaison Bulletin, 189-199*, September/October, pp. 127-128.

**Keywords:** DHKP-C; hunger strikers; Eren Keskin; PKK; TİKKO; TKV; Human Rights Association.

**Paçal, Jan**. (1996). Prison hunger strikers are near death. *Turkish Daily News*, June 10, reprinted in *Institut Kurde de Paris, Information and Liaison Bulletin, 134-135*, May/June, p. 140.

**Keywords:** hunger strikes; PKK; Ayten Anlas; DHKP-C; prison conditions; Devrimci Sol; Resistance Movement; TDP.

**PEN**. (2004). Caselist January to June 2004. *International Pen Writers in Prison Committee*, August, reprinted in *Institut Kurde de Paris, Information and Liaison Bulletin, 233*, August 2004, pp. 67-74.

**Keywords:** Emine Senlikoglu: writer, sentenced to 20 months in prison for her book, *Who's Victim am I?* challenging the ban on Muslim women wearing headscarves; the charge is "incitement to enmity"; Leyla Zana: released from prison on bail; Funda Uncu Irkli: translator of *Choke (Tikanma)*, Chuck Palahniuk's book, fiction that has nothing to do with politics in Turkey; charged with "insult to the morals of the people"; Ruhat Mengi: journalist; wrote article in *Vatan* criticizing plans to reduce sentences that can be served against rapists; the MPs that drafted the bill took out charges of defamation; Ahmet Onal: on trial for publishing a book by M. Erol Coskun, *Acinin Dili Kadin* (Women: Voice of the Pain); Coskun sentenced to 15 months in prison in 2003; Nevin Berktan: political prisoner detained since 1994 on charges of membership of a terrorist organization; wrote a book on her experiences in prison which she was also prosecuted for called, *Hucrem (My Cell)*; Nursel Tozkoparan: women and nationalism; on trial along with two other singers for performing a song on television that "insulted the leader of the 12 September coupe, Kenan Evran"; Gulçiçek Guen Tekin: writer; indicted for her book, *Dilimiz Varligimiz, Dilimiz Kulturumuz* (*Our Language is Our Entity, Our Language is Our Culture*); Ulviye Kiliç: editor-in-chief of *Yesil Gole*: arrested and freed shortly afterwards after discussions with the Governor of Gole; Gamze Mimaroglu: editor-in-chief of *Tavir*; beaten while being held following searches of her newspaper by the Istanbul Security Directorate; Asiya Guzel Zeybek: journalist and writer, editor-in-chief of *Atilim*; arrested during demonstration protesting alleged links between the mafia and the government; accused of connections with Marxist-Leninist party, an illegal organization; accused of running and distributing their journal; tortured: raped while under interrogation; officers accused not prosecuted; Filiz Bingolce, Semih Sokmen: writer and publisher for Metis Publishing House; trial for "immoral publications" for a dictionary of women's slang which included terms of abuse used by both women and men to insult women; Kadriye Kanat: editor-in-chief of *Ozgur Kadinin Sesi* (Voice of Free Women); imprisoned for nationalist articles and for failing to appear at a hearing; Gulcan Kaya: editor of MEM Publishing House; charges of disseminating propaganda for KADEK; Nazan Yilma: journalist for *Kurtulus* (*Liberation*): accused of membership in an illegal organization; Iran: Malihe Maghezei: translator and writer; sentenced to 18 months' imprisonment for translating the book, *The Veil and the Male Elite*, by Fatima Mernissi, into Farsi; charged with insulting Islam; Narges Mohammadi: prominent journalist working for *Peyam Ajar*; one year in prison for granting interviews to media during the imprisonment of her husband; Fariba Davoudi: journalist for reformist press; sentenced for "anti-government propaganda" and "harming state security"; Tuka Maleki: writer; received prison term for involvement in the publication of ,*The History of Women's Music in Iran from Antiquity to Present*, and, *Men in Armor, Women in Veil*; Banafsheh Samgis: book critic; received prison term for involvement in the publication of, *The History of Women's Music in Iran from Antiquity to Present*, and, *Men in Armor, Women in Veil*.

**Pope, Nicole**. (2002). 150 prisonniers poursuivent une grève de la faim en Turquie [150 prisoners continue hunger strike in Turkey]. *le Monde*, April 5, reprinted in *Institut Kurde de Paris, Information and Liaison Bulletin, 205*, April, p. 2.

**Keywords:** hunger strikers; IHD; DKHP-C; Meryem Altun; Deniz Bakir; TIHV.

**Serpil**. (1992). Politisch Motovierte Gewalt Gegen Frauen [Politically motivated violence against women]. *Jiyan - Kurdische Frauenzeitschrift*, May, p.

9.

Keywords: Günay Korkut; sexual abuse in Turkish prisons; rape; torture; Bişeng Anık; Newroz atrocities in Turkey; cooperation of doctors with Turkish torturers.

*See also* Germany; Honour Killing; Rape

Sharrock, David. (1992). When the penalty for being a Kurd is death. *Kurdistan Report, 9*, May, pp. 7-8.

Keywords: Biseng Anik, a 16-year-old girl who died in police custody; torture; Sabriye Anik, the mother of Biseng; Turkish doctors' cooperation with torturers; PKK; Newroz.

Turkish Daily News. (1994). Politicians, intellectuals and scientists in prison at the end of November. *Turkish Daily News,* December 26, reprinted in *Institut Kurde de Paris, Information and Liaison Bulletin, 116-117*, November/December, pp. 209-210.

Keywords: Leyla Zana; Aslı Güneş; Merla Tikiz; Emine İğde.

Uksel, Y. (1995). Habille-toi, on t'emmène! [Get dressed, we'll take you!]. *Clara-Magazine, 36*, December, reprinted in *Institut Kurde de Paris, Information and Liaison Bulletin, 128-129*, November/December, p. 84.

Keywords: Kurdish women in Turkish prisons; torture; political prisoners.

Women Against Fundamentalism. (1994). Atrocities committed against Kurdish women. *5*(1), pp. 60. One illustration.

Keywords: Leyla Zana; Aysal Malkac; Gurbetelli Ersoz; letter writing; WAF participation at the Helsinki Citizens Assembly in Ankara: participated in facilitating a dialogue between Turkish and Kurdish women.

# V. POLITICIANS, JUDGES, AND ADMINISTRATORS

Barzani, Hishyar. (1995). *Les elites parlementaire kurdes iraqiennes* [The Iraqi Kurdish parliamentary elites; Master's thesis]. Université Lumièr Lyon II, 95 pages.

Keywords: interview-based study of the first Kurdish parliament elected in 1992 in Iraqi Kurdistan; six out of 105 deputies were women; rural-urban and geographic variables in parliamentary women;

all born in cities and speak the Sorani dialect; interview with two women parliamentarians; male-female relations among the deputies are conflictual, based on unequal relations of power in the interests of the males.

**Campbell, Mark**. (2000). Distant rumblings over Mount Ararat. *Kurdistan Report, 30*, Winter, pp. 39-40.

**Keywords:** Mukaddes Kubilay, the first woman to be elected mayor of Doğubeyazıt; the Khoybun; HADEP; women and war; domestic violence; women and poverty; positive influence of a female mayor on women's lives; PKK ceasefire; *Yeni Gündem.*

**Institut Kurde de Paris**. (2002). Women occupy important positions, says the first women judge appointed in Iraqi Kurdistan. *Institut Kurde de Paris, Information and Liaison Bulletin, 203*, February, p. 9.

**Keywords:** women occupying important administrative positions in Iraqi Kurdistan; Iraqi Kurdish women's roles; Kamila Ali Salim, the first woman judge in Iraqi Kurdistan appointed in May 1997 at Duhok Civil Court; quotes from her interview in Brayati (19 February); Ms. Nasreen Sideek, Minister of Reconstruction and Development (Arbil); appointment of the second woman judge in Suleimaniya; Ms. Narmeen Qaradaghi, lawyer at Arbil court talks about progress in amending laws in favor of women; the Kurdish government in Suleimaniya is the "first political authority in the Middle East" to abolish the law on "honour crimes"; amendment of old Iraqi laws as they pertain to women; Parliamentary Committee of Women's Rights.

**Institut Kurde de Paris**. (2004). Nesrin Barwari escapes an attack. *Institut Kurde de Paris, Information and Liaison Bulletin, 228*, March, p. 15.

**Keywords:** Nesrin Barwari, Minister of Public Works; assassination attempt at al-Karama, east of Mosul; Paul Bremer; PUK.

**Kak Ahmad, Hero**. (2005). Can Mehabad guard the Kurdish woman? *Hewler Globe, 1*(4), p. 3. Two photographs.

**Keywords:** the appointment of Mehabad Qaradaghi, a Kurdish feminist refugee in Sweden, as advisor to prime minister Nechirvan Barzani, the Kurdish Regional Government led by KDP; Qaradaghi, born in 1966 in Kifri, Iraqi Kurdistan, sentenced to jail in Iraq in 1980-81, until 1991 was member of "Kurdistan Ranjdaran Assembly," and lived in Sweden since 1993; poet, author, and feminist activist, and published 23 books; concern expressed about her loss of contact with

Kurdish women due to her stay abroad; Kurds have engaged in national liberation struggle led by men, and women have been marginalized; Qaradaghi should take a new approach if she is to succeed; even with appropriate legislation it would be difficult to change "people's attitudes and personal positions."

**Kakai, Falaq al-Din**. (1994). The Kurdish parliament. In *Iraq since the Gulf war* (pp. 118-33). Committee Against Repression and for Democratic Rights in Iraq. London: Zed Books. ISBN 1 85649 231 1 (Hb), ISBN 1 85649 232 X (pb).

Keywords: female deputies; educational background of deputies.

**Pope, Hugh**. (2002). The transformation of Iraqi Kurdistan. *Wall Street Journal,* reprinted in *Institut Kurde de Paris, Information and Liaison Bulletin, 203*, February 12, pp. 31-32.

Keywords: Nasreen Mustafa Sadeek, Minister of Reconstruction, recounts the exodus of Kurds in March 1991; health conditions; International Committee of the Red Cross; ethnic minorities in Iraqi Kurdistan.

**Schumann, Gerd**. (1994). Leyla Zana-Kurdin im türkischen Parlament [Leyla Zana-Kurd in the Turkish Parliament]. *Wir Frauen,* Düsseldorf, *2*, Summer, pp. 20-21. Z G 20.

Keywords: Turkey; human rights; human rights work; human rights violations; parliament; political prisoners; female politicians; Kurdish women.

**Tremblais, Jean-Louis**. (2003). Le pétrole au prix du sang [Oil at the cost of blood]. *Le Figaro Magazine,* p. 26, April 12, reprinted in *Institut Kurde de Paris, Information and Liaison Bulletin, 217*, April, p. 26.

Keywords: Nasreen Sideek Berwari, Minister of Reconstruction and Development of the Regional Government of Autonomous Kurdistan; the cost of reconstruction; Berwari comments on the price the British and American paid for the liberation of Iraq: the death of their soldiers; Berwari comments on the Oil for Food Program and its principal beneficiaries.

# RELIGION

## I. ALEVISM

**Becker, Markus**. (1993). Kurdische Frauen zwischen Islam und Feminismus [Kurdish women between Islam and feminism]. *Jiyan - Kurdische Frauenzeitschrift,* December, pp. 14-15.

> **Keywords:** Kurdish women and Islam; feminism; Alevi women; Dersim; Jewish Kurds; Christian Kurds; Zakho; comparison of the position of Alevi and Sunni Kurdish women; veiling; lack of veiling among Alevi Kurds; Turkish state's attempts to Islamize the Alevis; deportations of Alevi Kurds; Alevis and migration.

**Chater, Melville**. (1928). The Kizilbash Clans of Kurdistan. *National Geographic Magazine, LIV*(4), October, pp. 485-504. 22 black and white photographs (pp. 486, 487, 488, 490, 491, 492, 493, 494, 495, 496, 497, 498, 499, 500, 501, 502, 503, 504).

> **Keywords:** Kharput; a nursing home for Armenian mothers of Kurdish men's babies; the forcing of Armenian women "into Moslem harems during the deportations"; Dersim; tribalism; American missionaries' views of the inhabitants of the Dersim and Kharput region; religion; massacres of Armenians; religious practices of the Alevis; poverty; veiling; Kurdish women's dress; prevalence of monogamy among the Alevis; Alevi women's "free choice among her Kizilbash suitors"; marriage rituals of the Alevis; the "savage coquetry" which "marks Kurdish women."

**Eckhardt-Aktaş, Doris**. (1993). *Beziehungsweise Frauen: Streit - Solidarität - Tradition* [Or women: Quarrel - solidarity - tradition]. Frankfurt am Main: Ulrike Helmer Verlag. ISBN 3-927165-16-X. Contents (pp. 5-6), introduction (pp. 7-11), text (pp. 12-209), endnotes (p. 210), bibliography (pp. 211-216). Nine black and white photographs (unnumbered centre pages).

> **Keywords:** Alevis; Dersim; women's work; male-female socialization; women's education; honour; women's bodies; women accepted by society; "bad" women; marriage partners; mother-daughter relationships; women's position in the family; male violence against women; women's resistance to male violence; women's acceptance of male violence; female violence against women; marriage; bride price; men's fear of women; solidarity among women; hierarchy among women; discord among women; women's friendships; control; migration; changes in women's relationships wrought by migration;

immigration and women; solidarity among women within a family; Alevi Kurdish women in Germany.

**Gökalp, Emre**. (1993). Sivas incident remains on country's agenda. *Turkish Daily News,* August 6, reprinted in *Institut Kurde de Paris, Information and Liaison Bulletin, 101-102,* August/September, pp. 24-25.

**Keywords:** Sivas massacre; Islamists; Hezbullah; Refah Party; Aziz Nesin; SHP; Sivas riots; Sunni riots in Kahramanmaraõ; Kahramanmaraõ pogrom; Alevis; 1980 military coup; Unity Party.

**Kinzer, Stephen**. (1998). For the Turks, rising tension over religion. *International Herald Tribune,* October, reprinted in *Institut Kurde de Paris, Information and Liaison Bulletin, 162-163,* September/October, pp. 135-136.

**Keywords:** Kurdish quarter of Safranbolu; discrimination against Kurds in Safranbolu; unequal distribution of wealth along ethnic lines; fundamentalism and women.

**Muermann, Michael**. (1984). *Musto, Sahhe und Ousso...: Eine Geschichte aus Kurdistan* [Musto, Sahhe and Ousso ...: A story from Kurdistan]. Bornheim-Merten: Lamuv Verlag. ISBN 3-88977-004-5. Introduction (pp. 7-8), map (p. 18), text (pp. 10-159).

**Keywords:** living conditions in Tunceli (Dersim) Province; poverty; Zaza language forbidden; health conditions; women's work; Kurdish women's headdress; veiling among women; importance of hard work as a measure of a woman's value; Alevi religious practices; Duzgun Baba; Alevi shrines; education; prison; Kortu; Tunceli; exile in Germany; Turkish-Kurdish tensions in Germany; difficulties facing Kurdish women in German workplaces; racism; arranged marriage; honour.

*See also* Germany; Language

**Neyzi, Leyla**. (1999). Gülümser's story: Life history narratives, memory and belonging in Turkey. *New Perspectives on Turkey, 20,* Spring, pp. 1-26.

**Keywords:** migration; war; memory; belonging; Dersim (Tunceli); globalization/transnationalism; identity politics; structures of power; education; assimilation; Islamism; Kurdish and Alevi political projects; Pulumur district of Tunceli; gender and identity; Kemalism; Dersim Genocide; deportations; orphans; opposition to Sunni-Alevi marriages; Düzgün Baba; Alevi religious practices; popular religion among the Alevi Kurds of Dersim; PKK; 1980 military coup; exile;

experiences of racism in Turkish cities; Sunni discrimination against Alevis; racism against Alevis in compulsory religion courses in public schools.

## II. SUFISM

**Böttcher, Annabelle**. (1998). L'élite féminine kurde de la Kaftâriyya, une confrérie naqshbandî damascene [The Kurdish female elite of Kaftâriyya, a naqshbandî Damascene brotherhood]. In Martin van Bruinessen (Ed.), with the assistance of Joyce Blau, *Islam des Kurdes* (pp. 125-39). Les Annales de L'Autre Islam, No. 5, Paris: Equipe de recherche interdisciplinaire sur les scodiétés méditerranéennes musulmanes. ISSN 1246-7731.

**Keywords:** study of the female elite of Kaftâriyya, a branch of Naqshbandi religious order, in the Kurdish quarter of Damascus; pacifist Sufi group cooperates with the Syrian regime.

**Böttcher, Annabelle**. (2001). Portraits of women in contemporary Sufism. In Shahrzad Mojab (Ed.), *Women of a non-state nation: The Kurds* (pp. 195-208). Costa Mesa: Mazda Publishers. ISBN: 1-56859-093-8 (pb).

**Keywords:** Kurdish quarter of Damascus; Shaykha Wafā'Kaftārū; Ba'ath Party; Kaftāriyya sisterhood; Naqshbandiyya; Alawis; Hawwā' al-Millī; Ānisa Najāh; Ānisa da al-Kurdī; Rufaida Dīb; Sabāh al-Ġabrī.

## III. SUNNISM

**Howe, Marvine**. (2000). *Turkey today: A nation divided over Islam's revival*. Boulder: Westview Press. ISBN: 0-8133-3764-x (hc). Contents (pp. vii-viii), illustrations (p. ix), preface (pp. xi-xii), acknowledgements (p. xiii), brief guide to Turkish pronunciation (p. xv), map (p. xvii), text (pp. 1-284), notes (pp. 285-295), selected bibliography (pp. 297-300), index (pp. 301-310), 20 black and white photos (pp. 2, 13, 20, 24, 35, 65, 70, 71, 84, 91, 108, 115, 137, 162, 183, 201, 212, 235, 246, 256), map of sites of faith in Turkey (pp. 58-59).

**Keywords:** Atatürk; Refah Partisi; *Imam Hatip* schools; sufism; Fethullah Gülen; Department of Religious Affairs; Alevis; Hizbullah; Greek Orthodox Christians; PKK; Armenians; the Kurdization of Turkey; Leyla Zana; widows; refugees; Human Rights Association; HADEP; Jewish minority of Istanbul; the "Headscarf War"; women banned from universities for wearing the headscarf; Rainbow (a platform for Turkish Islamic women's groups); bride price; WWHR; virginity tests; honour killings; Merve Kavakçi; Fazilet Partisi; female literacy statistics; rural women's organizations; solidarity between Turkish and Kurdish women; KA-DER; polygamy; ÇATOM; women organizing against oppression.

**Kinzer, Stephen**. (2000). Turks uncover more victims of Muslim terrorist group. *International Herald Tribune,* January 25, reprinted in *Institut Kurde de Paris, Information and Liaison Bulletin, 178,* January, pp. 66-67.

Keywords: Hizbullah; torture; Konca Kuris (an Islamist feminist murdered by the Hizbullah); Sivas massacre.

**Turkish Probe**. (1994). Sivas Case, 29 Face Death Penalty. *Turkish Probe,* August 12, reprinted in *Institut Kurde de Paris, Information and Liaison Bulletin, 113-114,* August/September, p. 40.

Keywords: Sivas; Aziz Nesin; Satanic Verses; Demiral; Islamist activists; Islamist attacks on Alevi cultural festival in Sivas; arson attacks which left 37 people dead.

**Yalçın-Heckmann, Lale**. (1998). Some notes on the religious life of Kurdish rural women. In Martin van Bruinessen (Ed.), with the assistance of Joyce Blau, *Islam des Kurdes* (pp. 141-60). Les Annales de L'Autre Islam, No. 5, Paris: Equipe de recherche interdisciplinaire sur les scodiétés méditerranéennes musulmanes. ISSN 1246-7731.

Keywords: lack of interest in studying the ethnic, class, and rural dimensions of religion in Turkey; research based on filed work in the village of Sisin in Hakkari region in 1980-82; prayers at mosque for males only; division of time based on religious practice; good and bad days for washing, working, cleaning, etc.; the gendered nature of visiting graves and shrines, mourning, belief in evil eye, religious interpretations of male/female differences.

## IV. YEZIDISM

**Lescot, Roger**. (1975). Vie familiale [Family life]. In *Enquête sur les Yezidis de Syrie et du Djebel Sindjar* (pp. 148-57). Beirut: Librairie du Liban.

Keywords: familial structure: patriarchal, father's absolute authority over his children; marriage: generally at a young age: men at 15 and women at 12; polygamy is practiced: limit to four and in some cases five wives; bargaining for marriage; women as property; marriage price sometimes based on beauty of the woman, the status of her family and the place of her clan within the tribe; abduction as a last resort.

**Menant, Joachim**. (1892). *Les Yéziziz: Épisodes de l'histoire des adorateurs du diable* [The Yazidiz: Episodes from the history of the devil worshipers]. Paris:

Ernest Leroux. Two illustrations.

**Keywords:** dress of Yezidi women before and after marriage; polygamy is generally forbidden except for religious and political leaders; respect for women; adultery is punished by death but is very rare; arranged marriages; women can be repudiated and sent back to her parents for misconduct or bad behaviour; women cannot remarry whereas men can; wife and women as property of their families and husband; dowries.

# SOCIAL AND ECONOMIC ORGANIZATION

## I. COMMUNISM AND SOCIALISM

**Morgan, David.** (1999). Trade unions in the forefront of Kurdish freedom struggle. *Kurdistan Report, 28,* July-September, pp. 54-55.

**Keywords:** resistance to women's participation in unions from feudal culture still prevalent in Kurdish society; "women prisoners within the home"; domestic violence; prevented from sharing the platform with any other man besides their husbands; comprise about 5% of trade union members and even less amongst the executive; women's secretariat within the executive committee of KESK to advance women's organization; the Turkish state has responded with attacks on female workers: arrest, torture, sexual abuse (raids on Mus and Urfa).

**Fischer-Tahir, Andrea.** (2004). "Ich war eine, die keine Angst hatte": Biographische Annäherungen an Frauen im organisierten Widerstand im irakischen Kurdistan der 1980er Jahre ["I was someone who wasn't afraid": Biographical approaches to women in organized resistance in Iraqi Kurdistan in the 1980s.]. In Siamend Hajo, Carsten Borck, Eva Savelsberg, & Şükriye Dogan (Eds.), *Gender in Kurdistan und der Diaspora, Kurdologie Series Vol. 6* (pp. 59-105). Münster: UNRAST-Verlag. ISBN 3-89771-014-5 (pb).

**Keywords:** opposition to the central Iraqi government in the 1980s; martyrs; peshmerga; oral history; biographical interviews with former activists in Suleimaniya; Mehabad, a Kurdish woman activist born in Suleimaniya whose husband was martyred in the 1991 uprising; poverty; Iraqi Communist Party; KDP; PUK; Marxist-Leninism; Komele; collective towns; Behar, a Kurdish woman from a poor district of Baghdad who recruited girls for membership in a communist youth organization then joined the peshmergas; literacy;

329

Kurdayetî, the feeling of Kurdishness; communist youth and student organizations; Noširwan Mistefa Emîn; shame/honor; gender roles among the peshmerga/Komele; Jalal Talabani; revolution; an informal network called Ala-î Şoreş (Banner of the Revolution); Runak, a Kurdish woman born in Suleimaniya who joined the Iraqi Communist Party and was tortured and raped by Iraqi police; Maoism; Stalinism; patriarchy; al-Anfal; torture; electric shock; raping of female prisoners in front of their brothers; 1991 Uprising; Kurdish society's views of former female prisoners who were raped; the shame of formerly imprisoned women; Communist Party of Kurdistan.

**Ignatieff, Michael**. (1993). The last Marxists. *The Sunday Review, The Independent on Sunday,* October 31, London, pp. 18-20. Four photographs, one map.

> **Keywords:** Abdullah Öcalan; guerillas; PKK; Marxism; KDP; Northern Iraq; women's role in the PKK.

**KIC/KSC Publications**. (1993). *A gun barrel in the back of the neck: Trade Unions and the struggle in Kurdistan and Turkey.* KSC/KIC Publications: London. Text (pp. 1-36), 17 black and white photographs (pp. 2, 5, 7, 11, 12, 15, 19, 23, 27, 28), map (unnumbered front page).

> **Keywords:** interview with a Kurdish woman employed at the Batman Tobacco Company; women cotton pickers; Hizbullah; HEP; PKK; Amnesty International; Human Rights Association; Turkish Labour Laws; nomads.

**Kurdish Media**. (2000). Communist Party of Iraq accuses PUK of despotism. *Kurdish Media,* September 7, reprinted in *Institut Kurde de Paris, Information and Liaison Bulletin, 186,* September, pp. 32-34.

> **Keywords:** PUK close Iraqi Communist Party's offices, radio, and TV stations, as well as the Independent Organisation of Women, the Women's Shelter and the Children Protection Centres; security police raid women's shelter; domestic violence; imprisonment of women who sought shelter in women's shelter; potential return of women to their families by PUK; honor killing; threats to women posed by families and by Islamists; arrests and murders of defenders of the Iraqi Communist party by the PUK.

**Metcalf, Mark**. (1993). Kurdish women visit the pits: Internationalism is the key to the struggles of working people. *Kurdistan Report, 15,* July/August, pp. 34-35.

**Keywords:** Hackney Miners Support Committee; Kurdistan Solidarity Committee; links between Kurdish people in Britain and Women Against Pit Closures; Patriotic Women's Association of Kurdistan; PKK; working class movements and women; women and solidarity; comparison of the struggles by miners, miners' wives, and Kurds; Kurdish women's magazine *Jina Serbilind*, *Özgür Gündem*.

**Oral, Kezban**. (1995). Women in the trade union movement: Kezban Oral speaks to Berfin Sayli. In *Resistance: Women in Kurdistan* (p. 24). London: KIC/KSC Publications.

**Keywords:** sexism of union officials and employers: see trade unions as man's domain; not taking female trade unionists seriously; seeing them as weak; struggle first against patriarchy in addition to struggle of trade unions; union officials did not accept a proposal to celebrate March 8, International Women's Day; local branches of Tek Gida-Is food workers suffered repression because of their political positions on March 8; double burden of housework and working outside the home; weakness of the women's movement in Turkey; failure to integrate working class women into the movement; EKB: Unity of Working Women was formed to address this concern; workers and women both as vanguards of society.

*See also* Women's Movements; Women's Journalism

**Revolutionary Worker**. (1980). Inside the revolutionary war in Kurdestan. *Revolutionary Worker,* July 11, pp. S1, S3, S4, S5.

**Keywords:** Pasdaran; peshmerga; Komoleh; Peshmergas of the Oppressed and Toiling Masses of Kurdestan; Kurdish women's dress; Kurdish women's role in the struggle; SAVAK; Marxist study groups; Abasabad refugee camp; Women's Society of Baneh.

## II. FEUDALISM AND CAPITALISM

**Aydin, Zülküf**. (1986). *Underdevelopment and rural structures in Southeastern Turkey: The household economy in Gisgis and Kalhana.* Londong: Ithaca Press. ISBN 0-86372-034-X 301 pages. Introduction (pp. 1-21), text (pp. 22-262), bibliography (pp. 263-281), appendix (pp. 282-293), index (pp. 294-301), map of Turkey (p. 52), map showing location of Gisgis and Kalhana (p. 73).

**Keywords:** the development of capitalist relations in two villages to the north of Diyarbakir; nuclear and extended families; domination of the head of the household; relations of production with the peasant household (chapter 7); the age and sex division of labor; centrality of female labor in the reproduction of the labor force; statistics regarding gender; division of labour by sex; females as objects of monetary transactions; buying and selling of women; bride price; arranged marriages; girls committing suicide; persistence of polygamy; widows; difficulties widows over 30 face in remarrying; marriage of young girls; honour; the tradition of marriage between widowed women and their brothers-in-law; migration; population growth; women's participation in farming/agriculture; land tenure; marketing of produce by women; women shopping for necessities; diet; poverty; underdevelopment; women's migration due to marriage; blood feuds; health; Turkish Workers' Party; education; state policies; economic structure of Turkish Kurdistan.

*See also* Patriarchy

**Dziêgel, Leszek**. (1981). *Rural community of contemporary Iraqi Kurdistan facing modernization.* Krakow: Agricultural Academy in Krakow, The Institute of Tropical and Subtropical Agriculture and Forestry. Preface (p. 6), introduction (pp. 7- 8), text (pp. 9-198), references (pp. 198-208), map of Northern Iraq (p. 11).

**Keywords:** modernization in the period following the collapse of the Barzani Revolution; farming; domestic life; the interior of Kurdish homes; diet; segregation of the sexes; Chaldean women; Kurdish women's work; superstition; women's private property; Kurdish kitchens; women's dress; children's dress; the dressing of young boys as girls in order to protect them from the evil eye; Europeanization of dress; infant mortality rates; hygiene; medical care; birth rates; polygamy; lack of veiling in rural areas; education; women in the workplace.

**Lamb, Harold**. (1946). Mountain Tribes of Iran and Iraq. *National Geographic Magazine, LXXXIX*(3). March, pp. 385-408. 15 Black and White Photographs (pp. 387, 388, 389, 390, 391, 392, 393, 394, 398, 399, 402, 403, 404, 405, 406), map (pp. 396-397).

**Keywords:** Yezidism; women's work; Iran; Iraq; Soviet Republic of Armenia; Yezidis who took refuge from massacres and fled to Russia; Bakhtiaris; Lurs; Yezidi rites and religious beliefs; Herki migrants; Sheikh Mahmud's war with the RAF; blood feuds; Turkomans; Zoroastrianism; Nestorians; Kurdish hospitality; girls' school in Sulaimaniya.

*See also* Armenians; Assyrians/Chaldeans; Yezidism

**Plogstedt, Sibylle, and Ute Remus**. (1991). Weine nicht, meine Seele: Kurdinnen in der Türkei [Don't cry, my soul: Kurdish women in Turkey]. In Deutscher Frauenrat (Ed.), *Informationen für die Frau* (pp. 7-8).

**Keywords:** Lice; women farmers; Kurmanci; woman shot in a protest; living conditions in rural Kurdistan; PKK; assimilation; Turkification; Kurdish ghettos of Istanbul; poverty; gecekondus; education system; language rights; Deng; girl labourers; Silvan; Hüsniye Ölmez; rape in prison; suicide out of fear of rape; women murdered by their husbands in order to prevent their being raped; Newroz; Alevis; relatives of the disappeared; female political prisoners; military coup of 1980.

*See also* PKK; Political Prisoners; State Violence; Urban Life

**Vega, Anne**. (1994). Tradition et Modernité au Kurdistan et en Diaspora [Tradition and modernity in Kurdistan and the diaspora]. *Peuples Méditerranéens, 68-69*, July-December, pp. 107-142. ISSN 0399 1253.

**Keywords:** statistics regarding the number of Kurds in Kurdistan and in the various diaspora countries; social organization of Beytussebab; family organization; marriage amongst relatives; feudalism; marriage; comparison of Kurdish, Turkish, and Arab marriage patterns; the role of the parents in the choice of a marriage partner; endogamic marriages; the difficulties in inter-communal marriage (Sunni-Alevi-Yezidi); bride price; women's roles; women's work; childbirth; pregnancy; evil eye; birth rites; nursing; birth control; sterility; conception; the importance of women's virginity; the effects of the economy on Kurdish women's status in Istanbul; problems facing women in the Kurdish diaspora in Paris: social and community isolation; lack of support for childcare; problems with maintaining marriage traditions; women as child bearers and homemakers; preference for male children; childbirths in non-clinical settings; women in the diaspora returning to Kurdistan to give birth; childrearing traditions; pressure from male relatives to maintain child rearing traditions; abortion; contraceptives; sterility: mythology associated with sterility; sex openly discussed amongst couples and women; honour killing.

*See also* Diaspora; Marriage

**Yalçın-Heckmann, Lale and Pauline van Gelder**. (2000). Das Bild der Kurdinnen im Wandel des politischen Diskurses in der Türkei der 1990er Jahre - einige kritische Bemerkungen. In Eva Savelsberg, Siamend Hajo, & Carsten Borck (Eds.), *Kurdologie: Kurdische Frauen und das Bild der kurdischen Frau* (pp. 77-104). Münster: Lit Verlag.

**Keywords:** PKK; migration; immigration; Azadî; Hakkari; urban-rural dichotomy; kofî; fistan kiras; rural Kurdish women's dress; Özgür Halk; Öcalan; nationalism; Roza; female guerrillas; female politicians; mothers; PKK and women; Kurdistan Report; DEP; Leyla Zana; women as icons of the nation; women and reproduction; women's roles in national, economic and political struggles; importance of motherhood.

*See also* Layla Zana; Political Parties; PKK; Kurdish Nationalist Movements

## III. TRIBAL AND NOMADIC LIFE

**A., N.** (1932). "L'hospitalité kurde: Une femme, chef de tribu," *Hawar: Qovara Qurdî, Revue kurde*, Année 1, Numéro 6, 8 Tebax, pp. 7-8.

**Keywords:** author's 20 years of visiting Kurdish villages and tribes; Kurds have maintained their patriarchal customs, including their famous oriental hospitality; the chief of the Kurdish tribe of Ezdinan in the *nahié* of Nordouz, in the Ottoman province of Van was a woman named Fatma, known under the nickname of Kralitsa; was chief of the tribe after the death of her two brothers; after the Ottoman constitutional revolution of 1908, the author hospitalized and received with seven or eight companions for 12 days in the tent of Fatma.

**Beşikçi, İsmail.** (1986). Passages from transformation and structural problems of the East. *Kurdish Times, 1*(2), Fall, pp. 43-44.

**Keywords:** patriarchy among nomads in Kurdistan (Turkey); gendered nature of inheritance and ownership of property; wedding; "head-price" or bride price.

**Hütteroth, Wolf-Dieter.** (1959). *Bergnomaden und Yaylabauern im mittleren kurdischen Taurus* [Mountain nomads and Yayla farmers in the central Kurdish Taurus]. Marburg: Geographischen Institutes der Universität Marburg. Foreword (p. 3), table of contents (pp. 5-7), maps (pp. 17-18, 123-124, and unnumbered back pages), text (pp. 9-171), bibliography (pp. 173-188).

**Keywords:** women's work; women's production of dairy products; women's production of carpets; women's weaving; migration, nomadism.

**Kramer, Carol.** (1982). Ethnographic households and archaeological

334

interpretations: A case from Iranian Kurdistan. *American Behavioral Scientist,* July/August, pp. 663-675.

**Keywords:** archaeology; social patterns in extinct societies; ethnographic study of an Iranian Kurdish village; social relationships.

**Kurdistan Report.** (1993). The Beritans: Lovers of the mountains. *Kurdistan Report, 13,* February/March, pp. 20-21.

**Keywords:** Elazığ Massacre of 1514; Mazdaism; Zoroastrianism; Kosa tribe; Melemeran tribe; Kerkulagan tribe; marriage among the Beritans; feudalism; women's lack of right to inheritance among the Beritans; dowry; polygamy; women's role in the family; sharing of labour between men and women; Newroz traditions; Kurdish songs; Kurdish dance; Berti (women who milk sheep); effect of emergency rule on seasonal migration.

**Von Schweiger-Lerchenfeld, A.** (1880). Nomadic life of the Kurds (A. S. Meyrick, Trans.). In *Woman in all Lands* (pp. 65-74). New York: Chas. F. Roper & Co. Four illustrations (pp. 65, 67, 68, 72).

**Keywords:** nomadic life; religious customs; social customs; physical conditions of Kurdistan; Kurdish music; Kurdish women; blood feuds; women preventing blood feuds; slavery; insurrections; Nestorians; Kurdish women warriors; Kara Fatima; tattooing; piercing; women's work; Yezidis.

**Yalçın-Heckmann, Lale.** (1989). *Kurdish women and ethnic identity* [Documentation of the International Conference on "Human Rights in Kurdistan"] Initiative for Human Rights in Kurdistan, Bremen, April 14-16.

**Keywords:** ethnic identity; Hakkari; Mustafa Barzani; refugees; stereotypes of Kurdish women; tribal groups; socio-economic development of Hakkari; migrant women; tribal identity; Kurmanji; Yilmaz Güney; ethnic consciousness; ethnic barriers; Kurds; Arabs; Turks.

**Yalçın-Heckmann, Lale.** (1991). *Tribe and kinship among the Kurds.* Frankfurt am Main: Peter Lang Verlag GmbH. Contents (pp. 5-7), list of tables (p. 8), list of illustrations, maps, and figures, (p. 9), acknowledgements (p. 11), notes on transliteration (pp. 13-14), map (p. 15), introduction (pp. 17-24), map (p. 25), text (pp. 27- 255), notes (pp. 257-93), appendixes (pp. 295-307), eight black and white photos (pp. 309-15), list of kinship abbreviations (p. 316), glossary (pp. 317-18), references (pp. 319-328). ISSN: 0721-3549, ISBN: 3-631-42702-6.

335

**Keywords:** tribal life; nomadic life; kinship, tribe and state; history of Hakkari; Nestorians in Hakkari; physical landscape of Hakkari; settlement patterns; woman and infant mortality in Hakkari; health services and attitude towards health; literacy; work; economic activities; tribes and tribal ideology in Hakkari; tribal organization; leadership in Hakkari; Sisin; gender roles; polygamy; learning gender and rank; politics of everyday life; wife inheritance; wife-kidnapping; kinship relations of women; bride price; elopement.

**Yalçın-Heckmann, Lale**. (1995). Gender roles and strategies among the nomadic and semi-nomadic Kurdish tribes of Turkey. In Şirin Tekeli (Ed.), *Women in modern Turkish society: A reader* (pp. 219-31). London: Zed Books. ISBN 1-85649-151-X (hb) and ISBN 1-85649-152-8 (pb).

**Keywords:** tribal and nomadic life; Hakkari; Sisin; nomadic/semi-nomadic modes of production; marriage; kinship; patriarchal ideology; pastoral economy; division of labour/women's work; polygamy; wife-kidnaping; eloping; İsmail Beşikci; female consumption of prestige goods; consumption patterns; women's inhertance; *ziz bu* (an institutionalized form of protest for women).

## IV. URBAN LIFE

**Le Floc'Hmoan, Annick**. (2000). Istanbul: La triste errance des enfants kurdes [Istanbul: The sad wandering of Kurdish children]. *Elle*, March 6, reprinted in *Institut Kurde de Paris, Information and Liaison Bulletin, 180*, March, pp. 19-23. Seven photographs by Marie Dorigny.

**Keywords:** child labour; drug addiction among Kurdish street youth; forced evacuations of Kurdish villages; Kurdish ghetto in Istanbul; centers for street youth; beatings of street youth.

**Hanson, Margreta**. (1992). Letter from Damascus. *Kurdistan Times, I(2)*, Summer, pp. 175-81. ISSN: 1057-8668.

**Keywords:** Damascus Kurdish Quarter; the Gulf War; Kurdish uprising against Saddam Hussein; Kurdish refugees in Syria; Kurdistan of Syria; girls executed by Iraqi soldiers; injured Kurdish women in Syria; poison gas; Al Hourle Camp; Kurdish Human Rights Watch.

**Houston, Christopher**. (2001). Profane knowledge: Kurdish diaspora in the Turkish city. In *Islam, Kurds and the Turkish nation state* (pp. 113-32). Oxford/New York: Berg, 2001. ISBN 1 85973 472 3 (Cloth), 1 85973 477 4 (Paper).

**Keywords:** village guard system; reasons for Kurdish migration to Istanbul; corruption; the role played by elder brothers in a sister's upbringing; ideology of patriarchy; women and Islam; women and literacy/education; PKK; Kurdish Islam; 1925 Sheikh Said Uprising and one family's flight to Syria; Independence Tribunal; urbanization; the publishing of Kurdish books, translated by a Kurdish woman, in Turkey; Med TV; Kurdish and Turkish nationalisms; the Kurdish diaspora; assimilation; squatter communities; feudalism; Kurdish aristocratic feudal class.

*See also* Feudalism and Capitalism

**Kurdistan Rundbrief.** (1998). Das Leben der Kurdinnen in den Großstädten der Türkei [The life of the Kurdish women in the big cities of Turkey]. *Kurdistan Rundbrief, 8*(21) p. 6. Originally appeared in *Dengê Kurdistanê*, No. 44.

**Keywords:** migration; racist state propaganda against the Kurds; language difficulties facing Kurdish women in the large Turkish-speaking cities; economic difficulties facing Kurds in the large Turkish cities; IHD Istanbul; child labour; poor nourishment of children and the resulting difficulties in schools; working conditions; police controls; slums/shanties.

*See also* Language

**Samuel, Sue.** (1993). There is no way we can give up the struggle. *Kurdistan Report, 13*, February/March, pp. 9-12. Three photographs.

**Keywords:** female workers in a tobacco factory in Turkey: women's complaints of unfair terms of employment; a female tobacco factory worker tortured in police detention; family: worker says if it was not for the family women would be more active; families fear their daughters would end up in police stations.

**Schubert, Brigitte and Beate Rudolph.** (1996). Kurdische Frauen: Überleben und Widerstehen im Krieg [Kurdish women: surviving and resisting war]. *Menschenrechte für die Frau/ Terre des Femmes Zeitschrift, 2*, pp. 23-26. ISSN 09460373.

**Keywords:** HADEP; IHD; women and war; migration; gecekondus; poverty; women and employment; child labour; sexual harassment of child labourers; new roles for women migrants; assimilation policies of the Turkish state; loss of identity; women's role in preserving Kurdish culture, language and traditions; use of female relatives to punish male prisoners; rape of female prisoners; honor; changes in attitudes regarding honor; mothers and wives of the disappeared; women and protest; women organizing in slum areas; HADEP women's commission; Women's Peace Conference; killing of Kurdish girls by the police; massacres; solidarity between German and Kurdish women.

*See also* Honour Killing; State Violence; Political Prisoners

**Wedel, Heidi**. (1997). Kurdinnen in türkischen Metropolen: Migration, Flucht und politische Partizipation [Kurdish women in Turkish metropolises: migration, flight and political participation]. In Carsten Börck, Eva Savelsberg, & Siamend Hajo (Eds.), *Ethnizität, Nationalismus, Religion und Politik in Kurdistan, Vol. 1* (pp. 155-184). Münster: Lit Verlag. ISBN 3-8258-3420-4.

**Keywords:** Kurdish women in Turkish cities; socioeconomic reasons for migration; political reasons for migration; *gecekondus* (shantytowns); housing; division in shanty towns based on religion and ethnicity; language difficulties of Kurdish women in Turkish cities; employment and women's work; changes in working women's status in the Turkish cities; ethnic identity and political orientation; dominance of Kurdish identity; Sunni Kurds support of the Welfare Party (Refah); the political dilemma of Alevi Kurds; dominance of Alevi identity; Alevi and Kurdish organizations in the shantytowns; ethnic identity and political alienation; Kurdish refugees living in tents in Turkish cities.

**Wedel, Heidi**. (2001). Kurdish migrant women in Istanbul: Community and resources for local political participation of a marginalized social group. In Shahrzad Mojab (Ed.), *Women of a non-state nation: The Kurds* (pp. 113-34). Costa Mesa: Mazda Publishers.

**Keywords:** migration and women; gecekondus; Alevis; Sunnis; community activism; Güzeltepe; Kazim Karabekir; language difficulties; illiteracy; Alevi-Sunni relations; marriage; family life; polygamy; women's networks; women's participation in politics; relations between Kurdish and Turkish women; resource allocation and women; ethnic identity; political orientation; PKK; SHP; Refah; DEP; female muhtars; public demonstrations; employment; education.

# WAR AND PEACE

## I. IRAQ

**Agence France Presse and Reuters**. (2004). Une journalist d'une television kurde et un juge assassinés [Kurdish TV journalist and judge murdered]. *Le Monde*, October 16, reprinted in *Institut Kurde de Paris, Information and Liaison Bulletin, 235*, October, p. 69.

> **Keywords:** Dina Mohammed Hassan: journalist for Al-Hurriya (Freedom) Television Station, the Arabic language station of Jalal Talabani's PUK; shot down as she left her house to go to work in Baghdad.

**A.L.F.** (2003). La Parole est aux Opposantes Irakiennes [The word is to the Iraqi opponents]. *Elle*, March 10, reprinted in *Institut Kurde de Paris, Information and Liaison Bulletin, 216*, March, p. 60.

> **Keywords:** Pascale Isho, member of the Association of Assyrian Women in Iraqi Kurdistan, living in Erbil, Kurdistan; Erbil; the destruction of churches and monasteries by Saddam Hussein; deportations of Assyrians; the burning of Assyrian villages; Pascale Isho speaks in favour of the U.S. war against Iraq; Nazand Begikhani, Coordinator of the Movement of Kurdish Women Against the Crime of Horror and founder of the Network of International Studies of Kurdish Women, living in Lille, France; the torturing to death of a Kurdish girl's father and the execution of her three brothers; memories of deportations and chemical bombardments; Nazand Begikhani speaks of her fears about the Turkish involvement in Iraqi Kurdistan and the patriarchal Iraqi Opposition; Zahra Mohammad, a Fayli Kurdish exile living in London; Fayli Kurds; Zahra Mohammad recalls her having been tortured for opposing the beating of her younger brother by the Iraqi authorities; Zahra Mohammad remembers her time in a women's prison; Zahra Mohammad recounts the deportation of Fayli women to Iran, and the deaths which resulted from the four-day journey on foot; the "disappeared" Fayli men; Zahra Mohammad speaks of exile in Britain and of her wish for a short war to depose Saddam Hussein.

*See also* Assyrians/Chaldeans

**Begikhani, Nazand**. (1997). La femme kurde face à la montée islamiste [The Kurdish woman in the face of the Islamist rise]. *Les cahiers de l'Orient: Femmes en Islam*, pp. 43-53.

**Keywords:** Iran-Iraq war: women forced to participate in the workforce; women in the Kurdish nationalist movement; women after 1991 Gulf War and Kurdish Revolt; political and socio-economic crisis post 1991: rise of Islamic fundamentalist movements; Islamist view of women: women as representative of stability, continuity, and community cohesion; ideas of "honour" and "shame"; Women's Union of Kurdistan; Zhinan Union of Kurdistan; Independent Women's Organization; Kurdish Women's Alliance; Union of Muslim Sisters of Kurdistan; link between the development of the women's movement and the nationalist movement; nationalism taking priority over feminism.

**Brooks, Geraldine**. (2002). We must attack Iraq and free its people. *The Guardian,* January 9, reprinted in *Institut Kurde de Paris, Information and Liaison Bulletin, 202,* January, pp. 28-29.

**Keywords:** atrocities of Saddam's regime against the Iraqis; women raped in Iraqi Kurdistan; raping rooms of the Iraqi regime; survival of Saddam and the need to be removed "for the sake of the Iraqis."

**Burke, Jason and Luke Harding**. (2003). Kurds in fear of Turkish motives. *The Observer,* March 2, reprinted in *Institut Kurde de Paris, Information and Liaison Bulletin, 216,* March 2003, pp. 20-21.

**Keywords:** women's groups in Arbil; Jwan Kamal Baban of the Women's Union of Kurdistan; Kurdish women opposed to the presence of Turkish troops in Iraqi Kurdistan; the presence of Turkish troops in Zewa, Iraqi Kurdistan; PKK; Turcomans in Iraqi Kurdistan.

**Chaliand, Gérard**. (2002). Menace sur le printemps kurd [Threat to the Kurdish Spring]. *GEO,* December, reprinted in *Institut Kurde de Paris: Information and Liaison Bulletin, 213,* December, pp. 107-114.

**Keywords:** the lack of veiling among Kurdish women; the participation of females among the peshmerga; religious and ethnic minorities of Iraqi Kurdistan; Anfal; Halabja; Kurdish political parties; Kurdish Islamist movements.

**Constable, Pamela**. (2004). Women in Iraq decry decision to curb rights. *Washington Post,* Foreign Service, pp. A12.

**Keywords:** negative effects of Islamic Law on Iraqi women, including Kurdish women; Amira Hassan Abdullah: Kurdish lawyer, spoke at a protest meeting; fears that Iraqi women face the same prospects as women in Afghanistan; vow to fight the introduction of the laws;

Nasreen Barawi: Iraqi minister of social welfare and public service of Kurdish origin; said that the secret way in which the decision was made was a shock.

**Dribben, Melissa**. (2004). Two visiting Iraqi Kurdish women thank the U.S. for invading. *The Philadelphia Inquirer*, July 19, pp. B1, B2. Photograph of visitors.

**Keywords:** visit to Philadelphia in the U.S. for "democracy training" by Raz Rasool, director of Women's Alliance for a Democratic Iraq, and Surood Ahmad Falih; visit to Philadelphia's Foreign Policy Research Institute; memoirs of the repression of the Kurds by Saddam Hussein; liberation of the Iraqis and Kurds by the U.S.

**Institut Kurde de Paris**. (2004). Two journalists killed in Baghdad and in Mossul. *Institut Kurde de Paris, Information and Liaison Bulletin, 235*, October, pp. 23.

**Keywords:** Dina Mohammed Hassan: journalist for Al-Hurriya (Freedom) Television Station, the Arabic language station of Jalal Talabani's PUK; shot down as she left her house to go to work in Baghdad.

**International Alliance for Justice and Society for Threatened Peoples**. (2003). Invitation to press conference: Unheard voices of Iraqi women. *International Alliance for Justice and Society for Threatened Peoples*, February 26.

**Keywords:** group of Iraqi women including some from Iraqi Kurdistan; absence of the voice of Iraqi women in German and in International media about the oppression and violence they have suffered during Saddam Hussein's reign; group of Iraqi women to document the suffering of Iraqi women; Shirin Aqrawi: representative of Kurdistan Women Union, Initiative for Women in Bonn and the IFZ; speaker at press conference; family members died or were permanently injured as a result of Saddam Hussein's campaign against the Kurds; Najat Mahwi: head of the organization of Kurdish Women in Exile in Berlin; speaker at the press conference; suffered physical and psychological torture while in prison in Iraq; Shamsa Baba Sheikh: active in the organization of Kurdish Women in Exile in Berlin; comes from well-known Yezidi family.

**Institut Kurde de Paris**. (2002). Paris: an international conference on "the future of the Kurds in Iraq" at the French National Assembly. *Institut Kurde de Paris, Information and Liaison Bulletin, 212*, November, pp. 1-5.

**Keywords:** Nasrine Berwari, Minister of Reconstruction; reconstruction of Iraq; education; infant mortality rates; minority language education; lack of veiling among female students at Suleimaniah University.

**Knowles, Catherine S**. (1998). Life and human dignity, the birthright of all human beings: An analysis of the Iraqi genocide of the Kurds and effective enforcement of human rights. *Naval Law Review, 45*, pp. 152-216.

**Keywords:** targeting of the families of peshmerga fighters during the Anfal campaign; "Fourth Anfal"; Valley of the Lesser Zab River; people were segregated by sex; women were taken to Chamchamal, told, "Your men have gone to hell"; "Final Anfal": those that were captured, separated by sex and women and children held in animal pens; the entire male population in the villages of Northern-most Kurdistan was killed; Topzawa concentration camp: some of the women held were raped.

**Kuhner, Jeffrey T**. (2002). Dethrone Saddam: Allow independent Iraqi state. *Washington Times*, February 22, reprinted in *Institut Kurde de Paris, Information and Liaison Bulletin, 203*, February, pp. 83-84.

**Keywords:** genocide; Al-Anfal; mass murder; ethnic cleansing; death squads; 1991 Gulf War; beheading of women deemed to be prostitutes; 2,000 women beheaded since 2000.

**Mukalled, Diana**. (2003). A journalist diary: On the horrors of war... Kurdish women in Iraq (M Sfeir, Trans.). *Al-Raida* [Beirut], *21*(103), Fall [Women and War in the Arab World], pp. 60-62. One photograph.

**Keywords:** the defeat of Saddam Hussein and the fall of Kirkuk in April 2003; Kurdish armed women in green uniforms enter the city; Tinor, took up arms and became a peshmarga in order to fight mass killings and forced displacement of the Kurds; interview with Lieutenant Sarwat Ismail, commander of women's brigade; interview with Sadriat, survivor of Anfal genocide; interview with Rahmeh, a forcibly displaced woman from Kirkuk.

**Nickels, Thom**. (2004). Two Iraqi women speak out. *The Weekly Press* [Philadelphia's Center City Community Newspaper], July 27. One photograph of visitors.

**Keywords:** visit to Philadelphia in the U.S. for "democracy training" by Raz Rasool, director of Women's Alliance for a Democratic Iraq, and Surood Ahmad Falih; visit to Philadelphia's Foreign Policy

Research Institute; memoirs of the repression of the Kurds by Saddam Hussein; liberation of the Iraqis and Kurds by the U.S.

**O'Donnell, Lynne.** (2003). Saddam "made sex slaves" of Kurd women. *The Scotsman*, August 17.

**Keywords:** 18 women and female children disappeared from their homes in Iraq in 1989; appears that they were abducted to be sold as sex slaves in Egypt; evidence uncovered in the debris of the Kirkuk offices of Saddam Hussein's intelligence and security agency; documents give the names of the females who were between the ages of 14 and 29 at the time; 10 of the women from the village of Nawjul and the rest from the province of Gemiyan; Kirkuk's new post-war Appeal Court told the women's families that they could not pursue claims against the leaders of the local and national secret services agencies because an amnesty issued by Saddam last October remained valid; the mayor's office assured them that they could instead pursue claims through a government-sponsored human rights organization to be established to help Iraqis take legal action against the former Ba'athist regime; Nazaneen Rashid: one of the founders of KWAHK; Kurdish women's rights activist based in London, United Kingdom said the documents were the first concrete evidence of what is believed to be a widespread campaign against Kurdish women; she said that this was "a strategy that Saddam used against the Kurds, to turn all their daughters into whores so that their honour was destroyed"; rape as a weapon against ethnic groups; Egyptian government official denied that any Kurdish women were trafficked to Egypt and that Cairo would not investigate the documents that were found.

**O'Loughlin, Ed.** (2003). What was their guild, Kurds ask of women and children killed by Saddam, *Sydney Morning Herald*, July 17.

**Keywords:** mass graves of Kurdish women and children in Hatra, Iraq; believed to be one of many sites used to murder and bury victims of Saddam Hussein's massacre of the Kurds in the 1980s.

**Rohde, David.** (2003). Kurdish Refugees make do, not for the first time. *The New York Times,* March 25, reprinted in *Institut Kurde de Paris, Information and Liaison Bulletin, 216*, March, p. 147. Two photographs.

**Keywords:** Gazank, a 21-year-old college student, speaks of her fears of chemical bombardment; displaced in 1991 war; Human Rights Watch: Kurdish government unprepared to handle refugee crisis.

**Rohde, David.** (2003). For Kurds, big menace is an incursion by Turks. *The*

343

*New York Times,* March 7, reprinted in *Institut Kurde de Paris, Information and Liaison Bulletin, 216,* March, p. 45.

**Keywords:** Nasreen Sideek, Minister of Reconstruction and Development; Women's groups hold vigil to protest Turkish military intervention in Iraq; the difficulties facing Iraqi Kurdish refugees in Turkey; chemical attacks.

**Sydney Morning Herald.** (2002). Kurds in Iraqi Kurdistan stuck in the middle. *Sydney Morning Herald,* November 30, reprinted in *Institut Kurde de Paris, Information and Liaison Bulletin, 212,* November, pp. 114-117.

**Keywords:** Iraqi Kurdistan; Nasreen Mustafa Sideek, Minister for Reconstruction in one of the regional governments of Iraqi Kurdistan; Irbil; refugee camps in Iraqi Kurdistan; displaced families; infant mortality rates; women's dress; a female poet whose poem "Islam Will not Kill Me" has angered the mullahs; Patriotic Union of Kurdistan MP and lawyer Galawzh Jabbari; the rape of female prisoners in Iraqi prisons; PDK's Minister for Peshmerga Affairs, Hamida Fandi.

**United Nations Development Fund for Women.** (2005). Gender profile of the conflict in Iraq. *United Nations Development Fund for Women.*

**Keywords:** political participation in the Kurdistan Regional Government; in 2003, two of the 26 cabinet members were women and women occupied numerous posts among ministry staff; Nesreen Mustafa al-Barwari: Kurdish woman; only woman to be nominated to the 25 person interim Iraqi cabinet in August 2003; in charge of water treatment, waste management, environmental sanitations, and municipal facilities; youngest member of the cabinet; worked as an administrator with UNHCR in the Kurdish autonomous area from 1991; later became the Minister of Reconstruction and Development in the Kurdistan regional government; female victims of Saddam Hussein's extermination campaign against the Kurds; female participation in the 1991 Kurdish uprising; establishment of the Peshmerga Force for Women in 1996; now has over 300 fighters; training of female fighters; fighting against Ansar al-Islam, a Kurdish Islamist group; suspension of Article 111 of the Iraqi Penal Code by Kurdish authorities, in essence, not allowing "honour" to be used as a defense for murder; according to women's rights groups, honour killings were still prevalent; PUK militias shut down a women's rights organization and a women's shelter in July 2000, imprisoning staff and shelter residence; after the shelter was closed honour killings and violence against women rose; widows after the Anfal campaign: stigmatization of widows as women without spouses; economic strife;

emergence of women's organizations under autonomous Kurdish rule; "Martyr Layla Qassim" conference: February 20-22, 1992; under the auspices of the Kurdistan Women's Union, 177 women representing the three northern governorates of Iraqi Kurdistan participated; called for more inclusive participation of women at all levels in Iraqi Kurdistan; modernization of health services for women; lifting of economic sanctions from Iraq; Independent Women's Organization: created in 1992 by female activists in response to high levels of violence against women in the Kurdish autonomous area including harassment, physical violence, mutilation, murder; campaign to repeal "anti-woman" legislation in Northern Iraq and end impunity for "honour killings"; women's shelter in Sulaymaniyah: established in 1998; when it was closed down by a PUK militia, women of the IWO sent out a written appeal for support; with the help of the Kurdistan women's union, nearly 400 literacy centres for women were created with money from the Oil for Food Program; Heartland of Iraq Women's Conference: October 4-7, 2003; participation of Kurdish women's delegation; Ala Talabani from Kirkuk; liaison between women's groups, the CPA and the Iraqi Governing Council; chaired the conference.

## II. PEACE MOVEMENTS

**Demir, Gül**. (2001). Women see peace as the solution to their problems. *Turkish Daily News*, April 2, reprinted in *Kurdistan Report, 31*, Autumn, pp. 79-81.

**Keywords:** The Solidarity of Women for Peace group's visit to Diyarbakir; Pinar Selek; women from western Turkey invited to meet Kurdish women; extrajudicial killings; migration; sexual harassment; assault; Diyarbakir Women's Platform; mothers of "martyrs," as Demir Gül refers to the mothers of Turkish soldiers killed in the war; mothers of killed guerrillas; village burnings; mothers of political prisoners; wives of political prisoners; Leyla Zana's sister Pirozhan Doğru; women and identity; the disappeared; suicide committed by young girls; health problems; urbanization; Ayşe Özkan; Pazartesi magazine; Diyarbakir Democracy Platform; exiled women; OHAL Emergency Region; Deniz Türkali; fashion show of traditional Kurdish clothes modelled by Kurdish girls; bride price; polygamy; birth rates; press censorship; arranged marriages; selling of women.

**Gözde, Mert**. (2000). Efforts to end PKK/PUK conflict move ahead. *Turkish Daily News*, October 2, reprinted in *Institut Kurde de Paris, Information and Liaison Bulletin, 187*, October, p. 6.

**Keywords:** Kurdish Mothers for Peace; PKK; PUK; Kurdistan National Assembly; Democracy Party; Kurdistan Democrat Party; Talabani; Barzani.

**Kurdish Observer**. (2000). HADEP Women Commission's Kurdistan trip ended. *Kurdish Observer*, May 9.

**Keywords:** Kurdish women working for peace; HADEP Women Commission.

**Kurdish Observer**. (2000). Grand congress of HADEP women. *Kurdish Observer*, October 10.

**Keywords:** HADEP Women Branch's First Congress; Filiz Uğuz; Fatma Kurtalan; women and war; martial law; Ayşe Karadağ, HADEP Mayor of Derik (Mardin); Fatma Öcalan; ÖDP; Eğitim-Sen Women Branch Secretary Elif Akgül; Hediye Aksoy; Pir Sultan Association; 2 Temmuz Association; Emel Süngür; Mothers for Peace; THYD-DER Chairwoman Meliha Ozcan; Leyla Zana; Eren Keskin; 1st Group for Peace.

**Kurdish Observer**. (2000). "Peace Mothers" delegation members tortured in detention. *Kurdish Observer*, October 17, reprinted in *Institut Kurde de Paris, Information and Liaison Bulletin, 187*, October, pp. 35-36.

**Keywords:** YNK; PKK; Fahriye Bikkin; Rahime İnce; Azize Yıldız; Müyesser Güneş; Şekernaz Çakar; torture.

**Kurdish Observer**. (2000). The Mothers for Peace were exposed to sexual harassment. *Kurdish Observer*, October 31, reprinted in *Institut Kurde de Paris, Information and Liaison Bulletin, 187*, October, p. 70.

**Keywords:** YNK; PKK; Fahriye Bikkin; Rahime İnce; Azize Yıldız; Müyesser Güneş; Şekernaz Çakar; torture; sexual harassment; Eren Keskin; verbal abuse of women; women resisting oppression; women protesting.

**Kurdish Observer**. (2001). The aim is meeting with women of the world. *Kurdish Observer*, April 11.

**Keywords:** Partiya Jyna Azad (Free Women's Party); Kurdish women in Europe; Newroz; women's roles in war and peace; March 8; YJWK; PKK; Kurdish women's movement; attempts at solidarizing with Turkish women.

**Kurdish Observer**. (2001). Let woman's name be peace. *Kurdish Observer*,

June 12.

**Keywords:** women peace ambassadors; Turkish female intellectuals visit Kurdish women in Amed; Sema Sezer; Turkish and Armenian women meet with Kurdish women in Batman.

**Kurdish Observer**. (2001). Justice against inequality, peace against war. *Kurdish Observer*, October 17.

**Keywords:** HADEP Women's Wings; Women's Conference in Amed; Kurdish women protest Turkish support for American military action in Afghanistan.

**Paçal, Jan and Erdinç Ergenç**. (1996). Mothers: We want peace. *Turkish Probe*, August 2, reprinted in *Institut Kurde de Paris, Information and Liaison Bulletin, 136-137*, July/August, pp. 132-133.

**Keywords:** mothers of prisoners; hunger strikes; deaths of prisoners; mother's role in ending the hunger strikes.

**Staff and Agencies**. (2001). Kurdish women call for peace. *The Guardian*, October 25.

**Keywords:** Kurdish women protest against the bombing of Afghanistan in London, United Kingdom; feared fighting would destabilize Kurdish areas in the Middle East; called on Prime Minister Tony Blair to use diplomacy instead of violence against terrorism; tore up headscarves in protests; Yashar Ismailoglu: protestor; said that women were compromising honour by removing their scarves but had to do it in protest; said they did not support PKK.

**Turkish Daily News**. (1994). Actions against civilians. *Turkish Daily News*, December 26, reprinted in *Institut Kurde de Paris, Information and Liaison Bulletin, 116-117*, November/December, p. 210.

**Keywords:** attacks on civilians.

**Van Gent, Werner**. (1994). Wie eine Kerze in tiefschwarzer Nacht. *Tages-Anzeiger*, October 6, reprinted in *Institut Kurde de Paris, Information and Liaison Bulletin, 115*, October, pp. 24-25.

**Keywords:** struggle by intellectuals in Turkey for freedom of opinion.

**White, Jenny B**. (1999). Amplifying trust: Community and communication in Turkey. In Dale F. Eickelman & Jon W. Anderson (Eds.), *New media in the muslim World: The emerging public sphere* (pp. 162-79). Bloomington &

347

Indianapolis: Indiana University Press. ISBN: 0-253-21329-0. Illustration (p. 165), charts (pp. 166, 167, 168), black and white photo (p. 174).

**Keywords:** statistics; women's social interactions; media; secularism; shanty towns; women organizing in Ümraniye; women opening schools; Refah's closing of schools organized by women; Ümraniye Women's Centre; women fund-raising; Refah's attacks on women; class.

## III. TURKEY

**Agence France Presse**. (2000). Plus de 20 tués dans des accrochages entre kurdes irakiens et turcs [More than 20 killed in clashes between Iraqi Kurds and Turks]. *Agence France Presse,* October 2, reprinted in *Institut Kurde de Paris, Information and Liaison Bulletin, 187*, October, p. 7.

**Keywords:** Kurdish Mothers for Peace; Fouad Maasoum; Abdullah Öcalan; PKK; PUK; Kurdistan National Assembly; Democracy Party; Kurdistan Democrat Party; Talabani.

**Alkan, Xane**. (1996). The Turkish government's dirty war in Kurdistan: Its toll on Kurdish women. *Kurdistan Report, 23*, March-May, pp. 39-40.

**Keywords:** war; human rights violations; torture; women and migration; rape; self-immolation; kidnaping; women political prisoners; contra-guerrillas; village guards; Kemalism; genocide; Armenians; Greeks; Assyrians; Welfare Party; German-Turkish cooperation; women members of the Kurdistan Parliament in exile.

**Berger, Andreas, Rudi Friedrich and Kathrin Schneider**. (1998). Ein blinder Fleck: Der Krieg und die Frauen [A blind spot: the war and women]. In Andreas Berger, Rudi Friedrich, & Kathrin Schneider (Eds.), *Der Krieg in Türkei-Kurdistan* (pp. 163-70). Göttingen: Lamuv Verlag GmbH. ISBN: 3-88977-502-0.

**Keywords:** women and war; effects of war; village guard system; sexual harassment; PKK; desecration of female guerrillas' bodies; women lawyers; Meryem Erdal; rape; women prisoners.

**Doğan, Mülkiye**. (1993). Confessions of a former contra-guerrilla: A damning indictment of the Turkish security forces. *Kurdistan Report, 16*, October/November, pp. 18-21. Also appeared as "Confessions of a former contra-guerilla" in *Resistance: Women in Kurdistan*. London: KIC/KSC Publications, 1995, pp. 18-23. Two photographs.

**Keywords:** Mulkiye Doğan, former contra-guerilla from 1990-1993

(17 years old to 21 years old); taken out of school at age 13; family pressure; sexual pressure from a relationship with an older man; physical abuse; surveillance; forced marriage; attempted suicide; death threats from older man (former relationship); use of "femininity" (sex appeal, seduction) against targets: sexual exploitation of female contra-guerillas; women and nationalism.

**Ersöz, Gurbetelli**. (1994). Mother Müzeyyen [Mother Müzeyyen] (S. Kaczynski, Trans.). In Friends of Özgur Gündem (Eds.), *Gurbetelli Ersöz's Defence: An Impassioned Plea for Free Speech in Turkey* (pp. 25-28). London: Friends of Özgur Gündem and Action for Kurdish Women, November. Also appeared as "Mother Müzeyyen" in *Resistance: Women in Kurdistan*. London: KIC/KSC Publications, 1995, pp. 10-11. One photograph.

**Keywords:** widow; health problems; village; tribe; extrajudicial killings; village guards; burning of villages; torture; Leyla Zana; Hatip Dicle; Newroz.

**Institut Kurde de Paris**. (2003). Children continue to fall victim to mines in Kurdistan. *Institut Kurde de Paris, Information and Liaison Bulletin, 224*, p. 15, November.

**Keywords:** four children, three girls and one boy, killed by a mine in Uludere Village in Sirnak Province; the region was site of intense fighting between Turkish Army and PKK.

**Laizer, Sheri**. (1997). Kurdish women and minorities in struggle. *Pax Christi International*.

**Keywords:** KDP; PKK; massacres; rape; execution; Turks; Iranians; Turkish army; South Kurdistan; PUK; NATO; torture; sexual abuse; refugees.

**Laizer, Sheri**. (1991). *Into Kurdistan frontiers under fire*. London: Zed Books. ISBN 0-86232-898-5 (hb) and 0-86232-899-3 (pb). List of abbreviations (p. vii), foreword by Peter Gabriel (p. ix), introduction by Helga Graham (pp. 1-4), text (pp. 7-128), appendices (pp. 129-42), select bibliography (pp. 143-46), index (pp. 147-50).

**Keywords:** Iraqi Communist Party; KDP; MIT; TKSP; UNHCR; feudalism; Feqiye Teyran; refugees; Shikak tribe; Celali tribe; Kurdish songs and music; *dengbej*; Şivan Perwer; djinn; evil eye; Yilmaz Güney; Kurdish clothes; women's work; midwives; birth control; Islam; Zoroastrianism; Yezidis; honour; Jelali Kurds; urban life; Pir Sultan Abdal; Massoud Barzani; genocide; ethnocide; Halabja; child labor;

349

assimilation; NATO; ARGK; United Kurdish Front; Treaty of Sevres.

**Mitterrand, Danielle.** (1997). Lettre de Mme Mitterrand aux responsables des quinze [Letter from Mme Mitterrand to the leaders of the fifteen], November 26, reprinted in *Institut Kurde de Paris, Information and Liaison Bulletin, 152-153*, November/December, p. 113.

> **Keywords:** Leyla Zana; destruction of Kurdish villages by Turkey; assassination of intellectuals and pacifist democrats; Musa Anter; Mehmet Sincar; displaced Kurds; Sakharov Prize; Erbakan; narcotics trade.

**Mitterrand, Danielle.** (1998). Mrs Mitterrand's letter to all French members of parliament, February 12, reprinted in *Institut Kurde de Paris, Information and Liaison Bulletin, 154-155*, January/February 1998, pp. 8-9.

> **Keywords:** visit of President Demirel to France; French Members of Parliament; French Senators and Deputies; human rights violations in Turkey; war between Turkish military and the PKK; exodus of Kurdish refugees to Italy; internal migration within Turkey; settlement of Kurdish refugees in the shanty towns of Turkish cities; depopulation of Kurdish lands; physical elimination of Kurdish political and cultural elites; DEP; Leyla Zana; France-Libertés; destruction of Kurdish villages by Turkey; assassination of intellectuals and pacifist democrats; Musa Anter; Mehmet Sincar; human rights lawyers; NATO; Council of Europe; Western governments' support for Turkey as a "secular democracy"; the deliberate destruction of the material and spiritual culture, the economic infrastructure and way of life of the native population; policy of genocide; mothers of the disappeared; banning of political parties; military modernization; debt; sale of French Cougar helicopters to Turkey; potential sale of Leclerc tanks; potential sale of Tiger Eurocopter helicopter gunships.

**Mönch-Buçak, Yayla.** (1991). Kurdistan: als Kolonie verkauft und verraten vom Leben und Widerstand kurdischer Frauen in einem vierseitig besetzten Land [Kurdistan: Sold as a colony and betrayed by the life and resistance of Kurdish women in a country occupied by four sides]. In Frauen in der Einen Welt, Zentrum für Interkulturelle Frauenalltagsforschung (Eds.), *Frauen in der Einen Welt Volume 3/4* (pp. 88-97). Nürnberg: Zentrum für Interkulturelle Frauenalltagsforschung. ISSN 0937-5848.

> **Keywords:** Kurdistan; history; Iraq; Syria; Turkey; Ottoman Kurdistan; Great Britain; France; Turkish policies regarding Kurds; linguistic-cultural oppression of Kurds in Turkey; position of women in Kurdish society; patriarchy; marriage; polygamy; division of labor;

bride price; marginalization; migration; urbanization; Kurdish women in rural areas; Kurdish women in cities; Kurdish women's reactions to national oppression; Necla Yüce; Tunceli (Dersim); PKK; wives of PKK guerrillas; mothers of prisoners; Diyarbakir; Batman; killing of prisoners; torture; use of prisoners' wives to extract confessions; Yeşilyurt; Cizre; Mardin; Günay Aslan; Nure Oğlak; Leyli Oğlak; rape; killing of Kurdish girls by Turkish police; Şirin Doğan; Geyiksuyu; Taşlı; deportations; women's resistance in Kurdistan; diaspora; military coup of 1980; demonstrations; hunger strikes; the disappeared; Rahince Şahin; Saliha Şener; self-immolation as protest; Zekiye Alkan; Dargeçit; gecekondus.

**Müller, Doris and Elisa Huber**. (1995). Kurdische Frauen im Aufbruch [Kurdish women on the move.]. *donnawetter: die saarländische frauenzeitschrift, 38*(IV), pp. 20-21.

**Keywords:** Terre des Femmes; women and war; Zeynep Baran; Berivan; Dritte Welt; IHD; Turkish authorities' attempts at preventing Kurdish women from speaking in Germany; state violence against Kurdish women; illegality of most Kurdish organizations in Germany; destruction of Kurdish villages; torture and rape of prisoners; women and migration; rape of murdered Kurdish women by Turkish soldiers; politicization of Kurdish women; hunger strikes; death penalty; Atik Zeycar.

**Neue Zürcher Zeitung**. (1994). Die Türkei auf dem Weg in die Isolation. *Neue Zürcher Zeitung*, August 17, reprinted in *Institut Kurde de Paris, Information and Liaison Bulletin, 113-114*, August/September, pp. 60-61.

**Keywords:** human rights violations; PKK; youth and women's organizations controlled by the PKK; DEP; bombing of villages in Turkish Kurdistan; forced migration.

**Neue Zürcher Zeitung**. (1994). Erschwerte Berichterstattung aus der Türkei [Difficult reporting from Turkey]. *Neue Zürcher Zeitung*, October 8-9, reprinted in *Institut Kurde de Paris, Information and Liaison Bulletin, 115*, October, pp. 29-31.

**Keywords:** PKK; Leyla Zana; *Özgür Ülke*; International Red Cross Committee; Helsinki Watch; migration to cities; assaults on the press; nationalism in Turkey.

**Peterson, Scott**. (1996). Kurds caught between Turks, Saddam, their own factions. *The Christian Science Monitor*, April 30, reprinted in *Institut Kurde de Paris, Information and Liaison Bulletin, 132-133*, March-April, pp. 202-203.

**Keywords:** women and war; the Kurds of Tily; PKK; U.N.; Mizory Tribe.

**Sullivan, Scott and Sami Kohen**. (1990). The dirty war in Kurdistan. *Newsweek,* pp. 20-21, May 21, reprinted in *Institut Kurde de Paris, Information and Liaison Bulletin, 62,* May, pp. 40-41.

**Keywords:** murder; torture; abuse; beatings; rape; PKK; war; Nusaybin; Diyarbakir; Cizre; Yeşilyurt; NATO.

**Yalçin-Heckmann, Lale**. (1991). Notizen zum Frauenalltag in einem Flüchtlingslager: Kurdische Frauen an der türkisch-irakischen Grenze [Notes on everyday life in a refugee camp: Kurdish women on the Turkish-Iraqi border]. In Frauen in der Einen Welt, Zentrum für Interkulturelle Frauenalltagsforschung (Eds.), *Frauen in der Einen Welt Volume 3/4* (pp. 186-90). Nürnberg: Zentrum für Interkulturelle Frauenalltagsforschung. ISSN 0937-5848. One photo (p. 187).

**Keywords:** Kurdish uprising in Northern Iraq; European reactions to the uprising; Hakkari; refugee camps in Turkish Kurdistan; UNHRC; relations between Kurds along the Iraqi-Turkish border; marriage; female guerrillas; Nestorian women.

# APPENDIX

International
Kurdish
Women's Studies
Network
Tora Navneteweyî ya Lêkolînên
Jinên Kurd
تۆزی نێونەتەوەیی لێکۆڵینەوەی
ژنی کورد

Note: A spelling error was noted on this manually-designed pamphlet. The correct text in the Sorani Kurdish is:

تۆڕی نێونەتەوەیی لێکۆڵینەوەی ژنی کورد

تۆڕی نێونەتەوەیی لێکۆڵینەوەی ژنی کورد

## FORMATION OF THE NETWORK

The *International Kurdish Women's Studies Network* was formed in the fall of 1996. It was started as a response to a growing need for opening a space for Kurdish women in international debates on women's rights, women's studies, and promoting gender justice among the Kurdish communities in the diaspora and the Middle East. The Network was founded by a number of Kurdish and non-Kurdish women activists and researchers.

The Network is an international body with individual and organizational membership from Europe, North America, and the Middle East.

## GOALS

The *International Kurdish Women's Studies Network* provides a forum for exchange of experience and knowledge among those who are interested in and work for improving the lives of Kurdish women; to act as a liaison for community-based, institution-based, academic and independent researchers and activists in all parts of Kurdistan and in the diaspora; to assist those engaged in Kurdish women's studies and activism in all regions of Kurdistan and in the diaspora; and to promote the theories and practices of feminism among the women of Kurdistan and the diaspora; to promote women's rights and gender equality in Kurdistan.

## ACTIVITIES

~ Acting as an information resource for scholars, activists, and policy makers.

~ Promoting interest in teaching and research about Kurdish women.

~ Publishing scholarly works on Kurdish women.

~ Contributing to the production of feminist knowledge on topics such as women and nationalism, violence, war, ethnicity, global market economy, and state.

~ Conducting oral historical research among Kurdish women.

~ Networking with women's groups and organizations.

~ Securing scholarships & fellowships for enhancing Kurdish women's access to higher education.

~ Undertaking action projects on gender justice.

~ Raising Kurdish women's voices in international women's gatherings.

Tora Navneteweyî ya Lêkolînên Jinên Kurd

**Contact:**

Dr. Shahrzad Mojab
Transformative Learning Centre
Department of Adult Education,
Community Development & Counselling Psychology

OISE - University of Toronto
252 Bloor Street West, Toronto, Ontario, Canada
M5S 1V6
Tel: 1-416-923-6641, Ext. 2242
Fax: 1-416-926-4749
E-mail: smojab@oise.utoronto.ca

Inga Rogg
Orleansstr. 31
81667 Muenchen
Germany
Tel: 49-089-48 47 48
Fax: 49-089-489 14 83
E-mail: IngaRogg@compuserve.com

Internet: http://www.oise.utoronto.ca/projects/kwnet

# Author Index

# Institutions and the Press Index

365

www.ingramcontent.com/pod-product-compliance
Lightning Source LLC
Chambersburg PA
CBHW051949270326
41929CB00015B/2589